VOLVO
OWNERS HANDBOOK

of

Maintenance & Repair

for

P 444   P 445   P 544

122S and P 1800 Cars

Printed in 1964

by

FLOYD CLYMER PUBLICATIONS

"World's Larger Publisher of Books on Volkswagen cars and Trucks"

222 North Virgil Avenue, Los Angeles, Calif. 90004

1

INTRODUCTION

Welcome to the world of digital publishing ~ the book you now hold in your hand, while unchanged from the original **1964** edition, was printed using the latest state of the art digital technology. The advent of print-on-demand has forever changed the publishing process, never has information been so accessible and it is our hope that this book serves your informational needs for years to come. If this is your first exposure to digital publishing, we hope that you are pleased with the results. Many more titles of interest to the classic automobile and motorcycle enthusiast, collector and restorer are available via our website at **www.VelocePress.com**. We hope that you find this title as interesting as we do.

NOTE FROM THE PUBLISHER

The information presented is true and complete to the best of our knowledge. All recommendations are made without any guarantees on the part of the author or the publisher, who also disclaim all liability incurred with the use of this information.

TRADEMARKS

We recognize that some words, model names and designations, for example, mentioned herein are the property of the trademark holder. We use them for identification purposes only. This is not an official publication.

INFORMATION ON THE USE OF THIS PUBLICATION

This manual is an invaluable resource for the classic **Volvo** enthusiast and a must have for owners interested in performing their own maintenance. However, in today's information age we are constantly subject to changes in common practice, new technology, availability of improved materials and increased awareness of chemical toxicity. As such, it is advised that the user consult with an experienced professional prior to undertaking any procedure described herein. While every care has been taken to ensure correctness of information, it is obviously not possible to guarantee complete freedom from errors or omissions or to accept liability arising from such errors or omissions. Therefore, any individual that uses the information contained within, or elects to perform or participate in do-it-yourself repairs or modifications acknowledges that there is a risk factor involved and that the publisher or its associates cannot be held responsible for personal injury or property damage resulting from the use of the information or the outcome of such procedures.

It is important that the reader recognizes that any instructions may refer to either the right-hand or left-hand sides of the vehicle or the components and that the directions are followed carefully. One final word of advice, this publication is intended to be used as a reference guide, and when in doubt the reader should consult with a qualified expert.

ANNOUNCEMENT

The popularity of Volvo automobiles in the United States has risen steadily since their introduction here only a few years ago. Like the rest of the world, this country has extended a welcome to the Swedish product based strictly on its merits. In a highly competitive market and in a section of the price range which includes more automobiles than any other, Volvo models have made noteworthy gains. Although there was much good-natured chaffing about the PV444's plain looks when it was first shown here, I reminded people in the automobile business that Volvo was capitalizing on this conservatism. The continued acceptance of this rugged two-door sedan has proven that clean, uncluttered looks, combined with fine engineering and construction outweigh flashy temporary stylizing.

Volvo's remarkably clean-lined and advanced P-1800 has, I am sure, exceeded the factory's expectations. It easily offers one of the best sports-touring automobile buys in the world.

To the owners of these, and all other Volvo models, we offer this book in the hope that it may serve them well in maintaining and repairing, when necessary, their well-built machines. This volume is as complete in detail as is practical. Few owners will desire to carry out repairs as extensive as those which are shown regarding gearbox, rear end and so on, but, this very detail may serve in good stead if the owner finds himself in an emergency situation far from an authorized Volvo garage. Any professional mechanic can follow the steps outlined to repair what may be a relatively unfamiliar unit. The reader will note that references are made throughout to Volvo special tools (many of which are also illustrated). This will aid the repair process in that a glance at the tool will explain its function and enable a substitute to be readily located or improvised. Certain tools are almost a necessity when completely disassembling the rear axle, for example, and such references can prevent the improper methods from being employed. In the ordinary situation, the amateur mechanic or owner can proceed with common garage tools with complete ease. It is always best of course to entrust repairs to the authorized Volvo dealer and his trained personnel.

My pleasant visit to Sweden and the Volvo factory may have prejudiced me in favor of this sound, honest, good-performing automobile, but I prefer to think that most of my enthusiasm stems not only from personal driving pleasure Volvos have given me, but from the many complimentary things our customers who own Volvos have said about their cars.

Floyd Clymer

Publisher

3

CONTENTS

ENGINES: B 14 and B 16 SERIES

DESCRIPTION

General

The four cylinder overhead valve engines employed by Volvo prior to the introduction of the new B-18 model, were well-proven designs, husky and in production for several years. Built by the wholly owned Volvo subsidiary, AB Volvo Pentaverken, located in Skovde, the B 14 A, B 16 A, B 16 B and B 16 D types are quite similar in construction, differing only in displacement, compression, camshaft timing and carburetion. The B-14 is a 70 B.H.P. engine of 1410 cc (86 cu. in.) displacement with 7.8 to 1 compression ratio. The B 16 A, B and D engines have a larger bore resulting in 1580 cc (96.4 cu. in.) displacement. The A and D types are "economy" models, fitted with a single Zenith downdraft carburetor. The B designation is fitted with twin SU carburetors of a larger size than the pair found on the B 14.

CONDENSED SPECIFICATIONS

Engine

Output, B.H.P./r.p.m.

    B 14 A—70/5500; B 16 A—66/4500; B 16 B—85/5500; B 16 D—72/5500

Torque, lb. ft./r.p.m.

    B 14 A—75.9/3000; B 16 A—85.4/2500; B 16 B—86.8/3500; B 16 D—86.1/2600

Cubic capacity, liters

    B 14 A—1.41; B 16 A—1.58; B 16 B—1.58; B 16 D—1.58 (cu. in.): B 14 A—86; B 16 A—96.4; B 16 B—96.4; B 16 D—96.4

Compression ratio

    B 14 A—7.8:1; B 16 A—7.4:1; B 16 B—8.2:1; B 16 D—8.2:1

CYLINDER BLOCK

The cylinder block is cast in one unit with the cylinders bored directly in the block. On the engine block for the B 16 A, B 16 B and B 16 D engines, the right side has been designed so that the oil cleaner on the B 14 A engine is connected by means of external lines.

CRANKSHAFT

The crankshaft is made of drop-forged steel with precision ground and (except for the B 16 A) surface-hardened main and connecting rod bearing journals. The crankshaft is statically and dynamically balanced and is carried in three main bearings in the upper part of the crankcase. These bearings consist of replaceable

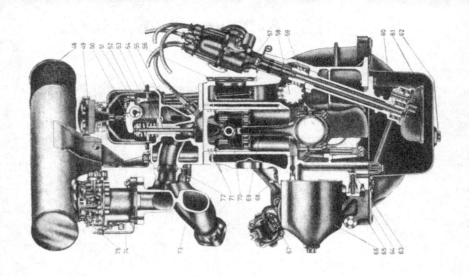

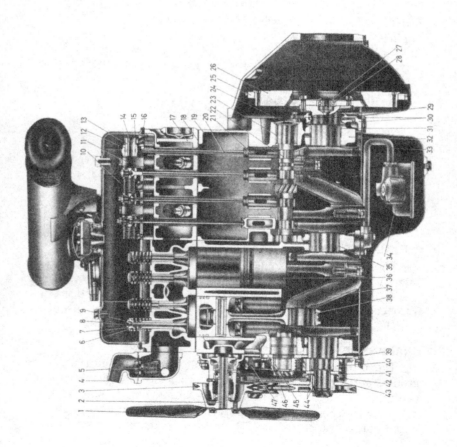

6

Longitudinal and cross sections of B 16 A engine.

1. Fan
2. Water pump
3. Fan belt
4. Thermostat housing, upper part
5. Thermostat
6. Valve spring seat
7. Rubber ring
8. Valve
9. Valve retainer
10. Spring
11. Bearing bracket
12. Bushing
13. Rocker arm shaft
14. Seal washer
15. Rocker cover
16. Gasket
17. Cylinder head
18. Cylinder head gasket
19. Cylinder block
20. Push rod
21. Valve lifter
22. Camshaft
23. Bushing
24. Seal washer
25. Ring gear
26. Flywheel
27. Retainer

28. Ball bearing
29. Felt seal
30. Sealing flanges, upper and lower
31. Main bearing shell (flange bearing)
32. Bearing cap
33. Oil pipe
34. Oil pump
35. Main bearing shell
36. Piston
37. Crankshaft
38. Connecting rod bearing shell
39. Seal plate
40. Crankshaft gear
41. Oil slinger ring
42. Timing gear casing
43. Felt seal
44. Key
45. Key
46. Guide flange
47. Camshaft gear
48. Air cleaner (right-hand illustration)
49. Cap with breather
50. Rocker arm

51. Setscrew with lock nut
52. Valve spring
53. Valve
54. Valve guide
55. Water distribution pipe
56. Inspection cover
57. Distributor
58. Camshaft gear
59. Pump gear
60. Oil pump
61. Oil pan
62. Drain plug
63. Relief valve plunger
64. Relief valve spring
65. Nut and washer for relief valve
66. Oil cleaner
67. Starter motor solenoid
68. Water drain cock
69. Connecting rod
70. Piston pin
71. Piston rings
72. Guide sleeve
73. Exhaust manifold
74. Carburetor
75. Rubber gasket

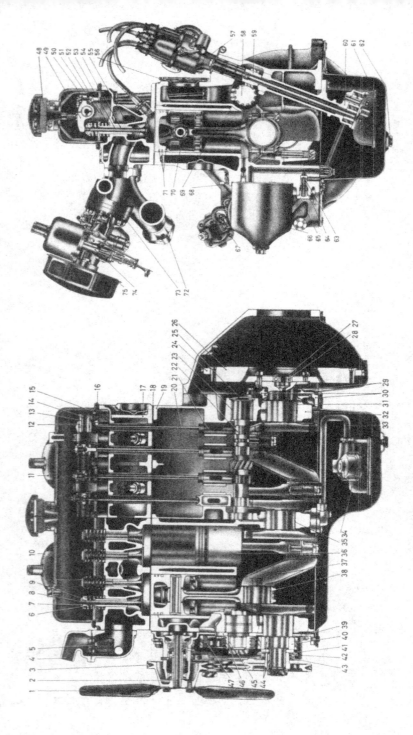

Longitudinal and cross sections of B 16 B engine

1. Fan
2. Water pump
3. Fan belt
4. Thermostat housing, upper part
5. Thermostat
6. Valve spring seat
7. Rubber ring
8. Valve
9. Valve retainer
10. Forward carburetor
11. Rear carburetor
12. Bushing
13. Rocker arm shaft
14. Seal washer
15. Rocker cover
16. Gasket
17. Cylinder head
18. Cylinder head gasket
19. Cylinder block
20. Push rod
21. Valve lifter
22. Camshaft
23. Bushing
24. Ring gear
25. Seal washer

26. Flywheel
27. Retainer
28. Ball bearing
29. Felt seal
30. Sealing flanges, upper and lower
31. Main bearing shell (flange bearing)
32. Bearing cap
33. Oil pipe
34. Oil pump
35. Main bearing shell
36. Piston
37. Crankshaft
38. Connecting rod bearing shell
39. Seal plate
40. Crankshaft gear
41. Oil slinger ring
42. Timing gear casing
43. Felt seal
44. Key
45. Key
46. Guide flange
47. Camshaft gear
48. Filler cap (right-hand illustration)
49. Rocker arm

50. Setscrew
51. Bearing bracket
52. Valve spring
53. Valve
54. Valve guide
55. Water distribution pipe
56. Inspection cover
57. Distributor
58. Camshaft gear
59. Pump gear
60. Oil pump
61. Oil pan
62. Drain plug
63. Relief valve plunger
64. Relief valve spring
65. Nut and washer for relief valve
66. Oil cleaner
67. Starter motor solenoid
68. Water drain cock
69. Connecting rod
70. Piston pin
71. Piston rings
72. Exhaust manifold
73. Intake manifold
74. Carburetor (rear)
75. Air cleaner

9

bearing shells. The rear bearing journal also gives axial location. Apart from standard sizes there are also undersize bearing shells available to provide the correct clearance without shaving or filing even after the bearing journals have been reground.

MAIN BEARINGS AND CONNECTING ROD BEARINGS

The main bearings and the connecting rod bearings are of the tri-metal type. They are made of steel with lead-bronze alloy linings. This lining is coated with a very thin layer of lead-indium. On the B 16 A engine, however, the bearing metal consists of a special lead-bronze alloy for the connecting rod bearings while the main bearings consist of specially designed babbit-lined units.

On all engine types the crankshaft thrust bearing, which has a greater bearing surface than the other main bearings, is babbit-lined.

CAMSHAFT

The camshaft is made of special steel with hardened and ground cams and bearing surfaces. The camshaft is guided axially by means of a washer at the front end. The camshaft on the B 16 A engine has lobes with a design that differs somewhat from the other engines.

PISTONS AND PISTON RINGS

The pistons are made of light-alloy and are coated with a thin layer of tin. The piston pin hole is slightly displaced from the center line of the piston. A letter is stamped in the top of each piston showing the class to which it belongs and there is an arrow showing in which direction the piston should be fitted. Each piston has two compression rings and one oil control ring. The upper ring on each piston is chromed.

CONNECTING RODS

The conecting rods are made of drop-forged, I-section steel giving maximum rigidity combined with low weight.

On B 16 engines, the cylinder bores are not directly over the connecting rod bearings but are somewhat displaced along the longitudinal axis of the engine. The consequence of this is that the center line of the connecting rods is displaced relative to the center line of the bearing surface.

The connecting rod bearings consist of replaceable shells while the piston pin bearings consist of precision finished bushings.

PISTON PINS

The piston pins are made of low carbon steel which has been surface-hardened and ground. This ensures a tough core which

1. Rear carburetor
2. Forward carburetor
3. Fuel pipe between carburetors
4. Fuel pipe from pump
5. Thermostat housing (cooling water outlet)
6. Oil cleaner
7. Fan
8. Water pump
9. Setting mark
10. Pulley
11. Oil pipe (pump—cleaner)
12. Generator
13. Engine support
14. Oil relief valve
15. Oil pan
16. Starter motor
17. Cover plate
18. Flywheel housing
19. Serial number plate
20. Exhaust manifold
21. Air cleaners

Fig. 1. B 14 A engine (carburetor side).

11

1. Air cleaner
2. Fuel pipe
3. Rocker cover
4. Thermostat housing
5. Timing gear casing
6. Mark for top dead center
7. Generator
8. Engine support
9. Oil cleaner
10. Oil relief valve
11. Starter motor
12. Serial number plate (number stamped directly into block on distributor side, late production engines)
13. Cylinder block
14. Exhaust manifold
15. Cylinder head
16. Carburetor

Fig. 2. B 16 A and B 16 D engine (carburetor side).

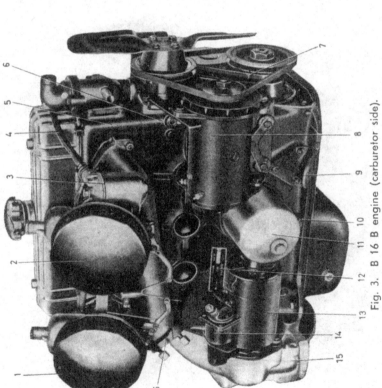

1. Rear air cleaner
2. Forward air cleaner
3. Float bowl (forward carburetor)
4. Fuel line
5. Cylinder head
6. Cylinder block
7. Ignition setting mark (T.D.C.)
8. Generator
9. Engine support
10. Oil relief valve
11. Oil cleaner
12. Serial number plate (number stamped directly into block on distributor side, late production engines)
13. Starter motor
14. Starter solenoid
15. Flywheel housing
16. Exhaust manifold

Fig. 3. B 16 B engine (carburetor side).

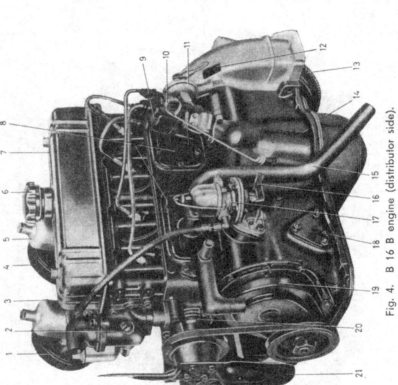

1. Forward air cleaner
2. Thermostat housing
3. Forward carburetor
4. Rear air cleaner
5. Rear carburetor
6. Oil filler cap
7. Rocker cover
8. Inspection cover
9. Distributor
10. Oil dipstick
11. Vacuum regulator
12. Inspection hole
13. Flywheel
14. Oil pan
15. Crankcase breather
16. Hand primer pump
17. Fuel pump
18. Engine support
19. Timing gear casing
20. Water pump
21. Fan

Fig. 4. B 16 B engine (distributor side).

14

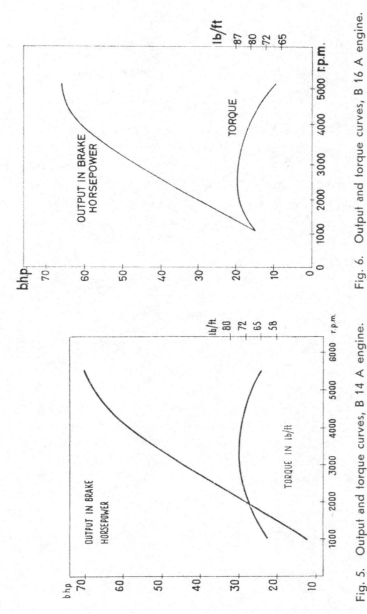

Fig. 5. Output and torque curves, B 14 A engine.

Fig. 6. Output and torque curves, B 16 A engine.

15

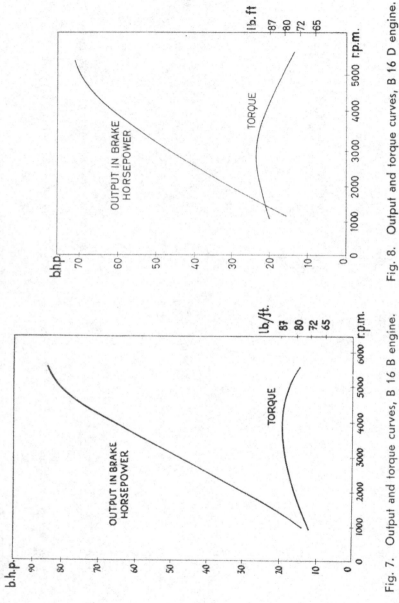

Fig. 7. Output and torque curves, B 16 B engine.

Fig. 8. Output and torque curves, B 16 D engine.

16

can stand the stresses caused by the high combustion pressure to which the pistons are subjected as well as hard surface to resist abrasion. The piston pins are fully floating, i.e. they can rotate both in the connecting rod bushing and in the piston boss. Axial movement is prevented by means of circlips in the piston bosses.

VALVES

The valves are made of special steel. There are spherical recesses in the valve heads. This means low weight which is a great advantage particularly at high engine speed. This recess in each valve also ensures a certain amount of elasticity and better sealing properties.

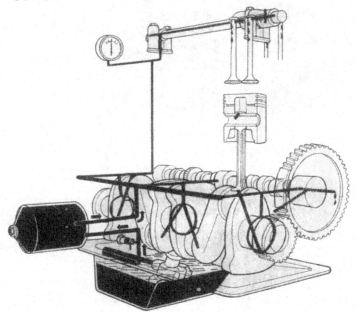

Fig. 9. Lubricating system.

LUBRICATING SYSTEM

The engine is provided with a pressure lubricating system. The oil cleaner is of the full-flow type and all oil on its way to the lubricating points must first pass through the oil cleaner. On the B 16 engine the oil cleaner is fitted directly on the right side of the cylinder block and there are no external oil lines. Oil passes to and from the oil cleaner through external oil lines.

The oil cleaner element consists of a replaceable paper unit. The cleaner is fitted with a by-pass valve which permits oil to by-pass the element if resistance to flow exceeds a certain value. A relief valve in the system prevents the oil pressure from becoming to high.

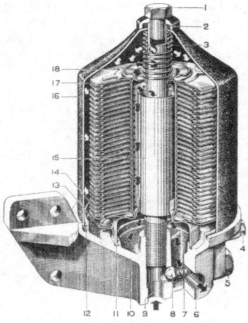

1. Center bolt
2. Washer
3. Spring
4. Drain plug
5. Nut for bypass valve
6. Outlet
7. Spring
8. Valve
9. Inlet
10. Bracket
11. Gasket
12. Gasket
13. Retainer
14. Screw
15. Level tube
16. Housing
17. Filter element
18. Washer

Fig. 10. Oil cleaner (B 14 A engine).

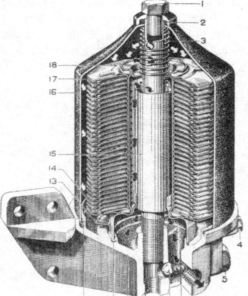

1. Drive gear
2. Lock pin
3. Bushing
4. Shaft
5. Housing
6. Pressure pipe connection
7. Gear (driven)
8. Lock ring
9. Strainer
10. Strainer housing
11. Inlet
12. Gear (driving)
13. Cover

Fig. 11. Oil pump.

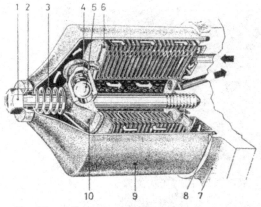

1. Bolt
2. Washer and seal
3. Spring
4. Valve spring
5. Valve ball
6. Filter element
7. Cylinder block
8. Gasket
9. Housing
10. Valve housing

Fig. 12.   AC oil cleaner (B 16 A, B, D engines).

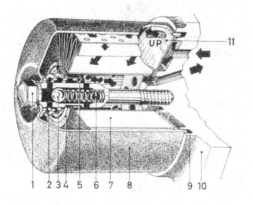

1. Bolt and washer
2. Spring
3. Valve ball
4. Sealing sleeve
5. Gasket
6. Valve spring
7. Filter element
8. Housing
9. Gasket
10. Cylinder block
11. Intermediate plate
    (late production
    engines, independent
    of cleaner make)

Fig. 13.   Mann oil cleaner (B 16 A, B, D engines).

IGNITION SYSTEM
Distributor

The distributor in the electrical system is fitted with both centrifugal and vacuum ignition regulators. Ignition timing on the B 14 engine can easily be altered manually by means of a screw adjuster device on the distributor. This device is not fitted on B 16 engines.

When the crankshaft is standing still, its position can be checked both by markings on the flywheel and with the aid of a raised spot on the timing gear casing. In the top dead center this raised spot is opposite a groove in the pulley.

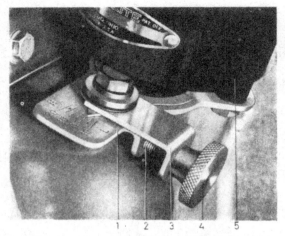

Fig. 14. Ignition timing adjuster (B 14 A only).

1. Attaching plate
2. Stud
3. Retainer
4. Nut
5. Distributor

COOLING SYSTEM

In order to obtain effective cooling water circulation there is an impeller type pump fitted in the cooling system and this is driven from a pulley on the forward end of the crankshaft. The pump shaft is carried in two ball bearings. The fan is fitted on the forward end of the pump shaft. This forces a powerful current of air through the radiator which is filtered in front of the engine.

In order to shorten the warming-up period of the engine after starting from cold condition, there is a thermostat in the cooling system and this is located in the upper connection between the engine and the radiator. The thermostat prevents the cooling water from passing out to the radiator and being cooled during the warming-up period. Instead circulation is limited to the engine itself through a hole from the cylinder block to the pump inlet channel in the block. The thermostat is balanced, that is to say it does not open under the influence of the pressure exerted by the water pump.

WORK THAT CAN BE CARRIED OUT WITHOUT REMOVING THE ENGINE FROM THE CAR

Compression Test

The purpose of the compression test is to check the sealing conditions of the piston rings and the cylinder walls. It is carried out by using a compression tester graduated in kg/cm^2 or lb/sq. in. Before the test is carried out the engine should be run until it reaches normal operating temperature, the air cleaner should be cleaned, all spark plugs removed and the throttle fully opened. Check that the choke flap is also fully opened. The battery must be well charged to allow the starter motor to turn the engine over sufficiently fast.

The cylinders are checked one at at time by placing the compression tester in the spark plug hole where it is held securely while the engine is turned over by means of the starter motor until the highest reading is obtained on the gauge. The maximum for each cylinder should be noted unless the tester used is of the self-registering type. The compression pressures for the various types of engines are shown in the specifications at the end of this chapter. Deviations of up to 10% from this value are permissible. If the values obtained are low, a small quantity of heavy oil is introduced into each cylinder. Then repeat the test and note the readings.

By comparing the values of compression pressure obtained with and without oil, some idea can be obtained concerning the sealing efficiency of the piston rings and the valves. If the pressure is higher after the oil has been introduced, the piston rings are probably not tight. If the compression pressure is low in one or more of the cylinders with and without oil, the valves are probably leaky. If two adjacent cylinders have very low compression pressure, there is probably a leak in the cylinder head gasket between the two cylinders.

Tuning up the engine

The purpose behind the tuning up of an engine is to ensure that it starts more easily, develops full output and has minimal fuel consumption. Engines should be tuned up regularly at intervals of 10,000 - 20,000 km (6,000 - 12,000 miles).

The best way to tune up an engine is to carry out the operations in the following order:

1. Remove all the spark plugs. Clean, adjust and test them or replace them with new plugs. Clean the air cleaner. Measure the compression on all the cylinders.

2. Examine the degree of charge of the battery. If the specific gravity of the battery electrolyte is lower than 1.230, then the battery must be charged/ If any of the individual cell in the battery have a low specific gravity, the cause for this must be determined. Examine all cables. Make sure that they are correctly tightened to their connections. Replace burned or badly insulated cables.
3. Check the dwell angle or remove the distributor cap and adjust the contact breakers to the correct gap. Replace burned breaker points. Examine the distributor cap for cracks and scrape off any oxide on the contact surfaces. Check the ignition cables and make sure that they are free from oxidation.
4. Check the ignition timing.
5. Adjust the valve clearance.
6. Clean the carburetor and check that all the settings are correct. Check that there is no air leakage at the carburetor or the intake manifold. Tighten the nuts. Replace the gaskets if required. Clean out the sediment bowl.

ENGINE DECARBONIZING AND VALVE GRINDING
Disassembly procedure

The engine should be decarbonized and the valves ground after about every 30,000 - 40,000 km (20,000 - 25,000 miles). On engines used for hard driving, the intervals between decarbonizing can be longer.

1. Drain off the cooling water. Remove the air cleaner (B 16 A and D).
2. Remove the rocker cover with gasket.
3. Remove the rocker arm mechanism and the push rods.
4. Remove the upper radiator hose and loosen the temperature gauge sensitive unit.
5. Loosen the throttle and choke controls at the carburetor.
6. Remove the ignition cables from the spark plugs.
7. Disconnect the exhaust pipe at the exhaust manifold.
8. Loosen all the cylinder head nuts. Lift off the cylinder head.
9. Clean the piston heads and blow off carbon with compressed air. Do not use abrasive cloth since the abrasive material can easily come between the pistons and the walls of the cylinders. Clean the upper surface of the cylinder block using a soft steel brush and compressed air. Cover the openings to the valve lifters.
10. Clean the cylinder head. Also follow the instructions given under the heading "Valves and valve mechanism."

Assembly procedure

Make sure that the sealing surface of the cylinder block and the cylinder head are absolutely clean and perfectly flat. Check this with a steel rule. Place the gasket on the block. Make sure that the oil channel for the rocker arm mechanism is not blocked. Oil the cylinder walls with engine oil. Place the cylinder head in position. Tighten the nuts. See "Tightening torque" in the specifications. Make a preliminary adjustment of the valves before screwing in the spark plugs. Fit the other component parts and fill the cooling system. Start the engine and let it run for at least 15 minutes. Then retighten the cylinder head nuts and carry out final adjustment of the valve clearances.

Valve clearance	Inlet	Exhaust
B 14 A, B 16 B, B 16 D	0.50 mm (0.020")	0.50 mm (0.020")
B 16 A	0.40 mm (0.016")	0.45 mm (0.018")

The valves should be finally adjusted while the engine is idling. Then fit the rocker with its gasket. Make sure that it is turned the right way. Check the ignition timing and adjust if necessary. Adjust the engine idling speed. After running for some miles, retighten the cylinder head nuts, adjust valve clearances.

CHANGING THE PISTON RINGS

1. Follow instructions 1 to 9 under the heading "Engine decarbonizing and valve grinding."
2. Lift the front end of the car to supports until it is about 20 cm (8" above floor level. Drain off the engine oil. Remove the oil pan in accordance with the instructions given under "Removing and fitting the oil pan."
3. Check the connecting rod markings. (They should be marked 1-4, on the side away from the camshaft).
4. Scrape away the ridge in the upper part of the cylinders.
5. Disconnect the connecting rods at the lower end and push them upwards together with the pistons one at a time through the cylinder bores. Replace the bearing shells, bearing caps and nuts in position on the connecting rods.
6. Remove all the piston rings. Clean the pistons and connecting rods. (Note: do not clean the pistons and bearing shells in a degreasing tank). Clean the piston ring grooves and the drain holes in the groove bottom.
   Check that the oil channels in the crankshaft are not blocked.
7. Inspect piston pin clearance. If clearance is excessive, new bushings and oversize piston pins should be fitted. Follow the instructions under the heading "Pistons, piston rings and piston pins."

Fig. 35. Cleaning piston ring grooves.

8. Check that the piston rings have the appropriate clearances in the cylinder bores and the piston ring grooves. Follow the instructions given under the heading "Pistons, piston rings and piston pins."

9. Check and straighten the connecting rods if required.

10. When fitting the pistons make sure that the piston ring gaps are not located directly above each other or opposite the piston pin bosses. Check that the cylinder walls and connecting rod bearing journals are clean and dry. Lubricate the pistons, cylinder bores and connecting rod bearing journals. Check the marking on the piston tops so that the pistons are installed correctly. Use tool SVO 2278 for B 16 and SVO 2229 for B 14 engines.

11. Fit the connecting rods and pistons. The connecting rod bolts should be replaced each time the engine is reconditioned.

12. Fit the connecting rods on the crankshaft.

13. Fit the cylinder head.

14. Fit the oil pan. Fill up with oil and fill the cooling system with water. Make a rough adjustment of valve clearances.

15. Run the engine until it reaches normal operating temperature.

16. Tighten the cylinder head nuts, adjust the valve clearances and check the ignition timing and the carburetor. See "Running-in the engine."

Fig. 36. Fitting a piston.

1. SVO 2278 for B 16 A, B, D engines
    SVO 2229 for B 14 A engines

REPLACING MAIN BEARINGS

The main bearing shells can be replaced without removing the engine from the car. The oil pan must, however, be removed. This operation is described under "Removing and fitting the oil pan."

Remove the lock washers for the nuts on the main bearing bolts, remove the bolts and then remove the bearing caps and the lower bearing inserts.

The upper bearing insert is removed by inserting a pin into the oil passage and then turning the crankshaft in its normal direction of rotation. The bearing shell (2) then moves with the crankshaft and can be removed. Inspect the bearing journal with the help of a dial indicator, the point of which is touching the journal and then rotate the shaft. If the out-of-roundness is more than 0.05 mm (0.002"), the crankshaft must be removed and reground.

Fit new bearing shells. The upper and lower inserts are identical but take care that the keys lodge correctly in their grooves.

See the specification as far as sizes are concerned.

Fit the bearing caps and tighten the nuts to the torque shown in the table. Use new lock washers. Fit the oil pan and fill with oil.

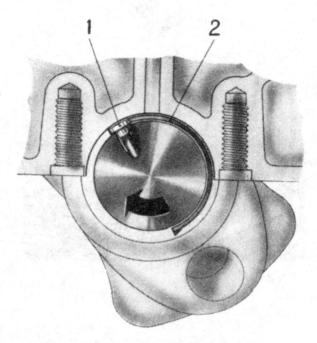

Fig. 37.   Removing a main bearing shell.

1. Pin
2. Bearing shell

REPLACING CONNECTING ROD BEARINGS

The connecting rod bearings can be replaced without removing the engine. Remove the oil pan in accordance with the instructions below. Remove the lock washers for the nuts and remove the nuts. The connecting rod bearing caps can then be removed as well as the lower bearing insert. Push the connecting rod slightly upwards and the upper bearing shell can then be removed.

Wipe the crank clean with a linen cloth and use a micrometer to measure partly the size and partly the out-of-roundness. If the out-of-roundness exceeds 0.07 mm (0.0028''), the crankshaft must be removed and reground since this can be the direct cause of the bearing failure. As far as sizes are concerned see under the heading "Main and connecting rod bearings."
Lubricate and fit the new bearing shells. Use new bearing bolts. Tighten the nuts in accordance with the tightening torques shown in the table and fit new washers. Fit the oil pan and fill with oil.

REMOVING AND FITTING THE OIL PAN

The oil pan can be removed without removing the engine from the vehicle, as follows:

1. Drain off the oil from the oil pan.
2. Remove the cover plates from the sides of the engine.
3. Remove the cover wheel from under the flywheel.
4. Loosen the nuts on the forward engine supports without removing them completely.
5. Lift up the engine by means of a jack placed under the front end (see fig. 38).

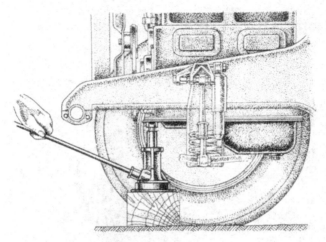

Fig. 38. Lifting the front end of the engine.

6. Slide in the spacers SVO 4124 and lower the jack.
7. Loosen the bolts round the oil pan and then remove the pan by pulling it downwards-backwards.
8. Assemble in the reverse order. Always replace a cork gasket that appears to be damaged or feels hard.

REPLACING THE CAMSHAFT AND/OR CAMSHAFT GEAR

1. Drain off the cooling water and detach the radiator blind cable.
2. Remove the radiator by loosening the hose clamps on the upper and lower radiator hoses and loosening the bolts on each side of the radiator. Lift up the radiator.
3. Remove the fanbelt and pull the pulley off the crankshaft. Use puller SVO 2279.
4. Remove the timing gear casing. Note the timing gear markings.
   If only the camshaft gear is to be replaced, the camshaft need not be removed.

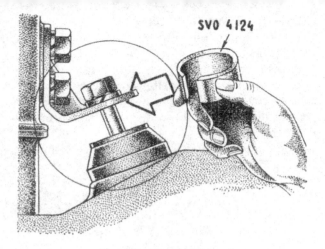

Fig. 39.   Fitting spacers.

Fig. 40.   Fitting the camshaft gear.

Remove the lock washer and the nut and then pull off the gear with tool SVO 2250. Fit the new gear by using tool SVO 1356A.

5. If the camshaft is to be replaced, the rocker arms, push rods and the fuel pump must be removed. Remove the covers on the side of the engine and remove the valve lifters. This work is facilitated if the distributor is also removed.

6. The camshaft can now be pulled out forwards after the thrust flange and radiator grille have been removed.

7. Fit in the reverse order. Make sure that the timing gears are returned in their original positions. Center the timing gear

casing by using tool SVO 1427 A. Check the cork gasket in the casing. Replace the gasket if it does not seal against the pulley hub.

8. Adjust the valve clearances and the ignition timing.

REMOVING THE ENGINE FROM THE VEHICLE

1. Drain off the cooling water, engine oil and transmission oil. Remove the battery, radiator and (on B 16 A and B 16 D engines) the air cleaner.

2. Disconnect all electrical connections, the fuel line at the fuel pump, the oil pipes, the pipe to the temperature gauge, the throttle and choke connections. Loosen the exhaust pipe at the exhaust manifold.

3. Loosen the forward engine supports, remove the gearshift lever.

4. Lift the vehicle on supports up to a height of about 20 cm (8")about the floor level.

5. Remove the cover plates on both sides under the engine. Disconnect the speedometer drive cable at the transmission and any remaining control linkages.

6. Put a jack under the transmission. Disconnect the propeller shaft at the flange on the driveshaft from the transmission and then remove the support member under the transmission.

7. Place the lifting chain SVO 4118 in position and lift the engine out of the vehicle. This is facilitated in the forward end of the engine is lifted first.

Fig. 41. Lifting out the engine.

DISASSEMBLING THE ENGINE

When the engine and the transmission have been removed from the vehicle they should be carefully washed and cleaned externally before disassembly is carried out. Use kerosene or solvent (less inflammable than gasoline). Then flush the engine with hot water and blow it dry with compressed air. Use only small quantities of kerosene or solvent at a time.

After washing, remove the transmission from the engine.

The engine is disassembled in the following order:

1. Remove the oil dipstick, crankcase breather, carburetor, fuel pump and distributor as well as the accelerator pedal linkage.
2. Place the engine in a suitable stand. Check that the oil has been drained off.
3. Remove the clutch. The clutch has been balanced as one unit together with the flywheel and the crankshaft and is marked with colored paint. Mark the component parts with punch marks so that they can be refitted in the correct positions.
4. Remove the oil cleaner, starter motor, generator and spark plugs.
5. Remove the inlet and exhaust manifolds, thermostat housing, water pump and water inlet elbow bend.
6. Remove the rocker arm shaft and lift up the push rods.
7. Remove the cylinder head. Remove the side covers and lift up the valve lifters.
8. Pull off the pulley from the crankshaft. Use puller SVO 2279.
9. Loosen and remove the timing gear casing.

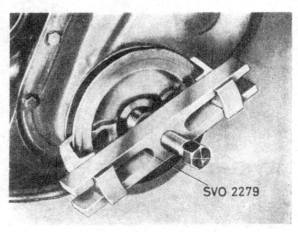

Fig. 42. Removing the pulley.

10. Check that the marking on the crankshaft timing gear is correct. Then pull off the camshaft gear with tool SVO 2250.
11. Pull off the crankshaft gear with tool SVO 1428 A.

Fig. 43. Removing the camshaft gear.

Fig. 44. Removing the crankshaft gear.

12. Turn the engine upside down and remove the oil pan.
13. Remove the lubricating oil pump complete with strainer and delivery pipe.
    Remove the relief valve plug and pull out the plunger using tool SVO 2079.
    Remove the rear crankshaft sealing flange.
14. Remove the camshaft thrust flange and pull out the camshaft.
15. Remove the connecting rod bearing caps and pull out the pistons complete with connecting rods through the cylinder bores. Return the caps and nuts to the respective connecting rods. Check the markings, 1-4, on the side away from the camshaft.
16. Remove the cover plate for the timing gear casing.
17. Remove the main bearing caps, lift up the crankshaft complete with flywheel and place it in some position where it is not likely to be damaged. The caps are marked with an arrow pointing forwards.
18. Remove the flywheel housing.
19. Separate the pistons from the connecting rods. Use tool SVO 1340 A.

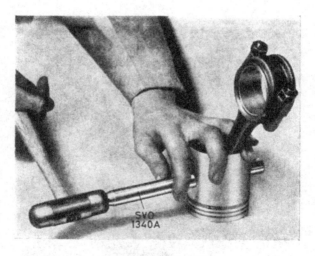

Fig. 45. Removing piston pin.

CLEANING THE ENGINE PARTS

After the engine has been disassembled all parts are first cleaned from carbon, oil sludge deposits and remnants of old gaskets. Kerosene or solvent are used to wash the parts. Make a habit of only using small quantities at a time and begin by washing the pistons, connecting rods, crankshaft and camshaft. Preferably use a degreasing tank which is electrically or steam heated. Engine parts can be cleaned to advantage in alkali in this type of degreasing tank. Only use cleaning agents which are marketed by reliable firms.

Take great care when washing parts made of light alloy. Such parts must not be left lying in the bath for more than half an hour. Pistons must not be placed in alkali solutions.

After washing the parts should be thoroughly flushed preferably with hot water. All oil passages should be flushed through and blown dry with compressed air. Use an air gun to ensure that all oil passages and narrow spaces are properly cleaned.

CYLINDER BLOCK
Gauging the cylinders
The cylinders become most worn at their upper ends and thus become tapered. They also become out of round. In order to obtain a complete impression of the appearance of a cylinder it must be measured at various points both parallel to and at right-angles to the piston pin. The cylinder is measured by using a special cylinder indicator, fig. 46. The dial indicator registers the

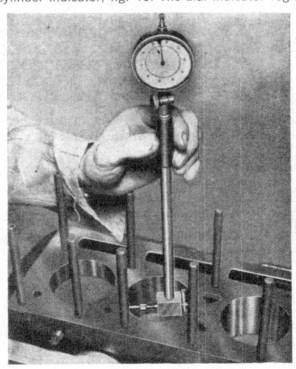

Fig. 46. Gauging cylinder bore.

relative wear in the cylinder walls by comparing the difference between the highest and lowest values obtained. The maximum cylinder wear can be established by zero-setting the indicator with the help of a micrometer gauge. On each cylinder bore there is a letter stamped showing the original bore (standard) in accordance with the table below. The micrometer is set to the lower limit in each cylinder bore range.

Range	Cylinder bore, standard
	B 16 A, B, D
A............	
B............	
C............	79.35-79.36 mm (3.1240"-3.1244")
D............	79.36-79.37 mm (3.1244"-3.1248")
E............	79.37-79.38 mm (3.1248"-3.1252")
F............	79.38-79.39 mm (3.1252"-2.1256")
G............	79.39-79.40 mm (3.1256"-3.1260")
H............	
	B 14 A
A............	74.96-74.97 mm (2.9512"-2.9516")
B............	74.97-74.98 mm (2.9516"-2.9520")
C............	74.98-74.99 mm (2.9520"-2.9524")
D............	74.99-75.00 mm (2.9524"-2.9528")
E............	75.00-75.01 mm (2.9528"-2.9531")
F............	75.01-75.02 mm (2.9531"-2.9535")
G............	75.02-75.03 mm (2.9535"-2.9539")
H............	75.03-75.04 mm (2.9539"-2.9543")

If the engine has been rebored, remove the carbon ridge in the upper end of the cylinder and then zero-set the gauge against this.

The amount of wear measured determines the remedy to be used. If the engine has abnormally high oil consumption and wear of up to 0.25-0.30 mm (0.10-0.012") is found or there are signs of scoring in the cylinder walls, reboring should be carried out.

REBORING THE CYLINDERS

Since demands as far as precision is concerned are extremely high, this work demands highly skilled and experienced workers. It is extremely important to ensure that cylinder bores are completely circular without taper and at right angle to the crankshaft with very close limits. Dealing with a reputable firm of automotive machinists is recommended.

Another important point is to ensure that the cylinder walls are machined to the very highest finish in order to shorten running-in time.

The cylinders are first measured in order to determine a suitable oversize (see specifications). They are then bored and honed to the exact size. (See under the heading "Piston Clearance"). After this has been done, the block should be cleaned, preferably in a degreasing tank, in order to remove any metallic particles.

CRANKSHAFT
Gauging crankshaft journals

The crankshaft should be checked for linearity and the journal should be checked for out of roundness, taper and score marks. Place the crankshaft in vee-block, move up the dial indicator against the center main bearing journal and then rotate the crankshaft. The dial indicator registers any distortion on the crankshaft and shows also the out of roundness of the journal. A micrometer should be used separately in order to determine the out of roundness of the journals. The maximum admissable runout of the center journal is 0.05 mm (0.0020").

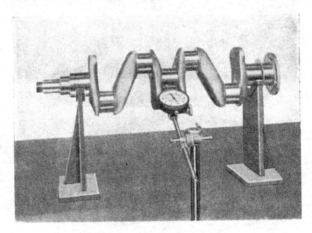

Fig. 47. Gauging the crankshaft journals.

Measurements should be made on at least 6 points around the periphery of the journal and at three points along the length. The maximum permissable out of roundness is 0.05 mm (0.0020") on the main bearing journals and 0.07 mm (0.0028") on the connecting rod bearing journals. The largest permissable taper is 0.05 mm (0.0020"). A distorted crankshaft can be aligned in a press. Out of round or tapered bearing journals should be ground to a suitable undersize, (see the information in the specifications). Scored bearing journals should also be ground. Grinding should be carried out in a special machine.

Grinding bearing journals

Maximum and minimum diameters when grinding the crankshaft to undersize are in the specifications. The width of the guide bearing depends on the journal size.

It is exceptionally important to follow the dimensions given on the table since they, together with the corresponding bearing shells, ensure the correct bearing clearance.

Fig. 48. Gauging bearing journal.

Fig. 49. Guide bearing journal width.

After the grinder has been dressed, the journal radii should be 2.75-3.00 mm (0.11"-0.12") as shown. After grinding, the journals should be lapped with fine grinding paste, edges removed from the oil hole and then the whole crankshaft should be thoroughly cleaned.

Oil passages

The crankshaft should be cleaned by boiling it in a degreasing tank and then flushed and cleaned with water and blown off with compressed air. Passages may also be cleaned up with a special brush.

MAIN AND CONNECTING ROD BEARINGS

Undersizes

Replacement bearing insert shells are available in the following undersizes: 0.010", 0.020", 0.030", 0.040".

All bearings have their respective part numbers stamped into the back.

Undersize bearings are also stamped with 01, 02, 03 or 04 to designate the respective undersizes.

The flange bearing shells have widths with oversizes 0.1, 0.2, 0.3, and 0.4 mm (0.004", 0.008", 0.12", and 0.016").

Fitting main and connecting rod bearings

Adjustment of bearing clearance may never be carried out by filing the bearing cap. The bearings are precision machined and must never be filed or scraped. Since they are replaceable, new shells should be fitted if there is any kind of damage or wear. If the bearing journals are damaged or out of round, they should be ground and undersize bearing shells fitted. Always inspect the oil flow to a damaged bearing.

Oil seal

The rear main bearing is fitted with a felt seal in two parts which is attached to the engine block with two flanges.

The front end of the crankshaft carries a sheet metal oilslinger clamped between the crankshaft gear washer and the pulley hub. The timing gear casing contains the felt ring which seals against the pulley hub. Inside both the forward and the rear felt seal there is a limited cavity with a draining hole at the bottom (B 16).

Always be careful to make sure that these holes are not blocked since they are intended to lead off any oil. Early production rear seals do not have this cavity.

In order to have the correct alignment between the casing and the crankshaft an aligning tool SVO 1427 should be used. Then fit the pulley.

As the end play of the crankshaft has a considerable influence on the efficiency of the seal, this play should always be between 0.01-0.1 mm (0.0004"-0.004").

PISTONS, PISTON RINGS AND PISTON PINS
Gauging
The pistons are measured with a micrometer at right angles to the piston pin on the lower edge of the piston, on B 14 A engines 9.5 mm (0.375") from the lower edge.

See the specifications for dimensions concerning pistons and cylinder bores.

Fig. 50. Measuring piston.

Piston clearance
The piston should have a certain clearance in the cylinder bore. This clearance is measured with a feeler gauge 0.045 mm (0.0018") for the B 16 engines (0.050 mm = 0.0020" for B 14 engines) and ½" wide fitted on a spring balance. The pull required should be 2-3 kg (4½-6½ lb.).

Measurement should be carried out in the direction of thrust of the piston along the complete length of the cylinder bore and at several diameters in the cylinder. The piston pin should not be fitted while this measurement is being carried out.

When checking the clearance of a piston in a standard bore cylinder, select the piston which corresponds to the class stamped on each cylinder bore. In cylinder E, for example, a piston of class E should always be fitted.

Note. This only applies to standard cylinder bores.

Fig. 51.   Checking piston fit.

Piston pin clearance

To obtain the correct clearance for the piston pins, use reamers with guides. Use these tools carefully and make only a slight cut with each pass. Correct fit is achieved when the piston pin slides into the bosses under thumb pressure. Pistons and piston pins should both be at normal room temperature when this is done.

Piston ring clearance

a)   New or rebored cylinder.

The gap between the piston ring ends, with the ring fitted into the cylinder bore, Fig. 55, should be 0.25-0.50 mm = 0.01''-0.02''. For B 16 engines and 0.35-0.45 mm (0.014''-0.018'') for B 14 engines. This should be checked with a feeler gauge. Piston rings must not bind anywhere in the groove. Check this by rolling the ring in the groove around the piston. Also measure clearance at a few places. The correct value for the clearance is 0.068-0.079 mm (0.0027''-0.0031'') for B 16

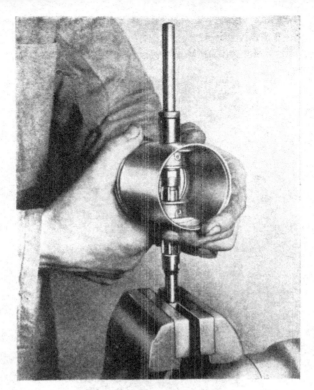

Fig. 52. Reaming piston.

Fig. 53. Checking piston pin fit.

engines and 0.035-0.069 mm (0.0014''-0.0027'') for B 14 engines.

b) Worn cylinder bore.

When checking piston ring clearance in a worn bore, the ring gap should always be checked at the bottom dead center position of the piston since the bore is worn to a taper. If the ring gap is faultily checked in the upper part of the cylinder, the ring ends can contact each other at the bottom dead center position, this causing a stress against the cylinder wall with consequent seizure. If the cylinder ridge is not removed, the upper edge of the top compression ring must be beveled.

Fig. 54.   Checking piston ring clearance in groove.

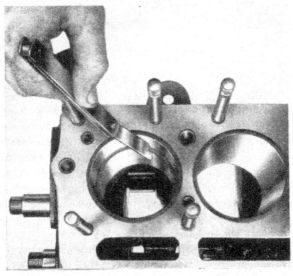

Fig. 55.   Checking piston ring gap.

Weighing pistons

It is important that all pistons in an engine have the same weight within certain specified limits in order to avoid the occurrence of vibrations in the engine. The pistons are checked by placing one of them on one pan of a balance and balancing the other pistons, one by one, against it. The difference in weight between the pistons registered by the balance pointer should not deviate by more than ± 5 grams (± 0.18 oz.) for B 16 engines and ± 3 grams (± 0.11 oz.) for B 14 engines.

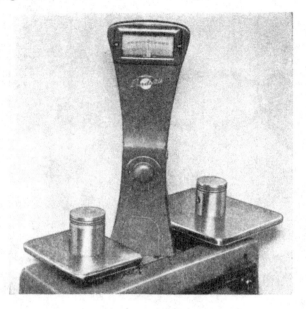

Fig. 56. Weighing pistons.

Assembling the piston and connecting rods

Before proceeding to assemble the pistons and connecting rods, check that the piston pin clearances in the piston bosses and the connecting rod bushings are correct. The connecting rod must also be absolutely straight. The piston rings are not placed on the piston until the piston and the rod have been assembled. The compression rings are beveled on the inside edge and they should be turned to face upwards. The top compression rod is chromed. When fitting the piston rings, use a special piston ring expander tool to avoid damaging the piston ring. Lubricate the piston pin and the bushing before assembling. Check that the piston is correctly assembled on the connecting rod. Since the piston pin hole in the piston is not exactly central, it is important to ensure that the correct side of the piston faces forward. For

Fig. 57. Fitting piston rings.

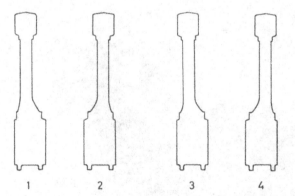

| 1 | 2 | 3 | 4 |

Fig. 58. Connecting rod locations in B 16 engines.

this reason the pistons are marked with an arrow which should face the front end of the engine. On B 16 engines, the connecting rods, which are displaced in the longitudinal axis of the engine, are fitted in accordance with Fig. 58. Fix the circlips in both bosses of the piston.

CONNECTING RODS
Replacement of piston pin bushing
Press out the old bushing by using tool SVO 1335A and press in a new bushing with the same tool. Use a suitable sleeve below. The bushing is then reamed to the correct size. Make only light

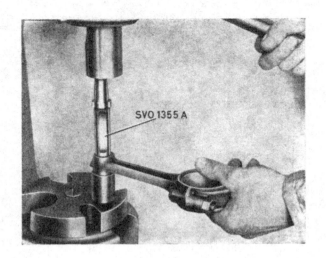

Fig. 59. Removing a bushing.

Fig. 60. Piston pin fit.

cuts and check repeatedly with the piston pin until it obtains a light thumb fit without noticeable looseness.

44

Fig. 61. Checking connecting rod.

Fig. 62. Checking connecting rod.

45

Straightening connecting rods

When extensive work is carried out on an engine, the connecting rods should always be straightened before they are replaced in the engine. The straightening can be undertaken with, or without, the piston being fitted on the rod. If the piston has been removed from the connecting rod, it is a good thing to straighten the connecting rods without the piston first and then make a final check with the piston fitted. Greatest deviations should not exceed 0.01 mm.(0.0004'') measured over a length of 100 mm (4'').

When a connecting rod has been straightened with the piston fitted, the piston rings should be removed.

Connecting rods should also be checked for freedom from S-distortion, due attention being paid to the fact that the connecting rods on B 16 engines are of displaced (offset) designs.

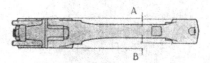

Fig. 63.   Connecting rod shank displacement,

B 16 engines.

A = 0.85 mm (0.035'')
B = 5.85 mm (0.230'')

Permissible deviation = ±0.25 mm (±0.010'')

Weight

The connecting rods of any engine should have the same weight within certain limits. By means of the classification system with various letters, connecting rods which lie within these limits are marked within the same letter. These letters are stamped on the connecting rods immediately above the bearing cap dividing line.

Only connecting rods which are marked with the same letter may be fitted in any one engine. Weights concerning a complete connecting rod with the fully finished bushing are shown in the specifications.

Mark the connecting rods with the correct letter when replacement is carried out.

CAMSHAFT

The camshaft should be inspected for linearity and for wear on the journals, cams and distributor gear. The camshaft must be straight to within 0.04 mm (0.0016''). A bent camshaft cannot be straightened but should be replaced.

The maximum permissible wear on the bearing journals is 0.075 mm (0.003) if new bearings are fitted.

If the cams, journals or ignition distributor gear are much worn, the camshaft should be replaced.

On B 16 A engine, two types of camshaft have ben used, one forged and one cast.

On engines fitted with a forged camshaft, a forged oil pump gear should always be selected and the same applies to the use of a cast camshaft together with a cast gear. Cast gears are phosphated (grey-black). These types of camshaft have various part numbers stamped on the rear end.

Camshaft adjustment

Timing gears are marked, showing the correct adjustment.

A

Fig. 64. Timing gear settings.

Replacing camshaft bearings

Camshaft bearings that have worn 0.05 mm (0.002") or more should be replaced. This operation requires the use of a boring machine. When pressing in a new bearing, make sure that the holes in the bushings index correctly with the oil passages in the block.

Replacing camshaft gear

The camshaft should be replaced when the backlash reaches

0.12 mm (0.0047"). The gear can be removed with the engine still fitted in the vehicle. See "Replacing the camshaft and/or gear." The new gear is fitted with the help of tool SVO 1356 A. Take care to ensure that the gear is not damaged.

VALVES AND VALVE MECHANISM

In order to obtain maximum power and acceleration combined with optimum fuel economy, it is important to ensure that the valves and the valve mechanism are in perfect condition. The greatest care should be exercised in all work on these parts and the measurements and clearances concerned should be closely observed.

Valves

Valve stems should be perfectly straight and the wear must nowhere exceed 0.02 mm (0.0008"). If the valve disk edge is so worn that it is less than 1 mm (0.04") wide after regrinding, the valve should be rejected.

Valve guides

The clearance between the valve stems and the valve guides should be checked with new valves. Make sure that an exhaust valve is used to check the exhaust valve guides and an inlet valve to check the inlet valve guides since the exhaust and inlet valve guides since the exhaust and inlet valve stems are of different thicknesses. Clearance with a new valve may not exceed 0.15 mm (0.0006").

Fig. 65.   Measuring valve guide clearance

Valve springs

The valve springs must conform to the specifications. The springs are close-wound at one end and this end should be placed downward when the valves are fitted.

Fig. 66.   Testing valve spring.

Push rods

The push rods should be perfectly straight. Check by rolling them on a surface plate. If they roll irregularly, they are distorted and must be rejected.

Replacing valve guides

Press out the old valve guides with tool (SVO 1459) fitted in a press. Use tool SVO 4158 when fitting since this gives the correct fitting depth. When the valve guides have been pressed in, the distance from the valve guide upper end to the cylinder head upper flat should be 21 mm (0.83).

New valve guides should be reamed with a special reamer SVO 4128. Use the same reamer for both the inlet and exhaust valve guides. Since the inlet valve stems are thicker than the exhaust valve stems, the clearance in the quide will be greatest for the exhaust valves.

Valve seat grinding

Before valve seat grinding is carried out, the cylinder head should always be carefully cleaned in the combustion chambers and gas ports and, if required, new valve guides should be pressed in and reamed.

Fig. 67. Fitting valve guides.

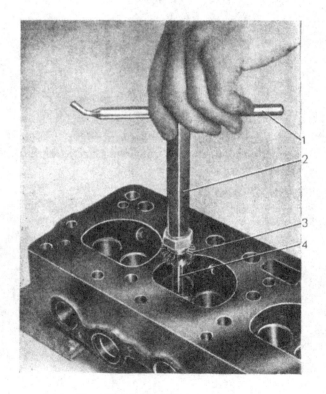

Fig. 68. Refacing valve seats.

When grinding take care not to remove more material than is absolutely necessary in order to obtain the correct angle and width of the seat.

Regrinding is carried out either with hand milling cutters, or, preferably, with electrically driven grinders. Grinding wheels used should be carefully dressed and adjusted to an angle of 45°. This should be carried out in a special attachment which can be adjusted to the desired angle.

When grinding, a pilot spindle, which is part of the equipment, is inserted in the valve guide where it centered and locked by means of an expander. The pilot spindle then should be lightly oiled with thin oil after which the grinding wheel is placed on the spindle and driven electrically under light pressure. The wheel should only be allowed to rotate for a few seconds at a time after which the machine should be switched off. It should not be lifted out until it has completely stopped rotating. Continue this procedure until the complete seating surface is perfectly smooth. If necessary, the width of the seat face is reduced from above by means of a 20° angle grinding wheel and inwards by means of a 70° wheel. After grinding is completed, the seat width should be 1.5 mm (0.060″).

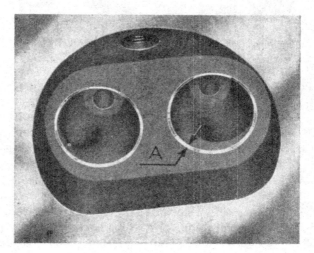

Fig. 69.   Valve seat width.

A = 1.5 mm (0.060″)

Valve grinding

Valve grinding comprises refacing of the valve sealing surface, cut-off grinding of the valve stem end and lapping-in of the valve against the valve seat with the help of an abrasive compound.

The facing of the valve is carried out in a special machine in which the valve is chucked and brought into rotation against the fine-grain grinding wheel which also rotates. The valve seat angle should be 44.5°. Before this operation is carried out, the valve should be cleaned completely free from carbon and oil. When the sealing face is finally ground, the edge of the valve should be at least 1 mm (0.04''). Otherwise the valve should be rejected since valves with thinner edge will soon be scorched and warp.

Fig. 70. Grinding valve mechanically.

To grind the end of the valve stem, place the valve in a vee-block and press the stem against the side of a grinding wheel at the same time as the valve is being rotated. The final lapping-in of the valve is carried out against the valve seat proper in the cylinder head. The valve sealing face should be smeared with a little abrasive grinding compound which has been mixed with oil. The valve is then placed in position, pressed against the seat, and rotated back and forth a few times, lift out the valve and thoroughly clean the valve and the seat. Then check the sealing surfaces by applying a coat of paint to the valve sealing face, insert the valve in the valve guide, press against the seat and give it about one-quarter of a turn. If the contact is satisfactory, the paint will cover the entire surface of the valve seat.

Fitting new valve seats

Note. Before a valve seat is replaced, always press in a new valve guide and ream it to the correct size.

If a valve seat is so heavily burnt that it cannot be reconditioned by milling or grinding, it must be removed and a new seat must be fitted. This is done by using a special end milling cutter and a new steel insert must be pressed into position. It is absolutely essential to ensure that the new seat insert is very carefully milled to size and pressed into place in order to ensure that it seats properly. This operation requires special equipment with a milling attachment and drifting tools.

The new seat insert is cooled with liquid carbon dioxide, and is then pressed into place with the particular tool required. The new seat is then ground to the correct width and angle as above.

Rocker arms

It is very important to ensure that the rocker arm bushings are not too much worn. The maximum permissable wear is 0.1 mm (0.0004"). Take care that the rocker arm pad has the correct form, that the oil passages are not clogged and that the locknut and the ball and thread on the adjusting screw are in good condition.

When fitting new bushings, take care to turn them the correct way. The passage in the bushing should form a 30° angle with the ball screw. Use tool SVO 4154 A Fig. 71. A suitable sleeve should be used as a rapport. the new bushings should be reamed with the special tool SVO 4153.

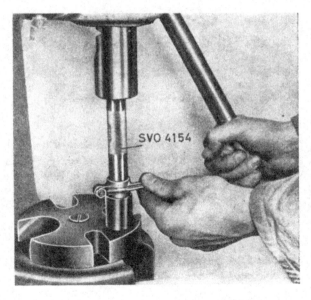

Fig. 71. Replacing rocker arm bushings.

The surface of the rocker arm pad is ground smooth with the help of a special tool. Remember that the pads are hardened and, for this reason, the grinding depth should be restricted to max.

0.5 mm (0.02"). The oil passages in the bushings should be blown clean with compressed air.

Defective adjusting screws and locknuts should be rejected and replaced if there is any fault whatsoever on the ball or the screw.

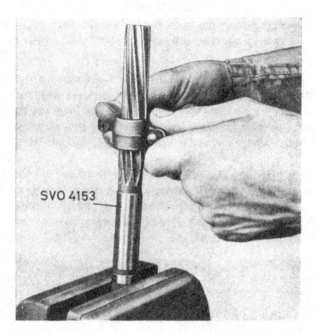

Fig. 72. Reaming rocker arm bushings.

Rocker arm shaft

The rocker arm shaft should be replaced when the rocker journals have worn more than 0.05 mm (0.002"). A good shaft should be blown clean with compressed air, and new seal washers should be fitted.

Valve lifters.

Valve lifters with worn or damaged bearing surfaces should be replaced.

Valve clearance adjustment

After an engine has ben reconditioned, the first thing to do is make a preliminary adjustment of the clearances on all the valves. This rough adjustment is carried out in the following way. All the spark plugs should be removed.

Number one piston is cranked to its firing position as observed by the closing of the exhaust valve on number four cylinder which occurs when number one piston is in its firing position.

Fig. 73.   Adjusting valve clearance.

Back off the locknut and turn the ball screw until the feeler gauge binds. Then slacken the ball screw enough to allow the gauge to be moved back and forth with some resistance. Tighten the locknut, taking care to ensure that the screw does not turn with it. Now move number four piston to the firing position by noting the closing of the exhaust valve in number one cylinder and adjust the valves on number four cylinder. Adjust the valves on cylinders two and three in the same way. When the exhaust valve on number three cylinder closes, this means that number two piston is in the firing position and vice versa.

Valve Clearances

	Inlet Valve	Exhaust Valve
B 14A, B 16 B, B 16 D	0.50 mm (0.020")	0.50 mm (0.020")
B 16 A	0.40 mm (0.016")	0.45 mm (0.018")

Fit the spark plugs when all the valves have been adjusted. Make sure that oil and water is added to the engine and then start it.

Final adjustment should be carried when the engine has reached normal operating temperature and is idling slowly.

FLYWHEEL

Replacing the flywheel bushing

If the flywheel center bushing is so much worn that the pilot bearing has become loose, the bore may be turned to increase the diameter to receive an insert ring. The diameter of the bearing should be 35 ± 0.006 mm. Maximum runout is 0.025 mm (0.001").

Refacing the flywheel

If the face of the flywheel is scored or blued, it may be refaced by grinding. Grinding should be carried out by using a special grinding attachment in a lathe. The total depth available for grinding is restricted to 0.75 mm (0.03").

Replacing the ring gear

Remove the old ring gear with a hammer and a drift. Heat the new ring gear to about 180° C (355°F) and place it on the flywheel, the beveled side of the teeth upwards. Then tap the gear lightly so that it seats well against the shoulder all round on the flywheel Do not strike too hard since this can damage the flywheel.

Pilot bearing

The pilot bearing in the flywheel should be replaced if play is evident or, if, after cleaning, there are signs of damage on the balls, ball races or retainers. Pull out the old bearing by using tool SVO 4090 and drive in a new one with tool SVO 1426.

LUBRICATING SYSTEM

Oil Pump

Reconditioning

The most important requirement is that the pump shaft does not have too much clearance in the housing. Clean the pump and check this clearance. Worn or damaged bushings or shaft should be replaced. If the housing is scored on the inside, it should be replaced. Shaft bushings should be pressed into position and reamed to size. Use a reamer with a guide bush. Holes for slotted pins are drilled after the gears have been fitted on the shaft. Before locking the driving gear in position, check that there is an axial clearance of 0.02 mm (0.008") and that gear backlash is between 0.15-0.35 mm (0.006-0.014"). The driven gear should be fitted with the ground side facing the pump housing cover. A scored cover can be refaced on a facing grinding machine.

Check the clearance between the cover and the gears before fitting the cover. This clearance should be 0.05 mm (0.002").

Fitting the oil pump

The installation of the pump is facilitated if the distributor is

Fig. 74.   Measuring backlash.

Fig. 75.   Checking axial clearance.

Fig. 76. Grinding the flywheel.

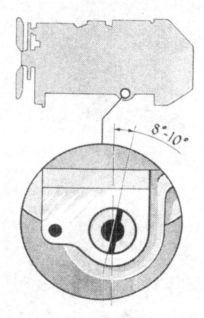

8°-10°

Fig. 77. Driving gear position.

removed and fitted back in position when the oil pump has been secured. With the engine cranked to 0° and with number one cylinder in its firing position, the driving gear should be in the position shown in fig. 77.

Relief valve

The relief valve plunger is extracted by using tool SVO 2079.

Clean the plunger before refitting it. The spring should be tested in the manner shown in fig. 66. If the spring does not hold the specified length, it should be replaced.

Oil passages

It is extremely important to ensure that the oil passages are perfectly clean and great care should be taken to ensure the removal of all obstructions. It is necessary to remove the seal plugs at the end and scrape the walls of the passages clean by using a special brush. Flushing with water should then be carried out and blowing dry with compressed air. The rocker arm system oil passage should also be cleaned. This passage goes through the block and the cylinder head beside the number four cylinder.

Oil Cleaner

The oil cleaner element should be replaced for the first time in a new reconditioned engine after 5000 km (3000 miles), the second change after a total mileage of 10000 km (6000 miles) and later replacements after every 10000 km (6000 miles).

The B 14 engine, however, can be run rather longer between normal changes, attention being paid to oil pressure. When this goes down to 2.5 kg/cm^2 (36 lb./sq. in.) during normal operation, the element should be changed.

Replacing the cleaner element, B 14 engine

1. Unscrew the drain plug on the side of the bracket and loosen the center bolt. Collect the oil that runs out.
2. Unscrew the center bolt and lift up the housing and then the element.
3. Clean the housing and the bracket by washing with solvent.
4. Fit a new, original Volvo element and gasket and then fit the housing and drain plug back in position. Top up with oil if the engine oil is not being changed at the same time.
5. Run the engine for several minutes and check for leakage.

Replacing element, B 16 A, B 16 B, B 16 D engines

1. Clean the oil cleaner housing and the adjacent parts of the engine to prevent dirt from getting into the lubricating system when removing.
2. Loosen the center bolt (3) on the cleaner housing. Collect the oil that runs out.
3. Remove the oil cleaner. Remove the old element and clean the housing with solvent. The element cannot be washed but should be replaced with a new, original Volvo element which is especially made for this type of oil cleaner. If the wrong type of element is fitted, there is a risk that the function of the lubricating system can be disturbed.

4. Check that the plate marked "UP" has the hole and the marking at the top (not fitted on early production unit). Fit the element and the gasket and then the housing. Guide the housing with the hand so that it comes into its groove correctly. Tighten the bolt with a torque of 2 kgm (15 lb. ft.).
5. If the element is replaced without changing the engine oil, topping up should be carried out by adding 0.75 liters (1½ U.S. pints).
6. Clean the parts around the oil cleaner. Start the engine and check for leakage at the gasket.

Crankcase breather

The purpose of the crankcase breather is to remove vapor and blowby gases from the crankcase. This is done by means of a pipe on the left side of the crankcase. If this pipe is blocked, there will be a pressure rise in the crankcase and this can cause oil leakage. The oil filler cap filter and this crankcase breather pipe should be cleaned out every time major work is carried out on the engine.

Fig. 78. Replacing the oil cleaner element,

B 14 A engine.

Fig. 79.   Replacing the oil cleaner element,

B 16 A, B, D engines.

1.   Element   2.   Housing   3.   Bolt

IGNITION SYSTEM
Ignition setting

Accurate adjustment of ignition timing should always be carried out with the help of stroboscope while the engine is running at a rapid idling speed. The basic setting when assembling the engine is carried out with the help of a small bulb which is connected to the distributor.

The ignition setting should preferably be suitable for high-octane fuel (93 octane Research Method). On the B 14 engine, there is a device which allows for manual adjustment.

Basic adjustment

1. Crank the engine to T.D.C. and the firing point for number one cylinder. Check that the driving gear on the oil pump is in the correct position as shown.
2. Turn the crankshaft about ¼ of a turn backwards and then forwards again to the firing position, i.e. 4° before T.D.C. on B 16 engines, 2° before T.D.C. on the B 14 engine and 5° on the B 18 engine. When rotating forwards, check that the indicator pointer, Fig. 83 is registering the correct reading and has not gone past this. If the crankshaft is rotated too far, it should be rotated backwards and then forwards again

to the correct position so as to avoid a faulty reading depend-ing on gear backlash.

3. Turn the distributor coupling to the correct position and push down the distributor into position. Connect the lamp (Max. 3 W.) as shown in Fig. 80. Switch on the current.

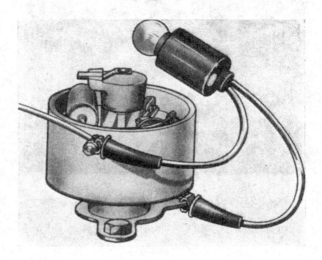

Fig. 80.   Adjusting ignition timing.

4. Loosen the clamp screw on the attaching plate and turn the distributor housing in a clockwise direction until the breaker points close, then slowly in a counter-clockwise direction until the bulb just lights up. Tighten the distributor in this position.
5. Check that the rotor points to the terminal leading to number one cylinder. Fit the distributor cap and cables as shown in Fig. 81. The rotor moves clockwise. The order of firing is 1-3-4-2.

Fine adjustment

1. Disconnect the distributor vacuum regulator by loosening one end of the pipe.
2. Mark out the graduation 21° for B 16, 20° for B 14, 18° for B 18 B, 23° for B 18 D before T.D.C. on the flywheel with chalk.
3. Connect up a lamp, Fig. 82 with the ignition cable to the spark plug in number one cylinder and the other cables to the battery.
4. Run the engine at 1500 r.p.m. and hold the lamp directed at the flywheel graduations. If the ignition setting is correct as described, then the chalk mark on the flywheel should appear

to be stationary opposite the indicator.

5. If necessary, adjust the setting by tuning the distributor after loosening the clamp screw. On the B 14 engine, the setting can be altered by turning the adjuster on the distributor.

6. Remove the lamp and retighten the vacuum pipe.

Fig. 81.   Order of firing 1—3—4—2.

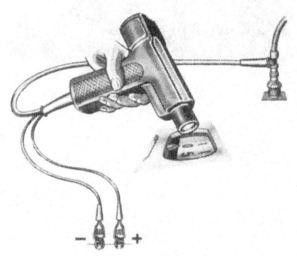

Fig. 82.   Checking ignition timing.

Testing spark plugs

After cleaning and adjusting spark plugs, test them in a special spark plug tester as it is impossible to judge their true condition from ocular inspection only. Mount the spark plug and place the pressure chamber of the apparatus under 7 kg/cm² = 100 lb./sq. in. pressure. Connect the lead to the plug ferrule; if the plug is in good working order, a powerful spark will then be seen in the inspection window when the switch is pressed.

Observe instructions accompanying the tester.

Fig. 83.   Flywheel markings.

COOLING SYSTEM
Water Pump
Removing pump
Drain cooling water. To remove water pump, first remove fan which is held by four screws in the pulley, then remove fan belt. Next remove four screws securing pump to engine block, and pump is free. The radiator need not be removed.

Dismantling
1. Remove lock screw retaining rear ball bearing. Use tool SVO 2266 to press out pump shaft, while guiding pulley with one hand to prevent binding. Remove impeller. Ball bearings and spacer sleeve generally come out with the shaft; if not, remove sealing ring and press out bearings using large end of tool SVO 2266.
2. Turn pump housing and take out sealing ring with tool SVO 2266. Unscrew grease cup.
3. Remove oilslinger. Place ring SVO 2271 in the press, large diameter end downward. Use tool SVO 2266 to press shaft through the ring so that the pulley, ball bearings, and spacer sleeve come loose.

Inspection
Wash all parts carefully before inspecting for damage. The bearings shall rotate freely without sticking, and the sealing ring must be free from cracks and press firmly and smoothly against the impeller.

Replace damaged and worn parts.

Assembly
1. Place the front bearing on ring SVO 2271 open side upwards. Press shaft into bearing until shaft end bottoms against press table, then into pulley until shaft end is flush with pulley face.
2. Place spacer sleeve on shaft, turn shaft round and press on rear bearing with ring SVO 2271 as support. The ball bearing is turned so as to show open side toward spacer. Place rings as shown in Fig. 97 but with drift tool against pulley face. Install grease nipple.
3. Install assembled shaft in housing. Take care that shaft does not bind when pressed into housing. Insert lock screw at rear bearing.
4. Install oilslinger, flange away from bearing. Install sealing ring 4 with tool SVO 2270.
5. Mount impeller with tool SVO 2266, placing large end against impeller.

Fig. 97.   Removing the pulley.

6. Check that pulley turns easily. Check impeller to housing flange clearance, which should be 0.3 mm = 0.012 in. Place a straightrule across housing end and check with feeler gauge. The clearance between impeller rear face and housing should be 0.5 mm — 1 mm. = 0.02-0.04 in.
7. Fill pump with heat-resistant grease.

Fitting pump

When fitting pump on engine, proceed in reverse order to removal. Always install a new gasket between pump housing and cylinder block. Inspect water hose and replace, if soft and mushroomed inside.

Thermostat

The thermostat has the important function of reducing the time for warm-up to normal operating temperature. If defective, it must not be removed, but should be replaced by a new one.

Cylinder wear and corrosion are especially prominent when the engine is cold. The function of the thermostat is to block the passage for the water from the engine to the radiator, and to re-circulate it through the engine. It is thereby rapidly brought to operating temperature, and cylinder wear is reduced. Inside the engine, the water can circulate through a bypass to ensure even heat distribution without local overheating.

If it is suspected that the thermostat has become stuck in the open position, or has sprung a leak, it should be taken out and tested. Tie thermostat to a piece of string and suspend it in a beaker of water, together with a thermometer. Take care that the thermometer does not stand on the bottom of the beaker. Heat the water and observe the thermometer reading when the thermostat begins to open. The opening temperature should be between 75° and 78° C, i.e. 167°-172° F. (72°-76° C $=$ 162°-169° F on early production engines). Raise temperature until thermostat is fully open, which should happen at 90° C (194° F) or 85° C (185° F) on early production engines. If the thermostat operating range is another, replace it.

Radiator

A leaky radiator shall be soldered. If the leak is somewhere in the cellular system, the radiator must be dismantled and tested to establish the correct location of the leak. Do not solder haphazardly.

The radiator is tested by connecting a compressed air hose to one radiator pipe and sealing off the other. Use a reducing valve to take the pressure down to max. 0.2 kg/cm² $=$ 3 lb./sq. in. Submerge the radiator in water and trace air bubbles issuing from it.

Removing radiator

Disconnect the radiator blind wire, and drain off the cooling water from the engine. If the water contains antifreeze, collect water in a clean vessel. After disconnecting upper and lower radiator hoses and removing screws on either side of radiator, lift off radiator.

Stopped radiator

Blockage can be avoided by using clean water (preferably rain water) with rust inhibitor added.

If it is suspected that the radiator may be wholly or partially blocked, check by feeling the front of the radiator while the engine is running. If part of the radiator front feels cold although the engine water is excessively hot, the radiator must be partially blocked. It is often rather difficult to clean out a stopped radiator perfectly. Dissolve approx. 250 grams of soda in 5 liters of hot water (9 oz. in 5 US quarts), fill solution in radiator and top up with water. Cleaners are also available commercially. If caustic soda is used, take about half amount in same quantity of water. Let this solution remain in engine for about 4 hours running, then drain cooling system and flush through carefully with water, preferably against the normal direction of circulation, engine and radiator separately with thermostat removed.

If necessary, repeat this cleaning procedure once more. If without result, have radiator cleaned by specialist, or replace it.

Anti-Freeze

To prevent freezing of the engine during cold weather, antifreeze is added to the cooling water.

Ethylene glycol is an effective anti-freeze agent which raises the boiling point of water above $100°$ C $= 212°$ F. Ethylene glycol is not volatile.

Denaturated spirit is sometimes used but has the disadvantage of vaporizing even at normal temperature, making a regular check necessary. Moreover, if spilled onto body parts, the spirit damages the paint.

Before adding antifreeze:

1. Flush out cooling system carefully.
2. Check radiator for leaks, and inspect all rubber hoses, not forgetting the hot water heating system.
3. Pull the cylinder head nuts, check all hoses and gaskets for leaks, replace collars and gaskets which do not seal properly, and also check radiator filler cap gasket.
4. Check that thermostat is in good order.

After draining anti-freeze in spring, flush out cooling system carefully in a reverse direction.

REASSEMBLING ENGINE

When reassembling engine, use a suitable stand or dolly to support the cylinder block. The order of reassembly is the reverse of that used when dismantling the engine.

It is very important that all parts are carefully cleaned before assembling, and oiled or greased where suitable. All gaskets, packings, and other sealing parts must be installed with care. The table in the specifications gives the torque values to be used for various bolts and nuts.

Pack in the flywheel ball bearing with heat-resistant grease before fitting. Use tool SVO 1426 to drive in bearing. Secure flywheel nuts with new washers.

Clutch, flywheel, and crankshaft are balanced together as a unit, and are marked with paint. Take care that they are mounted in their correct positions according to markings.

Use tool SVO 1356 A to install crankshaft gear and camshaft gear. Hammer in the sealing laths at the rear main bearing, and cut off flush with engine block.

Make sure that the generator tensioner is clean and free from paint on the contact surfaces to ensure good grounding.

Use only new gaskets and seals when reassembling engine. The timing gear casing must be perfectly centered in order to seal effectively. This is achieved by using pilot tool SVO 1427 A.

It is of utmost importance that the cylinder head nuts are pulled in the prescribed order, as the head may otherwise warp or crack. The proper torquing order of the nuts is shown. Always use a calibrated torque wrench.

Fig. 103. Tightening sequence for cylinder head nuts.

FITTING ENGINE IN VEHICLE

To fit engine in vehicle, proceed in reverse order to removal procedure. Take care not to damage engine, cables, or paint. Attach securely to engine supports, but not too tight. Secure nuts with new cotters.

RUNNING-IN

A reconditioned engine or on which new pistons, piston rings, main bearings or connecting rod bearings have been fitted must always be operated with great care during the first time of operation so that the new parts wear in correctly. This running-in is preferably made in a test stand, if available.

Check that oil and water have been filled.

The oil pressure gauge should show a reading immediately after the engine starts. If not, stop the engine and remedy the fault. A normal oil pressure is 2.5-3.5 kg/cm² (36-50 lb./sq. in.) on B 16 engines and 3-4 kg/cm² (43-57 lb./sq. in.) on B 14 engines.

If everything seems in order, let engine fast idle for a few hours, then load engine and raise the speed to about 1000 r.p.m. The total running time in the test stand should be some 3 hours. Drain and fill new oil at the end of the running-in period. If no test stand is available, running-in will have to be carried out with engine installed in the vehicle. Fill oil and water, start engine and observe oil pressure as above. Let engine fast idle for a few hours.

Check oil pressure and cooling water temperature at intervals. Look out for possible leakage of oil or water and listen for abnormal noises.

Before loading engine and increasing speed, retighten cylinder head nuts and adjust valve lash. Use tool SVO 2264, with extension bar and torque wrench, in order to avoid dismantling the rocker arm shaft. If the extension bar is so long that it penetrates through the tool and touches the cylinder head, shorten it by grinding. See specifications for tightening torques.

Change oil after running-in.

The fan belt (narrow belts on B 16 engines) should be tensioned so that the pulley begins to slip when a pull of 5.5-6.5 kg (12-14½ lb. is applied 150 mm (6") from the hub center. See Fig. 105.

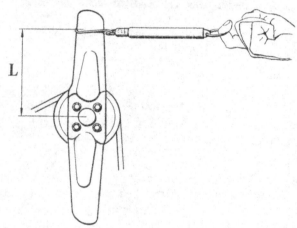

Fig. 105. Pulley belt tension.

L = 150 mm (6")

On B 14 engines (thicker belts), the belt should be tensioned so that it is possible to depress it about 10 mm (½") with the thumb at a point midway between the pulleys.

The running-in of the engine is not finally completed and the precautions detailed in the Instruction Book for the vehicle must still be observed.

SPECIFICATIONS
B 14 ENGINE

General

Output, B.H.P./r.p.m.—70/5500; Max. Torque: kgm/r.p.m.—10.5/3000, lb. ft./r.p.m.—75.9/3000; Number of cylinders—4; Bore: mm—75, in.—2.953; Stroke: mm—80, in.—3.15; Displacement: liters—1.414, cu. in.—86.; Compression ratio—7.8:1; Compression pressure at 200 r.p.m., kg/cm²—10-11; lbs. sq. in.—142-156; Weight, including clutch, carburetor, starter motor and generator: kg—145, lb.—320.

CYLINDER BLOCK

Material—Special-alloy cast-iron. The cylinder bores are drilled directly in the block; Bore, standard—75.00 mm, 2.953"; Bore, 0.010" oversize—75.25 mm, 2.963"; Bore, 0.020" oversize—75.51 mm, 2.973"; Bore, 0.030" oversize—75.76 mm, 2.983"; Bore, 0.040" oversize—76.02 mm, 2.993"; Bore, 0.050" oversize—76.27 mm, 3.003".

PISTONS

Material—Light-alloy; Weight—297 ± 3 grams, 10.48 ± 0.11 oz.; Permissable weight difference between pistons in same engine—6 grams, 0.21 oz.; Total height—86 mm, 3.390"; Height from piston pin center to piston top—46 mm, 1.81"; Piston clearance—0.04-0.06 mm, 0.0016"-0.0024"; Diameter, measured at right angles to piston pin at lower edge (9.5 mm = 3/8" from lower edge on B 14 engines), standard—74.95 mm, 2.9508"; 0.010" oversize—75.20 mm, 2.9606"; 0.020" oversize—75.46 mm, 2.9709"; 0.030" oversize—75.71 mm, 2.9807"; 0.040" oversize—75.97 mm, 2.9910"; 0.050" oversize—76.22 mm, 3.0004".

PISTON RINGS

Upper side marked "TOP". Piston ring oversizes—0.01" to 0.05".

Compression rings

Beveled on upper inner edge. Number on each piston—2; Height upper ring (chromed)—1.5 mm, 0.060"; Height lower ring—2.5 mm, 0.100"; Ring gap width—0.35-0.45 mm, 0.014"-0.018"; Ring clearance in groove—0.050-0.087mm, 0.0020"-0.0034".

Oil rings

Number on each piston—1; Height—5 mm, 0.200"; Ring gap

width—0.25-0.40 mm, 0.010"-0.016"; Ring clearance in groove—0.031-0.069 mm, 0.0012"-0.0027".

PISTON PINS
Fully floating. Circlips at both ends in piston.

Fit in connecting rod (18°C = 65°F)—Close running fit; Fit in piston (18°C = 65°F)—Slide fit; Diameter, standard—19 mm, 0.748"; Diameter, 0.05 mm oversize—19.05 mm, 0.750"; Diameter, 0.10 mm oversize—19.10 mm, 0.752"; Diameter, 0.20 mm oversize—19.20 mm, 0.754".

CYLINDER HEAD
Height measured from cylinder head contact surface to cylinder head nut flats—97 mm, 3.82".

CRANKSHAFT
Replaceable bearing shells for main and connecting rod bearings. Crankshaft end play—0.01-0.10 mm, 0.0004"-0.0040"; Main bearings, radial play, flange bearing—0.014-0.064 mm, 0.0005"-0.0025"; Main bearings, radial play, others—0.051-0.100 mm, 0.0020"-0.0039"; Connecting rod bearings, radial play—0.051-0.087 mm, 0.0020"-0.0034".

MAIN BEARINGS
Main bearing journals
Journal diameter, standard—53.950-53.960 mm, 2.1240"-2.1244"; 0.010" undersize — 53.696-53.706 mm, 2.1140"-2.1144"; 0.020" undersize — 53.442-53.452 mm, 2.1040"-2.1044"; 0.030" undersize — 53.188-53.198 mm, 2.0949"-2.0944"; 0.040" undersize — 52.934-52.944 mm, 2.0840"-2.0844"; Journal width, flange bearing, standard—38.935-38.975 mm, 1.5329"-1.5344"; 0.1 mm oversize (for 0.010" undersize shell)—39.035-39.075 mm, 1.5369"-1.5384"; 0.2 mm oversize (for 0.020" undersize shell) — 39.135-39.175 mm, 1.5407"-1.5423"; 0.3 mm oversize (for 0.030" undersize shell)—39.235-39.275 mm, 1.5447"-1.5463"; 0.4 mm oversize (for 0.040" undersize shell)—39.335-39.375 mm, 1.5486"-1.5502".

Main bearing shells
Flange bearing shells
Thickness, standard — 1.911-1.918 mm, 0.0752"-0.0755"; 0.010" undersize—2.038-2.045 mm, 0.0802"-0.0805"; 0.020" undersize—2.165-2.172 mm, 0.0852"-0.0855"; 0.030" undersize—2.292-2.299 mm, 0.0902"-0.0905"; 0.040" undersize—2.419-2.426 mm, 0.0952"-0.0955".

Other main bearing shells

Thickness, standard — 1.894-1.900 mm, 0.0746"-0.0748"; Thickness, undersize 0.010" — 2.021-2.027 mm, 0.0796"-0.0798"; Thickness, undersize 0.020" — 2.148-2.154 mm, 0.0845"-0.0848"; Thickness, undersize 0.030" — 2.275-2.281 mm, 0.0895"-0.0898"; Thickness, undersize 0.040" — 2.402-2.408 mm, 0.0946"-0.0948".

CONNECTING ROD BEARINGS
Connecting rod bearing journals

Bearing seat width—32.900-33.00 mm, 1.2953"-1.2992"; Journal diameter, standard — 47.589-47.600 mm, 1.8736"-1.8740"; 0.010" undersize — 47.335-47.347 mm, 1.8635"-1.8640"; 0.020" undersize — 47.081-47.092 mm, 1.8536"-1.8540"; 0.030" undersize — 46.827-46.838 mm, 1.8436"-1.8440"; 0.040" undersize — 46.573-46.584 mm, 1.8336"-1.8520".

Connecting rod bearing shells

Thickness, standard — 1.562-1.568 mm, 0.0615"-0.0617"; Thickness, 0.010" undersize — 1.689-1.695 mm, 0.0665"-0.0667"; Thickness, 0.020" undersize — 1.816-1.822 mm, 0.0715"-0.0717"; Thickness, 0.030" undersize — 1.943-1.949 mm, 0.0765"-0.0767"; Thickness, 0.040" undersize — 2.070-2.076 mm, 0.0815"-0.0817".

Connecting rods

Marked 1-4 on side away from camshaft. Classified A-D showing weight classification. Only connecting rods with same weight classification may be used in the same engine. Axial play at crankshaft—0.15-0.35 mm, 0.0060"-0.0140"; Length, center-center—150 ± 0.1 mm, 5.905 ± 0.004"; Weight, Class A—528-558 grams, 18.62-19.68 oz.;Weight, Class B—558-588 grams, 19.68-2p. 74 oz.; Weight, Class C—588-618 grams, 20.74-21.80 oz.; Weight, Class D—618-648 grams, 21.80-22.85 oz.

FLYWHEEL

Permissable axial play—0.20 mm, 0.008"; Ring gear (chamfer facing inwards)—116 teeth.

Flywheel housing

Permissable axial play for rear surface—0.08 mm, 0.0016"; Max. radial play for rear guide—0.15 mm, 0.0060".

CAMSHAFT

Drive—Fiber gear on camshaft; Number of bearings—3; Forward bearing journal, diameter—46.975-47.000 mm, 1.8494"-1.8504"; Center bearing journal, diameter—42.975-43.000 mm,

1.619"-1.6929"; Rear bearing journal, diameter—36.975-37.000 mm, 1.4557"-1.4567"; Radial clearance — 0.025-0.075 mm, 0.0010"-0.0029".

Valve clearance for check of camshaft setting (cold engine— 1.15 mm, 0.045"; Inlet valves should open at—0° (T.D.C.).

Camshaft bearings

Forward bearing, diameter—47.025-47.050 mm, 1.8514"-1.8524"; Center bearing, diameter — 43.025-43.050 mm, 1.6939"-1.6949"; Rear bearing, diameter—37.025-37.050 mm, 1.4577"-1.4587".

Timing gears

Crankshaft gear—20 teeth; Camshaft gear—40 teeth; Backlash—0.01-0.04 mm, 0.0004"-0.0016".

VALVE SYSTEM
Valves
Inlet

Disk diameter—37 mm, 1.46"; Stem diameter—7.859-7.874 mm, 0.3094"-0.3100"; Valve seat angle—44.5°; Cylinder head seat angle—45°; Seat width in cylinder head—1.5 mm, 0.060".

Exhaust

Disk resistant to ethyl fuel. Disk diameter—34 mm, 1.34"; Stem diameter—7.830-7.845 mm, 0.3082-0.3089"; Valve seat angle—44.5°; Cylinder head seat angle—45°; Seat width in cylinder head—1.5 mm, 0.060".

Valve clearances

Clearance, inlet, warm engine—0.50 mm, 0.020"; Clearance, exhaust, warm engine—0.50 mm, 0.020"

Valve guides

Length—62 mm, 2.44"; Inner diameter—7.905-7.920 mm, 0.311"-0.312"; Length above cylinder head upper surface—21 mm, 0.83"; Clearance valve stem—valve guide, inlet valves— 0.031-0.061 mm, 0.0012"-0.0024"; .Clearance valve stem—valve guide, exhaust valves—0.060-0.090 mm, 0.0024"-0.0035".

Valve springs

Springs close—wound at one end. This end should be turned downwards. Length, unloaded—42.5 mm, 1.67"; Length mm/loading, kg—37/27 ± 2; Length in./loading, lb.—1.46/60 ± 4½; Length, mm/loading, kg—28.5/78 ± 4; Length, in./loading, lb.— 1.13/172 ± 9.

LUBRICATING SYSTEM

Oil capacity of crankcase—3.25 liters, 7 US pints; Oil capacity, incl. oil cleaner—3.75 litters, 8 US pints, 7 Imp. pints; Oil pressure, warm engine (2000 r.p.m. = 50 km.p.h. (30 m.p.h.) (in top gear)—3-4 kg/cm², 43-57 lb./sq. in.; Lubricant—Engine oil (For Service MM, MS); Lubricant viscosity, below 0° C (32°F)—SAE 10W; Lubricant viscosity, from 0° C (32°F) to + 30°C (90°F)—SAE 20; Lubricant viscosity, above 30° C (90° F)—SAE 30.

Oil pump

Type—Gear pump; Number of teeth—10; Axial clearance—0.02-0.10 mm, 0.0008"-0.0004"; Radial clearance—0.00-0.10 mm, 0"-0.0004"; Backlash—0.15-0.25 mm, 0.006"-0.010".

Oil cleaner

Type—Fullflow; Make and designation—AC, A 700; Element, designation including gasket—AC 70; Bypass valve spring (in oil cleaner), length unloaded—50 mm, 2"; Spring length loaded with 1.5 ± 0.1 kg—35 mm; Spring length loaded with 3½ lb—1.38"; Material thickness—1 mm, 0.040".

FUEL SYSTEM

Fuel pump, make and type—AC diaphragm pump; Fuel pressure—Min. 0.14 kg/cm², 2 lb./sq. in., Max. 0.25 kg/cm², 3.5 lb./sq. in.; Capacity at idling speed—0.5 liters/min., 1 US pint/min.; Fuel gauge, type—Electric.

CARBURETORS

Make and type—SU H2; Number of carburetors—2; Size (air intake diameter)—32 mm, (1¼"); Fuel control jet, designation—AUC 2112; Fuel needle, designation—C2; Float level gauge (placed between the float bowl cover and the yoke-formed part of the needle arm), diam.—11 mm, 7/16"; Rapid idling, setting of rod in cam-shaped lever—Position 1; Idling speed—approx. 550 r.p.m.

IGNITION SYSTEM

Order of firing—1-3-4-2; Ignition setting, basic, (93 octane Research Method)—2° before T.D.C.; Ignition setting, basic, (83 octane Research Method); Ignition setting stroboscope setting 1500 r.p.m. with vacuum regulator disconnected—20° before T.D.C. (93 octane); Spark plugs—Champion Y 4A (10 mm), Champion J 6 (14 mm.) or similar; Spark plug gap—0.7-0.8 mm. (0.028"-0.032").

Distributor

Make and designation—Auto-Lite, IAT 4006; Direction of rotation—Clockwise; Contact breaker gap—0.45-0.55 mm., 0.018"-

0.022"; Breaker arm tension—0.48-0.57 kg., 17-20 oz.; Dwell angle—47°.

COOLING SYSTEM

Type—Pressure; Filler cap valve opens at—0.23-0.30 kg/cm², 3.2-4.2 lb./sq. in.; Thermostat marked—165; Starts to open at— 74 ± 2° C, 165 ± 4° F; Fully open at—85 ± 2° C, 185 ± 4° F; Fan belt, designation—11/16" x 34½".

WEAR TOLERANCES

Cylinders:

Rebore when worn (if oil consumption abnormal)—0.25 mm., 0.010".

Crankshaft:

Maximum main bearing journal out-of-round — 0.05 mm., 0.0020"; Maximum connecting rod journal out-of-round — 0.07 mm., 0.0028"; Maximum crankshaft end play — 0.15 mm., 0.0060".

Valves

Maximum valve stem to valve guide clearance — 0.15 mm., 0.0060"; Maximum valve stem wear—0.02 mm., 0.0008"; Minimum width of valve disk edge—1 mm., 0.04".

Camshaft:

Maximum out-of-round (with new bearings) — 0.075 mm., 0.0030"; Maximum bearing wear—0.02 mm, 0.0008".

TIGHTENING TORQUES

Cylinder head—7-8 kgm., 50-60 lb. ft.; Main bearings—8-10 kgm., 60-70 lb. ft.; Connecting rod bearings—4-5 kgm., 30-35 lb. ft.; Flywheel—2.3-2.7 kgm., 17-20 lb. ft.; Generator bolts (⅜"- 16) (B 16 A)—2.5 kgm., 18 lb. ft.;Oil cleaner center bolt—2 kgm., 15 lb. ft.; Spark plugs, 14 mm.—3.5 kgm., 25 lb. ft.; Spark plugs, 10 mm. (early production)—1.5 kgm., 11 lb. ft.

TOOLS

The following special tools are required when carrying out repair and service work on the engine and water pump.

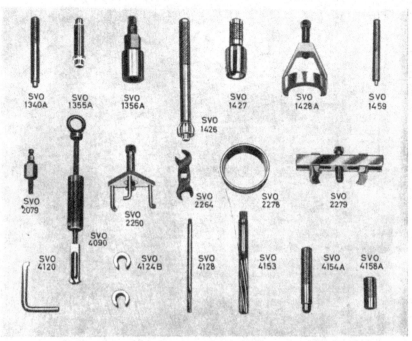

Fig. 107. Special tools for engine.

SVO 1340 A	Drift for removing and fitting piston pins	SVO 2250	Puller for camshaft gear
SVO 1355 A	Drift for removing and fitting connecting rod bushings	SVO 2264	Wrench for tightening cylinder head nuts under rocker arm shaft
SVO 1356 A	Press tool for camshaft gear and crankshaft pulley	SVO 2278	Installation ring for pistons, B 16 engines
SVO 1426	Drift for fitting ball bearing in flywheel	SVO 2279	Puller for crankshaft pulley and generator
SVO 1427 A	Centering tool for timing gear casing and crankshaft gear	SVO 4090	Puller for ball bearing in flywheel
SVO 1428 A	Puller for crankshaft gear	SVO 4120	Puller for water distributor pipe
SVO 1459	Drift for removing valve guides	SVO 4124 B	Spacer for engine supports (2)
SVO 2079	Puller for oil relief valve plunger	SVO 4128	Valve guide reamer
SVO 2229	Installating ring for pistons, B 14 engines	SVO 4153	Reamer for rocker arm bushings
		SVO 4154 A	Drift for removing and fitting rocker arm bushings
		SVO 4158 A	Drift for fitting valve guides

Illustration 1-A. Section through B 18 B engine

1. Front air cleaner
2. Front carburetor
3. Upper valve washer
4. Exhaust valve
5. Shield plate
6. Inlet manifold
7. Valve key
8. Inlet valve
9. Valve guide
10. Throttle control
11. Seal ring
12. Valve spring
13. Rocker arm
14. Rocker arm shaft
15. Breather (oil filler)
16. Spring
17. Lower valve washers (rubber and steel washers, rubber washer lowest)
18. Push rod
19. Bearing bracket
20. Rocker arm cover
21. Gasket
22. Water distributor tube
23. Cylinder head
24. Vacuum line
25. Distributor
26. Flywheel housing
27. Valve lifter
28. Retainer
29. Cylinder block
30. Gear
31. Lock ring
32. Pilot bearing
33. Flywheel
34. Bushing
35. Flange bearing shell
36. Sealing flange
37. Main bearing cap
38. Cover plate
39. Oil pan
40. Gasket
41. Oil pump
42. Main bearing shell
43. Oil pipe
44. Crankshaft
45. Camshaft
46. Piston
47. Piston rings
48. Connecting rod
49. Lock ring
50. Piston pin
51. Connecting rod bearing shell
52. Connecting rod bushing
53. Thrust washer and spacer
54. Camshaft gear
55. Timing gear casing
56. Crankshaft gear
57. Sleeve
58. Washer
59. Pulley
60. Bolt
61. Fan
62. Key
63. Oil jet
64. Key
65. Lock washer
66. Cooling water inlet
67. Gasket
68. Water pump
69. Generator
70. Pulley
71. Gasket
72. Seal
73. Tensioner
74. Cylinder head gasket
75. Thermostat
76. Gasket
77. Cooling water outlet

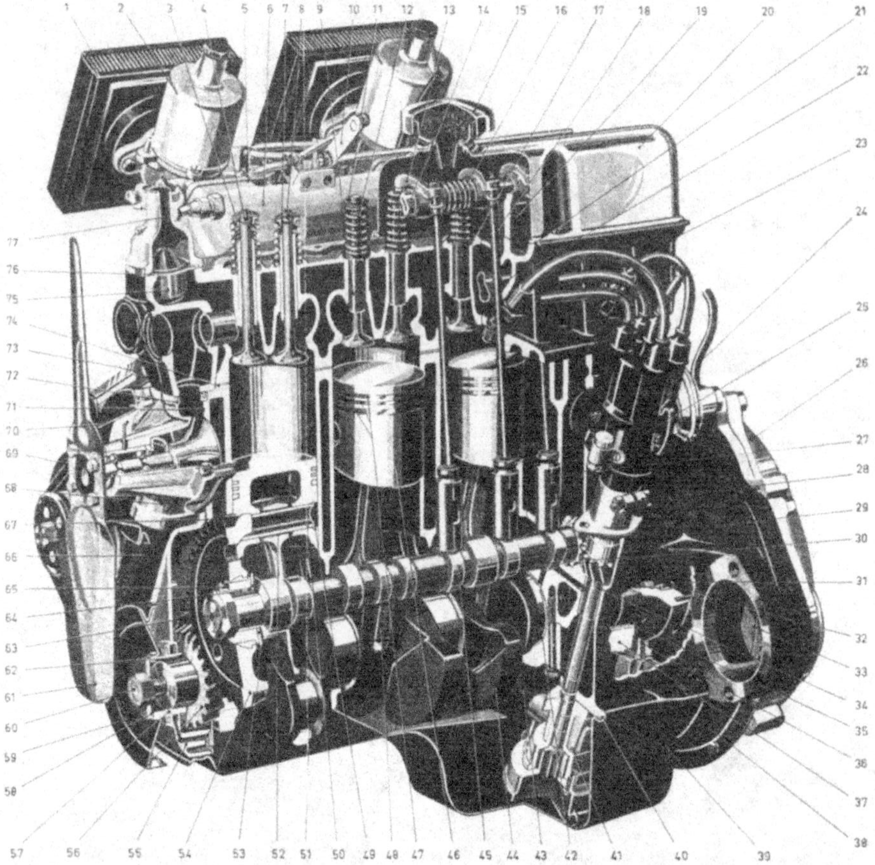

78

ENGINES: B 18 SERIES

The B 18 series of engines was put into production in 1961 with the first units going into PV 544-C units as of chassis number 330100 and in P 122 series as of chassis 84300. All P 1800 models are fitted with the B 18B. The new engine, of 1780 cc (109 cubic inch) displacement is of the same general configuration as the earlier four cylinder overhead cam B 16 series, but has five main bearings and a number of design refinements. Full specifications are given at the end of this book, but the distinguishing characteristics by which each type can be identified are given below:

Condensed Specifications

Engine	B 18 A	B 18 B	B 18 D
Output B.H.P/r.p.m.	75/4500	100/5500	90/5000
Torque, lb. ft./r.p.m.	103/2800	108/4000	105/3500
Compression ratio	8.5-1	9.5-1	8.5-1
Carburetion	Zenith 36	SU HS6	SU HS6

CYLINDER BLOCK

The cylinder block (29, Illustration 1-A) is made in one unit of special cast iron. The cylinder bores which are surounded by cooling water jackets, are machined directly in the block. The oil channels in the block are arranged in such a way that the oil cleaner, which is of the fullflow type is connected directly to the oil cooler on one side of the block.

CYLINDER HEAD WITH VALVES

The cylinder head (23) which is attached to the top of the block by means of bolts, covers the upper part of the cylinders and forms the combustion chambers. The cylinder head also contains the inlet and exhaust ports as well as cooling water jackets. The valves (4 and 8, illustration 1-A) in the cylinder head are of the overhead type and are made of special steel, being carried in replaceable guides.

CRANKSHAFT WITH BEARINGS

The crankshaft (44) is of forged steel and has ground and surface-hardened crankpins. It is carried in five main bearings, the rear one of which also functions as an axial guide thrust bearing. The crankshaft is drilled for lubricating oil.

The insert bearing shells consist of steel-backed, indium plated, lead-bronzed bearing metal.

Fig. 2. *The engine (right-hand side)*
(*oil cleaner only fitted on B 18 B*)

1. Shield plate
2. Rear air cleaner
3. Rear carburetor
4. Forward air cleaner
5. Forward carburetor
6. Breather (oil filler)
7. Inlet manifold
8. Exhaust manifold
9. Cylinder head
10. Water pipe (to oil cooler)
11. Water pipe (from heater)
12. Setting mark
13. Pulley
14. Pulley
15. Belt tensioner
16. Water pipe
17. Cylinder block
18. Oil cooler (B 18 B)
19. Plug for oil temperature gauge (B 18 B)
20. Drain cock for water
21. Oil cleaner
22. Drain cock for water

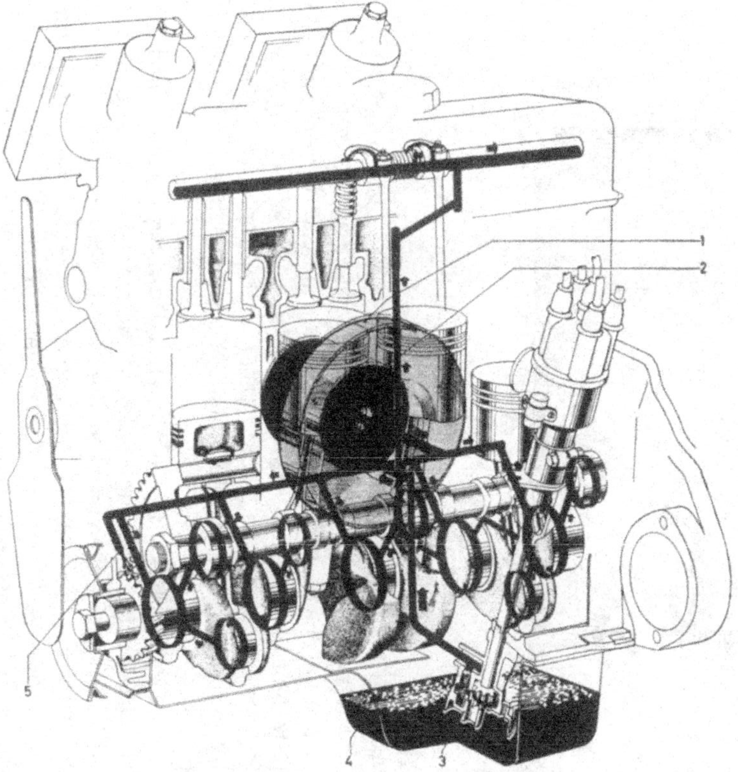

Fig. 1—3. The lubricating system

1. Oil cooler
2. Oil cleaner
3. Oil pump
4. Oil pan
5. Nozzle

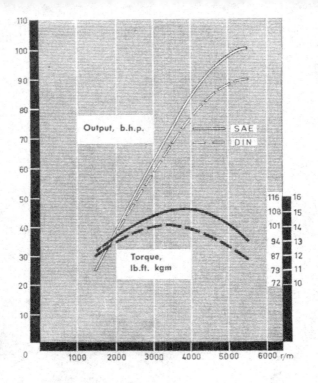

Fig. 1-4. Output and torque curves

CAMSHAFT AND VALVE LIFTERS

The camshaft (45) is made of special-alloy cast-iron and has surface-hardened cam lobes. The camshaft is driven from the crankshaft by means of gears with a ratio of 1.2 Axial guidance is obtained by means of a thrust washer on the front end of the shaft. The axial clearance is determined by a shim behind the camshaft gear.

The valve lifters (27) are operated directly by the camshaft. They are located in ground holes in the block above the camshaft and transfer the movement to the valves through push rods and rocker arms. There are no inspection covers for the valve lifters since the valve lifters are accessible from the top after the cylinder head has been removed.

CONNECTING RODS, PISTONS AND PISTON RINGS

The connecting rods (48) are of drop-forged steel and are fitted at the top with finely-finished bushings which act as bearings for the piston pins. The connecting rod bearings on the crankshaft consist of precision-manufactured, replaceable bearing shells. The pistons (46) are made of light-alloy and each has two compression rings and one oil scraper ring. The upper compression ring on each piston is chromed to reduce cylinder wear. The piston pins (50) are fully-floating in both the pistons and connecting rods. The axial movement of the piston pins is limited by the circlips in the piston pin holes.

LUBRICATING SYSTEM

The engine is lubricated by oil under pressure, see Fig. 1-3. The pressure is produced by a gear type pump, driven from the camshaft and located under the crankshaft in the oil pan. The gears in the pump force the oil past the relief valve (which is also located in the pump) and then through the oil cooler, oil cleaner and so out through the passages to various lubricating points. All the oil thus first passes through the oil cleaner before reaching a lubrication point.

OIL PUMP

When the pump gears start rotating, oil is carried through the spaces between the teeth along the inner walls of the pump from the suction side to the pressure side. The pressure pipe from the pump to the block has no screw unions and is tensioned in position when the pump attaching bolts are tightened. There are sealing rings of special rubber at both ends of this pipe. The relief valve is located directly in the pump.

OIL CLEANER

The oil cleaner is manufactured in one unit complete with insert cartridge which is made of special paper. In the oil cleaner there is a relief valve which releases oil past the cartridge if the resistance to flow should become too great.

OIL COOLER

The oil cooler is fitted between the oil cleaner and the cylinder block and consists of an inner part for the oil which is surrounded by a cooling jacket. When the oil passes through the cooler on its way to the oil cleaner, part of the heat from the oil is conducted away by the cooling water. The cooling water cannot go to the nearest way from the inlet (1) to the outlet (6) but is forced to circulate round the oil cooler by means of the stop plates (5). The oil is pressed through the pair of disks one after the other due to the stop plates (4) and then passes out finally to the air cleaner.

IGNITION SYSTEM

The distributor (25 Illustration 1-A) which is driven through a bevel gear from the camshaft is fitted with both centrifugal and vacuum governors. The direction of rotation is anti-clockwise and the order of firing is 1-3-4-2

COOLING SYSTEM

The cooling system is of the pressure type with a circulating pump.

While the engine is cold the water only circulates through the engine itself through a by-pass. When the engine warms up, the thermostat starts to open the outlet to the radiator whereby the spring-loaded plate on the underside of the thermostat closes the bypass. Circulation is then regulated by the thermostat so that the engine operating temperature is maintained within the correct limits. A tube in the cylinder head ensures that there is equal distribution of the cooling water through the warmest parts of the cylinder head. The cooling water round the walls of the cylinders circulates by the thermo-siphon principle.

WORK THAT CAN BE CARRIED OUT WITHOUT REMOVING THE ENGINE FROM THE CAR

NOTE: For illustrations relating to these operations see "B-14 & B 16 Engine".

MEASURING THE COMPRESSION

1. Run the engine until it obtains normal operating temperature. Check that the air cleaners are not blocked. Replace them if necessary.
2. Remove all the spark plugs. Depress the accelerator pedal and place a weight on it or block the carburetor linkage so that the throttle is completely open.
3. Insert a compression gage in the spark plug holes, one after the other, and turn the engine over with the starter motor until the pressure reaches a maximum value.
4. Note the pressure obtained on each cylinder.
5. If low or uneven values are obtained, repeat the compression test after pouring a small quantity of thick oil into each cylinder. If the pressure is low in one of hte cylinders, both with and without oil, this is a symptom of leaking valves. If the pressure is higher when the oil has been added, it is probable that the piston rings are worn.

TUNING THE ENGINE

The engine should be tuned up at regular intervals if it is to operate at greatest efficiency. Tuning up consists of adjusting all settings to the correct value and remedying small defects.

1. Run the engine until warm. Check and adjust, if necessary the dwell angle (contact breaker gap). Replace burnt contact breaker points. Check the ignition timing setting with a stroboscope while the engine is running at rapid idling speed with the vacuum governor disconnected.

2. Check the distributor cap and clean it. Check and clean the ignition cables and contacts.
3. Check the state of the charge of the battery and the battery connections.
4. Clean the fuel pump sludge trap. Remove the float bowl covers from the carburetors and blow the housing clean. Remove and clean the plungers of the suction chambers and clean the chambers in solvent. Re-assemble.
4. Check the air cleaners and replace if necessary.
6. Check the tightening torque of the cylinder head bolts and the tightening of the inlet and exhaust manifolds. Check that there are no air leaks.
7. Remove and adjust the spark plugs or fit new spark plugs.
8. Check the compression on all the cylinders.
9. Adjust the valve clearances. Check that there is no oil leakage.
10. Check and adjust when necessary the carburetor settings.

REPLACING THE WATER PUMP
1. Drain off the cooling water.
2. Release the tension on the fan belt. Loosen both the water pipes.
3. Remove the fan and pulley, remove the pump.
4. Fitting is carried out in the reverse order but make sure that the seal rings on the top of the pump are correctly located. Also press the pump upwards against the extension of the cylinder head, for example, with two robust screwdrivers in front of and below the screw union so that the seal between the pump and the cylinder head is good.
5. Make sure that the seal rings on the water pipes are in good condition and push the pipes carefully in when attaching.
6. Fill up with water. Test-run the engine and check that there is no leakage.

REPLACING THE CARBURETORS
To replace one of the carburetors, both the carburetors must be removed and attaching screws pulled off simultaneously. The intermediary shaft is pushed into and carried in the throttle levers. When fitting, put the intermediary shaft in position between the carburetors and then fit both carburetors at the same time.

REPLACING THE OIL COOLER
To replace the oil cooler follow the instructions.

REPLACING THE OIL CLEANER
When replacing the oil cleaner, this being normally carried out after every 10,000 km (6000 miles), follow the instructions.

REPLACING THE TIMING GEAR CASING
1. Release fan belt tension.
2. Remove the fan and the pulley on the water pump.
3. Remove the crankshaft pulley bolt. Remove the pulley.
4. Remove the timing gear casing. Loosen a couple of extra bolts for the oil pan and be careful to ensure that the oil pan gasket is not damaged.
5. Make sure that the drain holes are not blocked in the new casing that is to be fitted.
6. Oil in the seal ring lightly and fit a new gasket.
7. Assemble the parts. Make sure that the casing is correctly centered. Tighten the fan belt.

See the specifications for the tightening torque for the pulley bolt.

REPLACING THE TIMING GEARS
1. Drain off the cooling water and remove the hood and radiator.
2. Carry out the work described in points 1-4 in the previous section.
3. Remove the camshaft nut and pull off the camshaft gear by using tool SVO 2250. The sleeve of the crankshaft is forced out with the help of a medium-sized sharp-ground screwdriver. The crankshaft gear is pulled off by using tool SVO 2405.
4. Fit the crankshaft gear with SVO 2407. Fit the camshaft gear with tool SVO 2408. Do not push the shaft in so that the seal washer at the rear end of the camshaft is forced out. Check that the gears have the correct relationship according to the markings shown in Fig. 1-29. There are flats on tool SVO 2407 to turn the crankshaft.
5. Measure the tooth flank clearance. Also measure the shaft and play, this being determined by the shim behind the camshaft gear. See the specifications for the measurement value. Fit the sleeve on the crankshaft.
6. Refit the other parts.

VALVE-GRINDING AND DECARBONIZING
1. Drain off the cooling water.
2. Disassemble the throttle control by loosening the ball joints, cotter pin and bracket on the inlet manifold. Loosen the choke control.
3. Remove the carburetors. Both carburetors must be loosened and removed simultaneously since the intermediary shaft is carried and guided in the carburetor lever.
4. Disconnect the exhaust pipe from the exhaust manifold, disconnect the water hoses to the radiator and disconnect the other connections to the cylinder head.

Fig. 1-29. Timing gear setting
1. Jet for lubrication of gears   2. Markings

5. Remove the rocker arm, rocker arm shaft and push rods.
6. Remove the cylinder head bolts, loosen the water pipe at the thermostat housing, loosen the attachment at the rear exhaust manifold bolt. Loosen the generator tensioner. Lift off the cylinder head.
7. Clean the piston crowns, combustion chambers, inlet and exhaust ports thoroughly. Do not use emery cloth since small particles can get between the pistons and cylinder walls and cause damage.
8. Recondition the valve system according to the description under the heading "Cylinder head with valves."
9. Fit the valves. Fit a new cylinder head gasket and new seals for the water pump. Fit the cylinder head. See the specifications for the tightening order and tightening torque. Fit the other parts. Fill up with cooling water.
10. Adjust the valve clearances. Run the engine for a short while until warm. Re-tighten the cylinder head and re-adjust the valve clearances.

REPLACING THE THERMOSTAT
1. Drain off part of cooling water.
2. Remove the bolts for the outlet pipe over the thermostat and turn up the pipe.
3. Replace the thermostat. Use a new gasket.

4. Screw the pipe into position. Fill up with cooling water and check for a leakage.

REMOVING THE ENGINE

1. Jack up the car about 30 cm. (12") over the floor and fit trestles under it. Drain off the cooling water and engine oil. Remove the connection to the positive pole from the battery.
2. Remove the hood and the radiator. Be careful not to damage the finish on the hood.
3. Remove the throttle control joints at the front and rear of the shaft between the engine and the body. Remove the cotter pin and washer and pull out the shaft. Disconnect the vacuum tube at the front end of the inlet manifold and disconnect the water pipe on the right-hand side of the thermostat housing. Disconnect all connections round the rest of the engine. Remove the throttle control shaft behind the flywheel housing.
4. Loosen the exhaust pipe at the exhaust manifold and the attachment on the flywheel housing. Remove the nuts for the engine mounting blocks.
5. Remove the gearshift lever. Remove the control for the clutch (and the cables for the overdrive, if fitted).
6. Disconnect the forward propeller shaft joint. Place a jack under the transmission and raise the jack slightly. Remove the support cross-member.
7. Fit lifting tool SVO 2425 to the engine. Tighten the bolt on the tool in the hole at the front end of the cylinder head, locate the hooks under the manifold front and rear.
8. Lift the front end of the engine an inch or so to clear the engine mounting blocks. Lower the transmission but not more than necessary and pull the engine forwards at the same time as the front end is lifted. Lift out the engine by gradually raising the front end and lowering the rear end.

DISASSEMBLING THE ENGINE

After the engine has been lifted out of the car, disassembly is carried out as shown below. (See under the headings concerned for the separate components).

1. Place the engine in a suitable stand. Check that the oil has been drained off.
2. Remove the starter motor and the cover plate on the lower front edge of the flywheel housing together with the transmission and then remove the clutch and flywheel.
3. Remove the rear sealing flange, the generator, the water pump and distributor, the rocker arm cover, the rocker arms and the cylinder head. Remove the oil cleaner and oil cooler. Remove the valve lifters with tool SVO 2424.

4. Remove the timing gear casing and the timing gears. See under heading "Replacement of timing gears" for the tools concerned. Remove the camshaft.
5. Stand up the engine on its rear end on a bench. Place three wooden blocks under so that the crankshaft can rotate freely. Remove the oil pan, oil pump and connecting rod with pistons. Replace the bearing caps on their respective connecting rods.
6. Lay the engine with the bottom upwards and remove the crankshaft. Replace the bearing caps in their correct positions.

CLEANING
All the engine parts should be carefully cleaned after the engine has been disassembled. Parts made of steel or cast iron can be cleaned in a de-greasing tank with a lye solution. Light-alloy parts can easily be damaged by the lye and should therefore preferably be cleaned in solvent. Never clean pistons and bearing shells in lye. Rinse the parts with warm water and blow them dry with compressed air after washing. Clean out the oil passages particularly thoroughly. Clean them through by using a special brush and then blow them out with compressed air. All the seal plugs at the ends of the drilled passages in the cylinder block must be removed while cleaning is going on.

CYLINDER HEADS WITH VALVES
DISASSEMBLY
1. Remove the rubber seal. Remove the valve springs by first compressing them with a valve spring tool and then removing the valve keys and releasing the tool. Place the valves in order in a special stand.
2. Measure the clearance between the valve stem and the valve guides. With a new valve this clearance should not exceed 0.15 mm (0.006"). Also check that the valves are not too worn. See under the headings "Valve system" and "Wear tolerances" in the specifications.

CLEANING
Clean the valves, combustion chambers and channels with rotating brushes to remove carbon and combustion residues.

GRINDING VALVES AND VALVE SEATS
1. Grind the valves in a valve-refacing machine after they have been cleaned. If the valves are very worn, fit new valves.
2. Grind the valve seats. Use an electrically driven valve-seat grinder or a hand reamer. A pilot spindle must first be fitted accurately before the work is started and worn valve guides should be replaced with new guides.

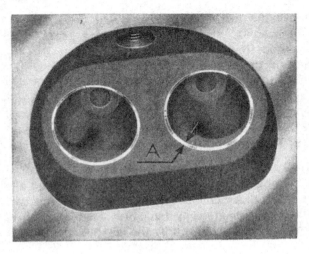

Fig. 1-35. Valve seat width
A = 1.5 mm (0.060")

Grind the seat until satisfactory sealing is obtained. The angle
is 45° and the width of the valve seat should be 1.5 mm
(0.060"). If the valve seat width is too wide after grinding,
it can be reduced from the inside with a grinding stone with
an angle of 70° and from the outside with a 20° grinding
stone.

3. Smear the valve seat surface with a thin layer of fine grounding compound and lap in the valves against their seats. Then
   clean the valves and seats and check for leakage.

REPLACING VALVE GUIDES

1. Press out the old guides with the help of tool SVO 1459.
2. Press in the new guides by using tool SVO 2289, which presses
   them in to the correct depth.
3. Ream the new guides to the correct diameter with a suitable
   reamer so that the correct clearance is obtained, see specifications.

ASSEMBLING

1. Check that the parts are in good condition and clean. Check
   that the springs hold the values shown in the specifications.
2. Fit the valves in position. Fit the lower rubber washer, steel
   washer, valve spring, upper washer and valve key. Finally fit
   the rubber ring.

REPLACING THE ROCKER ARM BUSHINGS
AND GRINDING THE ROCKER ARMS

1. If wear as much as 0.1 mm (0.004"), replace the rocker arm

bushings. Use tool SVO 1867 to press out and press in the bushings. Then ream the bushings with a suitable reamer to an accurate fit on the shaft. The hole in the bushing should index with the hole in the rocker arm.

2. If necessary grind the thrust surface against the valve in a special machine.

FITTING THE CYLINDER HEAD

1. Check that the cylinder head, cylinder block, pistons and cylinder bores are clean.
2. Check that the oilways to the rocker arm mechanism on the valve lifter side in the center of the block are clean. (In the cylinder head, the oil goes up through the screw hole between the screw and the wall of the hole and then out through a diagonal drilling to the attaching screw for the rocker arm shaft and then up in the shaft.)
3. Fit a new cylinder head gasket. Fit the cylinder head. Tighten the bolts in the right order and to the correct tightening torque. See Fig. 1-40 and the specifications.
4. Fit the rocker arm mechanism. Adjust the valve clearances. Fit the remaining parts.
5. Drive the car for a short distance to attain operating temperature. Retighten the cylinder head bolts and adjust the valve clearances.

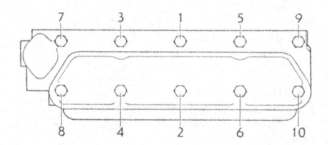

Fig. 1-40. Order of tightening for cylinder head bolts

ADJUSTING THE VALVE CLEARANCES

The valve clearance is the same whether the engine is cold or warm and is identical for both exhaust and inlet valves. For adjusting work use two feeler gauges, one 0.50 (0.02") and the other 0.55 mm (0.022"). The clearance is adjusted so that 0.50 mm (0.02") gauge is easy to insert while the 0.55 mm (0.222") gauge will not go in.

If the engine has been disassembled, the valve clearances should be roughly adjusted before starting. Then engine should then be turned over by hand by turning the fan. The spark plugs should be removed while this is done so that compression does not make the engine difficult to turn over.

CYLINDER BLOCK
Measuring the Cylinder Bores
The cylinder bores are measured by using an inside micrometer. There is a letter stamped on each cylinder bore showing its dimensions (only standard model), see specifications. Carry out measurements at various depths and at various points around the circumference. See the specifications for the dimensions.

PISTONS, PISTON RINGS, PISTON PINS
Measuring the Pistons
The pistons are measured by means of a micrometer at right angles to the piston pin hole, 12.5 mm (0.490") from the lower edge. See the specifications for the dimensions.

Fit of Pistons in Cylinder Bores
The fit of the pistons in the cylinder bores is checked without the piston pins fitted. The clearance at right angles to the piston pin hole is measured with a feeler gauge ½" wide and 0.04 mm (0.0016") thick attached to a spring balance. The pull required should be 0.5 - 2 kg (1 - 4½ lb.). This test should be repeated on several different diameters and at different depths. The standard bore cylinders have a letter stamped on which shows the dimension and the piston in this particular cylinder should be marked with the same letter.

Piston Ring Fit
In a new or rebored cylinder:
1. Push down the piston rings one after another in the cylinder bore. Use a piston upside down so that the rings come into their correct position.
2. Measure the ring gap with a feeler gauge. Fig. 1-44. The gap should be 0.25 - 0.50 mm (0.01-0.020"). If necessary widen the gap by using a file.
3. Check the piston rings in their respective ring grooves by rolling them in the groove. Also measure the clearance at several points. See the specifications for the dimensions.
In a worn cylinder:
When checking the fit of the rings in a worn cylinder bore, the rings must be tested at bottom dead center since it is there that the cylinder has the smallest bore.

Fig. 1-44. Measuring the piston ring gap

PISTON PINS

The piston pins are available in three oversizes: 0.05 mm (0.002"), 0.10 mm (0.0040") and 0.20 mm (0.008") larger than the standard diameter 22.00 mm (0.866"). If the piston pin hole in the piston is worn so much that it is necessary to fit an oversize, first ream up the hole to the corect dimension. Use a reamer fitted with a guide and remove only a small quantity of material at a time. The fit is correct when the piston pins can be pushed through the hole by hand and only light resistance felt.

CONNECTING RODS

If the old bushing is worn, it is pressed out by using tool SVO 1867 and a new bushing is pressed in with the same tool. Make sure that the lubricating holes index with the holes in the connecting rod. Then ream up the bushing to the correct fit. The piston pin should then slide through the hole with some pressure but without any noticeable looseness.

Check the connecting rods before fitting concerning alignment to make sure that they are straight, free from twist or S-distortion. If necessary, straighten them. Always fit new nuts and bolts when reconditioning is carried out.

Assembling and fitting pistons and connecting rods

When assembling make sure that the pistons are turned the right way with the arrow on the top of the pistons facing the front of the engine. The number marking on the connecting rods should be turned to face away from the camshaft side. The piston pins are then fitted, the circlips placed in position and the piston rings fitted.

Use a piston tool for the rings. The compression rings are marked "TOP" and the upper ring is chromed. Place the bearing

93

shells in position. Turn the rings so that the ring gaps are not immediately under each other, then lubricate the piston and bearing surfaces. Use the piston inserting tool SVO 2176, when fitting the piston in the bore. Tighten the connecting rod bolts with a torque wrench, see the specifications for the tightening torques.

CRANKSHAFT

After cleaning the crankshaft, measure its journals with a micrometer. This measurement should be carried out at several points round the circumference and along the width. Out-of-roundness on the main bearing journals should not exceed 0.05 mm (0.002") and on the connecting rod bearing journals, 0.07 mm (0.003"). Taper should not be greater than 0.05 mm (0.002") for any of the journals. If the measurement values obtained are in the neighborhood of or exceed the wear tolerances given above, the crankshaft should be ground to undersize. Suitable bearing inserts are available in five undersizes. See the specifications for the dimensions. Check that the crankshaft is straight to within 0.05 mm (0.02") by using a dial indicator. Lay the crankshaft in two ve blocks and adjust a dial indicator against the center bearing journal. Then rotate the crankshaft. If necessary, straighten the crankshaft in a press.

GRINDING THE CRANKSHAFT

Before the crankshaft is ground, its straightness should be checked as detailed above. Grinding is carried out in a special machine whereby the main and connecting rod bearing journals are ground to identical dimensions. These dimensions, which are given in the specifications, must be carefully followed to ensure that the correct bearing clearance is obtained with the precision bearing. Scraping of the bearing shells or filing of the bearing caps is absolutely forbidden in factory bulletins. The fillet radius at the ends of the bearing journals should be 2.0-2.5 mm (0.079-0.098") for all the journals. The width for the guide bearing is dependent on the size of the journal and should be ground to obtain the correct measurements. After grinding, the oil drilling openings should be carefully bevelled and all the bearing journals lapped with fine grinding compound to get the best surface texture. The crankshaft should then be washed. All the oil drillings should be cleaned particularly carefully to remove any traces of fillings.

MAIN BEARINGS AND CONNECTING ROD BEARINGS

Apart from the standard size, bearing shells are available in undersizes of 0.10", 0.020", 0.030", 0.040" and 0.050". The rear bearing inserts are fitted with flanges and have a larger width relative to their size. If the crankshaft has been ground to the correct dimensions, the correct bearing clearance is obtained when the corresponding bearing shells are fitted. The inserts may not be scraped and the bearing caps may never be filed to obtain closer bearing clearance. The bolts should be tightened with a torque wrench. See specifications for tightening torque.

FLYWHEEL PILOT BEARING

The pilot bearing lock ring is removed, the bearing pulled out with tool SVO 4090 and checked after washing in solvent. If the bearing is worn, fit a new bearing. Before re-fitting, pack the bearing with heat-resistant bearing grease. The bearing is fitted with tool SVO 1426 and the lock ring is then fitted.

GRINDING THE FLYWHEEL

If the wearing surface of the flywheel is uneven or burned, the surface can be ground flat in a saddle-mounted grinding machine. Never remove more than 0.75 mm (0.030") of the original thickness by grinding.

LUBRICATING SYSTEM

The oil cleaner is bolted to the oil cooler in one unit together with the cartridge and relief valve.

Replacement is carried out after every 10,000 km (6000 miles) when the oil cleaner is thrown away. In the case of a new or reconditioned engine, the oil cleaner is also changed for the first time after 5000 km (3000 miles) driving.

1. Remove the old oil cleaner with the help of a tool as shown in Fig. 1-58.
2. Smear oil into the rubber gasket on the new cleaner and make sure that the contact surface for the oil cleaner is free from dirt. If it is smeared with oil the gasket will slide better onto the sealing surface. Screw on the cleaner by hand until it just touches the oil cooler.
3. Tighten the oil cleaner a further half-turn but absolutely not more. Start the engine and check that the joints are not leaking. Top up with oil if necessary.

OIL PUMP WITH RELEASE VALVE

After the pump has been disassembled and cleaned, check that all the parts are in good condition. Check the spring for the relief valve.

Check that the tooth flank clearance is 0.15 - 0.35 mm (0.006-0.014"). Measure the axial clearance 0.02 - 0.10 mm (0.008 - 0.004"). Fit a new cover or check that the old cover is not noticeably worn. A worn cover can be ground true. If the

Fig. 1-57. Oil cleaner and oil cooler

1. Oil cooler   4. Water outlet
2. Water inlet   5. Drain cock for water
3. Oil cleaner   6. Drain cock for water

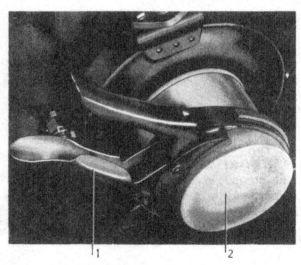

Fig. 1-58. Removing the oil cleaner
1. Tool   2. Cleaner

bushings or the shaft are worn, fit new units. Remember that the hole for the tubular pin in the driving gear may not be drilled right through since this would short-circuit the suction and pressure sides. The new bushings should be reamed after being pressed in. Use a reamer fitted with a guide. Check that the seal rings on the ends of the pressure pipe are in good condition or fit new seals. The pressure pipe must be clamped in the holes properly, first in the oil pump and then the oil pump and the pump together against the block. The pipe connecting flange should be flat against the block before being tightened.

OIL DRILLINGS

All the oil passages must be cleaned particularly carefully to avoid damage to the bearings, bearing journals and other parts. Before cleaning the cylinder block channels, remove the seal plugs and fit new plugs after cleaning them and blowing them dry.

REPLACING THE OIL COOLER

1. Drain off the engine cooling water.
2. Loosen the cooling water connections at the oil cooler. Remove the oil cleaner.
3. Remove the nut on the nipple for the oil cooler and pull out the cooler.
4. Fit the oil cooler in reverse order. The O-ring against the block must be replaced if necessary and, should it be replaced, a new ring should be glued in the groove on the oil cooler before the oil cooler is fitted. Smear the groove with a thin layer of glue, resistant to oil at temperatures up to 140° C = 285° F (for example, Plobond 20). Check during fitting that the oil cooler is in good top contact with the block all round when the nut has been tightened to a torque of 3-3.5 kgm (21 - 25 lb. ft.).
5. Fit the oil cleaner, see under the heading "Replacing the oil cleaner".
6. Fill up with cooling water and engine oil, if necessary.
7. Start the engine and check that there is no leakage.
8. If the nipple is replaced, the new nipple should be tightened to a torque of 4.5-5.5 kgm (32 - 40 lb. ft.).

REPLACING THE FUEL PUMP DIAPHRAGM
AND/OR VALVES B-18 Engines

Before disassembling the pump, first determine its pressure and capacity. If the values obtained (see specifications) are faulty, the pump should be disassembled for repair and this work most often consists in replacement of the diaphragm or valves.

1. Disassemble the pump.
2. Hold the pump as shown in Fig. 1-81. Remove the old diaphragm by pushing downwards and turning it a quarter of a turn.
3. Fit the new diaphragm by pressing with the rod and turning it a quarter of a turn. The distance between the end of the shaft and the support beneath should be about 2 mm (0.080") during assembly.
4. Check or replace the valves. Assemble and test the pump before refitting it on the engine.

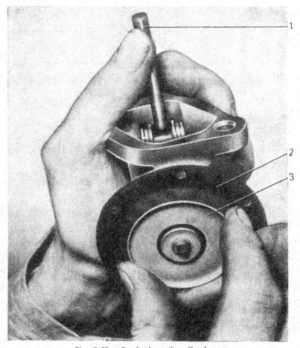

Fig. 1-81. Replacing the diaphragm
1. Lever   2. Diaphragm   3. Washer

COOLING SYSTEM

1. During the cold season ethylene glycol should be mixed with the cooling water together with an anti-corrosion agent in order to prevent the cooling system from freezing. See the specifications for the amounts required. Always use clean water (preferably rain water) together with anti-corrosion additive.

    Note: The water pump is made of light alloy.

THERMOSTAT

The thermostat can be tested after it has been removed, in a vessel full of water which is heated up. The thermostat should open and close at the temperatures shown in the specifications. Reject a faulty thermostat. Use a new gasket when assembling.

ASSEMBLING THE ENGINE

When assembling the engine follow the instructions for the parts concerned.

The order of working will be in the reverse way to that carried out when disassembling.

Check the marking on the bearings. The main bearings are marked 1-5, the connecting rod bearings 1-4, starting from the front.

Check that all component parts are clean and lubricate bearing surfaces with oil before assembling. Always use new gaskets, washers, cotter pins and lock washers. Shellac should not be used on sealing agent since it dries out and flakes off with the resultant risk that oil channels can be partially blocked. Seals on the ends of the pressure pipes, as well as the pipes on, and above the water pump, should be made of rubber. Make sure that these are in their correct positions and that the pipes are pressed in properly.

Make sure that the drain hole in the timing gear casing and rear sealing flange are open and that the seals are in good condition. Make sure also that the timing gear casing and flange are well centered.

Fit the new connecting rod nuts and bolts when reconditioning.

The cylinder head bolts must be tightened in a special order as shown in Fig. 1-88 in order to avoid unnecessary stresses. Check that the oil hole for the lubrication of the rocker arms is not blocked. The support bearing should be lubricated before fitting with heat-resistant bearing grease. The bearing is maintained in position by a lock ring.

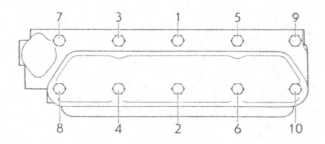

Fig. 1-88. The correct order to tighten the cylinder head bolts

The most important nuts and bolts should be tightened with a torque wrench, see the specifications for the correct tightening torque.

The fan belt should be tensioned so that the pulley starts to slip under a force of 6.5 - 8.5 kg. (14½ - 19 lb.) applied 150 mm (6") from the hub center. Exert pressure in the direction of rotation of the engine and use a spring balance.

FITTING ENGINE IN THE CAR

Use the lifting tool SVO 2425 when fitting the engine in the car. The order of operations will be the reverse of that used when removing, see under heading "Removing the Engine."

After all the components have been fitted, fill up with cooling water and oil. Make sure that all the controls have been correctly connected, see the sections concerned.

When the fan belts are vertical, the clearance to the radiator straight up should be at least 15 mm (0.59"). The clearance between the fan blades and the radiator straight forward where it is nearest should not be less than 11 mm (0.43").

Adjustment can be carried out by means of washers on the radiator mountings.

RUNNING IN

An engine that has been reconditioned either partly or completely must always be driven carefully during the first period, the running-in period. Do not run the engine at excessively high speeds but avoid running at very low speeds under loading.

Change the engine oil at closer intervals than usual.

If an engine test bench is available, it is a great advantage to run the engine in this if extensive reconditioning has been carried out.

Fig. 1-94. Tools for engine

SVO 1426 Tool for removing pilot bearing
SVO 1459 Tool for removing valve guides
SVO 1866 Tool for removing and fitting piston pins
SVO 1867 Tool for removing and fitting bushings in rocker arms
and connecting rods
SVO 2176 Tool for fitting piston rings (standard size)
SVO 2250 Puller for camshaft gear
SVO 2289 Tool for fitting valve guides
SVO 2405 Puller for crankshaft gear
SVO 2407 Press tool for fitting crankshaft gear
SVO 2408 Press tool for fitting camshaft gear
SVO 2424 Grip tool for removing and fitting valve lifters
SVO 4090 Puller for pilot bearings
SVO 2429 Press washer for removing impeller, water pump
SVO 2266 Tool for removing and fitting hub and impeller,
water pump
SVO 2430 Tool for fitting seal, water pump

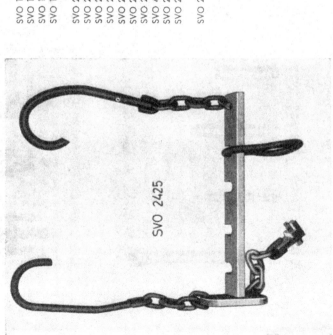

Fig. 1-95. Lifting tool for engine, SVO 2425

TOOLS

The following special tools are needed for work on the engine.

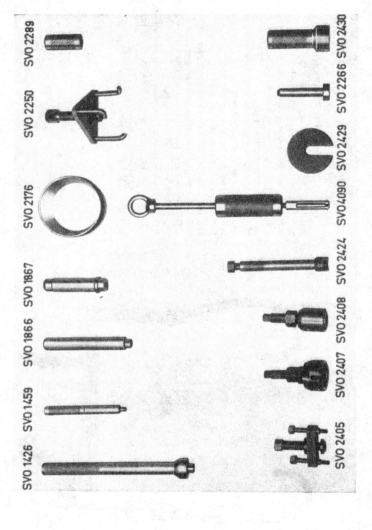

SVO 2289 SVO 2250 SVO 2176 SVO 1867 SVO 1866 SVO 1459 SVO 1426

SVO 2430 SVO 2266 SVO 2429 SVO 4090 SVO 2424 SVO 2408 SVO 2407 SVO 2405

TROUBLE SHOOTING ALL ENGINES

REASON	REMEDY

The engine stalls or runs very roughly at idling speed

REASON	REMEDY
Faulty spark plug or suppressor.	Check or replace spark plug and suppressor.
Air leaks at carburetor connections.	Check tightening. Replace faulty gaskets and washers.
Idling speed too low.	Increase idling speed and check that the induction sound is equally strong on both carburetors.
Uneven carburetor settings.	See "Carburetors settings after fitting".

Uneven running with cold engine and choke in use

REASON	REMEDY
The carburetors are not being influenced to the same extent by the choke.	Adjust settings. See "Adjusting the choke control and rapid idling".

The engine runs jerkily during acceleration

REASON	REMEDY
Dirty spark plug insulators.	Clean insulators.
Faulty spark plugs.	Check or replace spark plugs.
Dirty, faulty or moist distributor cap.	Remove and clean or change distributor cap.
Faulty or moist cables.	Check, clean or replace cables. See also Part 10.
Oil in carburetor damping cylinders insufficient or too thin.	Top up with oil of the right grade and viscosity.
Dirt in carburetors.	Remove float bowl covers and clean housing.
Fuel/air mixture too lean.	Check carburetor settings.
Faulty fuel pump supplying too little fuel.	Check fuel pump pressure and capacity.

Engine output low

REASON	REMEDY
Air cleaners blocked.	Fit new air cleaners.
Poor fuel being used, too low octane rating.	Check fuel grade, use correct fuel.
Faulty ignition setting.	Adjust ignition setting at rapid idling speed by using stroboscope. See "Ignition setting".
Faulty and uneven settings on carburetors.	Check and adjust carburetor settings. See "Carburetor settings after fitting".
Faulty valve clearances.	Check and adjust valve clearances.
Low compression on one cylinder.	Measure compression pressure. If values are too low, remove cylinder head for closer investigation of engine.
Piston chafing.	Remove cylinder head for investigation.
Wheel bearings chafing or brakes faultily adjusted.	

Knocking noise from valve mechanism

Valve clearances too large.	Adjust valve clearances.
Worn or damaged parts in valve mechanism.	Recondition or replace parts where necessary.

Heavy regular knocking sound, more obvious when engine under loading

Worn main or connecting rod bearings, worn pistons and piston pins.	Locate sound by short-circuiting the spark plugs, one after another. Then disassemble as far as required to examine bearings and pistons.

Low oil pressure

Low pressure at idling speed.	When the engine has been run hard and then allowed to run at the lowest idling speed, the oil pressure is normally quite low.
Oil cleaner blocked. (The engine must run for a longer time than usual after starting before pressure is registered).	Change the oil cleaner.
Faulty oil pressure contact, pressure gauge or pipe.	Measure pressure with extra pressure gauge. Replace faulty contact, pressure gauge or pipe.
Faulty spring in relief valve or worn oil pump.	Remove oil pump. Check spring and pump.
One or more bearing worn.	Examine and replace bearing shells.
Large general wear.	Replace or recondition engine.

High oil consumption

Hard driving.	No procedure necessary. Oil consumption can increase to a certain extent when the car is driven very hard.
Leakage at joint.	Tighten bolts and screws, replace faulty or poor gaskets and washers all round.
Oil level too high.	Do not top up with oil until the level starts to go down towards the lower mark on the dipstick.
Worn valve guides.	Recondition valve system.
Worn piston rings.	Replace piston rings.

High fuel consumption

Hard driving on highways or much city driving.	No procedure necessary. Normal under these conditions.
Blocked air cleaners.	Replace air cleaners.
Carburetor flooding.	Check and, if necessary, replace float valves. Also check pump pressure.
Faulty carburetor setting, excessively rich fuel/air mixture.	Adjust settings.
Poor suppressors on spark plugs. Faulty contact breaker points.	Replace spark plug suppressors. Adjust distributor.
Faulty dwell angle and ignition setting.	Adjust dwell angle and ignition setting. Use stroboscope for adjustment of ignition settings.

Engine runs abnormally warm

Not enough cooling water.	Fill up with cooling water.
Faulty gauge.	Check or replace temperature gauge.
Fuel has too low octane rating (knocking).	Fill up with fuel of correct octane rating.
Faulty thermostat.	Replace thermostat.
Faulty ignition settings.	Adjust ignition settings.
Faulty carburetor settings (excessively lean fuel/air mixture).	Adjust carburetor settings.
Blocked cooling system.	Clean out cooling system.
Fan belt insufficiently tensioned.	Adjust belt tension.

Loss of cooling water

Leaking hose connections.	Check or replace hoses and clamps.
Faulty radiator cap.	Replace radiator cap.
Faulty cylinder head gasket (oil in cooling water).	Replace cylinder head gasket.

1. Nut for damping plunger
   (also for oil filling)
2. Suction chamber
3. Float bowl cover
4. Rapid idling adjuster screw
5. Idling adjuster screw
6. Cam plate
7. Throttle shaft
8. Throttle shaft lever
9. Link rod
10. Link
11. Lift pin for piston

Fig. 16. Rear SU carburetor from control side.

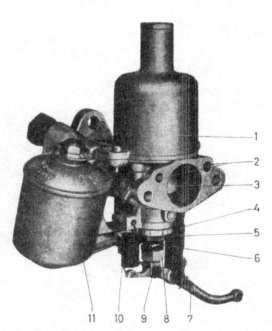

1. Suction chamber
2. Air channel
3. Piston
4. Seal washer
5. Lock nut
6. Spring
7. Lever
8. Adjuster nut
9. Lower part of jet
10. Spring
11. Float bowl

Fig. 17. Rear SU carburetor from float bowl side.

FUEL SYSTEM

B 14 A and B 16 B engines are fitted with twin SU H-2 and H-4 horizontal carburetors which are connected together. B 16 A and B 16 D engines are fitted with single Zenith 34 VN downdraft carburetors. B 18 B and B 18 D engines are fitted with twin SU HS-6 carburetors.

CARBURETORS, SU H-2, H-4

Both the carburetors are fitted with a rapid idling device. The front carburetor in each pair is not fitted directly with this device but receives the same impulse through the shaft connecting the carburetors together.

There is an equalizer tube between both the inlet manifolds which are very short. There is only one jet in each of the carburetors. Fuel flow is varied by a tapered needle which is guided by a plunger in the carburetor, this plunger being influenced by

Fig. 15. SU carburetors (B 14 A and B 16 B engines).

1. Forward carburetor
2. Fuel pipe between carburetors
3. Retainer for controls
4. Shaft between carburetors
5. Rear carburetor
6. Rapid idling adjuster screw
7. Idling adjuster screw
8. Equilizer tube
9. Couplings
10. Idling adjuster screw
11. Fuel line from pump

the degree of partial vacuum in the carburetor barrel. There is no choke in the normal sense of the term. Instead there is a cold starting device which, when engaged, gives a richer fuel/air mixture by depressing the jet whereupon the fuel flow area increases.

The function of the carburetor can be divided into the following groups:

1. Float system
2. Running
3. Cold starting
4. Rapid idling
5. Idling

1. **Float system.**

The fuel flow is controled by the float system so that the correct fuel level is obtained in the carburetor.

The float system consists of a float bowl (6) which is flexibly attached to the carburetor housing through the medium of rubber gaskets, as well as a float (5), cover (1) and the flexibly attached lever (4) together with the needle valve (3) which is attached to the cover. There is a strainer (2) with a spring in the cover. The float is guided by a center bolt in the float bowl.

When fuel is forced by the pump to the float bowl, it first passes through the strainer which removes all impurities. When the fuel level rises, the float is lifted upwards and when the fuel level has reached the height, the needle is pushed up by the lever so that the flow of fuel is stopped. When the level sinks, the valve opens again and more fuel flows in.

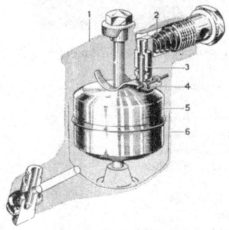

1. Float bowl cover
2. Strainer
3. Needle valve
4. Lever
5. Float
6. Float bowl

Fig. 18. Float system.

2. Running

The amount of fuel/air mixture which flows to the engine is regulated with the aid of the butterfly throttle (6) in the carburetor housing (7). The housing is in the shape of a channel but is also a body on which the various parts of the carburetor are assembled.

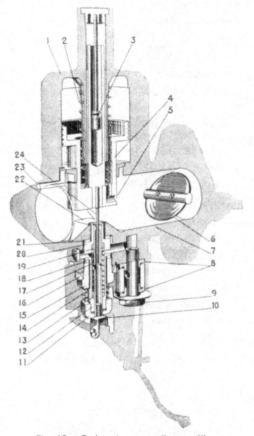

1. Suction chamber
2. Spring
3. Damping plunger
4. Piston in suction chamber
5. Channel
6. Butterfly throttle
7. Carburetor housing
8. Rubber gasket
9. Bolt for float bowl
10. Jet
11. Adjuster nut
12. Lower jet bearing
13. Seal with washer
14. Spring
15. Lock nut
16. Seal washer and gland
17. Spring
18. Washer
19. Seal ring and washer
20. Upper jet bearing
21. Washer
22. Bridge
23. Channel
24. Fuel needle

Fig. 19. Carburetor, operating position.

Above the jet (10) which is fitted from below, the channel narrows due to the projection known as the bridge (22) and the piston (4) which is situated above the bridge. The air flow speed increases when it passes through this restriction whereby the fuel is picked up more easily.

Opposite the bridge on the top of the carburetor, there is a suction chamber (1) with the piston (4). There is a tapered needle (24) attached to the lower section of the piston.

The piston is guided by a centrally located spindle which runs in the center part of the suction chamber where there is a bushing. The upper part of the piston is precision fitted into the suction chamber. The lower section functions as a shutter and restricts the cross-sectional area of the main air passage above the jet as the piston moves downwards. The piston, under the influence of its own weight and assisted by the spring (2) always shows a tendency to assume its lowest position. When the piston is in its lowest position it rests against the bridge by means of the pin fitted in it.

When the engine is running and the butterfly throttle opening increases, the degree of vacuum in the space between the bridge and the throttle increases and then the cavity above the piston is connected through a little channel (5) to the above-mentioned cavity and the piston moves upwards. The space below the upper section of the piston is connected to the outer air by means of a channel (23). (There are two channels on B 16 B carburetors).

When the piston rises, the carburetor channel cross-section above the jet is enlarged and an additional quantity of air is permitted to pass through. Since the fuel needle is attached to the piston, it also moves upwards and the effect of opening between the fuel needle and the jet is enlarged. A quantity of fuel corresponding to the larger quantity of air is then sucked in. The amount of fuel is regulated partly by the piston (fuel needle) position and partly by the air flow speed.

The jet is fed with fuel from the space in the carburetor housing at the float bowl connection through the hole in the jet walls.

The position of the piston will be stable for any given air flow through the carburetor. The degree of this air flow is determined by the degree of throttle opening as well as the speed of the engine and the loading on the engine. Every tendency on the part of the piston to move downwards will be accompanied by a reduction of the flow area between the bridge and the under side of the piston with the consequent increase of the degree of partial vacuum between the piston and the throttle. This immediately results in an increase in the partial vacuum in the upper part of the suction chamber. The piston will then be raised so much that balance is once more restored. There is a damping device in the recess in the piston spindle to prevent the piston from coming into any pendular motion or moving excessively rapidly. This device consists of a damping plunger (3) attached to the rod. The hollow interior of the spindle contains a quantity of light engine oil. The retarding effect of this damping device on rapid movement of the piston prevents the engine from stalling due to an excessively lean fuel/air mixture when the accelerator pedal is depressed rapidly.

Opposite the throttle (rear carburetor) there is a connection for the pipeline to the vacuum regulator on the distributor.

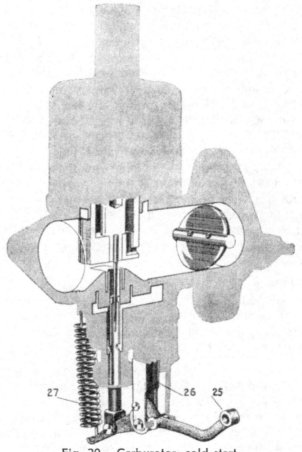

Fig. 20.   Carburetor, cold start.

25. Lever
26. Link
27. Spring

3. **Cold Starting**

In order to enrich the fuel/air mixture when starting a cold engine, there is a carburetor device by means of which the jet can be lowered. When the jet is lowered there will be a wider flow area for the fuel since the needle in the jet is tapered. There is no choke shutter on the carburetors. The jet, the lower part of which is yoke formed, is not fitted directly in the carburetor housing but is carried in two bearings (12 and 20) so that it can move up and down. When the lock nut (15) is loosened the jet can also be moved laterally (for centralizing). The upper bearing has a flange which with the aid of a washer (21), seals against the recess in the carburetor housing, the lower bearing flange sealing with the help of a washer (18) against the top of the lock nut. The lock nut seals against the carburetor housing by means of a washer and a gland (16). Inside the bearings there is a spring (17) exerting pressure against two washers with sealing glands (13 and 19) which prevent any leakage of fuel at the jet. When a cold engine is being started the outer end of the lever (25) is pulled upwards by means of a control system, the movement being transmitted to the link (26) so that the jet, which is connected to the inner end of the lever, is pulled downwards. This movement is limited by means of a projection on the lever and return to the normal position is taken care of by the return spring (27) when the control is pushed in. At the same time as this lever is operated, the throttle is opened slightly by means of the rapid idling device described below.

4. **Rapid Idling**

When the rapid idling device is operated, a larger throttle opening is obtained than is usual during normal idling and this is used during the engine warming-up period in order to obtain a somewhat higher idling speed. See fig. 21.

This device, which is connected to the cold starting device, consists of a link rod (31) connected to the lower lever which influences a cam-shaped plate (30) attached to the carburetor housing. There is an adjuster screw which contacts this plate when the rapid idling device is in operation. This screw is attached to the throttle lever (28). When the lower, outer end of the lever is lifted, the cam-shaped plate is turned by which the throttle is opened slightly. (The end of the lever can be lifted slightly before the jet is influenced depending upon the large clearance in the lever hole on the link).

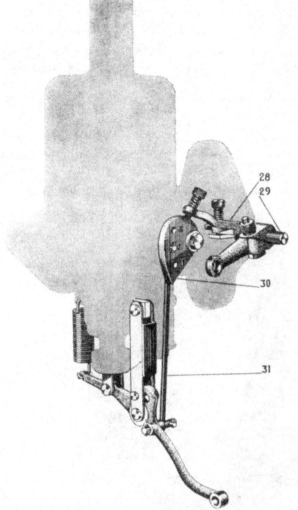

Fig. 21. Carburetor, rapid idling.

28. Lever for throttle
29. Throttle shaft
30. Cam plate
31. Link rod

5. **Idling**

When the engine is idling the carburetor piston is in its lowest position and rests on the bridge at the jet on a pin. The small opening which remains between the bridge and the piston allows the required amount of air to pass for idling without there being a sufficiently great degree of partial vacuum to raise the piston.

The amount of fuel required for idling is very small and the tapered needle almost entirely fills the jet opening.

The jet is pressed upwards by the spring (10 figure 17) so that the lower part of the jet is supported against the adjuster nut (8) which is locked in position by means of a spring (6). This nut is used to set the amount of fuel passing through since the fuel needle is tapered.

If the nut is screwed upwards a leaner fuel/air mixture is obtained and if the nut is screwed downwards, the mixture will be richer.

The relationship between fuel and air is set at idling for the complete speed range.

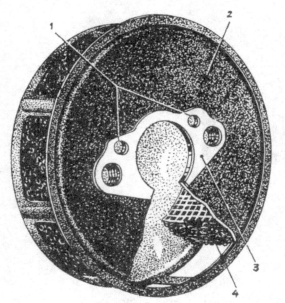

1. Air holes
2. Housing
3. Gasket
4. Wire filter

Fig. 22. Air cleaner (SU carburetors).

AIR CLEANERS FOR SU CARBURETORS

The air passing to the H2 & H4 carburetor is cleaned when it passes through the wire filters in the cleaners. The space below the piston in the suction chamber in each carburetor is connected with the air cleaner through the air holes. Air passing to these spaces is thus cleaned to prevent the pistons from binding. The gasket (3) must not be turned the wrong way since this will block the holes (1). (There is only one hole on each B 14 A carburetor). HS-6 carburetors are fitted with AC removable paper cartridge filters. (See HS-6 section.)

SU CARBURETOR TYPE HS-6

The operating principle of this carburetor (found on the B 18 B and B 18 D engines) is identical to that described above. Except for variations in the design of the float system and in the cold starting enrichment method, they can be treated in the same fashion. Illustrations accompanying make the differences plain. See "Engine Specifications" for needle designations and other specifications.

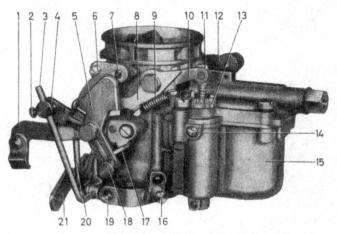

Fig. 23. Zenith carburetor from the right.

1. Bracket
2. Screw for rapid idling adjustment
3. Link for rapid idling
4. Attachment
5. Lever for choke flap (with cam)
6. Choke lever
7. Choke spindle
8. Rear part of acceleration pump lever
9. Spring
10. Forward part of acceleration pump lever
11. Pump plunger rod
12. Economiser valve
13. Washer for adjustment of acceleration pump stroke
14. Plunger check screw
15. Float bowl
16. Idle fuel adjusting screw
17. Stop
18. Attachment for choke control
19. Hole for vacuum line
20. Acceleration pump rod
21. Throttle lever

ZENITH CARBURETOR

B 16 A and B 16 D engines are fitted with a single down-draft carburetor made by Zenith, which has type designation 34 VN. The appearance of this carburetor is shown in fig. 23 and fig. 24.

Fuel flow is metered by fixed jets which are fitted in an emul-

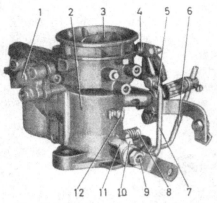

1. Economiser valve
2. Carburetor housing
3. Choke flap
4. Choke flap spring
5. Spring for lever
6. Link for rapid idling
7. Link for acceleration pump
8. Idle adjusting screw
9. Throttle shaft
10. Stop on lever
11. Short lever for throttle
12. Adjuster screw for venturi

Fig. 24.   Zenith carburetor from the left.

sion block terminating in a pointed nozzle projecting into a throat of the carburetor. In the emulsion block there are also air channels so that the fuel is mixed with a certain amount of air at a very early stage. The carburetor has a rapid idling device as well as an acceleration pump and an economizer valve system. The functions of the carburetor are treated separately as follows:

1. Float system
2. Choke system with rapid idling.
3. Idling system
4. Main and compensation jets. Economizer valve.
5. Acceleration pump

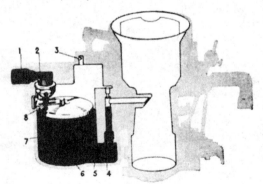

Fig. 25.   Float system.

1. Fuel inlet
2. Float valve with washer
3. Ventilation hole
4. Jet
5. Emulsion block
6. Float bowl
7. Float
8. Arm

1. Float system

The float keeps the fuel at the correct level. When the fuel has increased to the correct level, the float (7) lifts upwards and pushes the needle against the seat, through the medium of the float arm so that the flow of fuel is cut off. When the fuel level goes down the same procedure is repeated in the reverse direction.

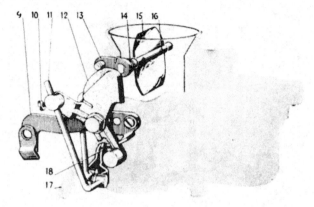

Fig. 26.   Choke device and rapid idling.

9.   Control attachment
10.   Rapid idling adjuster screw
11.   Link rod for rapid idling
12.   Lever for choke flap
13.   Lever on choke spindle
14.   Spring
15.   Choke flap
16.   Spindle
17.   Lever for throttle
18.   Lever for rapid idling

2. Choke device and rapid idling

In order to enrich the fuel/air mixture when a cold engine is started, the choke system is used and this is operated from the knob on the dash-board. When the choke control is pulled out when starting a cold engine the cam-shaped lever (12) moves. This influences the choke flap (15) by means of the spring (14) on the shaft so that it closes whereby a high degree of vacuum and consequently a larger supply of fuel is obtained. When the engine has started and the degree of vacuum increases the choke flap can open to a certain extent since the tendency to close comes from the spring on the flap shaft. In this way an excessively rich fuel/air mixture is avoided. The choke lever also operates the throttle through the link rod (11). This means that the throttle will open as the choke flap is closed. The degree to which the throttle opens relative to the closing of the choke flap is determined by the various settings of the link rod by means of the screw (10). Through this rapid idling device the engine can be given a higher idling speed from the driver's seat during the warming-up period to avoid the risk of the engine stalling.

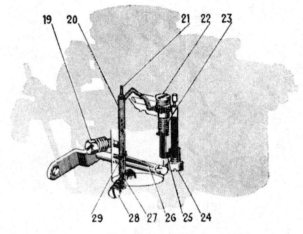

Fig. 27. Idling.

19. Idling adjuster screw
20. Channel
21. Air hole
22. Idling air jet
23. Idling jet
24. Main jet
25. Fuel hole
26. Throttle
27. Hole (variable flow)
28. Idling fuel adjuster screw
29. Transition hole

3. Idling system

When the engine is idling, the throttle flap is almost completely closed (this can be adjusted by means of a stop screw) so that the degree of vacuum around and under the throttle flap is comparatively high. There is powerful suction through the idling hole (27) and this sucks up fuel from the channel above the main jet (24) through a calibrated hole (25) and the idling jet (23) to the idling passage which terminates in the barrel of the carburetor with one large hole (27) and two small holes (29). Air is added to the fuel partly through a hole (21) under the choke flap and partly through an air jet (22) above the idling jet.

The fuel/air ratio is controlled by means of a screw (28) through which the fuel/air mixture is varied. Since a certain amount of air passes the throttle flap, the fuel/air mixture supplied to the engine during idling will be richer if the screw is screwed outwards and leaner when it is screwed inwards. The two small holes (29) just above the throttle flap supply fuel/air mixture as the throttle flap is opened, these last-mentioned holes operating together with the variable ones. This insures a smooth supply of fuel as the throttle is opened.

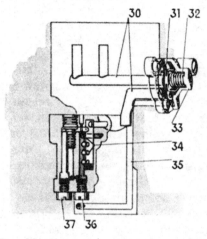

Fig. 28. Jets and economiser valve.

30. Air channels
31. Diaphragm with valve disk
    and gaskets
32. Spring
33. Casing for economiser valve
34. Hole for supplementary air
35. Vacuum channel
36. Main jet
37. Compensating jet

4. Main and compensation Jets. Economizer valve

A large amount of fuel for the engine when it is under loading and running at high speeds passes through the main jet (36). The main jet alone cannot supply a sufficiently accurate amount of fuel during all conditions of operation and, for this reason, it has been combined with a compensation jet (37). This compensation jet operates mostly at average engine speed and loading.

Both the jets are fitted in an emulsion block which terminates in a "beak" in the carburetor venturi. When it passes through the emulsion block, the fuel is mixed with a certain quantity of air so that it mixes easier with the large amount of air streaming into the engine through the barrel of the carburetor. The air passing into the emulsion block passes partly through a hole drilled above the main jet space and partly through channels (30) where the amount of air supplied is varied with the help of the economizer valve.

The space above the compensation jet forms a reservoir for the fuel. High speed means an increased flow. The fuel then passes more rapidly through the hole in the wall to the main jet passage so that the level of fuel sinks to the hole and an increased air flow is obtained. Air passes to the three holes in the wall to the space above the main jet from the air channels (30). When the fuel level in this space goes down more air is supplied which is mixed with fuel. With the help of the economizer valve, the fuel/air mixture is supplied with extra air when the degree of vacuum in the barrel of the carburteor is large. A valve is attached in a diaphragm (31) and held against its seat by means of a spring (32). Air is thus only supplied through the small upper hole at the diaphragm. The back side of the diaphragm is connected to the lower part of the carburetor barrel through a passage. When the degree of vacuum in the lower part of the carburetor barrel increases, for example during steady driving without any great degree of loading, the valve lifts from its seat and air passes out to the emulsion block also through the center passage at the valve disk.

If the degree of loading on the engine should increase for example during acceleration the degree of vacuum decreases and the spring presses the disk against its seat so that the fuel/air mixture again becomes richer.

5. **Acceleration pump**
   When the throttle flap is rapidly opened, the fuel/air mixture tends to become too lean due to the fact that air moves more quickly than fuel and thus reaches the engine earlier.

   In order to compensate for this tendency for the mixture to become leaner, a certain amount of fuel is sprayed in with the help of the acceleration pump directly into the barrel of the carburetor.

   The pump plunger (44) is fitted in a cylinder located inside

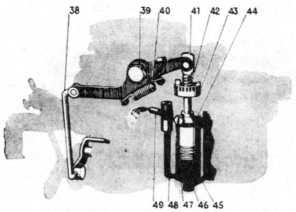

Fig. 29. Acceleration pump.

38.	Link rod	44.	Plunger
39.	Jointed lever	45.	Return spring
40.	Spring	46.	Inlet valve
41.	Plunger rod	47.	Check screw
42.	Spring	48.	Outlet valve
43.	Washer for pump stroke adjustment	49.	Acceleration jet

the float bowl and the plunger is pressed down by a lever with a spring-loaded joint. The travel of the pump plunger can thus be easily varied by turning a cam washer (43), the forward part of the lever stopping against the check in a higher or lower position depending on the position of the washer. The last part of the rear lever section movement is absorbed by the spring (40) at the joint.

At the inlet in the bottom of the pump cylinder there is an inlet valve (46) and the outlet, behind the accelerator jet, there is an outlet valve (48). The outlet valve is fitted with a ball which lifts and closes the air hole above during the pump stroke so that the fuel is sprayed in through the acceleration jet (49). During normal operation, this ball closes the connection to the float bowl and supplies instead air from the air hole to the acceleration jet. This prevents fuel from streaming through the jet when the pump is in its rest position.

AIR CLEANER FOR ZENITH CARBURETOR

The air cleaner consists of a metal casing containing a wire filter. Air for the engine is cleaned when it passes through the oiled-in filter and impurities are thus prevented from entering and damaging the engine. This air cleaner also functions as an intake silencer.

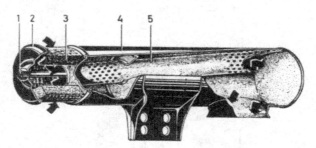

Fig. 31.   Air cleaner for Zenith carburetor.

1. Nut
2. Cover
3. Wire filter
4. Housing
5. Intake silencer

FUEL PUMP

The engine is fitted with a fuel pump of the diaphragm type feeding fuel from the fuel tank to the carburetor and driven by an eccentric on the camshaft. There is also an idling device through which the pump stops operating when the needle valve in the carburetor float bowl is closed. The pump is adjusted for a maximum pressure of 0.25 kg/cm² (3.5 p.s.i.).

The camshaft eccentric operates a rocker (16) journalled on a pin (17) and this influences a rocker link (18). The inner end of the rocker is coupled to the pump pull rod (2). The diaphragm (4) center is attached to the upper end of the pull rod. The circumference of the diaphragm is clamped between the two halves of the pump body.

When the diaphragm is pulled downwards, fuel is sucked from the tank through a sediment bowl (9), strainer (12) and inlet valve (13) into the pump chamber. When the eccentric has reached its highest point and begins to recede, the level is pulled back by a spring (3). The diaphragm is then pressed upwards by the thrust spring which was compressed during the suction stroke and forces the fuel past the outlet valve (7) to the carburetor. When the carburetor float bowl is filled with fuel, the needle valve closes and a counter-pressure builds up in the pump chamber. The diaphragm comes to a stop in the down position and the spring cannot force it upwards for a new suction stroke until more fuel is being consumed. The fuel pump has an external lever (1) for hand priming.

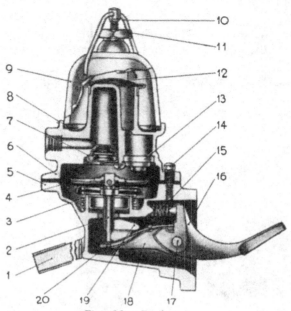

Fig. 30. Fuel pump.

1.	Lever	11.	Nut
2.	Diaphragm rod	12.	Strainer
3.	Spring	13.	Inlet valve
4.	Diaphragm	14.	Screw
5.	Lower section	15.	Spring
6.	Upper section	16.	Rocker
7.	Outlet valve	17.	Pin
8.	Gasket	18.	Link
9.	Sediment bowl	19.	Lever
10.	Bowl retainer	20.	Lock spring

CARBURETORS, SU H-2, H-4
Disassembly
1. Blow the carburetors clean externally.
2. Loosen and remove the air cleaners and the control retainer with the control rod between them.
3. Remove the fuel line connections and the vacuum line connections (to the distributor).
4. Loosen the nuts on the connections on the shaft between the carburetors. Move up the connections on the shaft. Loosen the throttle controls. Remove the carburetors.

Disassembly and cleaning
Float Bowl
1. Loosen the float bowl from the carburetor housing.
2. Remove the nut on the float bowl cover. Remove the cap and lift out the float.
3. Remove the float arm by pulling out the pin upon which it pivots.
4. Loosen the needle valve in the cover and the hollow bolt and strainer.

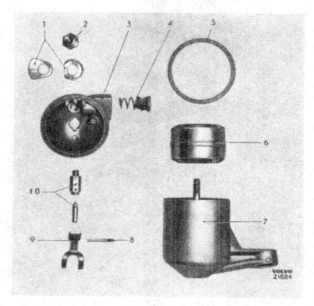

Fig. 84. Float-bowl assembly (SU).

1. Washers	6. Float
2. Nut	7. Float bowl
3. Float bowl cover	8. Pin
4. Strainer and spring	9. Lever
5. Gasket	10. Needle valve

Jet unit
1. Remove the return spring for the jet lever and the link rod between the lever and the cam-shaped plate.
2. Remove the bolt for the jet head and the upper bolt for the link and then remove the lever.
3. Remove the lock nut and take out the jet bearings with the spring and gland. Pull out the jet. Screw off the adjuster nut and remove its spring.

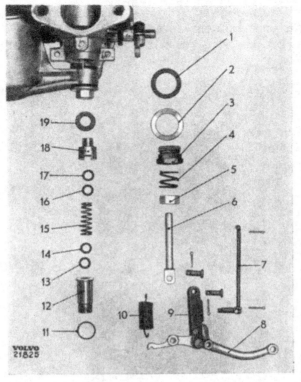

Fig. 85. Jet unit disassembled (SU).

1.	Washer	11.	Washer
2.	Seal washer	12.	Lower jet bearing
3.	Lock nut	13.	Seal ring
4.	Spring	14.	Washer
5.	Adjuster nut	15.	Spring
6.	Jet	16.	Washer
7.	Link rod	17.	Seal ring
8.	Lever	18.	Upper jet bearing
9.	Link	19.	Washer
10.	Spring		

Suction chamber with piston and fuel needle

The suction chamber and the piston are matched as units and if one of these is replaced then the other must be replaced at the same time. The suction chamber has three attaching screws which are staggered to ensure that it is fitted the right way. B 14 carburetors have two screws. Do not turn suction chamber.

1. Remove the damper from the suction chamber.
2. Loosen the screws on the suction chamber and lift out.

3. Lift up the spring and the piston. Take care to ensure that the needle is not damaged (bent).

4. Screw out the lock screw on the fuel needle and pull it out.

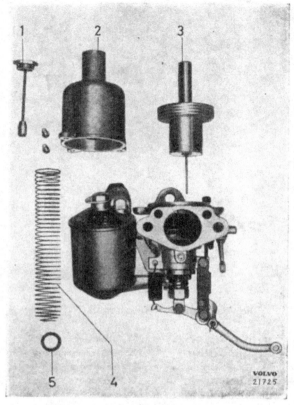

Fig. 86. Suction chamber disassembled (SU).

1. Damping plunger
2. Suction chamber
3. Piston
4. Spring
5. Washer

Cleaning

After disassembly, all parts should be cleaned in kerosene and then be blown clean with compressed air.

Assembly and fitting

Assembly and refitting on the engine is carried out in reverse to that used when disassembling and removing.

Before assembling, check that all gaskets and sealing glands are free from damage. Replace these if necessary. Make sure that all other parts are neither damaged or worn.

Neither the suction chamber nor the piston may be filed or rubbed with emery paper since this will change the fit and this has been very carefully calculated so that the carburetor will function properly. Any small unevenness can, however, be carefully rubbed away.

When attaching the needle in the piston it is very important to ensure that the needle assumes the right position as far as gap is concerned. See under the heading "Replacement of fuel needle." The piston in the suction chamber is grooved and a guide projection in the carburetor housing fits into this groove. Lubricate the piston spindle lightly with thin engine oil before reassembling.

When the jet is fitted, it must be centralized before it is tightened. Otherwise the needle can jam or, under unfavorable circumstances, become damaged. See under the heading "Centralizing the jet."

Add oil (engine oil SAE 5 W) to the damping cylinders after reassembling the carburetors. The air holes in the air cleaners must not be blocked.

Fig. 87.   Jet unit assembled (SU).

1.   Jet and associated parts

Checking the fuel level

The fuel level can be checked indirectly after removing the float bowl cover.

1. Loosen the fuel line and remove the float bowl cover.
2. Turn the float bowl cover upside down.
3. Measure the distance from the float bowl cover to the arm by means of a gauge with diameter 27/64" (11 mm). (This gauge can be made from a rod about 3⅛" long). When the needle valve is closed, the needle valve arm should just contact the gauge.
4. If necessary, bend the arm where it joins the yoke-shape section in order to maintain the clearance mentioned in point 3 above.

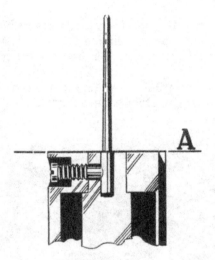

Fig. 88. Attachment of fuel needle (SU).

A = Attaching level

Replacement of fuel needle

1. Remove the suction chamber and the piston and fuel needle.
2. Loosen the screw on the fuel needle and pull out the fuel needle.
3. Fit a new fuel needle. Check that this is marked as mentioned in the Specifications. Push the needle so far into the piston that only the tapered working section is outside it. Tighten the lock screw.
4. Fit the parts into the carburetor. Then check that the piston

moves easily up and down. The piston can be lifted slightly without having to remove the air cleaner with the help of the pin. When the pin is slowly released, the piston should be heard to meet the bridge with a characteristic sound.

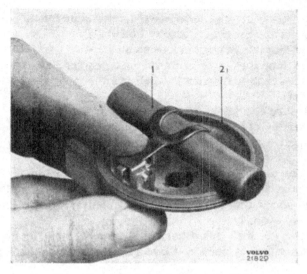

Fig. 89. Checking fuel level (SU).

1. Gauge (27/64" diameter)
2. Float bowl cover

Replacement of jet
1. Remove the jet as described under the heading "Disassembly and cleaning, jet unit." The adjuster nut does not need to be removed. If the carburetor is fitted on the engine the wire on the jet lever should be loosened.
2. Fit the new jet in the lower bearing and then fit the lower seal washer and packing, the spring, the upper seal washer with packing and the upper bearing with its copper washer. The brass washers for the upper and lower seals should be in contact with the spring.
3. Push in the jet together with the assembled parts into the carburetor housing. Screw on the lock nut loosely. Centralize the jet as shown below and then fit the lever and the other disassembled parts.

Centralizing the jet
In order to ensure that the carburetor functions in the correct way it is extremely important to make sure that the fuel needle moves easily up and down in the jet without jamming against

the walls of the jet. For this reason a very careful fit (centralizing) of the jet relative to the fuel needle is necessary.

The jet bearings are attached with quite a large lateral clearance so that they can be moved laterally when adjustment is carried out.

1. Remove the air cleaner. Screw up the adjuster nut as far as possible against the carburetor housing.
2. Check that the lock nut is loosened.
3. Check that the jet is in its highest position, i.e. that the jet heads is in contact with the nut and the needle is in its lower position.
4. Centralize the jet by carefully turning the lower jet bearing. Be careful not to disturb the adjuster nut. If the jet bearing requires moving slightly this can be carried out by slightly tapping the adjuster nut.
5. Lift the piston and the needle. When the piston is released it should strike against the bridge with a fully audible sound on condition that the jet is correctly centralized and the piston is running easily.
6. Tighten the lock nut. Check the pre-movement of the piston as described in point 5 above. Fit the air cleaner and make sure that the ventilation channels are not blocked.

Idling settings and the coupling together of the carburetors

Idling setting is carried out partly by means of the screws on the throttle arms which regulate engine speed, and partly by turning the adjuster nuts on the jet heads whereby the richness of the fuel mixture is altered. When the nuts are screwed down, a richer fuel mixture is obtained. If the nuts are screwed up the mixture will be leaner. The richness of the mixture is set during idling to cover the whole speed range of the engine.

When the correct idling speed has been obtained and both carburetors have been adjusted to the same level, they are then connected together. Individual settings should be carefully carried out before the carburetors are connected together in order to get the highest output for the engine.

1. Run the engine until it is thoroughly warmed up. If the jets have not been adjusted, a rough adjustment can be first carried out by screwing the adjuster nuts to their upper position and then screwing them down again one complete turn.
2. Loosen one of the couplings on the shaft between the carburetors. Make sure that the jets on both the carburetors are pressing against the adjuster nuts and that the screw for rapid idling is not in contact with the cam-shaped plate on each carburetor.

3. Adjust both throttles to the same position by screwing out the throttle adjuster screws and then screwing them in again until contact with the stop projections is just made. Then screw down each screw exactly one turn.

4. Start the engine. Check that the throttles are open to the same extent in both carburetors by listening to the sound with the aid of a rubber pipe placed in contact with the same point on the air cleaner of each carburetor. Adjust the idling screws until the air intake sound on both carburetors has exactly the same strength.

5. Adjust the jets by turning the adjuster nuts so that the idling speed is as high as possible with unchanged throttle opening. Adjust the carburetors one at a time. First screw the adjuster nuts upwards (leaner mixture) until the engine runs unevenly and then in the opposite direction until the engine runs perfectly smoothly. If the idling speed is too high it can be decreased by unscrewing the idling screws on the throttle shaft levers. Then check again as specified above that the air intake sound is equally strong on both carburetors.

6. Check that the fuel-air mixture is correct on both carburetors. First lift the piston on one of the carburetors slightly by means of the pin beside the air intake. Then release the pin and carry out the procedure on the other carburetor. The degree of uneven running on the engine should be the same in both cases. If the engine stalls when the piston on one of the carburetors is lifted, this usually means that the mixture on the other carburetor is too lean. The jet adjuster nut on the carburetor in question should be screwed carefully downwards to remedy this.

7. Connect the carburetors together by tightening the couplings on the shaft. Adjust the rapid idling screw. This is done by screwing the screw until it is in contact with the cam plate and then screwing it back until a certain clearance is obtained. Check once again that the air flow through both carburetors is the same. See point 4 above.

Rapid idling and control mechanism

The rapid idling system can be adjusted to suit varying conditions by means of the adjuster screw against the cam plate. See the specifications.

When the choke control is completely pushed in, the clearance between the adjuster screw and the cam plate should correspond to one turn of the screw.

The clamp on the end of the choke cable should be attached so that the jets begin to go down when the choke button on the instrument panel has been pulled out about ½" (rapid idling movement). Increased resistance will be felt on the choke button when the jets begin to move downwards.

When the choke control button is pulled out as far as it will go, the long lever ends should be lifted so far that the jets are completely lowered, i.e. the levers should contact the stops in the links. Make sure that both levers are influenced to the same extent through the curved cable so that both jets start to move downwards at the same time.

CARBURETOR, ZENITH 34 VN

Removing

1. Blow carburetor clean externally.
2. Remove air cleaner, disconnect fuel and vacuum pipes, throttle and choke linkages.
3. Remove carburetor from intake manifold. Cover the hole in the manifold.

Disassembling and cleaning

1. Remove the four float bowl attaching screws and remove float bowl.
2. Remove float lever and float. Both are marked "TOP."
3. Remove the screws for the emulsion block, remove the block and remove the main jet, the compensation jet, the idling air jet and the idling jet.
4. Remove the acceleration jet, the outlet valve with the check screw, the pump plunger with spring and the inlet valve under the pump plunger.
5. Loosen the float valve. Be careful not to damage the valve washer. Remove the idling fuel screw.
6. Remove the attaching screws for the economiser valve and take out the valve.
7. Clean the carburetor in solvent (or alcohol which dissolves resin deposits better). Blow all channels and jets clean with compressed air. Do not clean jets with wire since this can damage their calibration.

Assembly

Assemble in the reverse order to that used when disassembling.

1. Check that all parts are in good condition and use new gaskets.
2. Make sure that the economiser valve seals correctly against its seat. Otherwise lap it with fine grinding compound but make sure that all traces of this compound are washed off before the valve is finally assembled.
3. Turn the float and float lever so that the mark "TOP" faces

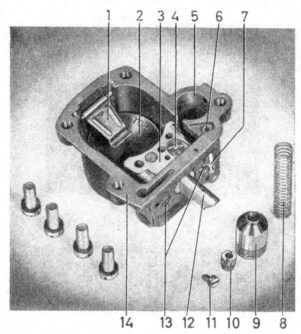

Fig. 90. Float bowl assembly (Zenith).

1. Float lever (marked TOP)
2. Float (marked TOP)
3. Emulsion block
4. Idling air jet
5. Barrel for acceleration pump
6. Outlet valve for acceleration pump
7. Acceleration jet
8. Spring
9. Plunger
10. Inlet valve for acceleration pump
11. Check screw
12. Emulsion block (beak)
13. Attaching screw for emulsion block
14. Float bowl

upwards. The lever spindle should be placed with the end points upwards.

4. Press the float bowl upwards and inwards against the carburetor body and then tighten the screws. Check that the emulsion block beak is in contact with the cross-stay on the venturi. Otherwise loosen the screw, push up the venturi, tighten the screw and secure it.

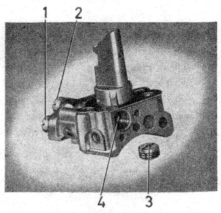

Fig. 91. Emulsion block (Zenith).

1. Compensation jet (fine thread)
2. Main jet (coarse thread)
3. Idling air jet
4. Idling jet

Fuel level

The fuel level, which should be 0.70" below the float bowl surface while the engine is running, is determined by the float lever and the needle valve washer. The thickness of the washer should be 0.040."

Acceleration pump stroke

The pump plunger can be adjusted to give a long or a short stroke by varying the position of the washer. To alter this adjustment, lift the washer upwards and give it half a turn. Normally the washer should be set for a short stroke, i.e. the highest cam turned towards the spring on the lever.

Adjusting rapid idling

When the carburetor is not fitted on the engine, rapid idling is adjusted as follows:

1. Place a 1.3 mm. wire gauge between the throttle and the wall of the carburetor throat on the idling air jet side. Make sure that the wire gauge does not come into contact with the venturi.
2. Loosen the screw for the attachment.
3. Close the choke flap completely and move over the cam-shaped lever until it is in contact with the stop.
4. With the lever against the stop and the wire gauge in the throttle as described in point 1 above, adjust the link rod so that the check on the lower lever just contacts the throttle

Fig. 92. Economiser valve (Zenith).

1. Float valve washer
2. Float valve
3. Economiser valve
4. Spring
5. Air hole and valve seat
6. Gasket
7. Diaphragm and valve disk
8. Gasket

lever and then lock the link rod by means of the screw (1). When the carburetor is fitted on the engine, the rapid idling setting can be checked as follows:

1. Screw out the idling adjusting screw so that the throttle closes completely. Then screw in the screw again until the throttle just begins to open (a piece of paper between the screw and the stop begins to be nipped). Then screw in the screw 3-2/3 turns corresponding to the opening when the wire gauge was inserted in the throttle in point 1 above. (In certain cases, it may be necessary to remove the spring from the screw).

2. Pull out the choke knob on the instrument panel as far as it will go and check that the cam-shaped lever contacts the stop. If the setting is correct the check on the lever should

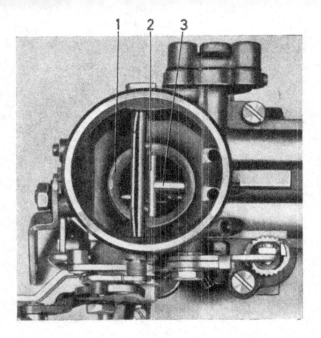

Fig. 93. Venturi position.

1. Venturi
2. Cross-stay
3. Emulsion block beak

just contact the stop on the throttle lever. Adjust, if required, by means of the screw for the link rod.

3. Replace the spring and adjust the idling speed.

Fitting

The carburetor is fitted in the reverse order to that used when removing. Make sure that the flanges are clean. Use a new gasket.

Adjusting idling

1. Run the engine until it is thoroughly warm.
2. Adjust the idling speed to 400-600 r.p.m. by means of the screw on the throttle shaft lever.
3. Adjust the fuel-air mixture with the aid of the idle fuel adjusting screw until the engine runs evenly and steadily. First screw the screw inwards (leaner mixture) until the engine runs unevenly and then outwards (richer mixture) until the best idling is obtained.
4. Adjust the idling speed by means of the screw if necessary.

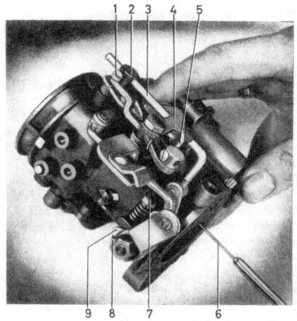

Fig. 94. Adjusting rapid idling.

1. Rapid idling adjusting screw
2. Attachment
3. Link rod
4. Cam-shaped lever
5. Stop
6. Wire gauge
7. Idle adjusting screw
8. Short lever for throttle
9. Check on rapid idling lever

FUEL PUMP—B 14, B 16 ENGINE
Testing

If no fuel arrives at the carburetor, disconnect fuel pipe on the carburetor and work fuel pump by hand. If no fuel issues from the open end of the fuel pipe, check that there is fuel in tank and that suction line is not stopped, or has sprung a leak through which air is drawn into the pump. If the suction line is in order, remove fuel pump.

Before dismantling pump, check pumping action with a special apparatus or in the following manner.

Connect a length of hose, not less than 80 cm = 32 in., to the suction side of the fuel pump and hold the other end of the hose in a vessel containing fuel. With pump 70 cm. = 28 in. above the fuel level, the pump shall draw up fuel when worked by hand. Otherwise, proceed by dismantling the pump for a check on diaphragm, valves and gaskets.

Replacing diaphragm

1. Remove screws securing upper and lower halves of pump housing, and separate body halves.
2. Take the lower half in the left hand as shown in Fig. 95, and press rocker with left thumb. Depress washer 3 with right hand thumb, rotate washer one-quarter turn, and remove washer, diaphragm 2, and pull rod.

Diaphragm, washer, and pull rod are assembled to a unit, and are replaced together. Reassembly of the pump is carried out in the reverse order. Take care that the pump pull rod is placed in its proper position on the rocker, and that the diaphragm is clamped evenly between the two pump housing halves.

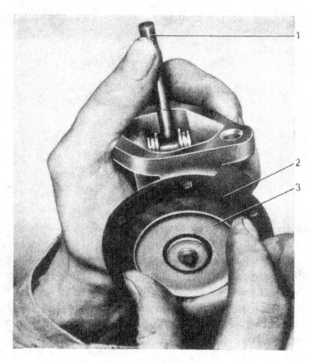

Fig. 95. Replacing the diaphragm.

1. Rocker   2. Diaphragm   3. Washer

Replacing the valves

To replace pump valves, separate the two halves of pump housing, then remove two screws fastening valve holder, and take out valves.

Check that replacement valves are turned the right way and that gaskets are in good order.

Repairing fuel tank

Leaky fuel tanks shall be soldered tight. Remove the tank from vehicle and drain all fuel. Then wash through tank carefully with hot water or with steam for at least 10 minutes in order to remove the last traces of fuel.

Clean carefully before soldering, and apply a smooth coat of tin, preferably using an electric soldering iron.

Flush through tank with compressed air during entire soldering process in order to prevent concentrations of gases which might produce an explosion.

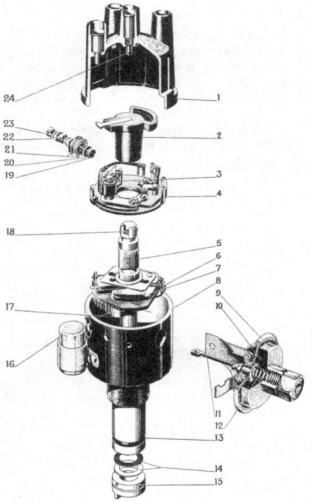

Fig. 5. Distributor.

1. Cap
2. Rotor arm
3. Contact breaker
4. Breaker plate
5. Breaker cam
6. Spring
7. Governor weight
8. Distributor housing
9. Vacuum regulator
10. Diaphragm
11. Link rod
12. Spring
13. Rubber seal
14. Washers
15. Flange
16. Capacitor
17. Distributor shaft
18. Felt packing
19. Screw
20. Flat washers
21. Insulating washers
22. Spring washer
23. Nut
24. Rod brush

IGNITION – 6 AND 12 VOLT

DISTRIBUTOR

Removing

1. Lift off the distributor cap.
2. Mark the position of the rotor arm on the distributor housing.
3. Disconnect the primary lead.
4. Disconnect the hose on the vacuum regulator.
5. Unscrew the clamping bolt and lift up the distributor.

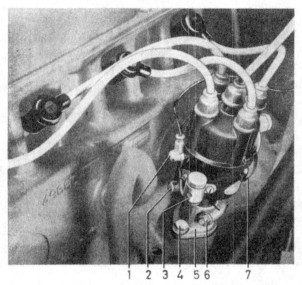

1 2 3 4 5 6   7

Fig. 56.   Distributor fitted.

1. Lead for coil	5. Flange
2. Lubricating cup	6. Clamping bolt
3. Capacitor	7. Clamping catch or cap
4. Attaching bolt for distributor	

Fitting

Fitting is done in the reverse order to removing. If the engine has not been moved while the distributor has been removed, fit the distributor in accordance with the marking made under point 2 above.

Dismantling the distributor

1. Pull off the rotor arm.
2. Disconnect the vacuum regulator by unscrewing the screws and then lifting it off.
3. Unscrew the primary terminal screw and remove the washers belonging to it.

4. Remove the breaker plate. This is done by unscrewing the two screws which hold the catch springs for the cap.
5. Lift off the stop spring (locking spring) and knock out the pin for the flange and pull this off. Mark the position of the flange in relation to the shaft.
6. Lift up the distributor shaft.
7. Remove the locking springs and springs between the centrifugal governor and contact breaker camshaft and lift this up.
8. Wash all parts in solvent and lay them out for inspection.

Inspecting
Distributor Plate
1. The surface of the contact should be flat and smooth. The color of the contacts should be grey. Oxidized or burnt contacts must be replaced. After a long period of use, the contact lip can be worn and the spring fatigued, so that the contact should be replaced.
2. The contact plate must not be loose or worn so that there is any burr.

Distributor Shaft
1. The play between the distributor shaft and the breaker camshaft must not exceed 0.1 mm (0.004").
2. The cams on the breaker camshaft must not be scored or worn down so that the closing angle is altered.
3. The holes in the centrifugal governor weights must not be oval or deformed in any other way. The fibre washers must be intact.
4. The governor springs must not be deformed or damaged.

Distributor housing
1. The clearance between the distributor housing and shaft should not exceed 0.2 mm (0.008"). In the event of excessive play, the bushings must be replaced and, if this is not sufficient, the shaft also.
2. The insulation washers for the primary terminal must not be cracked or soaked in oil, as this will cause leakage over the primary terminal.
3. The capacitor is tested with a glow lamp connected to direct current, or with a capacity bridge.
   When testing with a glow lamp at room temperature, there must be no discharging. When testing with warm capacitor (60—70°C = 140—158°F), up to 15 discharges per minute can be accepted.

Assembling

1. Place the Resitex washer on the distributor shaft and the fibre washers above this. Lubricate and place the centrifugal governor weights in position. Place on the locking springs.
2. Lubricate and fit the breaker camshaft and place on the springs.
3. Lubricate the distributor shaft and place it in the distributor housing. Check that the axial adjusting washers are positioned correctly. The fibre washer should contact the inside of the distributor housing. The steel washers should contact the flange.

   Fit the breaker plate and distributor cap catch springs.

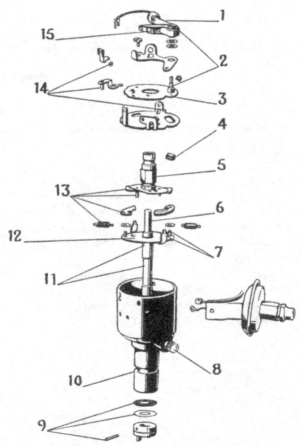

Fig. 64. Lubricating scheme for distributor.
(Lubricant Bosch or corresponding).

4. Fit the primary terminal and connect this to the breakers and capacitor.

5. If the contacts have been replaced, ensure that new ones lie correctly horizontally and that their faces close flush against each other. Adjustment can be made with a special tool, for example, Bosch EFAW 57 or similar. Only the fixed contact may be bent. Adjust the gap and check the contact pressure.

6. Fit the vacuum regulator.

7. Fit the flange and check the axial play. The fibre washer should lie against the distributor housing and the steel washer or washers against the flange. The axial play must be min. 0.1 mm (0.004"), max. 0.2 mm (0.008").

Adjusting the ignition control curve (centrifugal regulator)

Adjusting the curve is done by tensioning the centrifugal regulator springs. When doing this the shaft must be lifted up from the distributor housing and the screws on the other side of the flange slackened. If the flange is turned opposite to the direction of rotation, the springs are tensioned; that is to say, ignition is retarded and maximum control is reached later.

NOTE: Adjusting the curve must not be done by bending the flange spring loops.

CLUTCH

Borg and Beck single plate dry disc type clutches are fitted to all Volvo automobiles. Their size, spring tension, and method of actuation varies according to the year model and engine fitted. Complete specifications are given at the end of this volume. However, the essential difference to be noted between the 1800 clutch and others used with the same engine is in increased spring tension and greater diameter (8½"). When replacing any parts of this unit, make sure that the exact replacement part is used. (The heavy duty springs are color coded with black paint, for example.)

DESCRIPTION—PV 444, 445, 544, P 210

The pressure plate is operated by three release levers which are actuated from the clutch pedal by links, clutch fork and release bearing. The thrust required on the pressure plate is obtained from six strong pressure springs. The release bearing is guided by a tubular extension on the main drive pinion bearing cover.

From B 4 B engine No. 49746 the clutch is balanced together with the crankshaft and flywheel and is marked with a special color. Re-fitting after repair should be carried out in accordance with this marking.

On PV 544 and PV 444 from chassis No. 131918 the clutch control is slightly different. Thus the inner end of the intermediate shaft is journalled in a rubber bushing and the pressure link is made in two parts and provided with a spring loaded adjusting device. This is shown in figs. 2—4.

ADJUSTING CLUTCH PEDAL FREE PLAY

The clutch pedal should be adjusted so that the free play is 20—25 mm (0.79—0.98") on PV 444 A—K, PV 445, P 210 and 10—15 mm (0.39—0.59") on PV 444 from chassis No. 131918 onwards and PV 544. Adjusting is carried out from underneath if the protective plate on the lefthand side is not fitted. The adjusting nut (1, fig. 1) is also accessible from the top on the left-hand side. Adjusting is carried out by using a short set spanner. The adjusting nut is locked with the lock nut after adjustment.

REPLACING RUBBER BUSHING FOR
INTERMEDIATE SHAFT

1. Remove the return spring. Slacken the bolts and remove the rubber bushing.
2. Place the metal bushing in the rubber bushing and then place

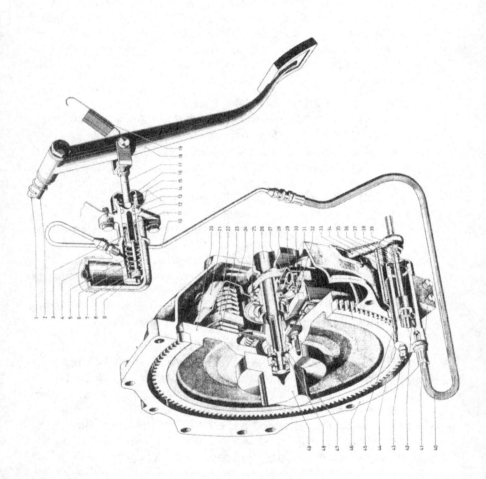

Illustration 1. Clutch and clutch controls.

1. Shaft
2. Spacing spring
3. Retainer
4. Cover
5. Spring
6. Thrust rod
7. Retainer
8. Non-return valve
9. Master cylinder
10. Pipe
11. Plunger packing
12. Plunger
13. Plunger packing
14. Washer
15. Locking ring
16. Rubber cover
17. Thrust rod
18. Pedal
19. Return spring
20. Flywheel
21. Clutch cover casing
22. Pressure plate
23. Clutch plate
24. Clutch spring
25. Clutch release bearing

26. Clutch disc shaft
    (main drive pinion, gearbox)
27. Spring
28. Cover for clutch disc shaft
29. Shaft pin
30. Lip
31. Clutch release lever
32. Eyebolt
33. Clutch release fork
34. Return spring
35. Thrust rod
36. Locking ring
37. Rubber cover
38. Locknut
39. Adjusting nut
40. Hose
41. Control cylinder
42. Spring
43. Bleeding valve
44. Plunger packing
45. Plunger
46. Flywheel housing
47. Locking ring
48. Support bearing in crankshaft
49. Crankshaft

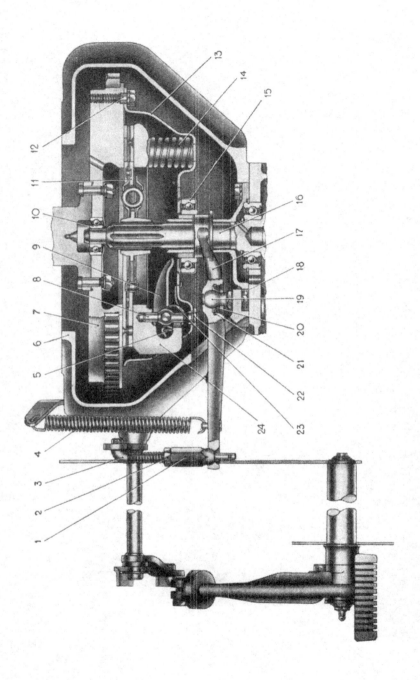

Fig. 1. Clutch and clutch control.

1. Adjusting nut
2. Lock nut
3. Pressure link
4. Return spring
5. Strut between release lever and pressure plate
6. Flywheel housing
7. Flywheel
8. Eyebolt for lever

9. Release lever
10. Flywheel pilot bearing
11. Driven plate
12. Clutch cover bolt
13. Clutch cover
14. Pressure spring
15. Release bearing
16. Main drive pinion (disc shaft)

17. Clutch release fork
18. Locking bolt for ball joint
19. Ball joint
20. Ball seat
21. Locking ring for ball seat
22. Adjusting nut
23. Release lever spring
24. Pressure plate

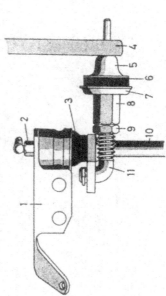

Fig. 2. Clutch control.

1. Bracket
2. Grease nipple
3. Rubber bushing
4. Release fork
5. Cup
6. Rubber cushion

7. Washer
8. Adjusting nut
9. Lock nut
10. Intermediate shaft
11. Pressure link

the rubber bushing in the bracket. Place the bracket with bushing on the intermediate shaft and then bolt in position. Hook on the return spring.
3. Check and adjust pedal free play.

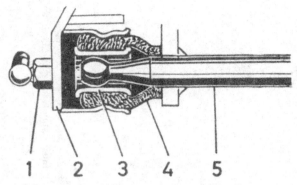

Fig. 3.   Journalling of intermediate arm.

1. Grease nipple
2. Bracket
3. Bushing
4. Rubber bushing
5. Intermediate arm

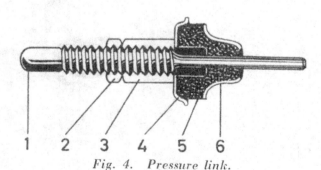

Fig. 4.   Pressure link.

1. Pressure link
2. Lock nut
3. Adjusting nut
4. Washer
5. Rubber bushing
6. Cup

REPLACING RUBBER CUSHION IN PRESSURE LINK

1. Remove the return spring. Remove the split pin and take off the pressure link.
2. Pull the pressure link apart and remove the rubber block. Fit on the new block and assemble the pressure link.
3. Fit the pressure link and lock it with the split pin. Hook on the return spring.
4. Check and adjust pedal free play.

REMOVING CLUTCH

1. Remove the gearbox.
2. Lift off the return spring (4, fig. 1) and disconnect the pressure link (3) at the release fork.
3. Remove the release bearing (15).
4. Remove the plate cover under the flywheel.
5. Remove the release fork (17) by first slackening the ball joint (19) a few turns with a 17 mm set spanner and hold this still whilst unscrewing the bolt (18) on which the ball joint is fitted. Then turn the release fork half a turn and remove it from the rear, fig. 5.

Fig. 5.   Removing the clutch release fork.

6. Check that the clutch and flywheel are marked with paint as shown in fig. 6. If this is not the case, mark the clutch and flywheel together with the pressure plate with a center punch. This must be done so that when refitting the clutch after repair it will resume the position in which it was previously fitted so that the original balance is maintained. Turn the flywheel round to make sure that no earlier marking exists.

Fig. 6.   Marking of clutch and flywheel.

7. Slacken the six clutch casing bolts transversely a little at a
    time in order to avoid stresses and remove them. Hold up the
    clutch so that it does not fall to the floor. The clutch and
    driven plate can now be removed downwards. See fig. 7.

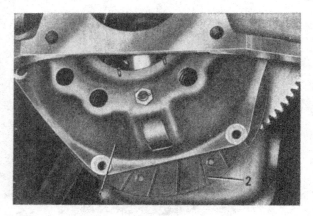

Fig. 7.   Removing clutch.

1. Clutch
2. Driven plate

REMOVING PEDAL SHAFT

1. Remove from both pedals the part which goes up through
    the toe plate. Disconnect the return springs and pressure links
    for the brake and clutch.
2. Remove the locking ring (12, fig. 24) from the inner end of
    the pedal shaft. Drive out the pedal shaft outwards and re-
    move the pedals.

3. Fit new bushings in the pedals. Use drift SVO 4088 with backing ring SVO 4089 for this. If necessary ream the bushings.
   If the shaft is worn at the pedal positions it should be replaced.

REPLACING PEDAL SHAFT

1. First fit washer (3) on the grooved end of the shaft, see fig. 24. Place the ring (2) in position outside the washer.
2. Lubricate the bushing in the clutch pedal, fit the narrow rubber ring (4) on the side which faces outwards and the rubber sleeve (6) on the side of the pedal facing the frame.
3. Fit the clutch pedal on the shaft (7) and move shaft into position in the frame.
4. Fit rubber sleeve (9) on the side of the brake pedal facing the frame. Lubricate the bushing and fit the pedal on the shaft.
5. Then fit on the brace bar (11). Press together the whole with cramp SVO 4084, fig. 23 and fit on lock ring (12).
6. Screw in the grease nipple (1) at the clutch pedal end and the plug (13) at the opposite end. Lubricate with chassis grease.
7. Connect up the pressure links and return springs for brake and clutch. Bolt on the upper part of the pedals and adjust clutch pedal free-play.

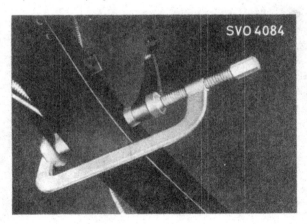

Fig, 23. Fitting the pedals.

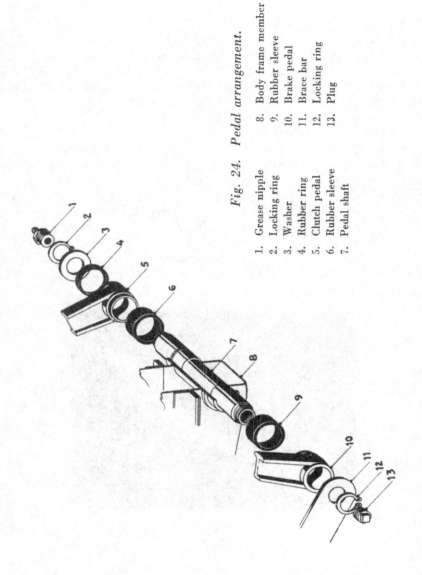

Fig. 24. Pedal arrangement.

1. Grease nipple
2. Locking ring
3. Washer
4. Rubber ring
5. Clutch pedal
6. Rubber sleeve
7. Pedal shaft

8. Body frame member
9. Rubber sleeve
10. Brake pedal
11. Brace bar
12. Locking ring
13. Plug

154

TOOLS

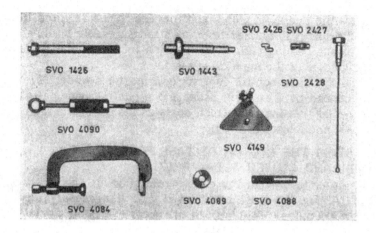

Fig. 26.

Clutch

SVO 1426   Drift for flywheel pilot bearing.

SVO 1433   Mandrel for centring driven plate and adjusting levers.

SVO 2426   Wrench for loosening and tightening gearbox bolts.

SVO 2427   Ball joint for SVO 2426.

SVO 2428   Wrench for fitting and removing gearbox bolts.

SVO 4090   Puller for ball bearing in flywheel.

SVO 4149   Dial indicator attachment.

Pedal shaft

SVO 4084   Cramp for assembling pedal shaft.

SVO 4088   Drift for pedal bushing.

SVO 4089   Backing washer for pressing in and out pedal bushing.

DESCRIPTION—122S, 1800

The pressure plate (22, Illustration 1) is operated by means of three levers (31) which are actuated from the clutch pedal (18) through the hydraulic clutch control. The thrust required on the pressure plate is obtained from six strong pressure springs (24). The release bearing (25) is guided by a tubular extension on the bearing cover of the main drive pinion.

The hydraulic control consists of a master cylinder (9) which is influenced by the clutch pedal and a control cylinder (41) on the flywheel housing (46) which operates the clutch via the clutch fork (33) and release bearing.

ADJUSTING THE CLUTCH RELEASE FORK
TRAVEL AND CLUTCH PEDAL PLAY

In order to prevent the clutch from slipping, the clutch fork travel (A, Fig. 1) must be checked and if necessary adjusted every 3000 miles (5000 km). In the event of trouble arising with declutching, the clutch pedal play (A, Fig. 2) should also be checked.

The clutch fork travel is adjusted by means of the nuts (1, Fig. 1). These are adjusted so that the clutch fork travel is 0.12" —0.16" (3—4 mm).

The clutch pedal play should be 5½" (140 mm) and is adjusted with the nut (1, Fig. 2).

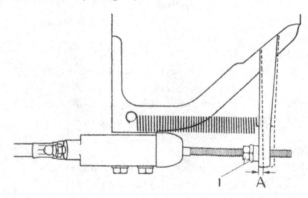

Fig. 1.   Clutch fork travel.

1.   Adjusting nut   A.   0.12"—0.16" (3—4 mm)

REMOVING CLUTCH, EARLY PRODUCTION

1.   Remove the gearbox.
2.   Disconnect the return spring.
3.   Remove the release bearing.
4.   Remove the cover under the flywheel.

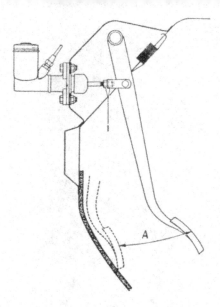

Fig. 2.   Clutch pedal play.

1. Adjusting nut   A. 5 1/2" (140 mm)

4. The six bolts which hold the clutch to the flywheel should be slackened crosswise a couple of turns at a time to prevent breakage and should then be removed. Hold up the clutch so that it does not fall to the floor. Lift off the clutch and clutch plate (23).

5. Remove the release fork by first slackening the ball joint a few turns with a 17 mm wrench and then holding it still while unscrewing the bolt on which the ball joint fits. Then turn the release fork half a turn and remove it backwards.

6. Check that the clutch and the flywheel are marked with paint. Otherwise, mark the clutch and flywheel with pressure plate with a center punch. This must be done in order to ensure that the clutch is refitted in the same position as before.

7. The six bolts which hold the clutch to the flywheel should be slackened crosswise a couple of turns at a time to prevent breakage and then removed. Hold up the clutch so that it does not fall to the floor. The clutch and the plate can then be removed downwards.

REMOVING CLUTCH, LATE PRODUCTION
1. Remove the gearbox.
2. Disconnect the return spring (34, Illustration 1), at the release fork (33). Remove the bolt for the control cylinder (41).

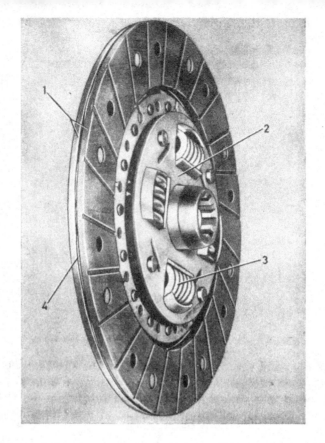

Fig. 3.   Clutch plate

1. Facing   2. Hub   3. Spring   4. Disc

Tie up the cylinder to the body. Remove the plate from the lower front part of the flywheel housing (46). Remove the bolts and take off the flywheel housing.
3. Remove the release bearing (25). Unscrew the bolt which holds the ball joint for the release fork. Remove the ball and fork.

REMOVING MASTER CYLINDER

Remove the pipe (10, Illustration I) from the master cylinder (9). Remove the pedal bolt. Unscrew the bolts and lift off the cylinder.

Disassembling
1. Remove the cover and empty out the brake fluid.
2. Take off the rubber cover (16) and remove the locking ring

(15). Take out the plunger (12) and the other parts from the cylinder.

3. Remove the retainer (3) for the non-return valve (8) from the plunger and separate the parts.

Inspecting

Wash all parts in alcohol or hydraulic fluid and then check them for wear or other damage.

The cylinder must be carefully examined internally. There must be no grooves or scratches on the polished surface. Small scratches can be cleaned up with very fine emery cloth.

Assembling

1. Fit the packings on the plunger (12). Fit together the non-return valve (8), retainer (3), spring (5) and plunger.
2. Dip the plunger and non-return valve in brake fluid and fit them in the cylinders. Fit the thrust rod (17), washer (14) and locking ring (15). Place on the rubber cover (16).

Fitting

Fitting is done in the reverse order to removing. Fill up with brake fluid and bleed the system.

REMOVING CONTROL CYLINDER

Remove the pipe (10) from the hose (40). Remove the hose from the retainer. Unhook the return spring (34). Remove the bolts and lift off the control cylinder (41).

Disassembling

Remove the rubber cover (37) and thrust rod (35). Remove the locking ring (36) and take out the plunger (45) and spring (42).

Assembling

Dip the plunger (45) and packing (44) in brake fluid and fit the packing on the plunger. Fit the spring (42) and plunger in the cylinder (41).

Fit the locking ring (36), thrust rod (35) and dust cover (37).

Fitting

Fitting is done in the reverse order to removing. Bleed the system and adjust the clutch travel.

BLEEDING THE HYDRAULIC SYSTEM

Check that the container is filled with brake fluid. Remove the rubber cap on the bleeding valve (43) on the control cylinder (41). Place a hose on the valve and immerse the other end of the hose in a container filled with brake fluid. Open the bleeding valve and depress the clutch pedal. Close the bleeding valve while the pedal is fully depressed. Then release the pedal. Repeat this procedure until brake fluid free from bubbles runs out. Fill the container with brake fluid up to the level mark (fluid level).

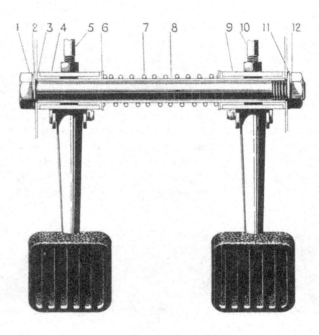

Fig. 15. Pedal shaft.

1.	Bolt	7.	Spring
2.	Washer	8.	Pedal shaft
3.	Nylon bushing	9.	Brake pedal
4.	Clutch pedal	10.	Thrust rod
5.	Thrust rod	11.	Locking washer
6.	Washer	12.	Nut

RENEWING THE PEDAL SHAFT

1. Remove the split pins and bolts in the pedals. Remove the return springs. Slacken the bolt and nut for the pedal shaft (8) Fig. 15. Remove the pedals (4, 9) and shaft.
2. Knock out the bushings (3) with a suitable drift. Press in the new bushings.
3. Inspect the pedal shaft for wear. If it is abnormally worn, it should be replaced.
4. Lubricate the bushings in the pedal with a thin coating of ball bearing grease. Fit the spring and pedals on the pedal shaft and place them in position. Fit on the bolt and nut for the pedal shaft. Place in the pedal bolt and hook on the return spring.

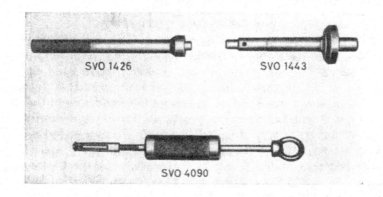

Fig. 17.   Special tools.

SVO 1426   Drift for support bearing in flywheel
SVO 1443   Mandrel for centering the clutch plate
SVO 4090   Puller for ball bearing in flywheel

TRANSMISSIONS

A number of different transmissions differing in internal and external configuration, ratios and operation have been fitted to Volvos. The first series, designated H-1 through H-6, (with the type designation stamped on the upper left hand side of the case) were three-speed-and-reverse gearboxes having synchromesh on second and third only. The M4 and M40 are four speed types of more recent design. M30 is a three speed unit using many of the same parts as the M40 with the exception that first gear is replaced by a blanking sleeve and thus second gear of the M40 becomes first in the M30. Gear ratios are different, of course. Both transmissions are fully synchronized, as is the M-4. Types M31 and M41 utilize a separate overdrive behind the main case.

The well known gear works, Koping Engineering Co., which has been responsible for all Volvo transmissions is now a part of the Volvo complex and the newer gearboxes do not have the firm name cast into the housing as in the past. The same high standards of manufacture and inspection prevail, however, and the Volvo gearbox is extremely rugged and serviceable.

It is not expected that the average owner will want to go so far as to completely disassemble the transmission in his car. However, the knowledge of exactly how the operation should proceed in the case of the most common types is extremely useful during an emergency. Note that certain Volvo tools are required to separate the gearbox from the clutch housing if it is removed without removing the engine.

A word on the operation of the overdrive unit fitted to boxes designated M31 and M41 will be found at the end of the chapter. Identification of the M series, part number and serial number will be found on the bottom of the case at the rear.

The M40 and M41 transmission fitted to the 1800 differs only in having a remote gear change lever. Here are ratios found in the various boxes:

	H 15	H 6	M 4	M 30	M 40
First	3.23	3.13	3.45	3.13	3.13
Second	1.62	1.62	2.18	1.55	1.99
Third	1.00	1.00	1.31	1.00	1.36
Fourth			1.00		1.00
Reverse	2.92	2.66	3.55	3.25	3.25

M-4 TRANSMISSION

The design of the gearbox is shown in fig. 1 and illustration I. All gears, with the exception of reverse, are in constant mesh. In neutral the gears on the main shaft rotate freely and they are therefore fitted with bronze bushings. When one of the gears is engaged the corresponding gear wheel is locked to the main shaft by means of an engaging sleeve.

The gear lever positions are shown in fig. 2. The power transmission path of the different speeds is shown in fig. 3-7.

Fig. 1. Gearbox type M 4.

Fig. 2. Gear lever positions.

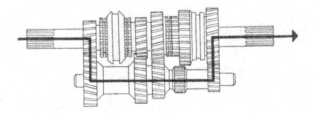

Fig. 3. 1st speed.

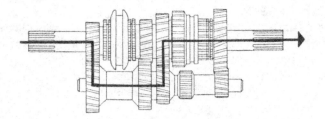

Fig. 4. 2nd speed.

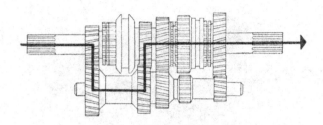

Fig. 5. 3rd speed.

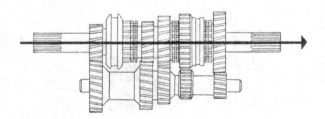

Fig. 6. 4th speed.

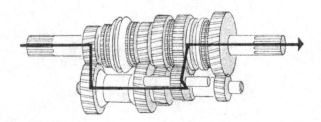

Fig. 7. Reverse.

Fig. 11. Gearbox in position.

1. Gearbox
2. Number plate
3. Rubber cushion
4. Supporting member

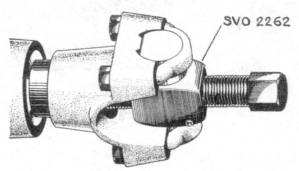

SVO 2262

Fig. 12. Removing flange.

REPLACING SEALING RING

1. Carry out operations 1-4 under the heading "Removing" as far as necessary.

2. Slacken the nut for the flange (42 illustration I). Use tool SVO 4035 as backing for round flanges. Pull off the flange with puller SVO 2261 for PV 444, 445, 544 and SVO2262 for P 1200.

3. Pull out the old sealing ring (41) with puller SVO4030, see fig. 13. Fit the new sealing ring with the help of sleeve SVO2305 and drift SVO 4028, see fig. 14.

4. Press on the flange with SVO 2304, see fig. 15. Fit on remaining parts.

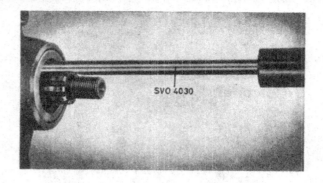

Fig. 13. Removing sealing ring.

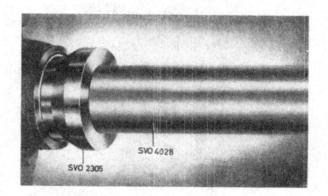

Fig. 14. Fitting sealing ring.

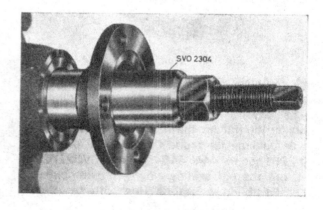

Fig. 15. Fitting flange.

REMOVING (without removing engine)

1. Drain off the coolant. Slacken the upper radiator and the hoses from the engine to the heater. Slacken the exhaust pipe at the manifold flange. Slacken the battery cable and the cable to the oil pressure gauge. Unscrew the thermometer body and the sensitive head of the oil pressure gauge. Uncouple the accelerator pedal pod.

2. Remove the rubber protector and gear lever.

3. Jack up the car and block up underneath. Drain the oil from the gearbox.

4. Place a jack beneath the gearbox to take the weight. Slacken and remove the supporting members beneath the gearbox. Uncouple the front universal joint from the gearbox flange. Slacken the speedometer cable. Place a wooden block between the engine and the cowl and lower the jack.

5. Slacken the bolts which hold the gearbox and clutch housing together. Spanner SVO 1456 for the lower bolts and SVO 4036 for the upper bolts will be required. Pull the gearbox out backwards.

DISMANTLING

1. Fit together SVO 4109 and jig SVO 2044 in a vice. Place the gearbox in the jig.

2. Slacken the gearbox cover (14 Illustration I) nuts. Remove the cover. Take out the springs (13) and interlock balls (12) for the selector rails.

3. Remove the cover (36) over the selector rails. Slacken the selector fork bolts. Move the selector fork (31) back to 1st speed position. Drive out pin (30) slightly (it must not foul 1st speed gear wheel). Then move the selector fork forwards sufficiently to allow the pin to pass in front of the gear wheel. Drive out the pin. Move the selector forks backwards and take them out.

4. Engage two gears and loosen the nut for flange (42).

5. Slacken the bolt and remove locking washer (55) for the intermediate gear wheel (44) with puller SVO 2301. Let the wheel fall into the bottom of the gearbox.

6. Slacken the bolts and pull out the main shaft.

7. Slacken the bolts and remove cover (2) over the main drive pinion (1). Drive out the main drive pinion. If necessary remove the locking ring and press off ball bearing (4) from the main drive pinion.

8. Take out intermediate gear wheel. Pull out reverse gear shaft (52) with puller SVO 2301, see fig. 16. Take out reverse gear wheel and lever (54).

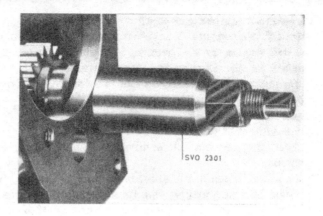

SVO 2301

Fig. 16. Removing reverse gear shaft.

DISMANTLING MAIN SHAFT

1. Move the clutch sleeve (23) for the first and 2nd speeds forwards. Place the shaft in a press and support beneath 1st speed gear wheel (33). Press out the shaft with a drift, see fig. 17.

2. Remove the synchronizing cone, thrust washer, engaging sleeve, guides and spring from the shaft.

3. Remove the locking ring on the front end of the shaft. Support beneath 2nd gear wheel (20) and press out the shaft, see fig. 18.

Fig. 17. Dismantling main shaft.

Fig. 18. Dismantling main shaft.

4. Dismantle 3rd and 4th speed synchronizing components.
5. Remove the sealing ring (41) from the rear cover (39) and take out the oil slinger (40) and speedometer gear wheel (38). If necessary remove the locking ring and press out the ball bearing (37).

INSPECTION

Before inspection all parts should be carefully washed in solvent. All sealing surfaces should be scraped free from gaskets and sealing compounds.

After cleaning all parts should be checked for wear, deformation or other damage.

Check the gear wheels especially for cracks or chips in the teeth.

Check the synchronizing cones and all the other synchronizing components. Damaged or worn parts should be replaced.

Check the ball bearings especially for scoring or cracks in the races or balls.

ASSEMBLING MAIN SHAFT

1. Press the ball bearing (37 Illustration I) into the rear cover (39), fig. 19 and fit the locking ring. There are different thicknesses of locking rings so select one which completely fills the locking ring groove.

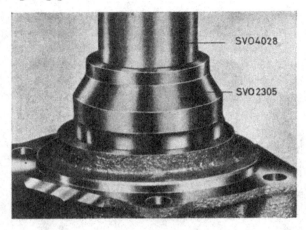

Fig. 19. Fitting ball bearing into rear cover.

2. Fit the speedometer gear wheel (38) and oil slinger (40) on the bearing in the rear cover. Press in the sealing ring (41) with sleeve SVO 2305 and drift SVO 4028, see fig. 20.

Fig. 20. Fitting sealing ring.

3. Assemble the synchronizing components, for 1st and 2nd speeds on the main shaft. Ensure that the spring rings are correctly fitted, see fig. 21.

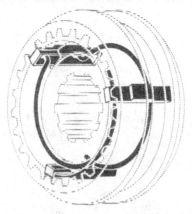

Fig. 21. Assembling synchronizing components.

4. Fit thrust washer, synchronizing cone, 1st speed gear wheel (33) and thrust washer (35). Fit the rear cover on the shaft. Ensure that the speedometer gear wheel and oil slinger are correctly located. Fit on the flange (42). Use a sleeve which fits into the recess in the flange, press on the cover and flange (see fig. 22).

Fig. 22. Fitting on rear cover.

5. Fit on the thrust washer (22), synchronizing cone (21) and 2nd speed gear wheel (20). Locate the locking ball (18) on the shaft with grease. Press on the bushing (17) with sleeve SVO 4028, see fig. 23. Ensure that the groove in the bushing comes centrally over the ball. Fit on 3rd gear wheel (16) and synchronizing cone.

Fig. 23.   Fitting bushing.

6. Assemble 3rd and 4th speed synchronizing components. Ensure that the spring rings are correctly fitted, see fig. 21. Turn the clutch sleeve so that the machined groove in one of the beveled surfaces faces rearwards. Then fit on the main shaft. Select a locking ring of correct thickness, see fig. 24, and fit on same.

ASSEMBLING GEARBOX

1. Fit lever (54) and guide stud (53). Fit on reverse gear wheel (52) and shaft for same (56).

2. Place locating tool SVO 2303 in the intermediate gear wheel (44). Put in spacing washers (47, 50) and needles (24 in each bearing). Use grease to hold the needles and washers in place.

3. Fit the washers (43, 48) to the housing with grease and guide them into position with SVO 2302, see fig. 25. Lay the inter-

Fig. 24.   Trying out locking ring for thickness.

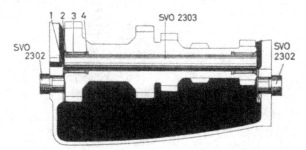

Fig. 25.   Fitting intermediate gear.

1.   Thrust washer
2.   Spacing washer
3.   Needle bearing
4.   Spacing washer

mediate gear in the bottom of the housing.

4.   Fit the oil slinger (5) and bearing (4) on the main drive pinion (1) with the help of tools SVO 2305 and SVO 4028, see fig. 26. Select a locking ring of suitable thickness and fit same. Press the main drive pinion into position in the housing. Fit on the cover (2) over the main drive pinion.

5.   Place the needle bearing (3) in position and then fit the main shaft into the housing.

6.   Turn the gearbox upside down. Fit intermediate gear wheel shaft (49). See that the thrust washers do not fall down. Fit the locking washer (55) for intermediate gear and reverse gear shaft.

7.   Fit selector rails and forks. Move selector fork (31) to 1st speed position when fitting pin (30). Use a new pin. Fit the end cover (36) over the selector rails.

8. Fit on washer and nut for flange.

9. Place the interlock balls and springs in position. Fit on the gearbox cover. Check that all gears engage and disengage easily.

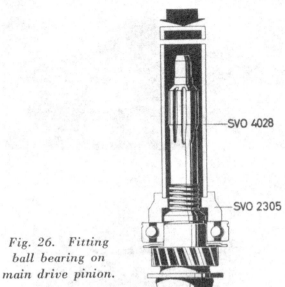

SVO 4028

SVO 2305

Fig. 26. Fitting ball bearing on main drive pinion.

Fig. 27. Fitting selector forks and rails.

FITTING

Fitting is done in the reverse sequence to removing. Fill up the gearbox with oil.

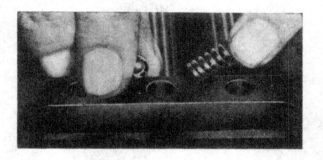

Fig. 28. Fitting interlock balls and springs.

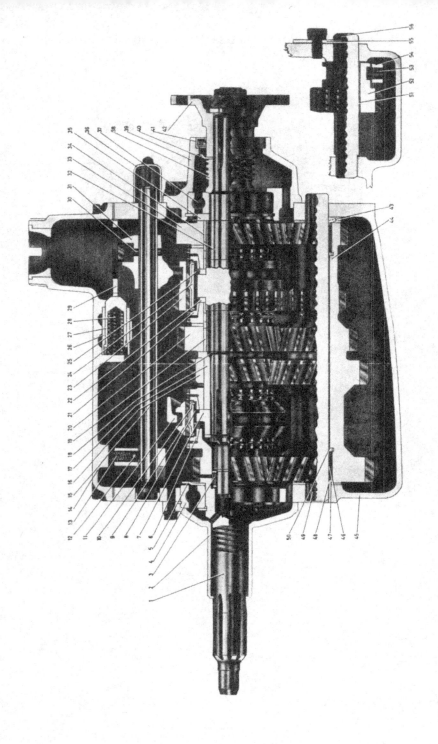

Illustration I. Gearbox type M 4

1. Main drive pinion
2. Front cover
3. Needle bearing
4. Ball bearing
5. Oil slinger
6. Synchronizing cone
7. Synchronizing hub
8. Spring
9. Engaging sleeve
10. Guide
11. Selector fork
12. Interlock ball
13. Spring
14. Cover
15. Selector rail
16. Gear for 3rd speed
17. Bushing
18. Ball
19. Bushing

20. Gear for 2nd speed
21. Synchronizing cone
22. Thrust washer
23. Engaging sleeve and gear for reverse
24. Guide
25. Spring
26. Sleeve
27. Sleeve
28. Spring
29. Locking plate
30. Pin
31. Selector fork
32. Main shaft
33. Gear for 1st speed
34. Bushing
35. Thrust washer
36. Cover
37. Ball bearing

38. Speedometer gear wheel
39. Rear cover
40. Oil slinger
41. Sealing ring
42. Flange
43. Thrust washer
44. Intermediate gear
45. Gearbox housing
46. Needle bearing
47. Spacing washer
48. Thrust washer
49. Intermediate gear wheel shaft
50. Spacing washer
51. Bushing
52. Reverse gear wheel
53. Guide stud
54. Lever
55. Locking washer
56. Reverse gear shaft

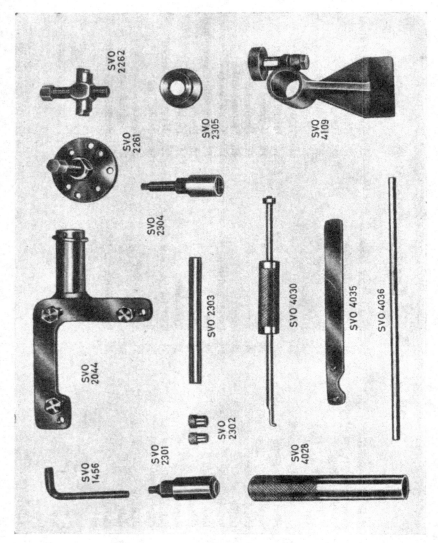

SVO 2262

SVO 2305

SVO 4109

SVO 2261

SVO 2304

SVO 2303

SVO 4030

SVO 4035

SVO 4036

SVO 2044

SVO 2302

SVO 2301

SVO 1456

SVO 4028

TOOLS

The following special tools are required for carrying out repairs to the **M-4** gearbox.

SVO 1456   Hexagon box spanner (angle) for lower gearbox bolts.

SVO 2044   Jig for dismantling and assembling. Used together with SVO 4109.

SOV 2261   Puller for flange in PV 544, 444—445.

SVO 2262   Puller for flange on P 1200.

SVO 2301   Puller for removing reverse gear shaft.

SVO 2302   Locating tool for thrust washer. Used together with 2303 when fitting intermediate gear.

SVO 2303   Locating tool for fitting intermediate gear plus 2 SVO 2302.

SVO 2304   Press tool for fitting flange.

SVO 2305   Fitting sleeve for main drive pinion bearing, bearing and sealing ring in rear cover. Used together with SVO 2304 and SVO 4028.

SVO 4028   Drift for bushing in 3rd speed gear wheel in main shaft.

SVO 4030   Puller for flange sealing ring.

SVO 4035   Key. Used as counter-hold when removing and fitting flange, PV 544, 444—445.

SVO 4036   Hexagon box spanner (straight) for upper gearbox bolts.

SVO 4109   Support for jig SVO 2044.

Fig. 1. Gearbox with overdrive.

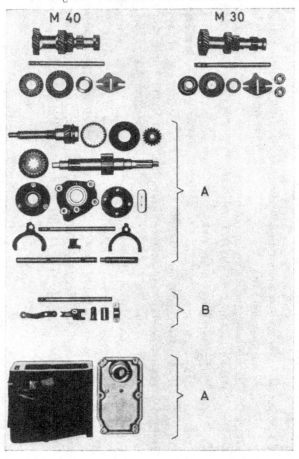

*Fig. 2. Comparing component parts,
M 30—M 40.*

A. Identical parts   B. Not included on M 30

TRANSMISSIONS — M30, M40, M31, M41

The chief difference between the gearboxes is that on the M 40 the 1st speed gear is replaced with a spacing sleeve and 2nd and 3rd speed gears have become 1st and 2nd respectively. The sliding reverse gear on the M 40 has been fixed by means of two spacing sleeves on the M 30.

The construction of the gearboxes is shown in Figs. 1 and 2 and Illustrations I and II. All gears with the exception of the reverse gears are in constant mesh with each other. In the neutral position the gears on the main rotate freely. For this reason they are provided with bronze bushings. When engaging a gear, the corresponding gear wheel is connected to the main shaft by means of an engaging sleeve.

The gear lever positions are shown in Fig. 3. The power transmission path of the different speeds is shown in Figs. 4—9.

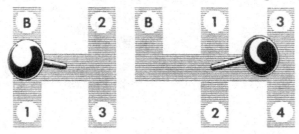

Fig. 3.   Gear lever positions.

B = Reverse

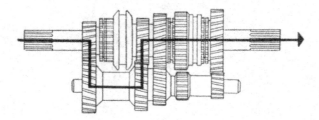

Fig. 4.   1st speed, M 40.

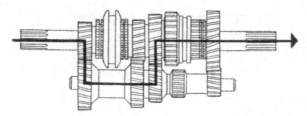

Fig. 5.   1st speed, M 30   2nd speed, M 40.

181

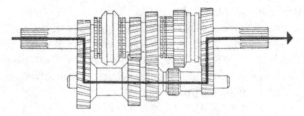

Fig. 6.   2nd speed, M 30   3rd speed, M 40.

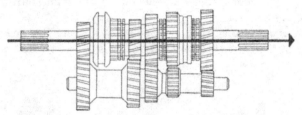

Fig. 7.   3rd speed, M 30   4th speed, M 40.

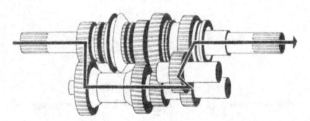

Fig. 8.   Reverse M 30.

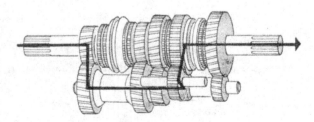

Fig. 9.   Reverse M 40.

REPLACING SEALING RING

1. Carry out operations 1—4 under the heading "Removing" as far as necessary.

2. Slacken the nut for the flange. Use spanner SVO 2409 as a counterhold, see Fig. 14. Pull off the flange. Use puller SVO 2261 for round flanges and SVO 2262 for other flanges, see Fig. 15.

3. Pull out the old sealing ring with puller SVO 4030, see Fig. 16. Fit the new sealing ring with the help of sleeve SVO 2413, see Fig. 17.

4. Press on the flange with SVO 2304, see Fig. 18. Fit on remaining parts.

REMOVING (without removing engine)

1. Drain off the coolant. Slacken the upper radiator hose and the hoses from the engine to the heater. Slacken the exhaust pipe at the manifold flange. Disconnect the battery cable and the cable to the oil pressure gauge. Unscrew the thermometer body and the sensitive head of the oil pressure gauge. Disconnect the accelerator pedal rod.

2. Remove the rubber protector and gear lever.

3. Jack up the car and block up underneath. Drain the oil from the gearbox.

4. Place a jack beneath the gearbox to take the weight. Slacken and remove the supporting member under the gearbox. Uncouple the front universal joint from the gearbox flange. Disconnect the speedometer cable. Place a wooden block between the engine and the cowl and lower the jack.

5. NOTE: Unscrew the bolts which hold the gearbox and clutch housing together with the help of spanner SVO 2426 (for B 16) or SVO 2431 (for B 18) and ball joint connector SVO 2427, see A, Fig. 19. Tool SVO 2428 (for B 16) or SVO 2432 (for B 18) is then used for screwing out, see B, Fig. 19. Pull out the gearbox backwards.

DISMANTLING

The above description applies to gearboxes without overdrive. If the gearbox is fitted with an overdrive, unscrew the bolts in the rear end of the gearbox and remove the overdrive. Then carry out the operations described below as far as necessary.

1. Fit together SVO 4109 and jig SVO 2044 in a vice. Place the gearbox in the jig.

2. Slacken the bolts for the gearbox cover. Lift off the cover. Remove the springs and interlock balls for the selector rails.

3. Remove the cover over the selector rails. Unscrew the

Fig. 13.   Gearbox in position.

1. Gearbox
2. Number plate
3. Rubber cushion
4. Supporting member

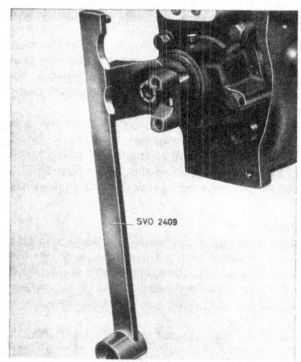

SVO 2409

Fig. 14.   Counterhold for flange.

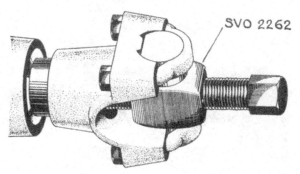

Fig. 15. Removing flange.

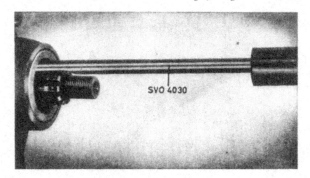

Fig. 16. Removing sealing ring.

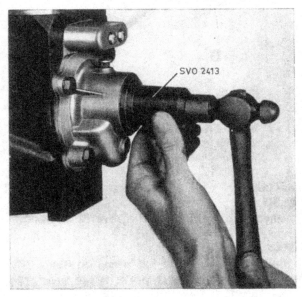

Fig. 17. Fitting sealing ring.

Fig. 18. Fitting flange.

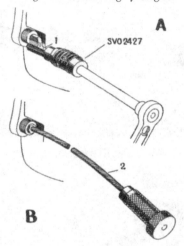

Fig. 19. Removing gearbox bolts.

A. Slackening and tightening
B. Screwing in and out
1. SVO 2426 (B 16) SVO 2431 (B 18)
2. SVO 2428 (B 16) SVO 2432 (B 18)

selector fork bolts.

4a. M 30:

Slide the selector fork back to the reverse position. Drive out the pin.

4b. M 40:

Slide the selector fork back to 1st speed position. Drive out the pin slightly (it must not foul the 1st speed gear wheel). Then move the selector fork forwards sufficiently to allow the pin to pass in front of the gear wheel. Drive out the pin.

5. Slide out the selector rails. When doing this, hold against the selector forks so that they do not come skew and jam on the rails. Remove the selector forks.

6. Unscrew the bolts for the rear cover. Turn the cover so that it does not lock the shaft for the idler and reverse gears. Drive out the shaft for the idler gear. **Note. The shaft must be driven out backwards.** Let the idler gear fall into the bottom of the gearbox.

7. Pull out the main shaft.

8. Unscrew the bolts and remove the cover over the input shaft. Prise out the sealing ring from the cover with a screwdriver or similar.

9. Drive out the input shaft. If necessary, remove the locking ring and press the ball bearing off the shaft.

10. Take out the idler gear. Pull out the shaft for the reverse gear with puller SVO 2301, Fig. 20. Take out the reverse gear and other parts.

Fig. 20. Removing reverse gear.

DISMANTLING MAIN SHAFT
M 30 Gearbox

1a. Gearbox with overdrive (M 31):

Remove the locking ring and press off the rotor for the overdrive oil pump. Remove the locking ring for the main shaft rear bearing. Slide the engaging sleeve for 1st speed and reverse forwards. Place the shaft in a press and support under the rear cover. Press out the shaft, Fig. 21.

1b. Gearbox without overdrive:

Unscrew the nut for the flange. Use tool SVO 2409 as a counterhold, see Fig. 14. Pull off the flange. Use puller SVO 2261 for round flanges and SVO 2262 for other flanges, see Fig. 15.

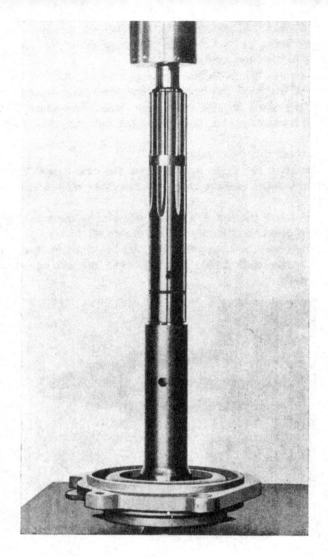

Fig. 21.   Dismantling main shaft, M 31.

Slide the engaging sleeve for 1st speed and reverse forward. Place the shaft in a press and support under the rear cover. Press out the shaft with a drift, see Fig. 22.

2. Remove the thrust washer, spacing sleeve, engaging sleeves, guides and springs from the shaft.

3. Remove the locking ring on the front end of the shaft. Pull off the synchronizer hub and 2nd speed gear wheel with a suitable puller, see Fig. 23. Remove the thrust washer.

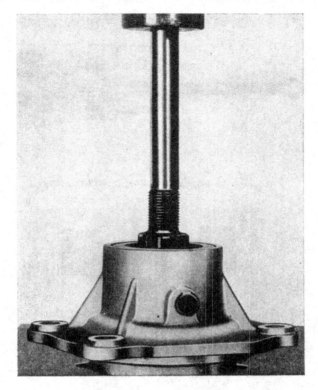

Fig. 22. Dismantling main shaft, M 30.

4. Remove the locking ring and then the thrust washer, 1st speed gear wheel, synchronizing cone and spring.

5. Remove the sealing ring from the rear cover and take out the speedometer gear. If necessary, remove the locking ring and press out the ball bearing.

M 40 Gearbox

1a. Gearbox with overdrive (M 41):

Support under the first speed gear wheel when pressing out the shaft. Then follow the instructions in point 1a under M 30 gearbox.

1b. Gearbox without overdrive:

Unscrew the nut for the flange. Use tool SVO 2409 as a counterhold on the flange. Slide the engaging sleeve for 1st and 2nd speeds forward. Place the shaft in a press and support under the 1st gear wheel. Press out the shaft with a drift, see Fig. 24.

2. Remove the synchronizing cone, thrust washer, engaging sleeves, guides and springs from the shaft.

3. Remove the locking ring on the front end of the shaft. Pull off the synchronizer hub and 3rd speed gear wheel with a

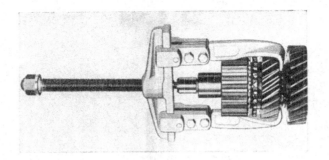

Fig. 23. Removing front synchronizer.

Fig. 24. Dismantling main shaft, M 40.

puller. Remove the thrust washer.

4. Remove the locking ring and then the thrust washer, 2nd speed gear wheel, synchronizing cone and spring.

5. Remove the sealing ring from the rear cover and take out the speedometer gear. If necessary, remove the locking ring and press out the ball bearing.

INSPECTION

Check the gear wheels particularly for cracks or chips on the tooth surfaces. Check the synchronizing cones and all the other synchronizing components. Damaged or worn parts should be replaced.

Check the ball bearings particularly for scoring or cracks in the races or balls.

ASSEMBLING
Assembling main shaft
M 30 Gearbox

1. Press the ball bearing into the rear cover with drift SVO 2412, see Fig. 25, and fit the locking ring. There are different thicknesses of locking ring so select one which completely fills the locking ring groove.

2. Gearbox without overdrive:

Place the speedometer gear on the bearing in the rear cover. Press in the sealing ring with drift SVO 2413, see Fig. 26.

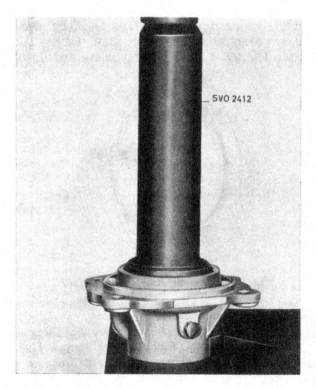

SVO 2412

Fig. 25. Fitting ball bearing in rear cover.

Fig. 26.   Fitting sealing ring in rear cover.

3. Fit the spring rings, guides and engaging sleeve for the 1st speed synchronizer on the main shaft. Fit the spring rings correctly, see Fig. 27. Fit the spacing sleeve and thrust washer.

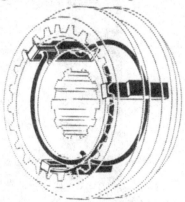

Fig. 27.   Assembling synchronizer.

4a.   Gearbox without overdrive:

Place the rear cover on the shaft. Ensure that the speedometer gear is positioned correctly. Place on the flange. Use a sleeve which fits into the recess in the flange and press on the cover and flange, see Fig. 28. Place on the washer and nut for the flange. Use tool SVO 2409 as a counterhold on the flange and tighten the nut.

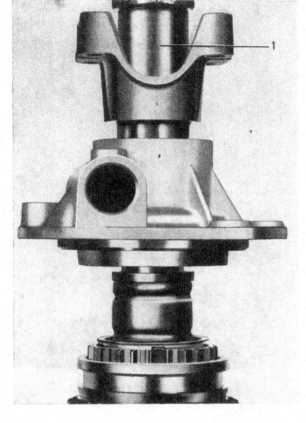

Fig. 28.   Fitting rear cover, M 30.
1. Sleeve

4b.   Gearbox with overdrive (M 31):

Place the rear cover and ball bearing on a support ring or sleeve as shown in Fig. 29. Place on the thrust washer and spacing sleeve. Press in the shaft. Select a locking ring of suitable thickness and fit same. Fit the key, eccentric for the oil pump and locking ring.

5.   Fit the synchronizing cone, 1st speed gear wheel and thrust washer on the shaft. Select a locking ring which fits well into the groove on the shaft and fit it.

6.   Fit the thrust washer, 2nd speed gear wheel and synchronizing cone on the shaft. Assemble the 2nd and 3rd speed synchronizing parts. Fit the spring rings correctly, see Fig. 27. Then fit the synchronizing ring on the main shaft. Select a locking ring which fits well into the groove and fit it.

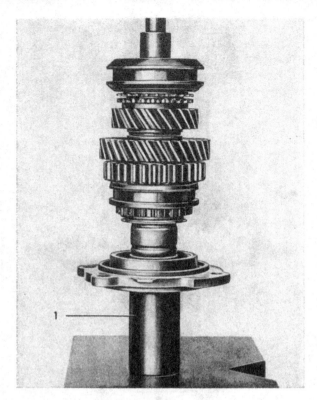

Fig. 29. Fitting rear cover.
1. Sleeve

M 40 Gearbox

1. Press the ball bearing into the rear cover, see Fig. 25, and fit the locking ring. There are different thicknesses of locking ring so select one which completely fills the locking ring groove.

2. Gearbox without overdrive:

Place the speedometer gear on the bearing in the rear cover. Press in the sealing ring with drift SVO 2413, see Fig. 26.

3. Fit the parts for 1st speed and 2nd speed synchronizer on the main shaft. Fit the spring rings currently, see Fig. 27.

4a. Gearbox without overdrive:

Fit the synchronizing cone, 1st speed gear wheel and thrust washer. Place the rear cover on the shaft. Ensure that the speedometer gear is positioned currently. Place on the flange. Use a sleeve which fits into the recess in the flange, press on the cover and flange. Use tool SVO 2409 as a counterhold on the flange and tighten the nut.

4a. Gearbox with overdrive (M 41):

See point 4b under M 30 gearbox.

5. Fit synchronizing cone, 2nd speed gear wheel and thrust washer on the shaft. Select a locking ring which fits well into the groove on the shaft and fit it.

6. Fit the thrust washer, 3rd speed gear wheel and synchronizing cone on the shaft. Assemble the 3rd and 4th speed synchronizing parts. Fit the spring rings correctly, see Fig. 27. Then fit the synchronizer on the main shaft. Select a locking ring of the correct thickness and fit it.

Fig. 30.   Fitting rear cover, M 40.
1. Sleeve

ASSEMBLING GEARBOX

1a. M 30 gearbox:

Fit the reverse gear, spacing sleeves and reverse shaft. Ensure that the groove in the reverse shaft is turned correctly.

1b. M 40 Gearbox:

Fit the lever and guide stud. Fit the reverse gear and reverse shaft. Ensure that the groove in the reverse shaft is turned correctly.

2. Place mandrel SVO 2303 in the idler gear. Place in spacing washers and needles (24 in each bearing). Use grease to hold the needles and washers in position.

3. Fix the washers to the housing with grease, and guide them into position with SVO 2302, see Fig. 31. Lay the idler gear in the bottom of the housing.

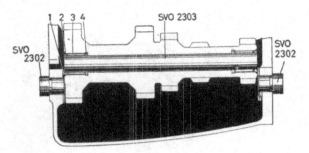

Fig. 31. Fitting idler gear.

1. Thrust washer   3. Needle bearing
2. Spacing washer   4. Spacing washer

4. Press the bearing onto the input shaft with the help of drift SVO 2412, see Fig. 32. Select a locking ring of suitable thickness and fit it. Place the 14 bearing rollers for the main

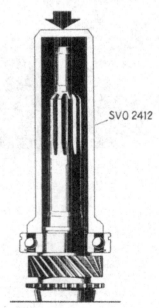

Fig. 32. Fitting ball bearing on input shaft.

shaft in position on the input shaft. Use grease to hold the rollers in place. Press the input shaft into position in the housing. Press the sealing ring into the cover with drift SVO 2010. Then fit the cover over the input shaft.

5. Place the main shaft in the housing. Turn the rear cover so that the countershaft can be fitted.

6. Turn the gearbox upside down. Fit the countershaft from the rear. Hold against SVO 2303 with the hand. Ensure that the thrust washers do not loosen and fall down.

7a. Gearboxes without overdrive:

Turn the rear cover correctly so that it locks the reverse shaft. Fit the bolts for the cover.

7b. Gearboxes with overdrive:

Turn the cover correctly so that it locks the reverse shaft. Ensure that the eccentric for the overdrive oil pump is turned upwards. Fit the overdrive unit.

8. Fit selector rails and fork. Move over the selector fork to the rear position when fitting the pin. Use a new pin. Fit the cover over the selector rails.

Note. If the end caps in the front end of the housing have been removed, these should be fitted in the same way as previously, that is to say, the centre end cap should project about 4 mm (5/32") outside the face of the housing, see Fig. 33.

9. Place the interlock balls and springs in position, see Fig. 34. Fit the gearbox cover. Check that all gears engage and disengage freely.

FITTING

Fitting is done in the reverse order to removing. Fill up the gearbox with oil.

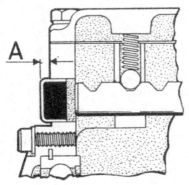

Fig. 33. Fitting end cap over selector rail.

A = approx. 4 mm (5/32")

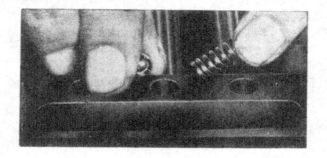

Fig. 34. Fitting interlock balls and springs.

OVERDRIVE

The overdrive on the M 31 and M 41 transmission is of the planetary gear type and is attached to the rear end of the main transmission. The design is shown in Fig. 3-32 and Illustration 111-B.

Fig. 3-32. Overdrive unit

The overdrive functions as follows:

In the direct gear position the clutch disk (41), illustration (III-B) is in the position shown in 1, Fig. 3-33. When driving forward, power from the transmission mainshaft (57) is transmitted through the free wheel (33, 34) to the overdrive output shaft (23). When reversing or using the engine as a brake, torque is transmitted through the clutch disk. This is possible since the clutch disk is pressed against the tapered portion of the output shaft by means of four springs (52). In the overdrive position the clutch disk is pressed against the brake drum (39), see II, Fig. 3-33. In this position the sun wheel is locked. When driving, the planet wheels (36) are therefore caused to rotate around the sun wheel (44). As a result of this the output shaft will rotate more quickly than the mainshaft.

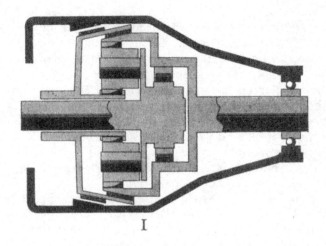

I

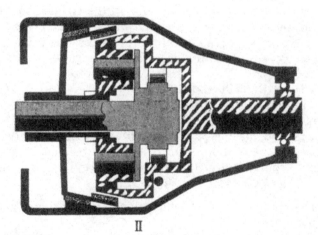

II

■ Non-rotating parts

▨ Rotating at same speed as input shaft

▨ Rotating at higher speed than input shaft

Fig. 3-33. Function of overdrive
I. Direct drive position   II. Overdrive position

Engagement of the overdrive is done electro-hydraulically. There is a contact on the transmission cover which cuts in when high gear is engaged. The overdrive can only be engaged when this contact is cut in.

When engaging the overdrive a contact fitted on the instrument panel is operated. Current passes through this contact and goes via the contact on the transmission to a solenoid on the overdrive, see Fig. 3-34. The solenoid has two windings, a heavy control winding and a fine retaining winding. The control winding influences the solenoid armature in such a way that a control valve in the overdrive is opened. When the valve has opened, current through the control winding is cut off. The valve is then held in open position by the retaining winding.

There is a plunger type pump in the overdrive (4 Fig. 3-35) which is driven by a cam on the mainshaft.

When the control valve (6) opens (position 1, Fig. 3-36), oil under pressure from the pump flows via the valve to two cylinders (1). The plungers in the cylinders then press the clutch disk forwards to make contact with the brake drum. When the overdrive is disengaged, the control valve shuts off the connection between the pump and cylinders. The clutch disk is then pressed rearwards by the springs. The oil in the cylinders flows out through the hollow valve rod into the overdrive housing, see II, Fig. 3-36.

WORK WHICH CAN BE CARRIED OUT
WITH THE OVERDRIVE UNIT FITTED
Checking Oil Pressure
1. Engage and disengage the overdrive 10-12 times (with the engine stopped) in order to remove any residual oil pressure.
2. Remove the plug over the control valve and connect oil pressure gauge SVO 2415, see Fig. 3-37.

NOTE. The spring (47, illustration III-B), stud (50) and ball (51) should remain in position.

3. Start and drive the car. (This test can also be done with the car jacked up). At a speed of 12.4 - 15.5 m.p.h. (20-25 km p.h.) with the overdrive direct drive engaged (16.2 - 20.6 m.p.h. equals 26 - 23 km p.h. on the overdrive), the gauge should show a pressure of 525-570 lb./sq. in. (37-40 kg/cm^2). If the gauge gives too low a reading, see "Fault tracing" concerning the reason and remedy.

CLEANING THE OIL STRAINER
The oil strainer should be cleaned at every oil change. First drain off the oil by removing the plug (3, Fig. 3-35, marked

Fig. 3-34. Electrical wiring diagram

1. Fusebox
2. Switch on transmission
3. Switch on instrument panel
4. Control lamp for overdrive
5. Relay for overdrive
6. Solenoid on overdrive

Wire color on relay:

C_1. Yellow — purple
C_2. Yellow
W_1. Yellow
W_2. Yellow — green

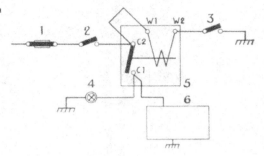

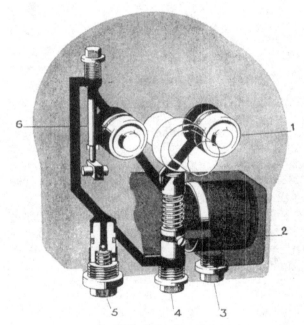

Fig. 3-35. Hydraulic system

1. Hydraulic cylinder and plunger
2. Oil strainer
3. Drain plug
4. Oil pump
5. Reducing valve
6. Control valve

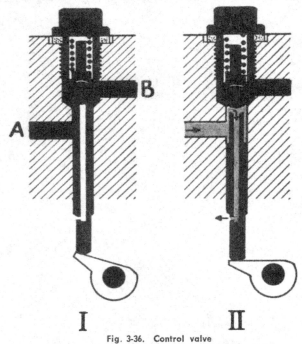

Fig. 3-36. Control valve

I. Overdrive position
II. Moving over from overdrive to direct drive
A. To hydraulic cylinder   B. From oil pump

"Drain") under the oil strainer. Cleaning should then be done as follows:

1. Remove the cover (2) and take out the oil strainer (1) see Fig. 3-38. Clean the oil strainer in gasoline or white spirit. Blow dry with compressed air.
2. Check that the gasket (3) is intact and place it in position. Fit the oil strainer, new gasket (4) and cover.

CHECKING AND ADJUSTING THE CONTROL VALVE

1. Jack up the car and place blocks under the front and rear axles.
2. Remove the cover over the control valve arm. Engage the overdrive (with the engine stopped and 4th speed engaged). If the control valve is correctly adjusted, it should be possible to push a 3/16" (4.75 mm) diameter pin through the hole in the arm and into the housing, see Fig. 3-39. If not, adjust until the correct position of the arm is obtained.
3. Check the current through the solenoid with the overdrive engaged. The current should be max. 1 amp. If the current is 18-20 amp., this means that the solenoid armature does not go in far enough to cut off the control current.

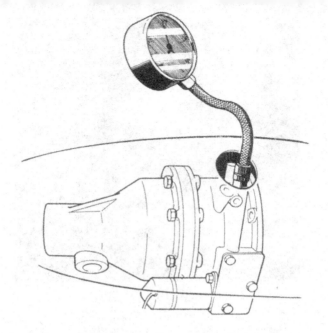

Fig. 3-37. Checking oil pressure with pressure gauge SVO 2415

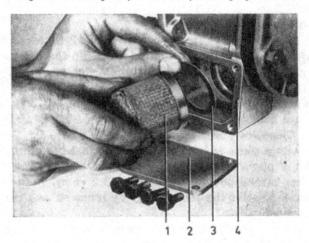

1 2 3 4

Fig. 3-38. Removing the oil strainer
1. Oil strainer
2. Cover
3. Gasket for oil strainer
4 Gasket for cover

NOTE. If the current through the solenoid is too high, the reason must be ascertained and the necessary measures taken, otherwise the solenoid can be destroyed.

Fig. 3-39. Adjusting the control valve
1. Control gauge, diam. 3/16" (4.75 mm)

CHECKING THE OIL PUMP

1. Engage and disengage the overdrive 10-12 times so that any residual oil pressure is removed. Jack up the car and place blocks under the front and rear axles. Remove the drain plug and let the oil run into the container.

2. Remove the plug and take out the spring (8) and ball (6). Remove the valve seating (7) with key SVO 2419, see Fig. 3-40. Clean and check the parts.

3. Feel with a piece of wire or similar against the pump plunger that the pump works when the output shaft is rotated. The plunger stroke should be 0.126" (3.2 mm). If the plunger stroke is shorter the pump must be removed and the reason ascertained.

4. The pump is removed in the following manner: Unscrew the bolt which holds the pump through the hole in the extension piece (56). Screw puller SVO 2418 into the place of the valve seating and pull out the pump, see Fig. 3-41. Disassemble and check the various parts of the pump.

5. The pump and pump valve are fitted in the reverse order to removing. Check that the gasket for the plug (4, Fig. 3-35) is intact. Fill up with oil.

204

Fig. 3-40. Removing the valve seating, oil pump

Fig. 3-41. Removing the oil pump

CHECKING THE REDUCING VALVE

1. Engage and disengage the overdrive 10-12 times so that any residual oil pressure is removed. Jack up the car and place blocks under the front and rear axles. Remove the drain plug and let the oil run out into a container.
2. Remove the plug and take out the spring (11) and valve (12). Pull out the valve seating (10) with the help of a small hook, see Fig. 3-42.
3. Clean and check all parts thoroughly. Fit the parts in the reverse order to removing.

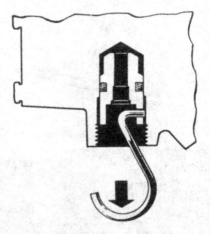

Fig. 3-42. Removing the valve seating, reducing valve

TOOLS

The following special tools are required for work on the overdrive unit

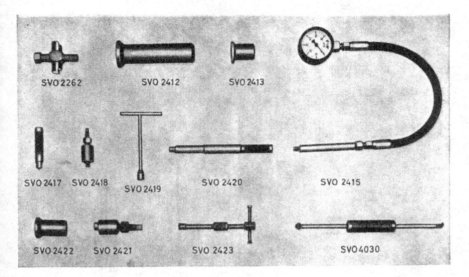

Fig. 3-58. Special tools

SVO 2262 Puller for coupling
SVO 2412 Drift for fitting front bearing on output shaft
SVO 2413 Drift for fitting rear bearing on output shaft
SVO 2415 Pressure gauge for checking oil pressure
SVO 2417 Drift for removing needle bearings in planet wheels and for fitting bearings in planet wheels and output shaft
SVO 2418 Puller for oil pump

SVO 2419 Key for valve seating, oil pump
SVO 2420 Centering mandrel for splines in planet wheel carrier and free wheel hub
SVO 2421 Press tool for fitting coupling
SVO 2422 Fitting tool for sealing ring, output shaft
SVO 2423 Puller for needle bearing in output shaft
SVO 4030 Puller for sealing ring, output shaft

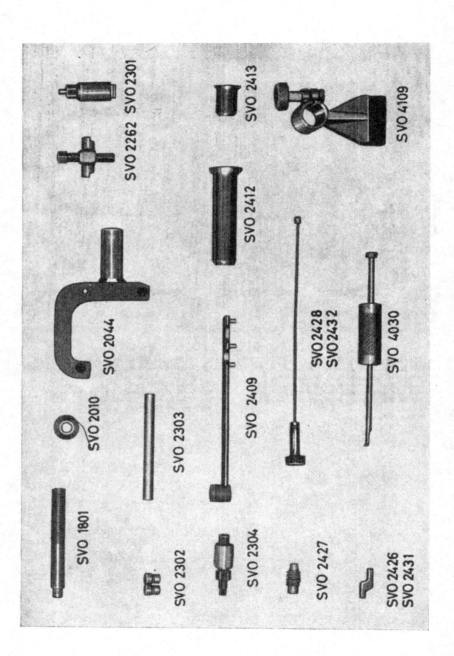

SVO 2262 SVO 2301

SVO 2413

SVO 4109

SVO 2412

SVO 2044

SVO 2010

SVO 2303

SVO 2409

SVO 2428
SVO 2432

SVO 4030

SVO 1801

SVO 2302

SVO 2304

SVO 2427

SVO 2426
SVO 2431

TOOLS

The following special tools are required for carrying out repairs to the gearbox.

SVO 1801   Standard handle 18×200 mm.
SVO 2010   Drift for fitting sealing ring in cover for input shaft.
SVO 2044   Jig for dismantling and assembling.
SVO 2261   Puller for flange on PV 444, 445, 544, P 210. (Not shown in the figure.)
SVO 2262   Puller for flange on P 1200.
SVO 2301   Puller for removing reverse gear shaft.
SVO 2302   Locating tool for thrust washer. Used together with SVO 2303 when fitting idler gear.
SVO 2303   Locating tool for fitting idler gear.
SVO 2304   Press tool for idling flange.
SVO 2409   Counterhold for flange.
SVO 2412   Tool for fitting bearing on input shaft in rear cover.

SVO 2413   Tool for fitting sealing ring in rear cover.
SVO 2426   Spanner for slackening and tightening gearbox bolts (used in connection with B 16 engine).
SVO 2427   Ball joint connector for spanner SVO 2426.
SVO 2428   Spanner for screwing in and out gearbox bolts (used in connection with B 16 engine).
SVO 2431   Spanner for slackening and tightening gearbox bolts (used in connection with B 18 engine).
SVO 2432   Spanner for screwing in and out gearbox bolts (used in connection with B 18 engine).
SVO 4030   Puller for sealing ring on flange.
SVO 4109   Support for jig SVO 2044.

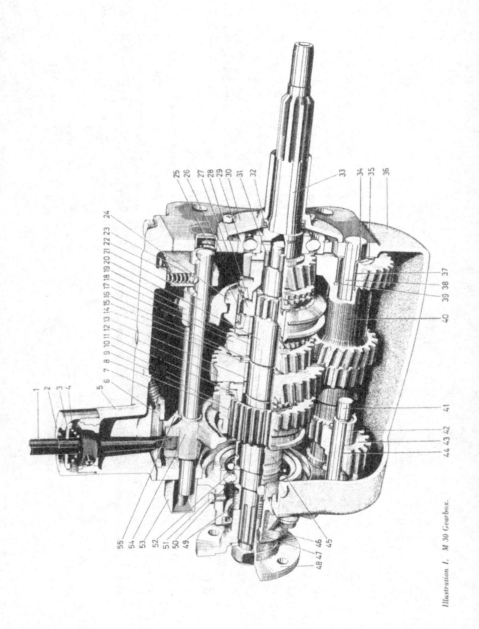

Illustration 1. M 30 Gearbox.

1. Gear lever
2. Cover
3. Washer
4. Spring
5. Cover
6. Sliding plate
7. Spring
8. Guide
9. Engaging sleeve and gear for reverse
10. Selector rail, 2nd and 3rd speeds
11. Synchronizing cone
12. Gear for 1st speed
13. Bushing
14. Thrust washer
15. Locking ring
16. Thrust washer
17. Gear for 2nd speed
18. Bushing
19. Selector fork for 2nd and 3rd speeds
20. Main shaft
21. Selector fork, 1st speed and reverse
22. Spring
23. Interlock ball
24. Engaging sleeve, 2nd and 3rd speeds
25. Guide
26. Spring
27. Synchronizer hub
28. Synchronizing cone
29. Ball bearing
30. Front cover
31. Roller bearing
32. Sealing ring
33. Input shaft
34. Spacing washer
35. Thrust washer
36. Housing
37. Needle bearing
38. Countershaft
39. Spacing washer
40. Idler wheel
41. Reverse shaft
42. Spacing sleeve
43. Reverse gear
44. Bushing
45. Spacing sleeve
46. Rear cover
47. Sealing ring
48. Flange
49. Speedometer gear
50. Ball bearing
51. Ventilation nipple
52. Thrust washer
53. Casing
54. Selector fork for 1st speed and reverse
55. Carrier

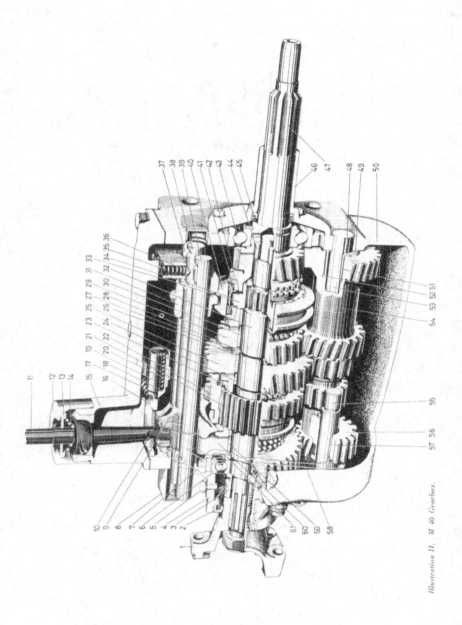

Illustration II. M 40 Gearbox.

212

1. Flange
2. Sealing ring
3. Speedometer gear
4. Rear cover
5. Ventilation nipple
6. Ball bearing
7. Carrier (X-ray picture)
8. Casing
9. Selector fork, 1st and 2nd speeds
10. Carrier
11. Gear lever
12. Casing
13. Washer
14. Spring
15. Cover
16. Sliding plate
17. Spring
18. Sleeve (reverse catch)
19. Sleeve
20. Spring
21. Guide
22. Engaging sleeve and gear for reverse
23. Synchronizing cone
24. Bushing
25. Gear for 2nd speed
26. Thrust washer
27. Locking ring
28. Thrust washer
29. Gear for 3rd speed
30. Bushing
31. Selector fork for 3rd and 4th speeds
32. Main shaft
33. Synchronizer hub
34. Guide
35. Spring
36. Interlock ball
37. Selector rail for 3rd and 4th speeds
38. Selector rail for 1st and 2nd speeds
39. Selector rail for reverse
40. Engaging sleeve
41. Spring
42. Synchronizing cone
43. Ball bearing
44. Roller bearing
45. Sealing ring
46. Front cover
47. Input shaft
48. Spacing washer
49. Thrust washer
50. Housing
51. Needle bearing
52. Spacing washer
53. Countershaft
54. Idler wheel
55. Reverse shaft
56. Reverse gear
57. Bushing
58. Lever (X-ray picture)
59. Bushing
60. Gear for 1st speed
61. Thrust washer

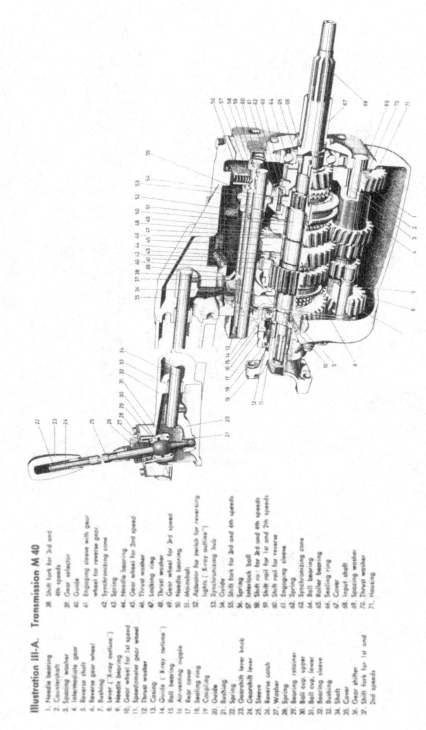

Illustration III-A. Transmission M 40

1. Needle bearing
2. Countershaft
3. Spacing washer
4. Intermediate gear
5. Reverse shaft
6. Reverse gear wheel
7. Bushing
8. Lever ("X-ray outline")
9. Needle bearing
10. Gear wheel for 1st speed
11. Speedometer gear wheel
12. Thrust washer
13. Casing
14. Guide ("X-ray outline")
15. Ball bearing
16. Air-venting nipple
17. Rear cover
18. Sealing ring
19. Coupling
20. Guide
21. Bushing
22. Spring
23. Gearshift lever knob
24. Gearshift lever
25. Sleeve
26. Reverse catch
27. Washer
28. Spring
29. Bearing retainer
30. Ball cup, upper
31. Ball cup, lower
32. Bearing sleeve
33. Bushing
34. Shaft
35. Cover
36. Gear shifter
37. Shift fork for 1st and 2nd speeds
38. Shift fork for 3rd and 4th speeds
39. Gear selector
40. Guide
41. Engaging sleeve with gear wheel for reverse gear
42. Synchronizing cone
43. Spring
44. Needle bearing
45. Gear wheel for 2nd speed
46. Thrust washer
47. Locking ring
48. Thrust washer
49. Gear wheel for 3rd speed
50. Needle bearing
51. Mainshaft
52. Actuator for switch for reversing lights ("X-ray outline")
53. Synchronizing hub
54. Guide
55. Shift fork for 3rd and 4th speeds
56. Spring
57. Interlock ball
58. Shift rail for 3rd and 4th speeds
59. Shift rail for 1st and 2th speeds
60. Shift rail for reverse
61. Engaging sleeve
62. Spring
63. Synchronizing cone
64. Ball bearing
65. Roller bearing
66. Sealing ring
67. Cover
68. Input shaft
69. Spacing washer
70. Thrust washer
71. Housing

214

Illustration III-B. Overdrive unit

1. Roller
2. Pump plunger
3. Spring
4. Lever
5. Pump cylinder
6. Ball
7. Valve seating
8. Spring
9. Rubber ring
10. Reducing valve
11. Spring
12. Valve cone
13. Lever
14. Plunger
15. Armature for solenoid
16. Valve rod ("X-Ray outline")
17. Solenoid
18. Plunger packing
19. Thrust bearing retainer
20. Housing, rear part
21. Bushing
22. Speedometer gear wheel, small
23. Output shaft
24. Coupling
25. Sealing ring
26. Ball bearing
27. Thrust washer
28. Spacing sleeve
29. Speedometer gear wheel, large
30. Ball bearing
31. Needle bearing
32. Thrust washer
33. Rollers for free wheel
34. Free wheel hub
35. Washer
36. Planet wheel
37. Needle bearing
38. Clutch facing
39. Brake drum
40. Locking pin
41. Clutch disk
42. Shaft
43. Planet wheel carrier
44. Sun wheel
45. Ball bearing
46. Housing, front part
47. Spring ("X-Ray outline")
48. Pressure plate
49. Air-venting nipple
50. Stud ("X-Ray outline")
51. Ball ("X-Ray outline")
52. Spring
53. Bushing
54. Pressure plate
55. Cam
56. Extension piece
57. Input shaft
   (transmission mainshaft)
58. Rear cover, transmission

215

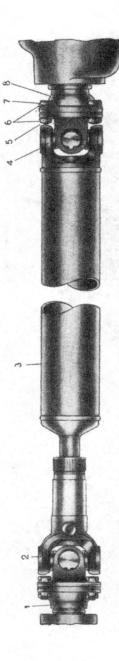

Fig. 1. Propeller shaft, early production.

1. Companion flange on gearbox main shaft.
2. Front universal joint.
3. Propeller shaft.
4. Stub ball yoke.
5. Rear universal joint.
6. Lock plate.
7. Screw.
8. Companion flange on drive pinion shaft.

DRIVE SHAFT

DRIVE SHAFT—PV 444, 445, 544, P 210

Description
The drive shaft on PV 444 up to chassis No. 2505 is tubular and made in one piece.

On PV 444 chassis No. 2506 and up, PV 445, PV 544 and P 210 it is made in two pieces. The front part is carried by a ball bearing at its rear end. The ball bearing rests in a bearing case suspended by two rubber mounted bolts. The shaft is fitted with three universal joints. Each universal joint consists of a cross with four ground journals, which are carried by needle bearings in flange yokes and stub ball yokes.

Drive shaft repair, one-piece model
This type of shaft can as a principle be repaired according to instructions given under "Drive shaft repair, two-piece model."

NOTE: When removing the one-piece shaft on PV 444, disconnect universal joints at gearbox and drive pinion shaft by removing the four companion flange screws. Shaft can then be removed.Punch-mark companion flange to ensure correct re-installation.

Follow instructions given for the two-piece shaft when repairing universal joints.

When installing shaft, check that the balance arrows, fig. 12, are exactly opposite each other and that only undamaged lock plates are used to lock the nuts. Connect parts according to punch marks.

Drive shaft repair, two-piece model
Removal of rear shaft with universal joints
1. Disconnect drive shaft front end at the universal joint by removing the four companion flange screws at collar bearing. Be careful not to drop shaft to avoid damage.
2. Disconnect shaft rear end in the same manner at drive pinion companion flange. Shaft can then be removed.

Removal of front shaft with bearing case and universal joint
After the rear shaft has been disassembled the front one can be removed as follows. There are two models of bearing case suspension (see fig. 3—4) and therefore the removal varies on the different cars.
1. Disconnect shaft front end by removing the four screws in companion flange on gearbox main shaft.
2. Early production only:

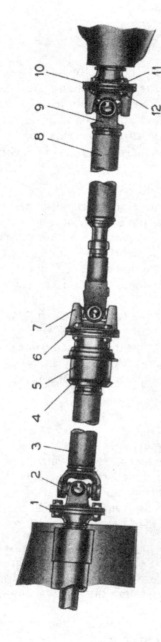

Fig. 2. Propeller shaft, later production.

1. Companion flange on gearbox main shaft.
2. Front universal joint.
3. Front propeller shaft.
4. Splash cap.
5. Collar bearing case.
6. Companion flange at collar bearing case.
7. Front universal joint on rear propeller shaft.
8. Rear propeller shaft.
9. Stub ball yoke.
10. Companion flange on drive pinion shaft.
11. Screw.
12. Lock plate.

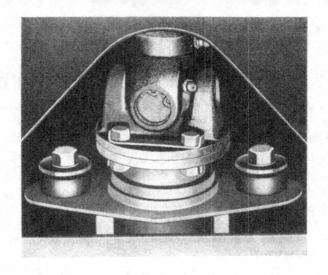

*Fig. 3. Bearing case suspension,
early production.*

*Fig. 4. Bearing case suspension,
later production.*

Loosen the two nuts (2) holding the bearing case (1), see fig. 3.

3. Shaft with universal joint and bearing case can be withdrawn backwards.

Both shafts can be removed at the same time by disconnecting universal joints at drive pinion shaft and gearbox and loosening the two nuts (early production) at the bearing case. Both shafts should then be withdrawn backwards at the same time.

Removal of bearing case with front drive shaft bearing

Place front shaft in vice. Be careful not to damage or deform it.

1. Punch-mark shaft and companion flange to ensure correct re-installation.
2. Remove bolt complete with washers holding companion flange with tool SVO 2261. (SVO 4068 also can be used).
3. Collar bearing case, with bearing can by now be removed.

Checking drive shafts with dial indicator

It is very important that a drive shaft is absolutely straight. As even small damage causes vibrations, a careful inspection should be carried out. Place the shaft between center and check it by means of a dial indicator all along its whole length when rotating. Should the runout exceed 0.25 mm (.01"), the shaft should be removed.

NOTE: **A damaged shaft must not be straightened or repaired but should be replaced with a new one.**

Disassembly and assembly of collar bearing

Press ball bearing out by means of an arbor press. Use driver SVO 4141 and SVO 4081 as a pad.

NOTE: **Ball bearing is factory packed with grease intended to last during its whole lifetime. Do not wash ball bearing in gasoline or any other solvent, causing lubricant to dissolve and run away. It should not be warmed up for the same reason.**

When pressing in the ball bearing, which is also done in an arbor press, make sure that it is not pressed askew into the bearing case. Use driver SVO 4080. Install bearing case in spacer SVO 4081 exactly under tool. Place ball bearing on the tool guide pin, true up and press it in as far as the tool permits. The ball bearing is similar on both sides and can consequently not be wrongly installed.

Inspection

Check ball bearing by pressing bearing races towards each other by hand and turn around. It should then run smoothly without sticking at any point. If not, reject the bearing and install a new one.

A dry bearing should also be replaced.

Disassembly of universal joint to change
cross and needle bearing

Install shaft (or universal joint if the middle one) in vice with the universal joint as close to the vice as possible. Remember that the shaft itself is a tube, which easily can be deformed. Mark the

universal joint in such a way that cross yokes can be re-assembled in their original positions. Line up marks with lubricator on cross.
1. Remove the four circlips locking needle bearing sleeve.
2. Remove lubricator.
3. Tap the free companion flange yoke as far as possible towards the cross center with a hammer. This will cause needle bearing sleeve to creep half-way out at the side you tap.
4. Then drive yoke in opposite direction as far as possible thereby forcing the remaining needle bearing sleeve to creep out in the same manner.
5. Empty rollers out of both bearings (22 rollers in each bearing),
6. Push one needle bearing sleeve entirely out by means of a thin metal driver.
7. Remove companion flange yoke and drive out the remaining needle bearing sleeve.
   The cross should be removed as follows:
1. Drive cross as far as possible in one direction by means of a hammer and a brass driver. Needle bearing sleeve will then creep about half-way out.
2. Drive cross in opposite direction in the same manner.
3. Empty rollers out of both needle bearings.
4. Drive one needle bearing sleeve entirely out by means of a thin metal driver.
5. Remove cross and drive the remaining needle bearing sleeve out.

Assembly of universal joint
1. Install shaft (or cross if the middle one) in vice with the universal joint as close to the vice as possible (in order not to damage tube).
2. Fit new cork seals and cork seal retainers on cross journals (cork seals at the outside).
3. Install cross in the same position as before disassembly. Check that lubricator is turned as fig. 11 shows.
4. Move cross in one direction as far as the needle bearing (4) can be fitted on the journal.
5. Press in needle bearing as far as the lock ring can be fitted. Use a driver the diameter of which is some less than the needle bearing sleeve diameter.
6. Handle the remaining bearing in the same manner and press it on as far as the lock ring can be fitted. Fit companion flange yoke on cross in the same way.
7. Install all lock rings.

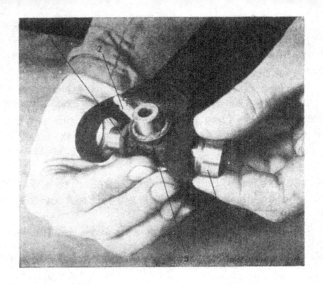

Fig. 11.   Assembling universal joint.

1. Cross.
2. Lubricator.
3. Cork seal.
4. Needle bearing.
5. Cork seal retainer.

NOTE: When pushing front universal joint, on rear shaft check that the arrow (1, fig. 12) stamped on the universal joint is placed exactly opposite the arrow (2) on shaft. If not, vibration will occur when propeller shaft revolves.

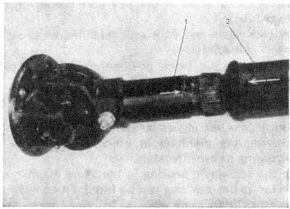

Fig. 12.   Assembling universal joint. Assemble universal joint with the arrows exactly opposite each other.

Fig. 13. Slip joint.

1. Cork seal.
2. Spring washer.
3. Retainer.

Renew cork packing ring (1, fig. 13), if necessary. It is split and easily changeable.

Installing bearing case with bearing

Fit bearing and collar bearing case on front shaft before installing.

1. Install drive shaft in vice.
2. Fit splash cap.
3. Push on bearing case with bearing.
4. Push on companion flange sleeve and check that the holes in companion flange sleeve are placed exactly opposite the holes in companion flange on gearbox mainshaft. Use driver SVO 4034.
5. Fit screw with washers and screws home. Hold companion flange sleeve with wrench SVO 4035.

Checking companion flange with dial indicator

Check companion flanges with a dial indicator before installing shafts. Place dial indicator as fig. 16 shows. Max. permissible out-of-roundness 0.07 mm (.003"). Max. permissible warping, 0.09 mm (.004").

NOTE. Companion flanges should be checked with a dial indicator after they are fitted to propeller shafts. Reject companion flanges not fulfilling demands above.

Installing drive shafts

Install the front shaft first.

1. Push it from behind through collar bearing case bracket.

2a. Early production:
Brace collar bearing case in bracket. Renew rubber bushings
if damaged. Washers at rubber bushings should be placed with
their convex side facing rubber.
2b. Later production:
Thrust the bearing case bushings on to the pins.
3. Connect universal joint and companion flange at gearbox.
Use new lock plates for nuts.
4. Connect front and rear shafts at collar bearing. Check that
all universal joints are placed in correct position in relation
to each other. See fig. 2.
5. Conect the rear shaft and companion flange on pinion shaft.
Use new lock plates.
Fill lubricating points with special lubricant.

Fig. 16. Checking out-of-roundness.

Fig. 17. Checking warping.

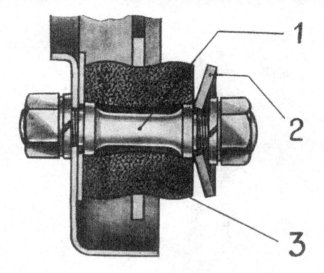

Fig. 18. Bearing case suspension,
early production.

1. Bolt.
2. Washer.
3. Rubber bushing.

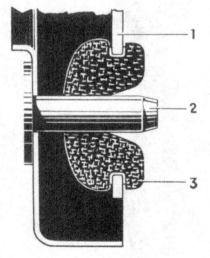

Fig. 19. Bearing case suspension,
later production.

1. Bearing case.
2. Pin.
3. Rubber bushing.

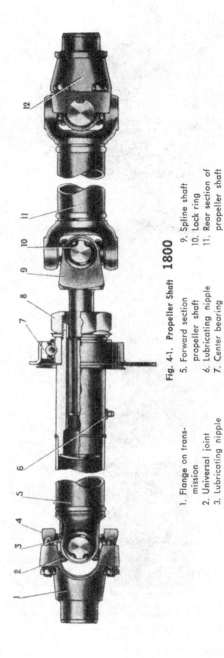

Fig. 4-1. Propeller Shaft 1800

1. Flange on transmission
2. Universal joint
3. Lubricating nipple
4. Clamp
5. Forward section propeller shaft
6. Lubricating nipple
7. Center bearing
8. Nut
9. Spline shaft
10. Lock ring
11. Rear section of propeller shaft
12. Flange on rear axle

DRIVESHAFT—122,1800
Description
The driveshaft is of the divided, tubular, type.

The forward section terminates in a slip joint at the rear end. In this there is a spline shaft which also forms one of the yokes on the intermediate universal joint.

The rear end of the forward section of the shaft is carried in a ball bearing. The ball bearing is carried in a bearing housing which is rubber-mounted on two pins.

The shaft is fitted with three universal joints. Each joint consists of a cross with four ground trunnions which are carried in the yokes by means of needle bearings.

REPLACING THE CENTER BEARING
1. Jack up the car and block up the front and rear axles. Loosen the clamps retaining the rear universal joint to the rear axle flange. Release the lock washer and remove the nut. Pull out the propeller shaft to the rear.
2. Loosen any springs fitted. Pull out the retainer with the center bearing to the rear. Press the center bearing out of the retainer with a suitable tool. Press the new bearing into the retainer with the help of ring SVO 4081. If the diameter of the press tool is less than the hole in the ring, lay a plate over the ring.
3. Fit the retainer with the center bearing and the rear section of the propeller shaft in the opposite order to that used when removing. Hook on the spring, if fitted. Lower the car.

   NOTE: When re-assembling make sure that the band on the rear universal joint is correctly positioned in the recess for it on the flange.

Removing
Jack up the car and block up the front and rear axles. Remove the clamps retaining the universal joints to the rear axle flange and the transmission flange. Loosen any springs fitted. Slide the drive shaft to the rear and remove it.

Disassembling
1. Loosen the lock washer and remove the nut for the center bearing. Remove the rear section of the propeller shaft. Remove the center bearing.
2. If necessary, press the center bearing out of the retainer with a suitable tool.

Disassembling the universal joints
The same disassembly principle is used on all the three uni-

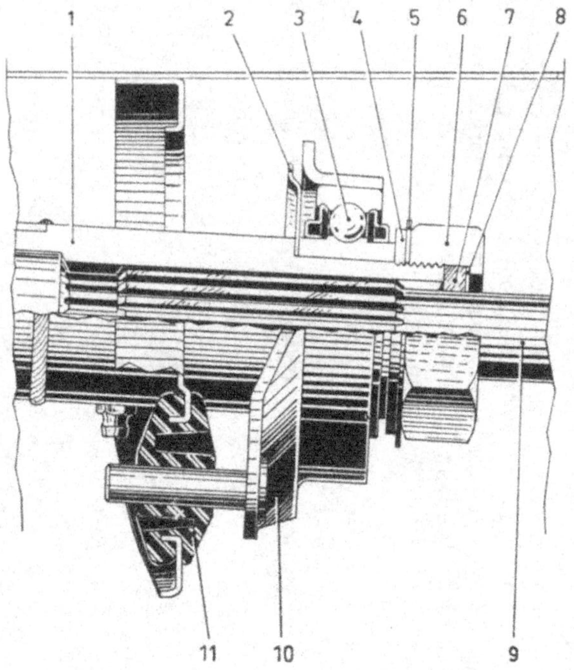

Fig. 4-2. Center Bearing 1800
1. Front section of propeller shaft
2. Cover plate
3. Ball bearings
4. Thrust washer
5. Lock washer
6. Nut
7. Felt washer
8. Washer
9. Spline shaft
10. Retainer
11. Rubber bushing

versal joints. The only difference is that on the center universal joints, there are two yokes from which the cross is loosened.

1. Remove the snap rings retaining the needle bearings in the yokes. Remove the lubricating nipple from the cross.
2. Set up the shaft in a vice, so that the universal joint is as near the vice as possible. Remember that the drive shaft is in the form of a tube and can easily be deformed.
3. Use a hammer and a metal drift to drive the cross as far as it will go in one direction. The needle bearing will then come about halfway out.
4. Then drive the cross in the same way as far as it will go in the opposite direction.
5. Drive out one of the needle bearings with a thin metal tool. Remove the cross. Drive out the other needle bearing.

Inspection

Set the shaft up between centers and check it with an indicator along its entire length while it is rotating. If the run-out should exceed 0.25 mm (0.010″) then the shaft should be replaced.

NOTE. **No attempt should be made to straighten a damaged propeller shaft—it should be replaced with a new shaft.**

Inspect the center bearing. The bearing should run smoothly without binding at any point. If this is not the case, fit a new bearing.

Assembling
Assembling the universal joints

1. Fit new cork washers on the joint cross trunnion. Fit the cross in the flange yoke in the same position as it was before being removed.
2. Move over the joint cross in one direction so far that the needle bearing can be fitted on the trunnion. Then press in the needle bearing so far that the snap ring can be fitted.
3. Fit the other needle bearing and snap ring in the same way.

Assembling the drive shaft

1. Press the center bearing in the retainer by using the ring SVO 4081. Fit the cover plate, center bearing, thrust washer on the forward part of the drive shaft.
2. Fit the nut, the washer and the left washer on the spline shaft. Lubricate the surface of the slip joint with a thin layer of molybdenum disulphide. Fit together the forward and rear sections of the drive shaft.
   NOTE. Make sure that the yoke on the forward section of the drive shaft and the yoke on the spline shaft are correctly lined up.

Fitting

Fitting is carried out in the reverse order to that used when removing.

NOTE. When fitting be very careful to ensure that the bands on the flanges in question. Tighten the nuts on the clamp to a torque of 1.40—1.65 kgm(10—12 lb. ft.)

REAR AXLE

REAR AXLE

Several types of rear axle-differential units have been fitted to Volvo models. The PV 444 early production between chassis numbers 1 to 8377 used ENV with non-hypoid type gears. From chassis 8378 forward and in PV 544 models, hypoid gear differentials will be found. These were either Hardy Spicer, Salisbury or ENV. Still later, a Spicer Model 27 was adopted and is in current use.

The ENV is distinguished by the fact that it is fitted in a special housing removable from the rear axle casing. The Spicer and Salisbury types are in one-piece castings. Also check manufacturer's plates on the housings.

Inasmuch as the repair and adjustment of the gear units in differentials is a specialized task calling for a good degree of skill and experience, the owner is cautioned against complete disassembly unless professional help is at hand. Many Volvo tools are employed in the shop to make this work simpler and easier. Substitutes can be fabricated in well equipped garages, of course, but a glance at the necessary procedure will reveal that this sort of repair is beyond the modest home workshop.

In order that the owner may have an emergency reference, the language and directions of the factory service manuals is followed here, relative to operations on the various axles. Complete specifications at the end of the book can be referred to.

WORK WHICH CAN BE CARRIED OUT WITH THE REAR AXLE FITTED IN POSITION
Replacing Drive Shaft Sealing Ring

1. Remove the wheel and pull off the hub, see fig. 1. Use puller SVO 1446 for hubs with four bolts and SVO 1791 for hubs with five bolts. Remove the brake backing plate after having placed a wooden block under the brake pedal and removed the brake pipe lines from the backing plate.
2. Pull out the drive shaft. Use puller SVO 2204 (SVO 1804 can be used on type I rear axles).
3. Pull out the sealing ring with the help of SVO 4078.
4. Drive in the new sealing ring. Ensure that it is driven in correctly. Use tool SVO 1803.
5. If necessary, wash off oil and grease from the brake backing plate. If any oil or grease has got onto the brake bands they must be replaced.
6. Fit the drive shaft and brake backing plate together with a new felt seal.

Illustration I. Rear axle suspension, PV 444 late production and PV 544

1. Shock absorber
2. Spring
3. Attachment in body
4. Torque rod
5. Rubber cushion
6. Track rod
7. Rear axle
8. Rubber bushing
9. Suspension arm

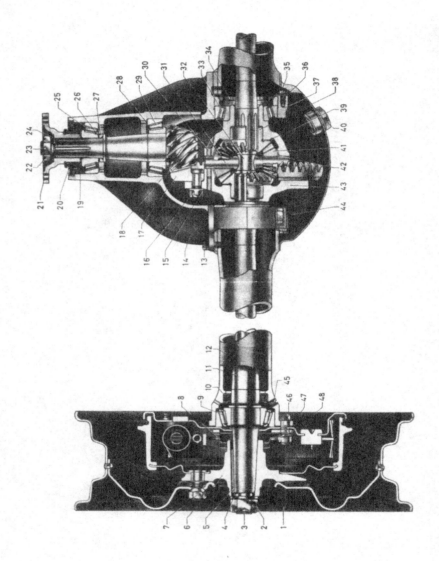

Illustration II. Rear axle, type I (ENV)

1. Rim
2. Castle nut
3. Split pin
4. Washer
5. Key
6. Wheel hub
7. Wheel nut
8. Retainer with felt seal
9. Roller bearing
10. Sealing ring
11. Drive shaft
12. Rear axle housing
13. Bolt with spring washer
14. Rear axle gear housing
15. Bolt with nut
16. Locking washer
17. Ring gear

18. Pinion
19. Washer
20. Sealing ring
21. Flange
22. Castle nut
23. Split pin
24. Washer
25. Front pinion bearing
26. Shim
27. Spacing ring
28. Shim
29. Rear pinion bearing
30. Locking pin
31. Shaft
32. Thrust block
33. Differential carrier bearing

34. Adjusting nut
35. Bolt
36. Locking washer
37. Cap for bearing
38. Differential side gear
39. Thrust washer, flat
40. Plug, oil filling
41. Small differential gear
42. Thrust washer, dished
43. Differential carrier
44. Bolt for bearing cap
45. Plug (early prod.)
46. Bolt with nut and spring washer
47. Shim
48. Washer

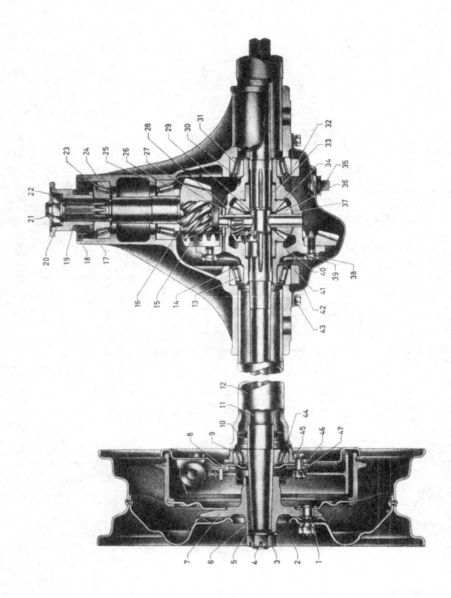

Illustration III. Rear axle, type II (Spicer, Salisbury)

1. Wheel nut
2. Rim
3. Castle nut
4. Split pin
5. Washer
6. Key
7. Wheel hub
8. Retainer with felt seal
9. Roller bearing
10. Sealing ring
11. Drive shaft
12. Rear axle housing
13. Differential carrier bearing
14. Shim
15. Ring gear
16. Pinion
17. Washer
18. Sealing ring
19. Cover plate
20. Flange
21. Nut
22. Washer
23. Front pinion bearing
24. Shim
25. Shim
26. Rear pinion bearing
27. Locking pin
28. Shaft
29. Thrust block
30. Shim
31. Differential carrier bearing
32. Cap
33. Differential side gear
34. Thrust washer, flat
35. Plug, oil filling
36. Small differential gear
37. Thrust washer, dished
38. Bolt
39. Locking washer
40. Differential carrier
41. Cap
42. Cover
43. Bolt with spring washer
44. Plug (early prod.)
45. Bolt with nut and spring washer
46. Shim
47. Washer

Fig. 1. Removing wheel hub.

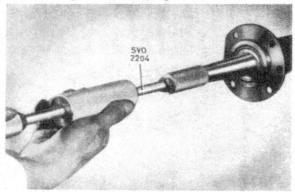

Fig. 2. Removing drive shaft.

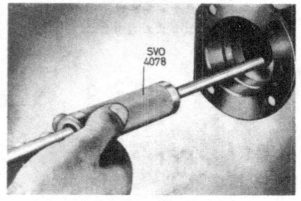

Fig. 3. Removing sealing ring.

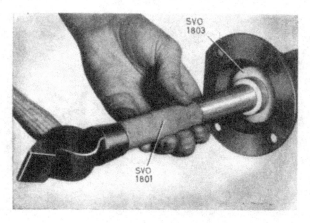

Fig. 4.   Fitting sealing ring.

7. Check the axial clearance of the drive shafts. See under heading "Assembling."
8. Fit the key if it was removed and then the wheel hub and wheel.
9. Bleed the brake lines and adjust the brakes.
10. Check the oil level in the rear axle.

REPLACING SEALING RING ON PINION
1. Disconnect the rear driveshaft from the flange on the pinion. Feel whether there is play in the pinion bearings. Any play should be taken up before the new sealing ring is fitted.
2. Remove the nut on the flange and then pull this off with SVO 2261. Remove the old sealing ring with SVO 4030.
3. Place in a new paper gasket and fit the new sealing ring with the SVO tool (concerning SVO tool numbers for the different rear axles, see the tool list).
4. Press on the flange with SVO tool.
5. Fit on the driveshaft.

REPLACING DRIVE SHAFT AND/OR/BEARINGS
1. Remove the wheel and pull off the wheel hub. Use puller SVO 1446 for hubs with four bolts and SVO 1791 for hubs with five studs. Remove the brake backing plate after having placed a wooden block under the brake pedal and removed the brake pipe lines from the brake backing plate.
2. Pull out the drive shaft. Use tool SVO 2204 (SVO 1804 can be used on type I rear axles). Check and if necessary replace the sealing ring.
3. Press off the bearing and then fit the new one (concerning SVO tool numbers for the different rear axles, see the tool list).

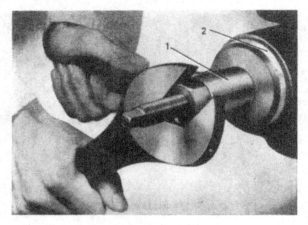

Fig. 7. Fitting sealing ring.

1. Press tool, see tool list.
2. Wrench, see tool list.

4. Fit the drive shafts, shims and brake backing plate.
5. Check and if necessary adjust the drive shaft axial clearance. Follow the instructions under the heading "Assembling."
6. Fit the key, wheel hub and wheel.
7. Bleed the brake lines and adjust the brakes.
8. Check the oil level in the rear axle.

REPAIR INSTRUCTIONS FOR REAR AXLE, TYPE I
Removing the Rear Axle

1. Slacken the rear wheel nuts (7, Illustration II) slightly, jack up the car and block up so that the wheels are about ⅜" clear of the floor. Unscrew the drain plug on the underside of the rear axle housing and let the oil run out while the shafts are removed.
2. Lift off the rear wheels and unscrew the rear axle nuts.
3. Pull off the rear wheel hubs with drums. Use puller SVO 1446 for hubs with four studs and SVO 1791 for hubs with five studs. (Handbrake released, brake shoes adjusted down if necessary).
4. Disconect the brake fluid pipe lines at the brake backing plates (place a wooden block under the brake pedal so that it cannot be depressed).
5. Unscrew the four bolts which hold the brake backing plates and remove these. Ensure that no shims are lost or damaged.
6. Pull out the drive shafts with tool SVO 2204 (SVO 1804 can be used).
7. Disconnect the propeller shafts from the pinion flange.

8. Unscrew the bolts which hold the rear axle housing and remove same.

Disassembling

1. Set up the rear axle in fixture SVO 4110. Check that the caps for the differential carrier have coinciding marks with the housing. If not, mark one of the sides with a center punch. Unscrew the bolts for the caps and remove these.
2. Remove the adjusting nuts and bearing rings. Lift out the differential with ring gear.
3. Unscrew the nut and pull off the flange with tool SVO 2261. Press out the pinion.
4. Pull out the sealing ring with puller SVO 4030 from the front end of the pinion housing. Remove the paper gasket, washer and roller bearing.
5. If necessary, drive out the bearing outer rings. Use SVO 4063 for the front and SVO 4064 for the rear bearing ring together with standard handle SVO 1801. Preserve the shims.
6. If necessary, pull the rear bearing off the pinion. Use puller SVO 2231 for PV 544. For PV 444, 445, use puller 2231 or SVO 4091.

There are two different types of pinion bearing. Since it is not possible to know in advance which bearing is fitted, this must first be carefully checked. If the wrong puller is used the bearing can be damaged so that it is impossible to remove.

	Volvo part number	SKF part number	Tool
Early type	181221	32207 W	SVO 4091
Late type	181233	231508	SVO 2231

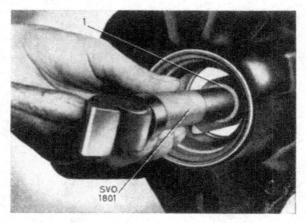

Fig. 10. Removing bearing ring.

1. Drift, see text.

241

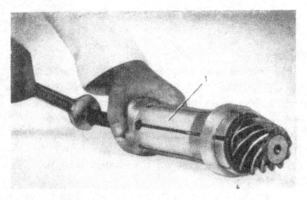

Fig. 11. Removing rear pinion bearing.

1. Puller, see text.

Disassembling Differential

1. Remove the bolts for the ring gear and take it out.
2. Drive out the locking pin for the differential gear shaft. Then drive out the shaft with the help of a suitable drift and remove the thrust block. The differential gears can now be removed together with the thrust washers.
3. Pull off the differential bearings if necessary. Use puller SVO 4042.

Fig. 12. Removing locking pin.

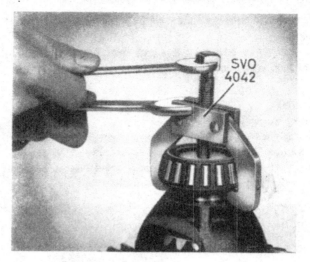

Fig. 13.   Removing differential bearing.

Inspection

In order to examine the various parts they must first be thoroughly cleaned. All bearing races and bearings should be examined. There should be no scratches or damage on races, rollers or roller retainers. All damaged bearings and bearing races must be replaced. Also thoroughly examine the pinion and ring gear to see that the teeth are not damaged. Cracks in the teeth surfaces can cause pieces to loosen while driving. These small pieces can get between the gear sand cause serious damage to the rear axle. If the gears are damaged or scratched, then both should be replaced with new ones. The rear axle drive gears (pinion and ring gear) are sold only in complete sets since they are manufactured together in special machines so that the correct tooth contact and silent running is obtained.

The differential gears should be examined for cracks and damage on the teeth. The differential gears should be refitted into the differential carrier in a clean and dry condition together with shaft and thrust washers, so that any play and wear can be determined more easily.

If any play is found, the parts concerned should be replaced. The thrust washers should be free from rough spots.

Also check to see whether the cylindrical portion of the flange which goes into the sealing ring is worn or scratched. If so, replace the flange together with the sealing ring.

Inspect the drive shafts. If these are bent or otherwise damaged, they should be replaced with new ones.

Examine the sealing rings and replace them if they are worn or damaged.

See that there are no cracks in the rear axle housing. Check that the brackets for the suspension arms and track rods are intact.

ASSEMBLING
Assembling the Differential

1. If the differential has been disassembled the differential side gears with thrust washers are first placed in the differential carrier. Then "roll" in the small differential gears (both together) with the dished thrust washers.

Fig. 14. Fitting differential gears.

2. Place in the thrust block and drive in the shaft.
3. Set up the differential carrier in a vise and insert a drive shaft into one of the differential side gears. The differential should now go so stiffly that it can only with difficulty be turned by hand on this shaft. If it turns too easily, fit new thrust washers. The flat washers are available in oversizes. Note that washers of the same thickness should be placed under two opposite gears. When adjustments have been completed, fit the locking pin for the shaft.
4. Fit the ring gear ensuring that the contact surfaces are clean and smooth. Tighten the bolts to the torque mentioned in the specifications and lock with tab washers.

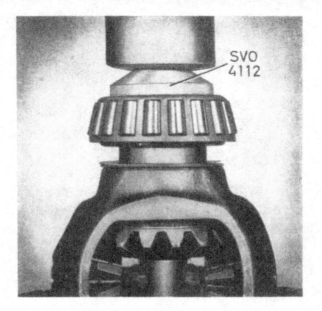

Fig. 15. Fitting differential carrier bearing.

5. Press on the differential carrier bearings. Use drift SVO 4112 and standard handle SVO 1801 for the bearings.

ASSEMBLING REAR AXLE

1. Place in position the number of shims which there were under the rear pinion bearing outer ring when disassembling, see fig. 16. Then press in the front and rear outer rings with press tool SVO 4047, see fig. 17. Ensure that the rings do not bind or come skew in the housing.

2. Press the rear pinion bearing on the pinion. Use tool SVO 4097.

3. Insert the pinion into the housing and fit on spacing ring, the number of shims that there were when disassembling and the front pinion bearing. Place on the intermediate ring SVO 4069, wrench SVO 4061 and fit press tools SVO 2304 and SVO 4049 respectively on the front end of the pinion. (SVO 2304 is used for pinions with ⅝"—18 thread and SVO 4049 for pinions with 18×1.5 mm thread). The simplest way of checking whether a pinion is of earlier or later type is to look at the flange nut. Earlier type pinions with 18×1.5 mm thread are fitted with a castle nut and split pin while later type pinions with ⅝"—18 thread have a "Nyloc" type locknut). Pull in the pinion with the help of the press tool.

4. After the pinion has been fitted, check and, if necessary, adjust the pinion bearing take-up. It should be relatively easy

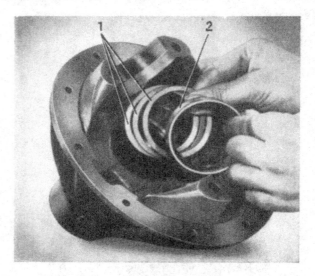

Fig. 16. Fitting shims.

1. Shims. 2. Bearing ring.

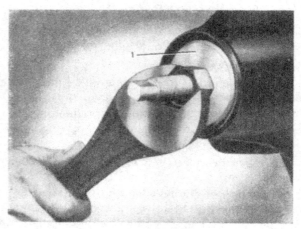

Fig. 17. Fitting bearing rings.

1. Press tool SVO 4047.

to turn the pinion around (2—4 kgcm = 1.75—3.5 lb. in.). There must, however, be no play. If the pinion turns too stiffly, the front bearing is taken off by pressing the pinion out and placing more shims there. If there is play or if the pinion turns too easily, shims are removed.

5. Fit the differential with ring gear together with bearing races, caps and adjusting nuts. Do not tighten the cap bolts so hard that the adjusting nuts cannot be turned.

6. The rear axle is now ready for adjusting of tooth contact and tooth flank clearance. Follow the instructions under the heading "Adjusting the rear axle."

7. After adjusting has been completed, remove press tool SVO 4049, wrench SVO 4061 and intermediate ring SVO 4061 and intermediate ring SVO 4069.

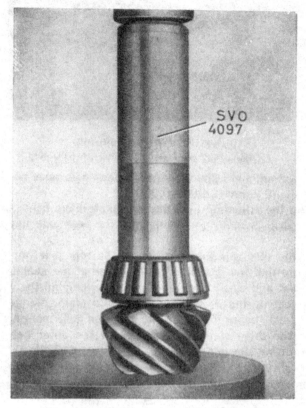

Fig. 18. Fitting rear pinion bearing.

8. Fit flat washer and sealing ring with gasket. For the sealing ring, use press tools SVO 2304 and SVO 4049 respectively and wrench SVO 4061. Then the flange is pressed on with the help of the press tool, see fig. 8. Fit washer and nut which should be tightened to the torque stated in the specifications.

9. Adjust finally the differential carrier bearings and lock the adjusting nuts. Taking up is done as follows: tighten up the cap bolts and then screw them ¼ of a turn. Place a dial indicator gauge against the rear side of the ring gear. Tighten the adjusting nuts so that the play disappears. Then tighten the adjusting nut on the tooth side of the ring gear a further

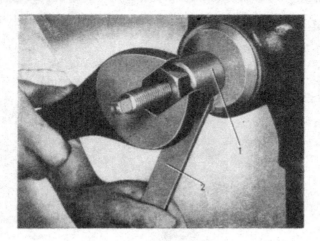

Fig. 19. Fitting pinion.

1. Press tool, see text.   2. Wrench SVO 4061.

1½—2 notches. Check the tooth flank clearance which should be 0.1—0.2 mm (0.004—0.008").

10. When the adjusting nuts and cap bolts have been locked, the rear axle is ready for fitting into the rear axle housing.

Fitting

1. Lift the rear axle into position in the rear axle housing. First ensure that the gasket is intact and that the sealing surfaces are flat and clean. Tighten the bolts evenly all the way round.

2. Connect up the propeller shaft to the pinion flange.

3. Pack ball bearing grease into the rear axle bearings and insert the drive shafts (11). Drive in the outer bearing rings with fitting sleeve SVO 1807.

4. Fit the brake backing plates, all shims which were taken out when removing and the felt sealing rings on both sides and tighten the bolts for good. Examine the rubber sleeve which seals the handbrake cable at the brake backing plate. Replace with a new one if necessary. Strike a few blows with a mallet on both drive shaft ends so that the bearing outer rings assume the correct position.

5. On late production the right-hand side shims are replaced by a 1.5 mm (0.060") thick washer. Adjusting must therefore be done on the left-hand side. Place a dial indicator gauge on this side on the retaining device SVO 4054 and SVO 4148 which is secured to the brake backing pate. Place the measurging point of the dial indicator gauge against the end of the drive shaft and zero the indicator.

248

Fig. 22. *Measuring axial clearance
on drive shafts.*

6. Pull the shaft in and out once or twice and note the indicator
   reading. This should be between 0.02 and 0.12 mm (0.008—
   0.047"). If it exceeds less than these limits, adjust with shims.
   These are available in the following thicknesses: 1.0, 0.35 and
   0.1 mm (0.0394", 0.0138" and 0.0039").
7. When adjustment of the drive shaft clearance has been completed, the brake fluid pipe line and handbrake cable is connected up on both sides. The hubs and drums are fitted, after
   which the wheels are placed on. The brakes should be bled
   and adjusted.
8. Fill up the rear axle with oil.
   Use only hypoid oil.

REPAIR INSTRUCTIONS FOR REAR AXLE, Type II
Removing

When working on the rear axle it is generally best to remove
the whole assembly. The instructions below apply principally to
PV 444 and PV 544 but also apply for PV 445 where appropriate.

1. Slacken the rear wheel nuts (1, Illustration III) and nuts on
   the drive shafts. Lift up the rear end of the car fairly high
   by placing a jack under the rear axle. Place chocks at the front
   wheels. Place blocks under the body in front of the rear wheels
   (on PV 445, the frame). Remove the rear wheels.

2. Disconnect the rear portion of the propeller shaft from the flange on the pinion and disconnect the brake pipe line from the master cylinder to the rear axle level with the rear universal joint (place a wooden block under the brake pedal).
3. Remove the track rods, shock absorbers, shock absorber bands and suspension arms from the rear axle and the handbrake cable from the body. On PV 444, chassis numbers 131918 onwards and PV 544 the torque rods are also removed, preferably at the body.
4. Lower the jack and remove the spring from the rear axle. Remove the rear axle.
5. Wash off the rear axle externally and drain out the oil from the rear axle housing.

Disassembling

Before disassembling it is best to measure up the drive shaft axial clearance and ring gear tooth flank clearance since in this way any defects can be discovered and remedied more easily.

1. Place the rear axle on a stand or a pair of trestles at suitable working height. Pull off the rear wheel hubs with puller SVO 1791.
2. Disconnect the brake pipe lines on the shaft from the brake backing plates. Remove the brake backing plates from the rear axle housing. Preserve the shims.
3. Remove the drive shafts. Use puller SVO 2204. If necessary, press the roller bearing off the shafts. When doing this, use support ring SVO 1806.
4. Remove the sealing rings with the help of puller SVO 4078.
5. Remove the inspection cover from the rear axle housing.
6. Check the markings on caps and housing. If these are lacking or have become obliterated, mark one side with a center punch. Remove the caps.
7. Fit tool SVO 2285 in the holes in the rear axle housing. Screw out the tensioning nut by hand as far as it will go and then turn it with a wrench until the differential carrier can be lifted out easily. Do not tighten the nut too much as otherwise the rear axle housing can be deformed. Lift out the differential carrier with ring gear.
8. Remove the nut for the flange and pull this off with puller SVO 2261. Press out the pinion.
9. Remove the sealing ring with the help of SVO 4030. Then remove washer, front pinion bearing and shims.
10. If necessary, drive out the bearing outer rings. Use standard handle SVO 1801 and drift SVO 4064 for the front and SVO 2207 for the rear ring. Preserve the shims under the rear ring.

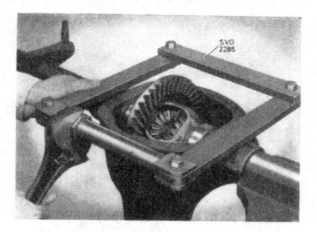

Fig. 23. Removing the differential.

11. If necessary, pull the rear bearing off the pinion (16) with puller SVO 2164.

DISASSEMBLING THE DIFFERENTIAL

1. Remove the bolts and take out the ring gear.
2. Drive out the locking pin and then the shaft for the differential gears. Take out the thrust block. Take out the differential gears and thrust washers.
3. Pull off the differential carrier bearings with puller SVO 4042. Preserve the shims.

Fig. 26. Removing locking pin.

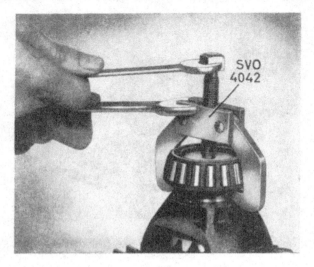

Fig. 27.   Removing differential carrier bearing.

ASSEMBLING
Assembling the Differential
1. Place the differential side gears with thrust washers in the differential carrier. Then "roll" in the small differential gears and the dished thrust washers (both gears at the same time).
2. Place in the thrust block and drive in the shaft.
3. Check the differential. If there is any play, fit the new thrust washers. The flat thrust washers can be replaced either by oversize washers or spring type thrust washers. Fit the spring type thrust washers correctly. The "back" should face the differential carrier.
   After checking and having fitted new washers if necessary, fit the locking pin.
4. Fit the ring gear. Ensure that the contact surfaces are clean and free from burr. Tighten the bolts to the torque shown in the specifications and lock with tab washers.

ASSEMBLING REAR AXLE
1. Press on the differential carrier bearings without shims. Use drift SVO 4112.
   Place the differential carrier with ring gear and roller bearings in the housing. Measure the axial clearance. This can be done in two ways, either with a dial indicator gauge or feeler gauge. Whichever method is used, measuring must be carried out with the utmost precision in order for the correct result to be obtained. If an indicator is used, this should be placed against the back side of the ring gear. The differential (also

Fig. 31. *Measuring differential axial clearance.*

the bearing outer rings) should first be moved over in one direction after which the indicator should be set to zero. Then the differential is moved over in the other direction and the clearance read off. If the feeler gauge method is used, two gauges are required. These are inserted between one of the outer rings and the bearing position in the carrier. Add 0.2 mm (0.008") to the reading obtained which gives the total thickness of the shims to be used when assembling.

2. Press the rear bearing onto the pinion. Use drift SVO 4097.
3. Replace the same number of shims for the rear pinion bearing outer ring which were there when disassembling, into the housing and then press in the outer rings using drift SVO 2206. Ensure that the rings do not bind or lie askew.
4. Insert the pinion into the housing and place on the same number of shims which were there when disassembling, the front pinion bearing and washer. Fit wrench SVO 2208 and press tool SVO 1845 on the front end of the pinion and tighten in the pinion.
5. Check the adjustment of the pinion bearings. The pinion should be relatively easy to turn (9—14 kgcm = 8—12 lb. in.), but there must be no play. Adjustment is carried out by means of shims on the front pinion bearing.
6. The pinion should have a certain nominal measurement (A, fig. 35) to the center line of the ring gear. Due to manufacturing tolerances, however, deviations from the nominal measurement occur. The deviation applying is indicated on the ground surface of the pinion by a figure and plus or minus sign. If there is a plus (+) sign, then the nominal measurement must be increased but if there is a minus (—) sign, the nominal measurement should be decreased. The figure marked on the pinion indicates the deviation in thousandths of an

253

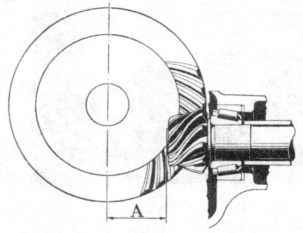

Fig. 35. *Pinion position.*

A. Nominal measurement = 2.25".

inch and, where necessary, must first be converted to mm, see conversion table.

The pinion piston is checked by using a dial indicator gauge, and indicator retainer SVO 2284 and measuring tool SVO 2283 which consists of two parts, a pinion gauge and adjusting jig. Checking is carried out as follows:

Place the pinion gauge on the ground surface of the pinion and the adjusting jig in the differential bearing positions. Place the indicator retainer on the rear axle housing and set the indicator to zero against the adjusting jig. Then move over the indicator retainer so that the indicator comes up against the pinion gauge. If the pinion is marked "O", the adjusting jig and pinion gauge should come level with each other, if it is marked with a minus (−) sign, the pinion gauge should come higher than the adjusting jig and if it is marked with a plus (+) sign, the pinion gauge should come lower than the jig for correct adjustment. Adjustment is carried out by adding or removing shims under the rear pinion bearing outer ring. If the pinion bearings had the correct adjustment, the same number of shims must at the same time be added or removed under the front pinion bearing.

Example. The pinion is marked +2. The pinion gauge should then come 0.002" = 0.051 mm under the adjusting jig. Measuring shows that the pinion gauge on the pinion comes 0.15 mm over the adjusting jig. The pinion should thus be lowered 0.15 + 0.05 = 0.20 mm so that shims corresponding to this thickness (measured with a micrometer) should be removed from under the rear pinion bearing outer ring.

Conversion table for inches to mm	
inches	mm
0.001	0.025
0.002	0.051
0.003	0.076
0.004	0.102
0.005	0.127
0.006	0.152
0.007	0.178
0.008	0.203
0.009	0.229

Fig. 36. Positioning the measuring tools.

Fig. 37. Setting the indicator gauge to zero.

Fig. 38. Measuring pinion position.

7. After the pinion position has been checked and adjusted if necessary, the tension on the pinion bearings should be checked once again.

8. Place the differential (without shims for the bearings) in the rear axle housing. Measure the differential axial clearance (clearance between the pinion and outer positions of the differential). This can be done either with an indicator gauge on the back side of the ring or with two feeler gauges. Note the clearance obtained.

9. The clearance obtained in accordance with the measurement carried out under point 8 should be decreased by the tooth flank clearance (backlash). In some cases this is stamped on the ring gear (for example, B/L .004). It is given in thousandths of an inch and, if necessary, must first be converted to mm, see conversion table.

The examples given below assume the use of the metric system but the same method also applies for measurements in inches except that no conversion will be necessary and assuming that the thickness of the shims used is also measured in inches.

Example: The ring gear is marked B/L .004 which according to the table corresponds to 0.10 mm. Shims required in accordance with point 1:

Measured clearance 1.5 mm + tension 0.2 mm = 1.7 mm.
Measured clearance in accordance with point 8 = 1 mm.
Shim thickness on ring gear side = 1 − 0.10 = 0.9 mm.
Shim thickness on opposite side = 1.7 − 0.9 = 0.8 mm.

If the tooth flank clearance (backlash) is not marked on the ring gear, use instead the average value (0.15 mm) of the clearance (0.10—0.20 mm).

Example: Measured clearance 1.4 mm + tension 0.2 mm = 1.6 mm.

Measured clearance in accordance with point 8 = 0.95 mm.

Shim thickness on ring side = 0.95 − 0.15 = 0.8 mm.

Shim thickness on opposite side = 1.6 − 0.8 = 0.8 mm.

10. Pull off the differential carrier bearings with puller SVO 4042. Place shims of the thickness calculated under the bearings and press these on again.

11. Fit tool SVO 2285 and a dial indicator gauge on the rear axle housing. Tighten the tensioning nut so that the rear axle housing is expanded max. 0.3 mm (0.012"). Remove the indicator. Place in the differential with bearings. Then remove tool SVO 2285.

12. Fit the caps with bolts and tighten the bolts. Place a dial indicator gauge against the back side of the ring gear. Pull the ring gear round and measure the run-out. This must not exceed 0.08 mm (0.003").

Fig. 39.   Expanding rear axle housing.

Fig. 40.   Measuring ring gear run-out.

13. Check the backlash. This should agree with the value given in the specifications or with the value stamped on the ring gear. This should be at least 0.10 mm (0.004").

Fig. 41. Measuring backlash.

14. Check the setting by marking up the tooth contact in accordance with the instructions under "Adjusting the rear axle."
15. After final adjustment, remove wrench SVO 2208.
16. Fit the flat washer and sealing ring together with paper gasket. Use press tool SVO 1845 and wrench SVO 2208 for the sealing ring. Then press on the flange using SVO 1845. Fit washer and nut. Tighten the nut to the torque shown in the specifications.
17. Remove the cap bolts. Then smear the threads on the bolts and in the holes with sealing compound—Permatex 3 Form—A—Gasket or corresponding. In this way sealing of the through-going holes and securing of the bolts is obtained. Tighten the bolts in accordance with values shown in specifications.
18. Fit the inspection cover and gasket.

ASSEMBLING REAR AXLE SHAFTS

1. Drive in the sealing rings for the drive shafts with drift 1803.
2. Press the bearings onto the drive shafts if they have been removed. Use SVO 1805. Ring SVO 1806 can be used as a counterhold if the smaller diameter of the hole is turned to face the flange on the shaft.
3. Pack the bearings with heat-resistant grease. Insert the drive shafts into the rear axle housing. Drive in the bearing outer rings with fitting sleeve SVO 2205 for PV 444, 544 and SVO 1807 for PV 445.
4. Fit the brake backing plates with shims and retainer with felt seal, see fig. 44. Check and if necessary adjust drive shaft

Fig. 44.   Fitting brake backing plate.

1. Shims.

*Fig. 45.   Measuring axial clearance
of drive shafts.*

axial clearance. The clearance is given in the specifications.
5. Fit the brake pipe lines at the brake backing plates and then the hubs and brake drums.

ADJUSTING THE REAR AXLE

When the rear axle gears are assembled it is extremely important to ensure that the ring gear and pinion are correctly fitted in relation to each other. This concerns not only backlash but also tooth contact. When the tooth contact is correct the stresses to which the teeth are subjected when the car is driven or distributed over the greater part of the tooth surfaces. In this way tooth breakage and excessive gear wear are avoided and the gears run quietly. The instructions given below can serve as a guide when this work is carried out.

First check the ring gear run-out with a dial indicator gauge. The run-out must not exceed the value given in the specifications.

In order to describe tooth contact in a simple manner, the various parts of the teeth have been given different names. See fig. 46 which shows a tooth on the ring gear. Note. Adjustment is carried out on the basis of the contact obtained on the ring gear teeth.

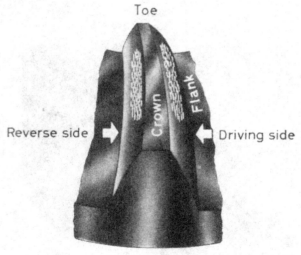

Fig. 46. Correct tooth contact.

The driving side is the side subjected to pressure from the pinion when the car is driven forwards.

The reverse side is the side which is subjected to pressure when the car is reversed and when the engine is used to brake the car in forward travel.

The narrowest and broadest ends of the tooth are called the toe and heel respectively. The toe lies nearest the center while the heel is furthest out on the ring side.

In order to obtain a clear picture of the tooth contact, both sides of the ring gear teeth are coated with marking paint consisting of a mixture of red lead and engine oil. The marking paint must not be too thinly mixed since this can cause a faulty impression of tooth contact. All the teeth should be coated with a thin coating of marking paint, see fig. 47. The pinion should then be rotated 10—12 turns in each direction at the same time as the ring gear is braked hard by using a wooden wedge or similar device as shown in fig. 48. The marking paint on the ring gear

Fig. 47. Coating the teeth with marking paint.

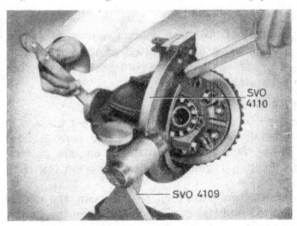

Fig. 48. Rotating the rear axle gears.

teeth is thus removed where the pinion teeth make contact so that a clear picture of the extent and position of the tooth contact is obtained. The correct tooth contact is shown in fig. 46.

Note. The pattern is almost rectangular in shape and is, on the driving side, half-way up the tooth but nearer the toe than the heel. On the reverse side it is rather higher than on the driving side but otherwise similar.

Tooth contact adjustment is carried out by altering the position of the pinion relative to the ring gear. This is done by adding or removing shims at the rear pinion bearing outer ring. At the same time, howeve, an equal number of shims must be added or removed at the front pinion bearing so that the pinion bearing adjustment is not altered.

Every time the pinion position is altered, the backlash must be checked and adjusted, see fig. 49.

Fig. 49. *Measuring backlash.*

The movement of the tooth contact pattern is somewhat different on spiral bevel gears (as fitted on the very first series of PV 444 cars produced) and on hypoid gears, so that both types are treated separately.

ADJUSTMENT OF SPIRAL BEVEL GEARS

On this type of rear axle, the tooth contact pattern moves in the same direction on both the driving and reverse sides.

If the pinion is moved inwards, the contact pattern moves from a high position (fig. 50) to a low position (fig. 51) on the tooth.

If the pattern comes too high on the tooth, the pinion should be moved inwards and if it comes too low, then the pinion should be moved outwards.

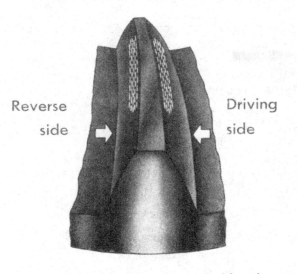

Reverse
side →   ← Driving
           side

Fig. 50.   Faulty tooth contact, spiral bevel gear.

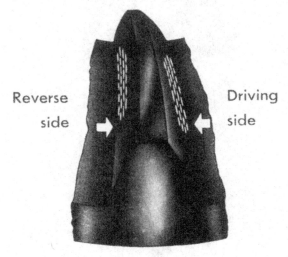

Reverse
side →   ← Driving
           side

Fig. 51.   Faulty tooth contact, spiral bevel gear.

When the pinion is moved away from its correct position, the pattern gradually assumes the shape of a narrow mark. It is thus easy to see when the gear is correctly adjusted since the tooth contact pattern then has the correct position on the teeth and the largest possible vertical width.

ADJUSTMENT OF HYPOID GEARS

On a hypoid gear the tooth contact pattern moves diagonally over the teeth and in different directions on the driving and reverse sides.

If the pinion is moved from outside and inwards, the contact pattern moves from a high position at the heel on the driving side, fig. 52, to a low position at the toe, fig. 53. On the reverse side the pattern moves at the same time from a high position at the toe, fig. 52, to a low position at the heel, fig. 53.

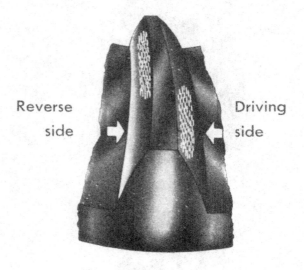

Reverse side →

Driving side ←

Fig. 52. Faulty tooth contact, hypoid gear.

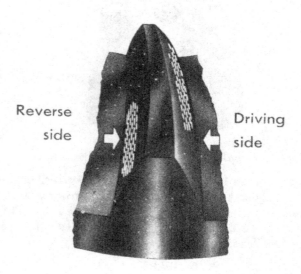

Reverse side →

Driving side ←

Fig. 53. Faulty tooth contact, hypoid gear.

The tooth contact pattern on the driving side thus moves in the same direction as the pinion. If the pattern comes too near the heel, the pinion is moved inwards, and if it comes too near the toe, then the pinion is moved outwards.

When the pattern has come into the correct position on the driving side, the pattern on the reverse side is noted. If the gear is correctly adjusted, then the two patterns should come opposite each other.

The adjustment procedure is carried out as follows:

1. Adjust the backlash to the value stated in the specifications.
2. Coat the teeth with marking paint and rotate the pinion while the ring gear is braked.
3. Note the position of the tooth contact pattern and adjust as described above. Every time the position of the pinion has been altered, the backlash should be checked and adjusted.

TOOLS

The following tools are required for carrying out repairs on the rear axle.

Tools for rear axle, type I

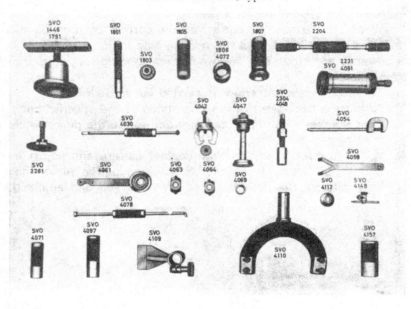

Tools for rear axle, type II

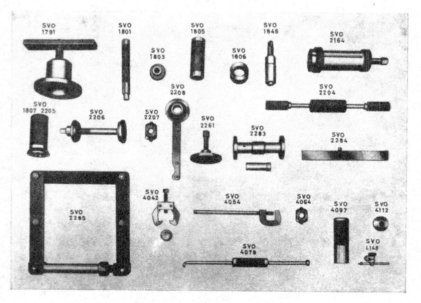

Number	Description	Remarks
SVO 1446	Puller for wheel hub	PV 444 chassis nos. 1—20004 PV 445 chassis nos. 1—1600
SVO 1791	Puller for wheel hub	PV 444 with effect from chassis no. 20005 onwards PV 445 with effect from chassis no. 1601 onwards, PV 544
SVO 1801	Standard handle 18×200 mm	
SVO 1803	Tool for fitting drive shaft sealing rings	
SVO 1805	Drift for fitting drive shaft bearings	PV 444 with effect from chassis no. 20005 onwards, PV 445, PV 544
SVO 1806	Counter-ring for removing and fitting drive shaft bearings	PV 444 with effect from chassis no. 20005 onwards, PV 445, PV 544
SVO 1807	Fitting sleeve for drive shaft bearing outer ring	PV 444 with effect from chassis no. 20005 onwards, PV 445, PV 544
SVO 2204	Puller for drive shaft	
SVO 2231	Puller for rear pinion bearing	For late production bearings, see page 5—4
SVO 2261	Puller for flange	
SVO 2304	Press tool for flange	For pinions with $^5/_8"$—18 thread
SVO 4030	Puller for pinion sealing ring	
SVO 4042	Puller for differential carrier bearings	
SVO 4047	Fitting tool for pinion bearing outer rings	SVO 4047A can be used for early production sealing rings
SVO 4049	Press tool for fitting flange	For pinions with 18×1.5 mm thread
SVO 4054	Attachment for dial indicator gauge	Used together with SVO 4148 and indicator gauge
SVO 4059	Wrench for adjusting nut	
SVO 4061	Wrench for flange and for fitting sealing ring and pinion	
SVO 4063	Drift for removing front pinion bearing outer ring	
SVO 4064	Drift for removing rear pinion bearing outer ring	
SVO 4069	Packing ring for adjusting rear axle gears	
SVO 4071	Fitting sleeve for drive shaft bearings	PV 444, chassis nos. 1—20004
SVO 4072	Counter-ring for removing and fitting drive shaft bearings	PV 444, chassis nos. 1—20004
SVO 4078	Puller for drive shaft sealing ring	
SVO 4091	Puller for rear pinion bearing	For late production bearings, see page 5—4
SVO 4097	Fitting sleeve for rear pinion bearing	
SVO 4109	Attachment for fixture SVO 4110	
SVO 4110	Fixture for rear axle gears	Used together with SVO 4109
SVO 4112	Drift for fitting differential carrier bearings	
SVO 4148	Retainer for dial indicator gauge	Used together with SVO 4054
SVO 4157	Fitting sleeve for drive shaft bearing outer ring	PV 444 chassis nos. 1—20004

Number	Description	Remarks
SVO 1791	Puller for wheel hub	
SVO 1801	Standard handle 18×200 mm	
SVO 1803	Drift for fitting drive shaft sealing ring	
SVO 1805	Fitting sleeve for drive shaft bearing	
SVO 1806	Counter-ring for removing and fitting drive shaft bearing	
SVO 1807	Fitting sleeve for drive shaft bearing outer ring	PV 445
SVO 1845	Press tool for fitting flange	Used together with SVO 2208 when adjusting backlash and fitting sealing ring
SVO 2164	Puller for rear pinion bearing	
SVO 2204	Puller for drive shaft	
SVO 2205	Fitting sleeve for drive shaft bearing outer ring	PV 444, 544
SVO 2206	Fitting tool for pinion bearing outer rings	
SVO 2207	Drift for removing rear pinion bearing outer ring	
SVO 2208	Wrench for flange and for fitting pinion sealing ring	
SVO 2261	Puller for flange	SVO 4068 can be used
SVO 2283	Measuring tool for adjusting pinion	
SVO 2284	Retainer for dial indicator gauge	
SVO 2285	Expanding frame for removing and fitting differential	
SVO 4042	Puller for differential carrier bearings	
SVO 4054	Dial indicator gauge attachment	Used together with SVO 4148 and indicator gauge
SVO 4064	Drift for removing front pinion bearing outer ring	
SVO 4078	Puller for drive shaft sealing ring	
SVO 4097	Fitting sleeve for rear pinion bearing	
SVO 4112	Fitting sleeve for differential carrier bearings	
SVO 4148	Retainer for dial indicator gauge	Used together with SVO 4054

FRONT AXLE AND STEERING
444-544

The independent front suspension of 444, 445, 544 and 210 models is by means of upper and lower control arms attached to a front cross member which is bolted to the frame (on 445 and 210) or to the integral body. The inner arms are pivoted on the member by means of bolts. They are separated by coil springs. Shock absorbers are mounted outside the member and attached to the steering knuckle support at the bottom, to the control arm at the top. The steering knuckle is carried in king pins. Axial thrust is taken by ball bearings. Stabilizer bars are attached to the lower control arm and to the body and frame.

The entire front cross member can be removed or work can be carried out on any portion of the system in the conventional manner by supporting the vehicle in the manner best suited to the task.

Removing complete front wheel suspension

1. Remove the hub cap and slacken the wheel nuts slightly.
2. Place a jack under the front axle member and lift up the front end of the vehicle so that the wheels are free. Place blocks under the body (in PV 445 and P 210 the frame) behind the front axle member.
3. Remove the wheel nuts and lift off the wheels.
4. Disconnect the stabilizers from the lower control arms.
5. Pull off the pitman arm. Use tool SVO 2370.
6. Put a wooden block under the brake pedal. Disconnect the front wheel brake line at the master cylinder. Plug the connections to prevent dirt from entering the brake system.
7. Screw off the nuts at the front engine mountings. Remove the front engine guard plate. Place a wooden block (size about 62 x 6 x 6 cm. = 24½ x 2½ x 2½") above the support members but under the fan hub. Insert the wooden block from below. In addition, on PV 445 and P 210 two blocks (size 4 x 6 x 6 cm = 1½ x 2½ x 2½") should be placed between the frame and the above-mentioned wooden block. On late production models a recess must be made in the block. If the vehicle is not to be moved and an overhead hoist is available, the engine can be suspended in this instead.
8. Unscrew the four bolts on each side which hold the front axle member to the body (on PV 445 and P 210, to the frame).
9. Lower the jack carefully. (Sometimes it is necessary to slacken one of the upper control arm inner attachments at the front axle member in order that the front suspension unit can be

lowered.) When the brake backing plates have reached the floor, the jack and front wheel suspension unit are pulled out.

Fitting complete front wheel suspension

1. Lift up the front wheel suspension unit on a hydraulic jack and move it under the vehicle.
2. Place two guide pins into the body (the frame on PV 445 and P 210). Raise the jack so that the front axle member comes into position and bolt it on.
3. Remove the wooden block for supporting the engine and tighten the engine down onto the front engine mountings. Connect the brake lines.
4. Fit the pitman arm.
5. Fit the stabilizers.
6. Air-vent the front wheel brake system.
7. Lift on the wheels after having cleaned the contact surfaces between wheel and hub free from sand and dirt, and tighten the nuts sufficiently so that the wheel cannot be disturbed on the hub. Lower the vehicle and tighten the wheel nuts. Tighten every other nut a little at a time until all are tightened to a torque of 10—14 kgm (72—101 lb. ft.). Fit the hub caps.
8. Check the wheel alignment.

Replacing and adjusting the front wheel bearings

When adjusting the front wheel bearings, first remove the wheel hub for inspecting the bearing races and rollers. If these are scored or worn they must be replaced. Below is described the procedure for complete replacement of bearings. For ordinary inspection and adjustment, disregard the points not applying.

For PV 444-445 A and B, other special tools are required in some cases. These tools are indicated in brackets.

1. Remove the hub cap and slacken the wheel nuts slightly.
2. Jack up the front part of the vehicle and place trestles under the lower control arms, remove the wheel nuts and lift off the wheel.
3. Remove the grease cap with tool SVO 2197 (Fig. 6.). Remove the split pin and castle nut. Pull off the hub with puller SVO 1791 (SVO 1446).
4. Drive out the bearing races. For the inner race use drift SVO 1799 (SVO 4003) and for the outer race drift SVO 1800 (SVO 4002), together with standard handle SVO 1801.
5. Pull off the inner bearing with puller SVO 1794 (SVO 4016) if necessary.
6. Clean the hub, brake drum and grease cap.
7. Press in the new bearing races. Use standard handle SVO 1801 together with drift SVO 1798 (SVO 4001) for the inner

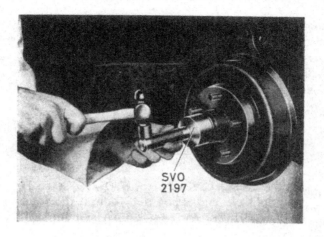

Fig. 6. Removing grease cap.

race and SVO 1797 (SVO 4000) for the outer race.

8. Pack the bearings with grease with the help of a lubricating device. If one of these is not available, pack the bearings by hand with sufficient grease that will find room between the roller retainer and the inner ring. Also coat grease onto the outer sides of the bearings and on the outer rings press end into the hub. The recess in the hub should be filled up with grease all round to the smallest diameter of the outer ring for the outer bearing.

   Place the inner bearing in position in the hub. Press in the sealing ring with drift SVO 1798 (SVO 4001) together with standard handle SVO 1801.

9. Place the hub on the spindle. Fit the outer bearing, washer and castle nut.

10. The front wheel bearings are adjusted by first tightening the nut with a torque wrench to a value of 7 kgm (50 lb. ft.). Then slacken the nut a third of a turn. If the slot in the nut does not correspond with the split pin hole, slacken the nut further to enable the split pin to be fitted. Check that the wheel rotates easily but without any play.

11. Fill the grease cap half-full with grease and fit it with drift SVO 2197.

12. Lift on the wheel after having cleaned the contact surfaces between wheel and hub free from sand and dirt, and tighten the nut sufficiently so that the wheel cannot be displaced on the hub. Lower the vehicle and tighten the wheel nut. Tighten every other nut a little at a time until all are tightened to a torque of 10—14 kgm (72—101 lb. ft.). Fit the hub cap.

Replacing king pin and outer control arm bolts with bushings

The clearance in the threaded bushings normally is 0.3—0.6 mm (0.012—0.023 ins). The maximum permissible clearance is 0.8 mm (0.032 ins.). The radial clearance of the king pin should not exceed 0.3 mm (0.012 ins.).

Removing

1. Remove the hub caps and slacken the wheel nuts slightly.
2. Lift up the front end of the vehicle so that the wheels are free and place trestles under the lower control arms. Remove the wheel.
3. Remove the grease cap with tool SVO 2197 (see Fig. 6). Remove the split pin and castle nut. Pull off the front hub with puller SVO 1791 (for PV 444—445 A and B, SVO 1446) as shown in Fig. 7. Pull off the inner bearing ring if necessary.

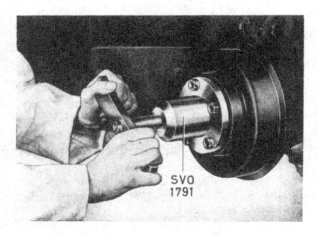

Fig. 7. Removing hub.

4. Remove the four bolts which hold the brake backing plate in place and splash guard to the steering knuckle. Lift off the brake backing plate, after which it should be tied up with a piece of wire or similar so that the brake hose is not damaged.
5. Remove the split pin and nut for the steering rod ball joint. Screw back the tensioning screw on tool SVO 2294 and place the tool on the ball joint. Press in the tool properly and ensure that the thread of the ball joint enters the countersink in the tool.
Screw in the tensioning screw until the ball joint releases.
6. Slacken the nut and screw out the upper control arm bolt. Take off the clamping bolt and remove the eccentric bushing.

7. (Only when replacing control arm bolts with bushings.) Slacken the nut and screw out the lower control arm bolt. Disconnect the shock absorber at the bottom. Lift off the steering knuckle support. Screw out the lower bushing.
8. Drive out the stop key with a drift. Remove the sealing washer with a pointed punch. Drive out the king pin downwards with tool SVO 2224. Place in the extensions as required. If the king pin fits very tightly it should first be knocked up a little with the help of a straight, thick drift.
9. Remove the grease nipples. Drive out the king pin bushings with drift SVO 1442.

Fitting

1. Clean the steering knuckle. Clean off any burr at the bushing positions. Press in the new bushings with drift SVO 1442. Make sure that the lubricating hole comes opposite the grease nipple and that short lubricating groove faces the sealing washer.
2. Ream the bushings with reamer SVO 1171. With a new king pin the play should then correspond to a running fit. Fit the grease nipples. Coat the bushings with chassis grease.
3. Place the steering knuckle, thrust bearing and adjusting shims in position and place the centering mandrel SVO 4005 in the upper bushing. Change the shims until the bearing take-up corresponds to a friction torque of 5—65 kg cm (4.34—56.4 lb. in.) when turning the spindle. A spring balance attached to the split pin hole of the spindle should then give a reading 0.3—4.4 kg (0.66—9.46 lb.) when pulled at right angles to the spindle. Then drive in the king pin ensuring that it comes in the correct position. Fit the stop key. Check that the steering knuckle turns easily. Fit the sealing washers by placing them in position with the dished side outwards and then knocking them flat with a hammer and drift.
4. Fit the steering knuckle support with bushings, guard plate and bolts. Fit the steering rod to the steering arm. Then turn the ball joint so that the split pin hole comes across the longitudinal direction of the rod. Tighten the castle nut to a torque of 3.2—3.8 kgm (23-27 lb. ft.).
5. Fit the brake backing plate and splash plate on the steering knuckle.
6. Fit the hub and wheel in accordance with points 8—12 under "Replacing and adjusting front wheel bearings."
7. Check the front wheel alignment.

Reconditioning the control arm system

Straightening of damaged control arms may only be carried out to a minor extent, and then only in a cold condition. If an old part differs considerably when compared with a new one, it should be replaced.

UPPER CONTROL ARM

Removing

1. Slacken the wheel nuts slightly.
2. Lift up the front end of the vehicle so that the wheel is free and place a trestle under the lower control arm.
3. Unscrew the wheel nut and lift off the wheel.
4. Disconnect the shock absorber attachment at the upper control arm bolt.
5. Unscrew the nut, after which the bolt is screwed out.
6. Unscrew the bolts which hold the pin to the front axle member, after which the control arm is lifted out.

Replacing pin

1. The pin is removed from the control arm by screwing out the grease nipples and then the threaded bushings at the ends of the pin.
2. Secure fixture SVO 2300 in a vice ensuring that the top edge of the plate is clear.
3. Fit the rubber protector on the new pin and insert this into the control arm. Screw the bushings onto the pin about two turns. It should then be possible to move the pin axially, if not the bushings must be screwed back slightly.
4. Place the control arm in the fixture so that the peg on the cap fits into the U-profile on the control arm and the holes in the shoulders of the pin fit on both the guide pins. Move the cap towards the control arm, tighten the wing nut slightly, screw in the stop screw and tighten up the wing nut.
5. Lubricate the bushings externally and screw them in until the hexagon comes against the control arm. Place the rubber protector in position on the bushings and fit the grease nipples.
6. Slacken the wing nut and stop screw and lift off the control arm.

Fitting

1. Place the control arm in the correct position after which the bolts which hold the pin to the front axle member are fitted. Tighten the bolts to a torque of 5.5—6.2 kgm (40—45 lb. ft.).
2. Fit new rubber seals and then the bolt (hexagon forward) with the nut. Do not forget the locking washers. Check that there is clearance. This should normally be 0.3—0.6 mm (0.012—0.023").

3. Lubricate the king pin and bushings and check that the grease penetrates through to all the lubricating points.
4. Fit the shock absorber and wheel. Lower the vehicle. Tighten the wheel nuts to a torque of 10—14 kgm (72—101 lb. ft.).
5. Check the wheel alignment, see under the heading "Wheel alignment."

LOWER CONTROL ARM
Removing
1. Slacken the wheel nuts slightly.
2. Lift up the front end of the vehicle so that the wheels are free and place trestles under the front axle member.
3. Remove the wheel. Disconnect the stabilizer from the attachment.
4. Place a jack under the control arm pin. Remove the nuts for the attachment in the front axle member and lower the jack. Remove the spring. Screw off the nut and bolt and lift off the control arm to the front.

Replacing pin or bushings
Remove the nuts and washers. Remove the two inner bolts which hold both parts of the control arm together and slacken the outer one slightly. Turn both the parts of the control arm away from each other and remove the pin and bushings. Fitting is done in the reverse order and is facilitated if the rubber bushings are coated with soap solution.

Fitting
1. Fit new rubber seals and then the bolt (hexagon forward) with locking washer. Place on the washer and tighten the nut. Check that there is a clearance of 0.3—0.6 mm (0.012—0.023") in the bushing.
2. Place the spring in position with the straight end downwards. Move up the control arm pin into position with the help of a jack. Secure the pin and lock with split pins.
3. Lubricate the bolt and check that grease penetrates through the bushing.
4. Fit the stabilizer and wheel. Lower the vehicle. Tighten the wheel nuts to a torque of 10—14 kgm (72—101 lb. ft.). Check the wheel alignment.

STEERING GEAR—PV 444, 445, 544, P 210
Description
There are several different types of steering box on these vehicles. Constructively they can be divided up into two main types, mainly "Ross, cam and levers" and "Gemmer, cam and roller." The Ross type steering box refers to those for PV 444—

445, early production (part numbers 27690 and 250024). The Gemmer type steering box refers to PV 444, late production (part number 250051), PV 445, intermediate production (part number 250051), PV 445, late production (part number 250081), PV 544, early production (part number 250080), PV 544, late production (part number 250084), P 210, early production (part number 250098) and for P 210, late production (part number 250096).

The turning circle is approx. 9.8—10.8 metres (34' 2"— 35' 5") depending on the vehicle model and steering gear. With effect from PV 544 C and P 210 B, and on a small series of PV 444 L and PV 445 M, the rods are provided with plastic lined ball joints. This means that it is not necessary to lubricate them so that the ball joints concerned do not have grease nipples.

Replacing the steering wheel, PV 444-445 not fitted with direction indicator switch housing

1. Remove the fuse for the horn.
2. Remove the horn ring by pushing it down and turning it a quarter of a turn anti-clockwise. Screw off the steering wheel nut.
3. Pull off the steering wheel. Use puller SVO 2368 (previously number SVO 1185 B) together with spacer SVO 1103 and claw SVO 1187. Spacer SVO 1453 and claw SVO 1454 can also be used.
4. Place on the new steering wheel so that the spokes come horizontally when the wheels point straight forward. Fit the nut and tighten it to a torque of 3.5 kgm (25 lb. ft.). Place the horn ring in position, press it down and turn it a quarter of a turn clockwise. Fit the fuse.

PV 444-445 with direction indicator switch housing

1. Remove the fuse for the horn.
2. Slacken the bolt on the left side of the steering wheel hub, turn and pull the horn ring upwards. Unscrew the steering wheel nut. On late production the locking washer is first removed.
3. Pull off the steering wheel. **When doing this the direction indicator switch must be in neutral position,** otherwise the the internal parts will be damaged.
4. Fit the new steering wheel. Check that the switch is in the neutral position and that two of the steering wheel spokes come horizontally when the front wheels are pointing straight forward. Tighten the steering wheel nut to a torque of 3.5— 5 kgm (25—35 lb. ft.). On late production the nut is locked with a locking washer.

5. Check that the switch housing does not come too near the steering wheel after fitting. The distance between the upper edge of the housing and the steering wheel hub should be 1—1.5 mm (0.04—0.06 ins.). The distance is adjusted by slackening the clamping bolt on the side of the switch housing and moving it in the required direction.
6. Fit the horn ring and screw in the locking bolt. Fit the fuse.

PV 544, P 210
1. Remove the fuse for the horn.
2. Unscrew the two attaching bolts, turn the horn ring slightly and lift it up. Bend down the locking washer and remove the steering wheel nut and washer.
3. **Check that the direction indicator switch is in the neutral position.** Pull off the steering wheel with puller SVO 2325.
4. Fit the new steering wheel. Check that the switch is in the neutral position and that corresponding points on the steering wheel spokes come horizontally when the front wheels are pointing straight forwards. Place on the locking washer and tighten the steering wheel nut to a torque of 3.5—5 kgm (25—35 lb. ft.). Lock the nut.

STEERING BOX
Removing
1. Remove the steering wheel, see points 1—3 under "Replacing the steering wheel."
2. Disconnect the horn lead on the steering box. Pull the lead with bushing, spring and cover, up through the steering column. Unscrew the screw and remove the housing for the direction indicator switch in cases where this is fitted.
3. Remove the jacket tube support under the instrument panel. Lift the driving seat out of the way.
4. Screw off the nut for the pitman arm. Pull off the pitman arm from the pitman arm shaft with puller SVO 2370. On PV 444-445, SVO 2195 can also be used.
5. Disconnect the steering box from the body (on PV 445 and P 210, the frame) and lift out the steering box with jacket tube forwards and upwards.

Gemmer
Clean all parts in white spirit.
Check the pitman arm shaft. The roller must not be scratched, scored or worn on the contact surfaces or be loose in the pitman arm shaft. If so, the pitman arm shaft must be replaced.
Examine the steering worm contact surfaces against the roller and the inner races of the ball bearings. If there are any scratches,

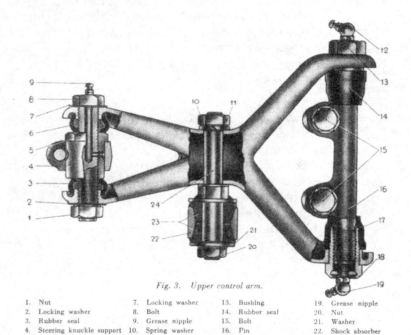

Fig. 3.   Upper control arm.

1. Nut	7. Locking washer	13. Bushing	19. Grease nipple
2. Locking washer	8. Bolt	14. Rubber seal	20. Nut
3. Rubber seal	9. Grease nipple	15. Bolt	21. Washer
4. Steering knuckle support	10. Spring washer	16. Pin	22. Shock absorber
5. Eccentric bushing	11. Nut	17. Rubber seal	23. Rubber bushing
6. Rubber seal	12. Grease nipple	18. Bushing	24. Bolt

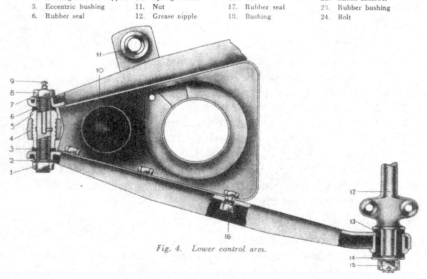

Fig. 4.   Lower control arm.

scoring or heavy wear, the steering worm with steering column must be replaced.

WHEEL ALIGNMENT

In order for the vehicle to have good steering properties and minimum tire wear, the front wheels must have certain, pre-determined settings which are generally known as wheel alignment. This includes caster, camber, king pin inclination, toe-out and toe-in.

Caster

This prefers to the longitudinal inclination of the king pin (forwards or backwards). This means easy steering since the wheels have a tendency to maintain the straight-forward position.

Camber

This refers to the inward or outward inclination of the wheel. Camber is reckoned to be positive if the wheel is inclined outwards and negative if it is inclined inwards. Positive camber is shown at C. Faulty camber means uneven tire wear.

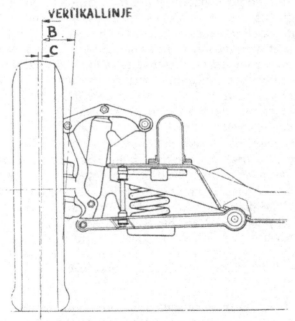

Fig. 44. Camber and king pin inclination.
Vertikallinje = Vertical line.

King Pin Inclination

This refers to the inward inclination of the king pin (B, Fig. 44). King pin inclination means that the center line of the king

279

pin and the wheel approach each other towards ground level. The wheel is thus easier to turn. The king pin inclination also influences the tendency of the wheels to run straight ahead since the vehicle is lifted slightly when the steering wheel is turned.

Toe-out

When driving around a curve, the wheels have varying radii of rotation. In order to have the same turning center with resulting minimum tire wear, the front wheels must be turned to a varying extent. This relationship, the toe-out, is determined by the construction of the steering rods and steering arms.

Toe-in

The difference in the distances between the wheels measured at hub height at the rear and front of the tires is called toe-in. The purpose of toe-in is to reduce tire wear.

Measuring and adjusting wheel alignment

Wheel alignment is measured by means of special instruments of which many different types are available. For this reason, no general instructions concerning the procedures to be adopted are given, with the exception of toe-out and toe-in. The principle of measurement is that camber is measured directly when the wheels are in the straight-forward position. Caster and king pin inclination cannot be measured directly. Instead, measurements of the angular differences are carried out on the instrument when the wheels are turned from 20° outwards to 20° inwards.

Most types of modern measuring tools for wheel alignment require that the wheels are locked by means of a pedal jack or similar device. This is not sufficient on vehicles equipped with Duo-Servo type brakes since the brake shoes in this system have a certain amount of reciprocating movement. On such vehicles, therefore, the brake drum should be locked mechanically to the brake backing plate when measuring. This can be done by applying welding pliers between the drum and brake backing plate on each front wheel, when it is not necessary to use a pedal jack.

When carrying out wheel alignment measurements, always follow the instructions given with the measuring instruments concerned.

Measures to be taken before adjusting wheel alignment

Before any adjustments are made, the following points must be checked and any faults corrected.
1. Check the tire pressure on all wheels.
2. Check that the front wheel tires are equally worn. If not, change around with a rear wheel or the spare wheel.

3. Check that the wheel warp and out of roundness do not exceed 2.5 mm (3/32"), and that the radial throw does not exceed 2.5 mm (3/32").
4. Check the front wheel bearings, king pin and bushings as well as the shock absorbers.
5. Check that the control arms are not damaged and that they are firmly attached to the front axle member. Check that the control arm bushings do not have excessive play.
6. Check that the springs are in good order and are not fatigued.
7. Check the play and adjustment of the steering mechanism. With the steering mechanism in the central position, the wheels should point straight forward.
8. Check the steering rods, steering arms, idler arm and intermediate tube.
9. Check that the vehicle has normal equipment (oil, water, gasoline and tools), but is otherwise unloaded.

Adjusting caster—444,544, P 210

Caster should be $-\frac{3}{4}°$ - $+\frac{1}{4}°$. This is adjusted by loosening the clamp bolt and then turning the eccentric bushing. Use wrench SVO 1411 if the bushing is early production with a width across flats of 28.5 mm (1⅛ ins.) and wrench SVO 2201 if the bushing is late production with width across flats of 34.3 mm (1-11/32 ins.). One complete turn alters the angle by ½°.

Note that if the wheel has the correct camber, one complete turn must be given, otherwise the camber will be altered. Tighten the clamp bolt before checking the caster.

Checking camber—444, 544, 210

After the caster has been checked, adjust the camber. This should be $-\frac{1}{4}°$ - $+\frac{1}{2}°$. It is adjusted by loosening the clamp bolt and turning the eccentric with wrench SVO 1411 or SVO 2201. Altering the camber also means a slight alteration of the caster, but this is negligible.

Adjusting toe-in—444, 544, 210

The toe-in should be 0—3 (0—0.12 ins.). This is adjusted by slackening the clamping bolts or locknuts respectively and turning the tie-rod in the required direction. By turning in the normal direction of rotation of the wheels, the distance between the tires at the front wheel is reduced, that is to say, toe-in is increased. A quarter of a turn of the tie rod represents a toe-in has been obtained, the clamping bolts are tightened to a torque of 1.1—1.4 kgm (8—10 lb. ft.). In the case of late production tie-rods the locknuts can be tightened to a torque of 7.5—9 kgm (55—65 lb. ft.).

Checking king pin inclination—444, 544, 210

As a precautionary measure, the king pin inclination should also be checked. This should be 5° when the camber is 0°.

Checking toe-out—444, 544, 210

1. Place the front wheels on turntables and ensure that they are pointing straight forward. When the vehicle is placed on them, the turntables should be set to zero and locked.
2. Turn one of the wheels 20° inwards and read off the turning angle of the other wheel. This should be 22±1°.
3. Turn the wheel in the other direction and read off the angle of turn on the other wheel in the same way.
4. There is no possibility of adjusting the toe-out. If it should be faulty, check the steering knuckles and steering rods and replace any damaged parts.

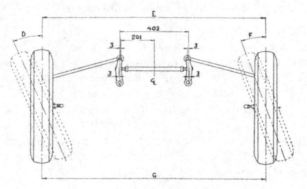

Fig. 45. Toe-out.

FRONT AXLE AND STEERING
122-1800

The 122 and 1800 have independent front wheel suspension. The front cross member which is bolted to the unitized body supports upper and lower control arms. Between them are interposed a pair of coil springs. The steering knuckles on each side pivot in ball joints and the front wheels are mounted in tapered roller bearings. It is possible to remove the entire front cross member as a unit for service. Less drastic procedures can be carried out in the conventional manner by supporting the front end of the car in various ways best suited to the operation at hand.

Adjusting caster—122-1800

On cars with chassis numbers up to 2610 the caster should be $0 \pm \frac{1}{2}°$ and with effect from chassis number 2611 onwards 0 to $+1°$. If it is the same on both sides, but incorrect, this is adjusted by means of shims between the front axle member and side member. When adjusting, the front end is lifted and trestles placed under the body at the jacking points. After the front axle member attaching bolts have been slackened, the requisite number of adjusting shims are added or removed in order to obtain the correct caster.

The attaching bolts are tightened before a new measurement is made.

Shims for adjusting the caster at the front axle member—side member are available in thicknesses of 2 and 3 mm (0.079 and 0.118"). The extent to which caster is altered by these shims is shown in the diagram.

NOTE: The alteration must be the same on both sides in order to avoid extra stress in the front axle member.

When the caster is different on the right and left sides, adjustment is done at the upper control arm shaft. Slacken the attaching bolts so that the adjusting shims can be lifted up. These are stocked in thicknesses of 0.15; 0.5; 1; 3 and 6 mm (0.006" 0.012; 0.039; 0.118 and 0.236"). The extent to which these alter the caster is shown in the diagram, Fig. 43. The same alteration is obtained if a shim is removed from one of the attaching bolts or if it is added to the other. In both cases the camber is altered slightly and the procedure will therefore partly depend on how much it is required to alter this. When the camber is correct, caster is adjusted by removing shims. Always tighten the attaching bolts to a torque of 4.8—5.5 kgm (35—40 lb. ft.) before making a new measurement. When the correct caster has been obtained, the attaching bolts are locked with the locking plate.

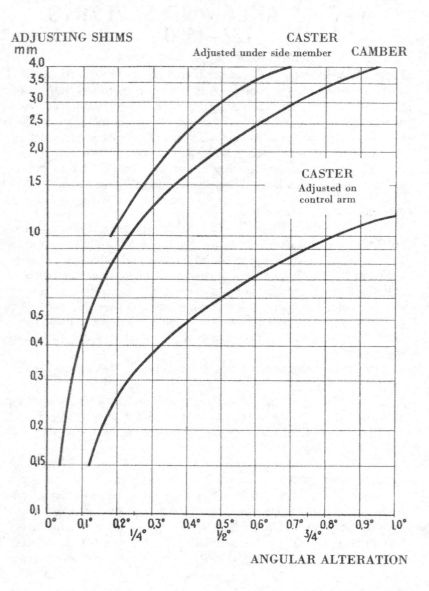

ADJUSTING SHIMS
mm

CASTER
Adjusted under side member

CAMBER

CASTER
Adjusted on
control arm

ANGULAR ALTERATION

Fig. 43. Diagram for alteration of caster
and camber.

Adjusting camber—122, 1800

The camber should be 0 to $+\frac{1}{2}°$ and is adjusted by means of shims at the upper control arm shaft. When doing this, the attaching bolts are slackened slightly. The number of shims is increased or reduced depending on the angular fault. After adjusting, the attaching bolts are tightened to a torque of 4.8—5.5 kgm (35—40 lb. ft.) and the camber checked. Adjusting shims are stocked in the following thicknesses: 0.15; 0.5; 1: 3 and 6 mm (0.006; 0.012; 0.039; 0.118 and 0.236"). the extent to which the shims alter the angle can be seen from the diagram.

NOTE: Adjusting shims of the same thickness must be removed or added to both the attaching bolts as otherwise the caster will be altered.

When the correct camber has been obtained, the attaching bolts are locked with the locking plate.

Checking king pin inclination—122, 1800

The king inclination, which on this car is represented by the inclination of the center line of the ball joints, should be 8° at a camber of 0°.

Checking toe-out—122, 1800

1. Place the front wheels of the car on turntables and ensure that the wheels point straight forwards. Before the car is placed on them, the turntables must be set to 0 and locked.
2. Turn the wheels to the left until the right wheel has turned 20° inwards. The scale on the left turntable should then read 22.5 ±1°.
3. Check the position of the right wheel in the same manner by turning the wheels to the right until the left wheel has turned 20° inwards, when the right turntable scale should give the same reading as previously indicated on the left. Both the measurements should thus lie within the above-mentioned tolerance, otherwise it means that the steering gear is deformed in some manner, or the front end distorted.
4. There are no adjusting possibilities but if the toe-out is incorrect, the steering arms and steering rod should be checked. Damaged parts should be replaced.

Adjusting steering limits—122, 1800
(early production)

It should be possible to turn the wheels a maximum of 40° in either direction. Turning is limited by stop screws on the pitman arm and idler arm. Adjustment is carried out as follows:

1. Set the front wheels to point straight forwards and drive them up onto turntables. When doing this, the turntables should be set to 0 and locked.

2. Release the turntable locking devices and turn the left wheel for a left-hand turn as far as it goes. Read off the turning angle. If this deviates from 38—40°, slacken the locknut for the eccentric head stop screw on the pitman arm. Turn the wheel to 40°. Adjust the stop screw so that it just contacts the pitman arm and tighten the locknut.

3. Repeat this procedure with the right wheel and stop screw on the idler arm.

Adjusting steering limits (late production)

Turning is limited by the stop screw on the pitman arm and idler arm, (see Fig. 45).

Adjusting is done as follows:

1. Turn the left wheel for a left-hand turn as far as it goes. Check that the distance between the tire and stabilizer measurement A) is 10—15 mm (25/64—19/32''). If not, slacken the locknut for the idler arm stop screw, after which this is turned until the correct value is obtained. Then lock the stop screw.

2. Repeat this procedure with the right wheel and the stop screw of the pitman arm.

Adjusting toe-in—122, 1800

Toe-in should be 0—4 mm (0—5/32''). Faulty toe-in is adjusted by slackening the clamping screws or locknuts respectively on the tie-rod after which the rod is turned in the required direction. The distance between the tires at the front is reduced, that is to say, toe-in is increased, by turning the tie-rod in the normal direction of rotation of the wheels.

Removing complete front end

1. Remove the hub caps and slacken the wheel nuts.
2. Lift up the front end so that the wheels are free. Place blocks under the body at the front jacking points.
3. Remove the wheel nuts and lift off the wheels.
4. Place a support under the front part of the engine.
5. Place a wooden block under the brake pedal. Disconnect the brake hoses from the body and plug the connections so that no dirt can enter.
6. Remove the pitman arm with the help of puller SVO 2282.
7. Disconnect the front engine mountings. Disconnect the idler arm and stabilizer from the body.
8. Place a jack under the front axle member. Screw out the front axle member attaching bolts. Take care of the adjusting shims.
9. Lower the front axle member and pull it out forwards.

Fitting complete front end

1. Place the front axle member on a jack and move it under the car.
2. Raise the jack so that the member comes in the right position. Place in the adjusting shims and tighten the bolts well.
3. Remove the support from under the engine and tighten down the engine onto the front engine mountings.
4. Fit the idler arm and stabilizer to the body.
5. Fit the pitman arm where the marks on the pitman arm shaft and pitman arm should coincide. Fit the spring washer and nut.
6. Connect the brake lines and air-vent the brake system.
7. Fit the wheels and lower the car. Tighten the wheel nuts to a torque of 10—14 kgm (70—100 lb ft.). Fit the hub caps.
8. Check the wheel alignment. See "Wheel Alignment."

Replacing and adjusting front wheel bearings

When adjusting the front wheel bearings, the hub should first be removed for inspecting the bearing races and rollers. Badly worn or scored bearings must be replaced. The complete replacement of the bearings is described below. When inspection and adjustment only are to be carried out, pass over the operations not involved.

1. Remove the hub and slacken the wheel nuts slightly.
2. Lift up the front end and place blocks under the lower control arms. Unscrew the wheel nuts and lift off the wheel.
3. (Applies only to cars with disc brakes). Disconnect the brake line and plug the connection. Bend up the locking washer and unscrew the attaching bolts. Lift off the caliper complete.
4. Remove the grease cap with tool SVO 2197. Remove the split pin and castle nut. Pull off the hub with puller SVO 1791. Pull off the inner bearing from the steering knuckle with puller SVO 1794 if the bearing remains in place.
5. Remove the bearing rings. For the inner bearing ring, use drift SVO 1799 and for the outer bearing ring, drift SVO 1800 together with standard handle SVO 1801.
6. Clean the hub, brake disc or brake drum and grease cap.
7. Press in the new bearing rings. In addition to the standard handle SVO 1801, drift SVO 1798 is used for the inner bearing ring and drift SVO 1797 for the outer bearing ring.
8. Press grease into the bearings with the help of a pressure lubricating apparatus. If one of these is not available, pack grease into the bearings by hand so that the space between the roller retainer and bearing inner ring is completely filled. Also coat the outer sides of the bearings and the outer rings

pressed into the hub with grease. The recess in the hub should be filled up with grease all around up to the smallest diameter of the outer ring for the outer bearing.

Place the inner bearing in position in the hub. Press in the sealing ring with drift SVO 1798 together with standard handle SVO 1801.

9. Place the hub on the spindle. Fit the outer bearing, washer and castle nut.
10. The front wheel bearings are adjusted by first tightening with a torque wrench to a value of 7 kgm (50 lb. ft.). The nut is then slackened a 1/3 of a turn and if the recess in the nut does not coincide with split pin hole in the spindle, slacken it further until the split pin can be fitted. Check that the wheel can rotate easily but without any play.
11. Fill the grease cap half full of grease and fit it with tool SVO 2197.
12. (Applies only to cars with disc brakes). Fit the caliper and lock the attaching bolts. Connect the brake lines. Air-vent the wheel unit cylinders.
13. Lift on the wheel after having cleaned the contact surfaces between the wheel and hub free from all dirt and grit, and tighten the nuts sufficiently so that the wheel cannot be displaced on the hub. Lower the car and tighten the wheel nuts. Tighten every other nut a little at a time until all are tightened to a torque of 10—14 kgm (72—100 lb. ft./ Fit the hub cap.

Reconditioning the control arm system

The ball joints cannot be dismantled or adjusted so that when worn they must be replaced.

The control arms may only be straightened to a minor extent and then only in a cold condition. If the old part deviates to any great extent when compared with a new one, it should be replaced.

Replacing the upper ball joint

1. Remove the hub cap and slacken the wheel nuts slightly.
2. Lift up the front end and place a trestle under the lower control arm. Screw off the wheel nut and lift off the wheel.
3. Screw off the nuts and remove the bolts. Lift the upper control arm.
4. Screw off the nut and remove the bolt. Remove the upper ball joint with sealing washer and rubber dust cover from the spindle.
5. Fitting is done in the reverse order. Fill up with grease between the rubber dust cover and ball joints.

On cars with chassis numbers lower than 84300 a special

ball joint for increasing the adjusting range of the front wheel alignment may be fitted. When fitting this ball joint, the attaching hole of which is displaced 2.5 mm (0.1") in relation to the ball stud, washers should be placed between the ball joint and control arm and longer attaching bolts used.

Replacing the lower ball joint

1. Remove the hub cap and slacken the wheel nuts slightly.
2. Lift up the front end and place a trestle under the lower control arm. Screw off the wheel nuts and lift off the wheel.
3. Screw off the nuts and remove the four bolts. Remove the split pin and nut.
4. (On cars with disc brakes). Disconnect the brake line from the retainer. It may be necessary to bend the brake line retainer to one side slightly. Turn the nut on the tool until it begins to tension. Then turn the nut until the ball joint releases, but not more than 1½ turns. If the ball joint is so tight that it does not release with this, strike a few light blows with a hammer and dolly on the ball joint attachment of the spindle.
5. Fitting is done in the reverse order. The castle nut is tightened to a torque of 4.8 5.5 kgm (35—40 lb. ft.). Fill up with grease between the rubber dust cover and ball joint. Air-vent wheel unit cylinders in cases where the brake line has been disconnected.

Replacing the upper control arm bushings

1. Remove the hub cap and slacken the wheel nuts slightly.
2. Lift up the front end and place a trestle under the lower control arm. Screw off the wheel nuts and lift off the wheel.
3. Screw off the nuts and remove the clamps.
4. Bend up the locking washer, screw out the attaching bolts and remove the shaft. Take care of the adjusting shims.
5. Remove the nuts, washers and bushings together with sleeves.
6. Fit the new rubber bushings and sleeves on the control arm shaft. The use of a soap solution as lubricant will facilitate fitting.
   Fit the washers and tighten the nuts. Then attach the control arm with its clamps loosely on both the bushings.
7. Fit the adjusting shims and attach the shaft and control arm. Tighten the attaching bolts to a torque of 4.8—5.5 kgm (35—40 lb. ft.) and lock them with the locking plate.
8. Tighten the attaching nuts for the clamps to a torque of 2—2.5 kgm (14—18 lb. ft.). Fit the other parts in the reverse order to removing.
9. Check the wheel alignment.

Replacing the upper control arm
1. Remove the hub cap and slacken the wheel nuts slightly.
2. Lift up the front end and place a trestle under the lower control arm. Screw off the wheel nuts and lift off the wheel.
3. Screw off the nuts and remove the clamps.
4. Remove the nuts and attaching bolts for the upper ball joint and lift off the upper control arm.
5. Fitting is done in the reverse order to removing. Tighten the nuts for the clamps to a torque of 2—2.5 kgm (14—18 lb. ft.). Check the wheel alignment.

Replacing the lower control arm bushings
1. Lift up the front end and block up under the front axle member.
2. Screw off the nuts and remove the clamps. Remove the nuts and washers.
3. Place a jack under the lower control arm inside the spring and lift so that the bushings are released. Pull off the bushings and sleeves.
4. Coat the rubber bushings and sleeves with soap solution and fit them on the control arm shaft. Fit the washers and nuts. When tightening the nuts, the outer part of the control arm should be lifted so that the distance between the rubber buffer and front axle member is about 40 mm (1½'').
5. Lower the control arm and fit the clamps and nuts. Tighten the nuts to a torque of 2—2.5 kgm (14—18 lb. ft.).
6. Lower the car. Check the wheel alignment.

Replacing the lower control arm
1. Remove the hub cap and slacken the wheel nuts slightly.
2. Lift up the front end and block up under the front axle member. Screw off the wheel nut and lift off the wheel.
3. Remove the nuts, washers and rubber bushings. Remove the bolt for the attaching washer. Remove the washer and shock absorber downwards.
4. Place a jack under the lower control arm immediately under the spring. Raise the jack until the upper control arm rubber buffer lifts.
5. Disconnect the stabilizer from the lower control arm. Remove the four attaching bolts and remove the lower ball joint from the control arm.
6. Lower the jack slowly and remove the spring when the control arm has come sufficiently far down.
7. Remove the nuts and clamps at the inner attachment, after which the control arm can be lifted off.

The car has a turning circle of about 9.5 m (32 ft.). The then lock with the locking washer.

8. Fitting is done in the reverse order. Tighten the nuts for the clamps to a torque of 2—2.5 kgm (14—18 lb. ft.). Check the wheel alignment.

STEERING GEAR—122, 1800
Description

The movement of the steering wheel is transmitted to the wheel via the steering column, steering box, pitman arm, tie-rod, idler arm and the steering rods and steering arms.

The steering box is of cam and roller type. The early type idler arms are caried in needle bearings and the late type in bushings. The steering column is divided into two parts joined with a coupling.

The upper part of the steering column is carried in bearings in the jacket tube. The ball joints in the steering system are lined with plastic making lubrication unnecessary.

The car has a turning circle of about 9.5 mm (32 ft.). The number of steering wheel turns from lock to lock is $3\frac{1}{4}$.

Replacing the steering wheel—122

1. Unscrew both the attaching bolts on the underside of the steering wheel spokes and remove the horn ring upwards.
2. Bend up the locking washer and remove the steering wheel nut. Mark the position of the steering wheel.
3. Set the direction indicator switch in the neutral position. Pull off the steering wheel with puller SVO 2263.
4. Fit the new steering wheel, paying attention to the marking. The steering wheel spokes should be horizontal when the wheels are pointed straight forwards. Tighten the steering wheel nut to a torque of 3.5—5.0 kgm (25—35 lb. ft.) and then lock with the locking washer.
5. Fit the horn ring and check its function.

STEERING GEAR
Removing

1. Disconnect the horn lead from the junction piece.
2. Unscrew the two nuts and remove the bolts.
3. Remove the pitman arm with puller SVO 2282 (Fig. 4).
4. Unscrew and remove the three attaching bolts (6, Fig. 23).
5. Lift up and turn the steering box as shown. Pull out the horn lead from the lower section of the steering column and steering box. Lift out the steering box but be careful when the carrier is moved past the brake line.

Fig. 4.   Removing the pitman arm.

Fig. 23.   Steering box.

1. Earth lead
2. Nut
3. Coupling disc

4. Nut
5. Carrier
6. Bolt

REPLACING THE STEERING WHEEL—1800

1. Pull out the horn cable from the junction block on the steering box.
2. Carefully remove the horn button with a screwdriver blade by prying up.
3. Bend up the locking tabs and remove the steering wheel nut. Mark the position of the steering wheel.
4, Pull the wheel off. Unscrew the housing and hub from the wheel.
5. Refit in reverse order, observing the markings so that the spokes will be horizontal. Tighten nut to a torque reading of 2.8 to 4.2 kgm (20-30 lb. ft.), then lock with the tabs.

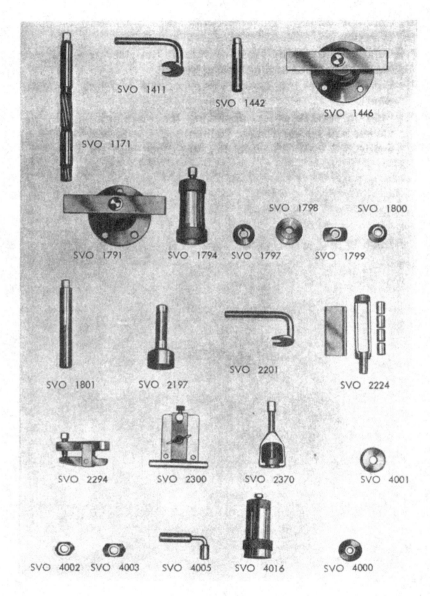

Fig. 48. Special tools for front axle.

TOOLS

The following special tools are required for carrying out repairs to the front axle and steering gear.

Front axle

SVO 1171   Reamer for king pin bushing.

SVO 1411   Wrench for eccentric bushing (PV 444 up to H, early production: PV 445 up to D, early production).

SVO 1442   Drift for removing and fitting king pin bushing.

SVO 1446   Puller for front wheel hub (PV 444—445 up to B).

SVO 1791   Puller for front wheel hub (PV 444 up to C: PV 544 up to D: (PV 544, P 210).

SVO 1794   Puller for inner bearing on steering knuckle (PV 444 up to C, PV 445 with effect from D, PV 544, P 210).

SVO 1797   Fitting drift for outer bearing ring in wheel hub (PV 444 with effect from C, PV 445 with effect from D, PV 544, P 210).

SVO 1798   Fitting drift for inner bearing ring and sealing ring in front wheel hub (PV 444 with effect from C, PV 445 with effect from D, PV 544, P 210).

SVO 1799   Removing drift for inner bearing ring in front wheel hub (PV 444 with effect from C, PV 445 with effect from D, PV 544, P 210).

SVO 1800   Removing drift for outer bearing ring front wheel hub (PV 444 with effect from C, PV 445 with effect from D, PV 544, P 210).

SVO 1801   Standard handle.

SVO 2197   Drift for removing and fitting grease cap.

SVO 2201   Wrench for eccentric bushing (PV 444 with effect from H, late production, PV 445 with effect from D, late production, PV 544, P 210).

SVO 2224   Removing tool for king pin.

SVO 2294   Removing tool for ball joint.

SVO 2300   Fixture for upper control arm.

SVO 2370   Puller for pitman arm.

SVO 4000   Fitting drift for outer bearing ring in front wheel hub (PV 444—445 up to B).

SVO 4001   Fitting drift for inner bearing ring and sealing ring in front wheel hub (PV 444—445 up to B).

SVO 4002   Removing drift for outer bearing ring in front wheel hub (PV 444—445 up to B).

SVO 4003   Removing drift for inner bearing ring front wheel hub (PV 444—445 up to B).

SVO 4005   Centring mandrel for king pin.

SVO 4016   Puller for inner bearing on steering knuckle (PV 444—445 up to B).

Steering gear

SVO 1103   Centre part for steering wheel puller SVO 2368.

SVO 1187   Tensioning claw for steering wheel puller SVO 2368.

SVO 1801   Standard handle.

SVO 1819   Puller for upper bearing outer ring (type Gemmer) and for pitman arm shaft bushings (PV 544).

SVO 2101   Puller for steering wheel (PV 444—445 with effect from B).

SVO 2199   Protecting sleeve for sealing ring when fitting pitman arm shaft (type Gemmer).

SVO 2225   Reamer for pitman arm shaft bushings (type Gemmer).

SVO 2226   Reamer for bushing in cover (type Gemmer with cast iron cover).

SVO 2227   Fitting drift for sealing ring (type Gemmer) and for bushing in cover (type Gemmer with cast iron cover).

SVO 2228   Drift for fitting pitman arm shaft bushing (type Gemmer).

SVO 2254   Guide for reamer SVO 2225 (type Gemmer).

SVO 2294   Removing tool for ball joint.

SVO 2395   Puller for steering wheel (PV 544, P 210).

SVO 2368   Puller for steering wheel (PV 444 A and PV 445 A). Previous number SVO 1185 B.

SVO 2370   Puller for pitman arm.

SVO 4025   Drift for removing and fitting idler arm bushing.

SVO 2498   Drift for fitting and removing bushings in idler arm bracket.

SVO 4075   Drift for removing and fitting pitman arm shaft bushings (type Ross).

SVO 4076   Reamer for pitman arm shaft bushings (type Ross).

SVO 4078   Puller for bearing in jacket tube.

SVO 4079   Drift for fitting sealing ring (type Ross).

SVO 4089   Backing ring for removing idler arm bushing.

SVO 4113   Drift for fitting upper bearing outer ring type Gemmer).

SVO 4153   Reamer for bushings in idler arm bracket.

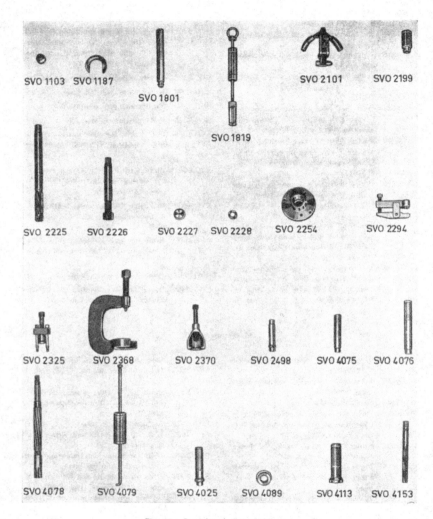

SVO 1103   SVO 1187

SVO 1801

SVO 1819

SVO 2101

SVO 2199

SVO 2225   SVO 2226   SVO 2227   SVO 2228   SVO 2254   SVO 2294

SVO 2325   SVO 2368   SVO 2370   SVO 2498   SVO 4075   SVO 4076

SVO 4078   SVO 4079   SVO 4025   SVO 4089   SVO 4113   SVO 4153

Fig. 49. Special tools for steering gear.

SPRINGS AND SHOCK ABSORBERS
122-1800

The 122 and 1800 models are fitted with coil springs front and rear. Upper ends of the front springs are seated in housings in the front cross member and the lower ends are carried in control arms fitted betwen the front member and the lower ball joints. Top ends of the rear springs are carried in housings in the body and lower ends are seated on pads on the rear axle housing. Rebound straps control excessive movement in the rear. A front stabilizer bar is also part of the suspension.

REMOVING THE FRONT SPRINGS

1. Jack up the front of the car and block it about 6 inches off the floor supporting it under the front cross member.
2. Remove the wheels.
3. Remove shock absorber nuts and washers, take off the outer rubber bushings (3, Fig. 9-1 and 1, Fig. 9-2), remove the bolts for the attaching plate and remove it and the shock absorber downward.
4. Jack up the lower control arm, with jack placed directly under spring, until the upper control arm rubber bumper fits.
5. Disconnect the stabilizer bar, remove the nut from the lower ball joint (12, Fig. 9-1).
6. Lower the jack slowly and remove spring.

REPLACING THE FRONT SPRINGS

1. Check the replacement spring against the·specifications for spring rate and the color code. Both front springs should be of the same rate.
2. Make sure that the rubber spacers are fresh and resillient. Replace when in doubt.
3. Fit spacer and washer first, then carry out removal procedure in reverse order.

REMOVING REAR SPRINGS

1. Jack up the rear of the car and block it off the floor by supporting at the jacking points.
2. Remove the wheels and release handbrake.
3. Place a jack under the rear axle housing and raise it until the rebound straps slacken.
4. Loosen lower shock absorber mount and upper attachment of the rebound strap. Slacken the front support arm attachment slightly.
5. Lower jack until spring is free. Remove spring and spacer.

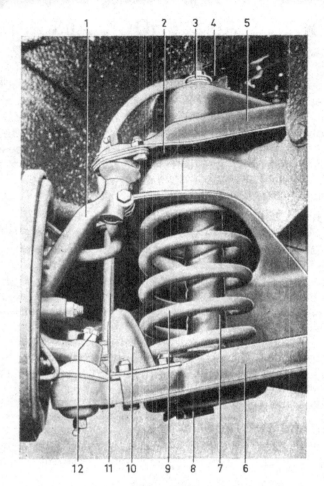

Fig. 9-1. Front spring and shock absorber

1. Steering knuckle
2. Upper rubber bumper
3. Rubber bushing
4. Washer
5. Upper control arm
6. Lower control arm
7. Shock absorber
8. Attaching plate
9. Spring
10. Lower rubber bumper
11. Stabilizer bar
12. Nut for lower ball joint

REPLACING REAR SPRINGS

1. Check color coding in specifications to make sure that replacement springs are identical for both sides. Check condition of rubber spacers and pads.

2. Make sure pads and spacers are in correct position. Proceed in reverse order.

REMOVING AND REPLACING A FRONT SHOCK ABSORBER

1. Remove the upper attaching nut, washer and rubber bushing (3 and 4, Fig. 9-1).
2. Remove the lower attaching nut, washers and bushing. (Fig. 9-2).
3. Remove the bolt for the attaching plate, remove shock absorber and attaching plate.
4. Shock absorbers are of the sealed type and must be replaced when faulty. Fit only a shock absorber designated for the car, either original equipment (Delco or Gabriel) or replacement type, for best results.
5. Refitting is carried out in reverse order of removal. Make sure washers are in correct position and tighten the nut until ⅛ inch of the threaded end of the bolt is visible.

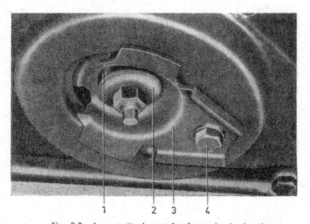

Fig. 9-2. Lower attachment for front shock absorber

1. Rubber bushing   3. Attaching plate
2. Washer for rubber bushing   4. Bolt

REMOVING AND REPLACING A REAR SHOCK ABSORBER

1. Remove the upper attaching nut, washer and bushing. Access in the 122 is through the baggage compartment; in the 1800 it is via a hole in the rear package shelf.
2. Remove lower attaching nut washer and bushing, remove downward.
3. Replacement is carried out in reverse of removal. Make sure that washers are in correct position. Tighten nut until ⅛" of threaded end of bolt shows on Delco type. On Gabriel, which has larger bolts, tighten until ⁷⁄₁₆ inch of threaded end is visible.

SPRINGS AND SHOCK ABSORBERS
PV 444 – 544

The 544 & 444 are fitted with coil springs both front and rear. The front springs extend from a housing on the front-axle member at the top to a control arm fitted to the front axle member and the lower end of the steering knuckle support.

The rear spring upper ends are fitted to the body with the aid of washers, bolts and rubber spacers. The lower ends are fitted to the rear axle support arms with washers and bolts.

REMOVING THE FRONT SPRINGS

1. Raise the front of the car until the wheels are about 15 cm (6") above floor level and block up the frame.
2. Disconnect the stabilizer.
3. Place a jack under the lower control arm and unscrew the four nuts on the front axle support member bracket.
4. Lower the jack slowly and remove the spring when the lower control arms is sufficiently released.

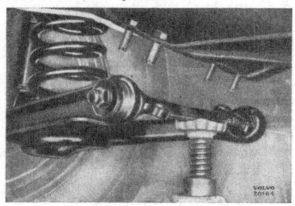

Fig. 1. Removing front springs.

CHECKING THE FRONT SPRINGS

Springs must be checked before fitting. Measure the compressed and extended length of the springs. These measurements are listed in the Specifications. Check the general condition of the springs. "Tired" or damaged springs must be replaced.

REPLACING THE FRONT SPRINGS

1. Place the spring in the attachment on the control arm. The straight end of the spring (A Fig. 2) must face downwards.
2. Lift up the control arm until the spring rests with the upper end in the seat on the front axle support member, then place a jack under the control arm.

Fig. 2. Front spring.

3. Make sure that the spring is correctly in position. The straight
    end should rest in the recess in the lower spring attachment.
    Raise the lower control arm by means of the jack and tighten
    the four nuts on the bolts in the front axle support member.
    Lock the nuts with cotter pins. Connect the stabilizer.
    Check, and if necessary, adjust the front wheel alignment.

REMOVING THE REAR SPRINGS

1. Release the handbrake.
2. Raise the rear end of the car with a jack and block up the
    frame. Chocks must be placed under the front wheels.

3. Disconnect the shock absorbers (5 Fig. 3) from the attachment in the rear axle housing.
4. Disconnect the shock absorber band (7) from its attachment (8) on the axle support arm.
5. Disconnect the spring from the axle support arm (screw 10).
6. Lower the rear axle housing sufficiently for the spring to be loosened.
7. Disconnect the spring from the body (screw) and remove the spring.

Fig. 3. *Rear spring fitted.*

1. Rear spring	6. Lower attachment for
2. Upper washer	shock absorber band
3. Bolt	7. Shock absorber band
4. Rubber spacer	8. Axle support arm
5. Shock absorber	9. Bolt
	10. Lower washer

REPLACING THE REAR SPRINGS

1. Place the spring and the rubber spacer (4) into position and attach the spring to the body. The straight part of the spring (A Fig. 4) must face diagonally inwards.
2. Raise the rear axle housing with the jack and attach the spring to the support arm. Attach the shock absorber band (7) to the rear axle support arm.
3. Connect the shock absorber (5) to the rear axle housing.

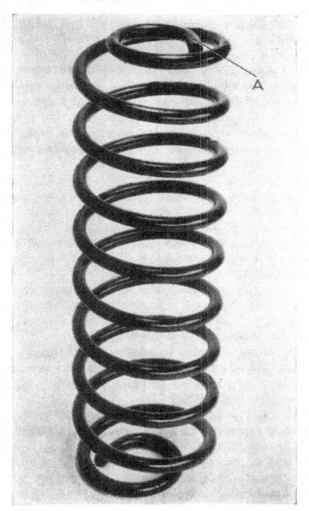

Fig. 4. Rear spring.

SHOCK ABSORBERS

The shock absorbers on the 544 and 444 are hydraulic, double-acting and telescopic. Rebound straps are fitted between the support arms and the body. These prevent damage to the shock absorbers by limiting wheel travel downwards. Wheel travel upwards is limited by rubber blocks. On early production cars, the straps were fitted behind the springs while on late production cars, they are fitted in front of the springs (7, Fig. 3).

Since chassis number 10001 they have been of the sealed type and must be replaced rather than repaired.

When the shock absorber is compressed or extended during travel, the plunger (5) slides in the pressure tube (2), forcing the fluid to flow through the valve operated channels in the plunger. The plunger sliding speed depends on how quickly the fluid passes from one side of the plunger to the other. As the channels are very narrow, the fluid can only pass through very slowly, and the plunger movement is braked and consequently the spring movement. With rapid compression or extension, the brake action on the plunger increases owing to the turbulence in the fluid passing through the channels in the plunger.

Volume does not change at the same degree on both sides of the plunger when the shock absorber is compressed or extended, as the plunger rod displaces a certain volume. Through this, some fluid will flow out through the valve (6) to the reservoir when compressed and the fluid will penetrate into the pressure tube (2) at the lower side of the plunger when the shock absorber is extended.

The dampening properties of a shock absorber cannot definitely be determined without using special instruments. In most cases, however, a fairly accurate idea of the state of the shock absorbers can be determined in the following way.

Test the shock absorber by working it up and down several times. There should be equal resistance in both directions. The shock absorber should be in an upright position with the dust cover uppermost when testing.

A preliminary investigation can be carried out by swaying the car before removing the shock absorbers. A strong damping effect should be noticeable.

Noise may be caused by worn rubber bushings on the shock absorbers eves, insufficient fluid or damaged integral parts. Worn or damaged parts must be replaced with new.

FITTING THE SHOCK ABSORBERS

Before fitting, air-vent the shock absorber by holding it in an upright position with the dust cover uppermost and work the unit up and down four or five complete strokes or until one feels the shock absorber resisting in both directions. Fit in the reverse order to that used when removing. The shock absorber attachment are assembled as shown in Figs. 6—9.

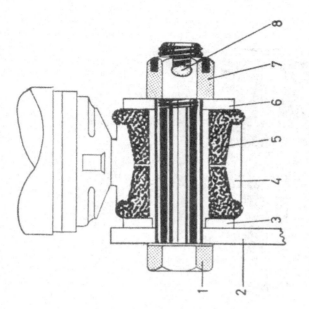

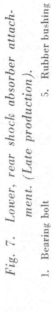

Fig. 7. Lower, rear shock absorber attachment. (Late production).

1. Bearing bolt
2. Bracket
3. Washer with spacer sleeve
4. Shock absorber attaching eyelet
5. Rubber bushing
6. Washer
7. Nut
8. Cotter pin

Fig. 6. Upper, rear shock absorber attachment.

1. Nut
2. Washer
3. Rubber bushing
4. Washers welded in body plate
5. Shock absorber attaching bolt

3 MM

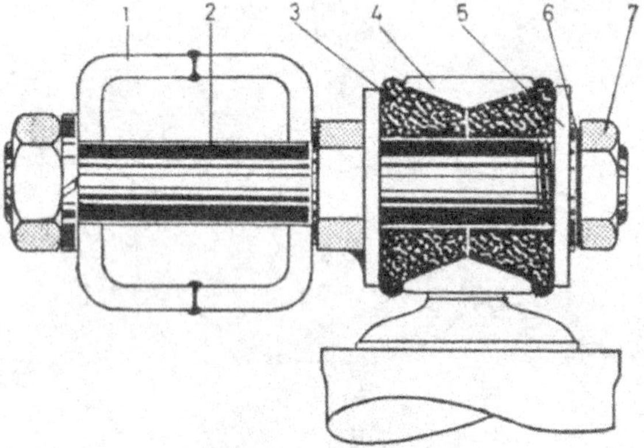

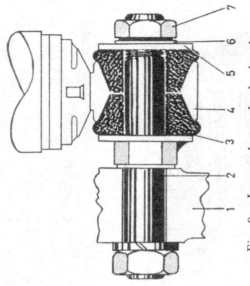

Fig. 9. Lower, front shock absorber attachment.

1. Steering knuckle support
2. Bearing bolt
3. Rubber bushing
4. Shock absorber attaching eyelet
5. Washer
6. Lock washer
7. Nut

Fig. 8. Upper, front shock absorber attachment.

1. Upper control arm
2. Bearing bolt
3. Rubber bushing
4. Shock absorber attaching eyelet
5. Washer
6. Lock washer
7. Nut

306

BRAKES

Four types of brakes have been fitted to Volvo production automobiles. (1) drum brakes with two-leading shoes; (2) drum brakes with duo-servo action; (3) combination of disc front, drum, rear; (4) disc front, drum rear with power assist. Identification of the different varieties is easily made through reference to photos and diagrams in this chapter but we will generally speak of "early production" and "late production" to designate the two-leading shoe and duo-servo, respectively. Both types will be found on 544 and 122 S, but, following chassis number 207866 all 544 models are equipped with the 'late' type and all current 122 models are so equipped.

The 1800, by virtue of its higher performance potential, utilizes the power assist of a servo mechanism which will be explained at the end of this chapter. It is not recommended that repairs be undertaken on the servo unit unless the mechanic is in possession of a Volvo Service Manual (SS 5013/3) which gives details lack of space precludes here. The 1800 handbrake is also slightly different and it is covered at the end of the handbrake section.

It is also important to note that the disc units use a different type of tapered hydraulic brake line and replacement should only be made with parts designated for them.

While the Volvo special tools mentioned are of great assistance, nominal brake tools or substitutes devised in the shop are equally valid. The important factor in hydraulic brake repair is cleanliness. The orifices in the system are tiny and mere specks of dirt, grease, fillings or grindings can easily foul the operation. Cylinders and components should be cleaned in hydraulic fluid or alcohol, but never gasoline or solvent, and blown off with compressed air, rather than wiped with rags or waste.

Replacement brake fluid for all cars except the 1800 should conform at least to SAE 70 R1. The 1800 requires heavy duty fluid meeting SAE 70 R3 specifications and no lesser grade should be used.

FOOT BRAKE

This can either be of the drum type or of the disc type. The arrangement of the foot brake system is shown in Figs. 1 and 3 respectively.

WHEEL BRAKE UNIT, DRUM BRAKES, EARLY PRODUCTION

The front wheel brakes (Figs. 5 and 6) are of the two leading shoe type, that is to say, each wheel has two brake cylinders with

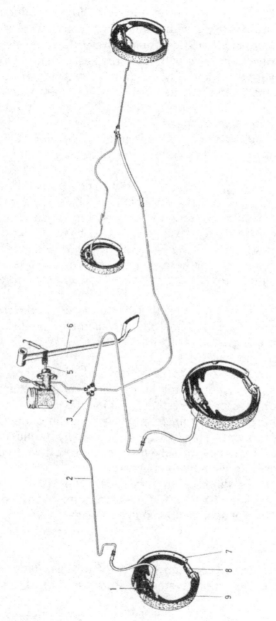

Fig. 1. Foot brake system, drum brakes.

1. Wheel unit cylinder
2. Brake line
3. Brake contact
4. Master cylinder
5. Push rod
6. Brake pedal
7. Rear brake shoe
8. Adjusting device
9. Front brake shoe

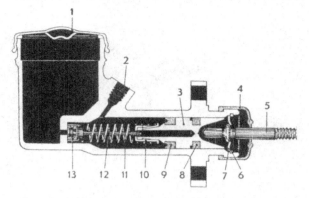

Fig. 2.   Master cylinder, early production.

1. Cap	8. Packing
2. Connection for brake line	9. Packing
3. Plunger	10. Spring retainer
4. Rubber cap	11. Spring
5. Push rod	12. Valve rod
6. Locking ring	13. Valve
7. Washer	

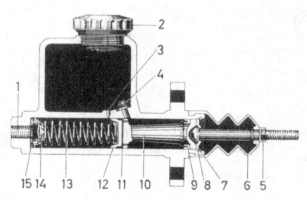

Fig. 4.   Master cylinder, late production.

1. Connection for brake line	6. Rubber cap	12. Packing
2. Cap	7. Locking ring	13. Spring
3. Equalizing hole	8. Stop washer	14. Valve
4. Strainer	9. Packing	15. Washer
5. Push rod	10. Plunger	
	11. Washer	

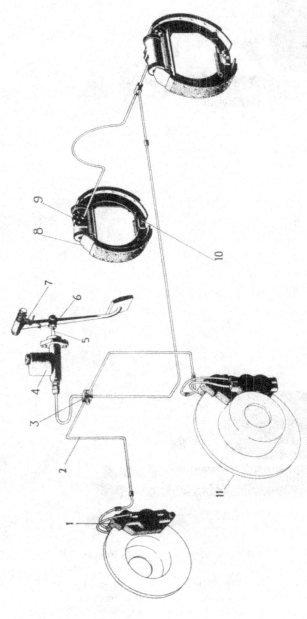

Fig. 3. Foot brake system, vehicle with front wheel disc brakes.

1. Front wheel brake unit
2. Brake line
3. Brake contact
4. Master cylinder
5. Push rod
6. Brake pedal
7. Return spring
8. Brake shoe
9. Wheel unit cylinder
10. Adjusting device
11. Brake disc

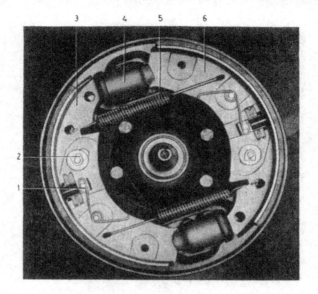

Fig. 5.   *Wheel brake unit, early production,*
left-hand front wheel.

1. Self adjusting device
2. Locking washer
3. Front brake shoe
4. Wheel unit cylinder
5. Return spring
6. Rear brake shoe

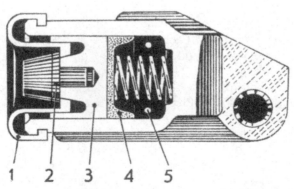

Fig. 6.   *Wheel unit cylinder, front wheel.*

1. Rubber cap
2. Plunger rod
3. Plunger
4. Plunger packing
5. Connection for
   brake line

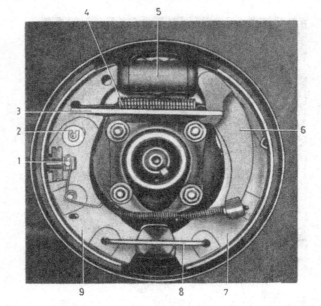

Fig. 7.   Wheel brake unit, early production,
left-hand rear wheel.

1. Self-adjusting device
2. Locking washer
3. Handbrake link
4. Return spring
5. Wheel unit cylinder
6. Lever
7. Rear brake shoe
8. Spring
9. Front brake shoe

a plunger in each. By means of this arrangement both the shoes function as primary shoes. Each shoe has a self-adjusting device.

The rear wheel brake units (Figs. 7 and 9) have a wheel unit cylinder with two plungers. At the bottom the shoes rest against a support attached to the brake backing plate. The front shoe is provided with a self-adjusting device and the rear shoe has a shorter lining.

Since the shoes can be displaced radially, they are self-centering. The clearance between the brake lining and drum can be adjusted by means of an eccentric which can be turned.

The self adjusting device (Fig. 8) functions as follows:

A contact plug (4) is fitted in a hole in the brake shoe. The outer end of this plug is held in contact with the brake drum by means of a spring (2). As the brake lining becomes worn, the contact plug moves inwards and influences the lever (7) by means of a stud (3), pressing the lever against the eccentric (6). This widens the distance between the guide lip (8) on the brake shoe

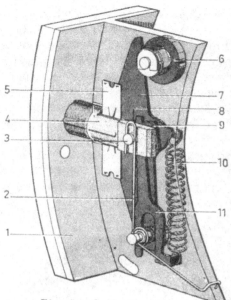

Fig. 8.   Self-adjusting device.

1. Brake shoe	7. Lever
2. Spring	8. Guide lip
3. Stud	9. Lip
4. Contact plug	10. Spring
5. Damping spring	11. Key
6. Cam	

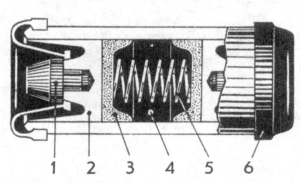

Fig. 9.   Wheel unit cylinder, rear wheel.

1. Plunger rod
2. Plunger
3. Packing
4. Connection for brake line
5. Spring
6. Rubber cap

and the lips (9) on the lever (7). The notched key (11), which is influenced by a spring (10), is then pulled in between the lips (8 and 9). The return movement of the brake shoe is thus limited so that the clearance between the brake lining and drum remains constant regardless of the wear on the brake lining.

When the contact plug reaches the web of the brake shoe as a result of brake lining wear, the self-adjusting function ceases. Further brake lining wear will then increase the clearance between the lining and drum. If the pedal stroke increases, that is to say, it can be pressed further down towards the floor, this means that the brake linings are worn and need replacing. In order to prevent vibration in the contact plug, a damping spring (5) is fitted between the brake shoe and contact plug.

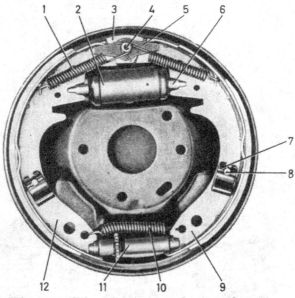

Fig. 10. Wheel brake unit, late production, right-hand front wheel.

1. Return spring
2. Wheel unit cylinder
3. Centring block
4. Anchor stud
5. Guide plate
6. Plunger rod
7. Clip
8. Guide pin
9. Front brake shoe
10. Locking spring
11. Adjusting device
12. Rear brake shoe

WHEEL BRAKE UNIT, DRUM BRAKES, LATE PRODUCTION

The brake shoes (12 and 9, Fig. 10) are movably attached to the brake backing plate by means of guide pins (8) and spring clips (7). The upper ends of the shoes are kept pressed against the rotating centering block (3) by the return springs (1). The lower ends are joined by means of the adjusting device (11) against which they are held pressed by the spring (10) which also locks the toothed wheel of the adjusting screw. This arrangement means that the brake shoes are self-centering and both shoes partially self-applying (Duo-servo).

When the brake is applied, the wheel unit cylinder plungers press out the shoes against the brake drum by means of the plunger rods (6, Fig. 10). Because of the friction between the drum and lining, the shoes will follow round in the direction of rotating of the drum. Due to the "floating" attachment of the shoes, the primary shoe (9) is pressed downwards and the secondary shoe (12) upwards until its upper end encounters the centering block (see Fig. 13). The end of the secondary shoe is then displaced by the block so that the shoe is centered in relation to the drum. Since the pivoting center of the secondary shoe is at the anchor stud (4, Fig. 10) and that of the primary shoe at the adjusting device, friction between the drum and lining will assist with applying the brake, see Fig. 13. This action is also assisted by the fact that the primary shoe tends to follow round in the direction of rotation of the drum, which assists the application of the secondary shoe.

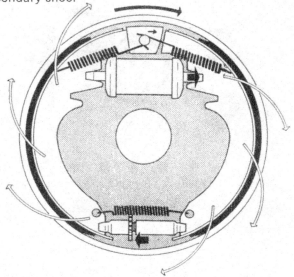

Fig. 13.   Method of application of wheel brake unit.

In order to give the brake linings as long life as possible, the rear shoes of the front wheel brake units (secondary shoes) are provided with thicker and eccentrically ground linings.

Wheel brake units of this type were at first provided with longer linings than those shown in Figs. 10 and 11.

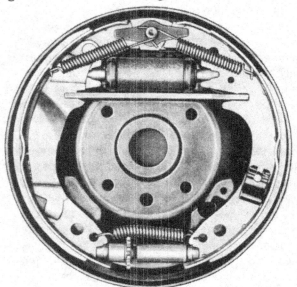

*Fig. 11.   Wheel brake unit, late production,
right-hand rear wheel.*

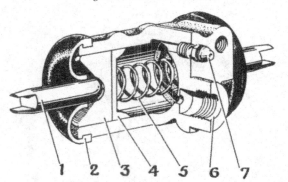

Fig. 12.   Wheel unit cylinder, late production.

1. Plunger rod
2. Rubber cap
3. Plunger
4. Plunger packing
5. Return spring
6. Connection for brake line
7. Air-venting nipple

WHEEL BRAKE UNITS ON VEHICLES
FITTED WITH DISC BRAKES AT FRONT

In this arrangement the front wheel brakes are of the disc type. The discs (11, Fig. 3) are made of steel and are attached to the hubs with which they rotate. At each steering knuckle there is a retainer for the wheel unit cylinders and brake pad assemblies, in future called the front wheel brake unit (1). In addition, protecting plates for the brake discs are attached to the steering knuckles. The brake pad assemblies (9, Fig. 14) are provided with moulded-in linings. During braking, one of the linings is pressed against the inner face of the brake disc by a large hydraulic plunger (10) and the other against the outer face of the disc by two smaller plungers (2). When braking ceases, the linings move back such an amount that they are always at a certain minimum distance from the brake disc, so that the front wheel brake units are self-adjusting.

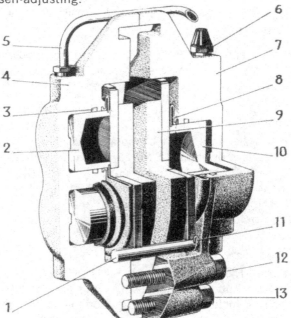

Fig. 14. Front wheel brake unit.

1.	Guide pin	8.	Dust cover
2.	Outer plunger	9.	Pad assembly
3.	Plunger packing	10.	Inner plunger
4.	Outer housing	11.	Locking spring
5.	Bridge pipe	12.	Bolt
6.	Brake line	13.	Bolt
7.	Inner housing		

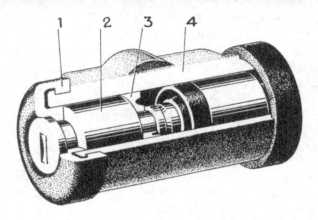

Fig. 15.   Rear wheel brake unit cylinder on vehicles fitted with disc brakes at front.

1. Rubber seal	3. Plunger packing
2. Plunger	4. Housing

The rear wheel brake units are of the drum type. The upper ends of the brake shoes (8, Fig. 3) rest against a double-acting wheel unit cylinder, and the lower ends against an adjusting device (10).

HANDBRAKE

The handbrake lever is floor-mounted on the outside of the driving seat. The movement of the lever is transmitted by means of a shaft, lever and pull rod to the clevis (3, Fig. 16). From there the movement is transmitted by means of cables (5) to the rear wheel brake unit levers (11). The upper end of this lever is attached to the rear brake shoe. When the lever is pulled forwards, the shoes are forced outwards by means of the links (10), causing the handbrake to be applied.

DISMANTLING THE FRONT WHEEL BRAKE UNIT EARLY TYPE

1. Remove the hub cap and slacken the wheel nuts slightly. Lift up the vehicle and block up under the lower control arm. Remove the wheel.
2. Remove the grease cap with tool SVO 2197 (Fig. 17). Remove the split pin and castle nut. Pull off the hub with tool SVO 1791 (Fig. 18). If the inner bearing does not come out, pull it off the spindle with tool SVO 1794 (Fig. 19).
3. Remove the locking washer and other washers from the stud for the adjusting cam on the front brake shoe. Remove the shoe and springs as shown in Fig. 20. Remove the rear shoe in the same way.

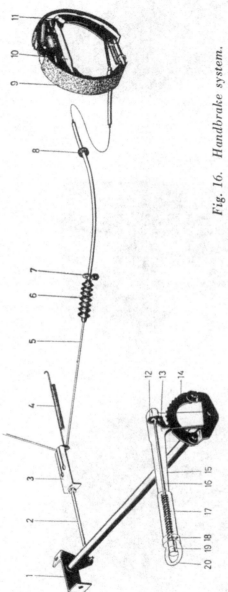

Fig. 16. Handbrake system.

1.	Bearing support	11.	Lever
2.	Pull rod	12.	Pawl
3.	Clevis, early production	13.	Pin
4.	Spring	14.	Ratchet segment
5.	Handbrake cable	15.	Handbrake lever
6.	Bellows	16.	Push rod
7.	Attachment for outer casing	17.	Spring
8.	Bushing	18.	Screw
9.	Brake shoe	19.	Button
10.	Link	20.	Loop

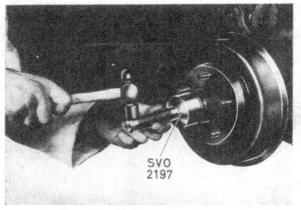

Fig. 17.   Removing the grease cap.

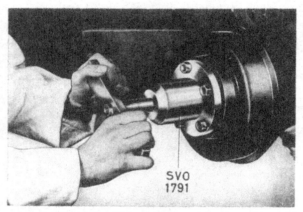

Fig. 18.   Removing the hub.

Fig. 19.   Removing the inner bearing.

Fig. 20. Removing the brake shoe.

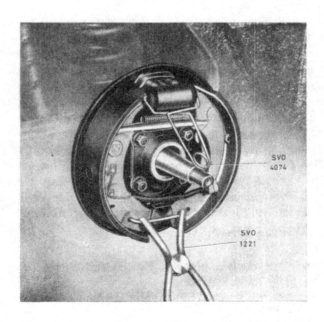

SVO
4074

SVO
1221

Fig. 21. Removing the lower spring.

DISMANTLING THE REAR WHEEL BRAKE UNIT

1. Remove the hub cap and slacken the wheel nuts slightly. Lift up the vehicle and block up the rear axle. Remove the wheel.
2. Release the handbrake. Remove the split pin and castle nut. Pull off the hub with tool SVO 1791 (Fig. 18).
3. Place clamp SVO 4074 on the wheel unit cylinder so that the plungers cannot be pressed outwards. Remove the lower spring with the help of pliers SVO 1221 (Fig. 21). Remove the locking washer and other washers from the front shoe. Then turn the shoe outwards so that the handbrake link can be removed. Lift off the front brake shoe and return spring. Disconnect the handbrake cable and remove the rear shoe.

REPLACING THE BRAKE LININGS

Although most owners prefer to replace worn shoes with units already having lining applied, the old linings can be removed in a band-type grinding machine. They can also be chiseled off, after which the brake shoe should be cleaned with emery cloth. In both cases, take care not to damage the shoe.

After having ben cleaned up, the brake shoe should be washed in clean solvent and then allowed to dry. If the linings are to be bonded on, the contact surface on the shoe must not be touched or made dirty after cleaning.

The dimensions of the new linings are given in the specifications. When fitting, make sure that the linings do not lie diagonally on the shoe and that the holes come opposite the contact plugs. The rear lining of the rear wheel brake unit is fitted on the upper part of the shoe.

When bonding, use only adhesive specially manufactured to withstand the high temperatures which arise during prolonged braking. The procedure for bonding varies with the different makes of adhesive and oven, so that a generally applicable description cannot be given. Follow the manufacturer's recommendations.

When riveting, begin at the center of the lining. Use a rivet press and rivet punches corresponding to the size of the rivets. Check that the lining beds down properly along its whole length.

SELF-ADJUSTING DEVICE
Dismantling

1. Press in the contact plug (4, Fig. 8) and check that the key (11) is in its lower position.
2. Disconnect the spring (10) for the key and the spring (2) for the contact plug.
3. Remove the lever (7), key (11), contact plug (4) damping spring (5) and guide lip (8).

322

Assembling

1. Fit the guide lip (8, Fig. 8). Replace the contact plug and fit the new one in position in the brake shoe. Place the key (11) in position with the smooth side towards the guide lip.
2. Press in the contact plug so that the hole in it comes opposite the hole in the brake shoe, and fit the lever (7) and spring (2) for the contact plug.
3. Hook on the spring (10) for the key and fit the dampening spring.

Testing

Testing is carried out as follows. While the contact plug is held pressed in, the key is moved to its outer end position, see Fig. 22, after which the pressure is taken off and the key released. When the contact plug is pressed in again, the spring should be able to pull the key inwards, see Fig. 23. While retaining pressure, the key is moved back to its outer position and the brake shoe is now ready for adjustment of the contact plug.

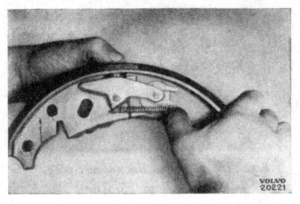

Fig. 22. Testing the self-adjusting device.

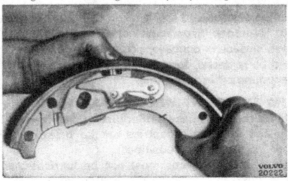

Fig. 23. Testing the self-adjusting device.

Adjusting the Contact Plug

The contact plug is adjusted with the help of a file and an adjusting jig (part number 210030).

With the contact plug in the outer position, the brake shoe is secured in a vice. The lip of the lever (2, Fig. 24) should rest against one of the jaws in order to prevent the plug from being pressed in when adjusting, thus making the adjustment incorrect.

Place the adjusting jig (1) over the contact plug and file this off flush with the jig (see Fig. 24). The plug will then come 0.1 mm (0.039") above the surface of the brake lining.

A jig can be made from sheet steel 0.1 mm thick (1½" x 4½" rectangle).

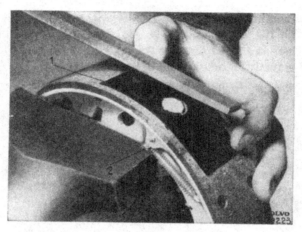

Fig. 24.   Adjusting the contact plug.

1. Adjusting jig   2. Lip

BRAKE DRUM

The friction surface and radial throw of the brake drum should be checked. The radial throw must not exceed 0.15 mm (0.006"). If the friction surface is concave, scratched or cracked, the brake drum should be replaced. Rust spots and minor scratches can be polished or ground off in a machine.

ASSEMBLING THE FRONT WHEEL BRAKE UNIT

1. Check that the key in the self-adjusting device is in its outer position and that the eccentrics on the brake backing plate are turned to their lowest position.

    The self-adjusting devices must not be lubricated since this results in dust and dirt adhering to the parts, impairing the function of the device.

2. Place the rear shoe in position. Fit the flat washer, spring washer, flat washer and locking washer on the adjusting cam stud. Squeeze up the locking washer slightly after fitting.
3. Hook on the return springs to both shoes and fit the front shoe, see Fig. 20. Fit the locking arrangement as described above.
4. Check that the return springs and locking washers are properly in place and that the linings are free from burr, grease and dirt.
5. If the inner front wheel bearing has been removed, fit it in place in the hub. If necessary, pack it with wheel bearing grease. Press in the sealing ring with the help of drift SVO 1798 and standard handle SVO 1801.
6. Fit the hub and brake drum on the steering knuckle. Place on the outer bearing, washer and castle nut. Adjust the bearings by first tightening the nut to a torque of 7 kgm (50 lb. ft.). Then slacken the nut a third of a turn and lock it. Fill the grease cap with grease and fit in with drift SVO 2197.
7. Fit the wheel. Adjust the brake, see under "Adjusting the front wheel brake unit". Lower the vehicle. Tighten the wheel nuts to a torque of 10—14kgm (70—100 lb. ft.). Fit on the hub cap. grease cap with grease and fit in with drift SVO 2197.

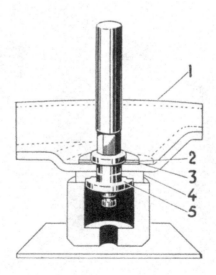

Fig. 25. Removing the stud.

1. Brake backing plate   4. Adjusting cam
2. Internally toothed washer 5. Stud
3. Spacing washer

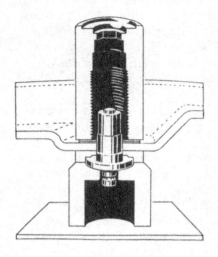

Fig. 26. Fitting the washers.

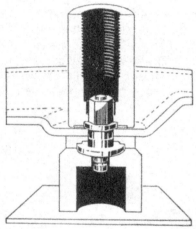

Fig. 27. Pressing together.

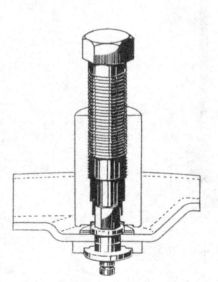

Fig. 28. Removing the tool.

ASSEMBLING THE REAR WHEEL BRAKE UNIT

1. Proceed in accordance with operations 1 and 2 under "Assembling the front wheel brake unit."
2. Hook the return spring onto the shoes, place the front shoe in position in the wheel unit cylinder, turn the shoe outwards, fit the handbrake link and place the shoe in position. Fit the locking arrangement.
3. Fit the lower spring with the help of pliers SVO 1221. Hook on the handbrake cable. Remove the clamp SVO 4074.
4. Check that the springs and locking washers are properly in position and that the linings are free from burr, grease and dirt.
5. Fit the hub, brake drum, washer and castle nut. Lock with a split pin after the nut has been tightened. Fit the wheel. Adjust the brake, see under "Adjusting the rear wheel brake unit." Lower the vehicle. Tighten the wheel nuts to a torque of 10—14 kgm (70—100 lb. ft.). Fit on the hub cap.

Fig. 29. Removing the return spring with brake spring tool (Snap-on BT 11 or corresponding).

ADJUSTING THE FRONT WHEEL BRAKE UNIT

Rotate the wheel backwards and turn the eccentric for the front brake shoe anti-clockwise on the right-hand wheel and clockwise on the left-hand wheel until the wheel is locked by the brake shoe. Then slacken the eccentric just sufficiently so that the wheel can rotate freely. Adjust the rear brake shoe in the same way.

ADJUSTING THE REAR WHEEL BRAKE UNIT

Check that the handbrake is released. Rotate the wheel backwards and turn the eccentric for the front brake shoe anti-clockwise on the right-hand wheel and clockwise on the left-hand wheel until the wheel is locked by the brake shoe. Then slacken the eccentric just sufficiently so that the wheel can rotate freely. Adjust the rear brake shoe by rotating the wheel forwards and applying the eccentric in the opposite direction to the front shoe.

DISMANTLING THE FRONT WHEEL BRAKE UNIT—Late Type

1. Remove the hub cap and slacken the wheel nuts slightly. Lift up the vehicle and block up under the lower control arm. Remove the wheel.

2. Remove the grease cap with tool SVO 2197 (Fig. 17). Remove the split pin and castle nut. Pull off the hub with tool SVO 1791 (Fig. 18). If the inner bearing does not come out with it, pull this off the spindle with tool SVO 1794 (Fig. 19).

3. Fit on the clamp SVO 4074 as shown in Fig. 30 so that the plungers in the wheel unit cylinder cannot be pressed outwards. The procedure for removing the shoes depends on which tool is used.

   The two return springs are first disconnected with a brake spring tool as shown in Fig. 29, after which the locking clamps are removed and the shoes lifted off together with the adjusting device.

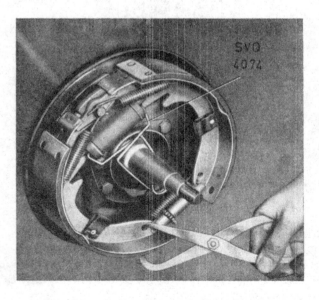

Fig. 30. Removing the locking spring.

The locking spring is disconnected with the help of the brake spring pliers as shown in Fig. 30. Pull apart the shoes and remove the adjusting device. Hold against the guide pin on the rear side of the brake backing plate and remove the locking clamp. Turn the shoe outwards until the push rod of the wheel unit cylinder is released, see Fig. 31. Then turn the shoe inwards until the return spring can be disconnected and the shoe lifted off. Remove the other shoe in the same way.

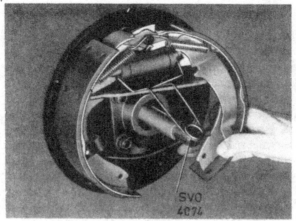

Fig. 31. Removing the brake shoe.

DISMANTLING THE REAR WHEEL BRAKE UNIT

1. Apply the handbrake. Remove the hub cap. Remove the split pin and slacken the castle nut and wheel nuts slightly. Lift up the vehicle and block up under the rear axle. Remove the wheel.
2. Release the handbrake. Remove the castle nut. Pull off the hub with tool SVO 1791 (Fig. 18).
3. Place the clamp SVO 4074 over the wheel unit cylinder so that the plungers cannot be pressed outwards. Disconnect the handbrake cable from the lever. The procedure when removing the shoes depends on which tool is used. With a brake spring tool as shown in Fig. 29, the two return springs are first disconnected, after which the locking clamps are removed and the shoes lifted off together with the adjusting device. With the help of brake pliers, the locking spring is disconnected as shown in Fig. 30. Pull apart the shoes and remove the locking clamp for the rear shoe. Turn the shoe outwards until the push rod from the wheel unit cylinder together with the handbrake link are released, see Fig. 31. Then turn the shoe inwards until the return spring can be disconnected and the shoe lifted off. Remove the other shoe in the same way.

REPLACING THE BRAKE LININGS

The vehicle can be equipped with different types of brake lining. The linings can be riveted or bonded onto the shoes, the primary shoes can have long or short linings and the linings can be of two different qualities. These can be differentiated since the earlier type is marked brown or green and stamped H 3142. **In order to avoid uneven braking effect, both wheels on the same shaft must have the same type of brake lining.**

In case of unavailability of shoes with lining applied the brake linings are replaced as follows.

Riveted Brake Linings

Remove the old linings by pressing out the rivets in a rivet press. Then wash the shoes in clean solvent and dry them.

Fit ready-made original linings. **When doing this, note that the thicker and eccentrically ground linings which are marked on the wearing side as shown in Fig. 32, should be fitted on the rear brake shoes (secondary shoes) of the front wheels. The thicker part (marked) should face upwards. On types with shorter primary linings, these are fitted as shown in Figs. 10 and 11 respectively.**

Use rivet sizes in accordance with those given in the specifications. Begin riveting at the middle of the lining and make sure that the lining beds down properly on the shoe along its whole length. Use a rivet press and rivet drifts corresponding to the rivet sizes.

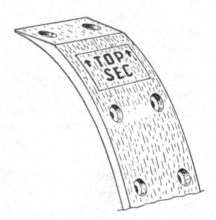

Fig. 32.   Rear brake lining of front wheel.

Bonded Brake Linings

The old linings should preferably be removed in a band-type grinding machine.

They can also be chiseled off, after which the brake shoe be cleaned up with emery cloth. In both cases care should be taken to ensure that the shoe is not damaged. After cleaning up, the shoe should be washed in clean solvent and then allowed to dry. After this, the contact surface for the lining must not be touched or made dirty.

For bonding purposes use only adhesives which are specially made to withstand the high temperatures arising during prolonged braking. Volvo original brake linings are ready-prepared with suitable quantities of such adhesive. The procedure when bonding varies with different makes of oven so that a generally applicable description cannot be given. Follow the manufacturer's instructions carefully.

When fitting, make sure that the lining does not come diagonally on the shoe and that it is placed as shown in Figs. 34 and 35 respectively. ¼" linings (part number 661279) should be fitted on the rear brake shoes (secondary shoes) of the front wheels and ³⁄₁₆" linings on the others.

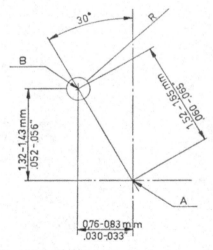

Fig. 33. Eccentricity for brake lining 661279.

After bonding, the linings should be ground to the correct measurements. Since the rear brake linings of the front wheels must be ground eccentrically, this requires a grinding machine which can be specially adjusted for this type of lining. There are different types of these machines, so that the grinding procedure varies accordingly. Fig. 33, shows how much the pivoting center

331

should be displaced in relation to the brake shoe center when grinding the eccentric lining (part number 661279). For other linings the pivoting center coincides with the brake shoe center. The grinding radius (R) equals half the diameter of the brake drum less 0.1—0.2 mm (0.004—0.008''). Machines which are graduated for the drum diameter should thus be set to a value which is 0.2—0.4 mm (0.008—0.016'') less than the diameter of the brake drum. Before the linings are ground they should be chamfered.

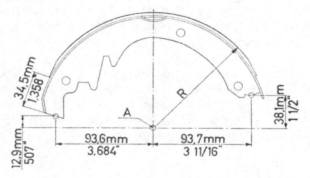

Fig. 35. Adjusting measurements for brake shoe, rear wheel.

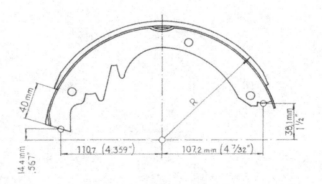

Fig. 34. Adjusting measurement for brake shoe, front wheel.

BRAKE DRUM

The friction surface and radial throw of the brake drums should be checked. The radial throw must not exceed 0.15 mm (0.006''). If the friction surface is concave, scored or cracked, the brake drum must be replaced. Rust spots and minor scratches can, however, be polished or ground off in a machine.

ASSEMBLING THE FRONT WHEEL BRAKE UNIT

1. Check, and if necessary, face the surface of the lips on the brake backing plate against which the shoes and centering block slide. Clean up the sliding surfaces on the shoes and centering block. Coat the surfaces with a very thin layer of heat-resistant grease. Place the centering block (3, Fig. 10) in position with the rounded side forwards **when the stamped-in arrow should point in the direction of rotation of the brake drum.** Place on the guide washer (5).

2. Hold the front shoe in place so that the return spring can be hooked on. Turn the shoe outwards so that the wheel unit cylinder push rod can be placed in position, see Fig. 36. Fit the guide pin (8) and clip (7).

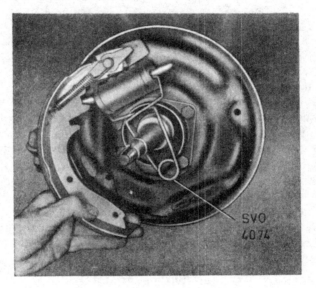

Fig. 36.   Fitting brake shoe.

Fit the rear shoe in the same way. Remove the clamp SVO 4074. Fit the adjusting device and its locking spring. If a brake spring tool as shown in Fig. 37 is available, it is possible to begin instead by fitting the adjusting device and locking spring, after which the shoes are placed in position. The locking clips are then fitted and the return springs hooked on with the pointed end of the tool, see Fig. 37.

3. Check that the springs and locking clamps are located properly, that the linings are free from burr, grease and dirt and that the thicker part of the lining on the rear shoe is turned upwards.

Fig. 37. Hooking on return springs.

4. If the inner front wheel bearing has been removed it should be placed in position in the hub. If necessary, pack with wheel bearing grease. Press in the sealing ring with the help of drift SVO 1798 and standard handle SVO 1801.

5. Fit the hub with cleaned brake drum on the spindle. Place on the outer bearing, washer and castle nut. Adjust the bearings by first tightening the nut to a torque of 7 kgm (50 lb. ft.) Then slacken the nut a third of a turn and lock it. Fill the grease cap with grease and fit it with drift SVO 2197.

6, Fit the wheel. Adjust the brakes, see under "Adjusting the wheel nuts to a torque of 10—14 kgm (70—100 lb. ft.) Fit on the hub cap.

ASSEMBLING THE REAR WHEEL BRAKE UNIT

1. Proceed in accordance with operations 1 and 2 under "Assembling the front wheel brake unit."
   Place the handbrake link with spring in position in the front shoe before fitting the rear shoe. Connect on the handbrake cable.

2. Check that the springs and locking clips are properly located and that the linings are free from burr, grease and dirt.

3. Fit the hub with cleaned brake drum, washer and castle nut. Fit the wheel. Adjust the brakes, see under "Adjusting the wheel brake units." Lower the vehicle. Lock the castle nut with a split pin after the nut has been tightened properly. Tighten the wheel nuts to a torque of 10—14 kgm (70—100 lb. ft.). Fit on the hub cap.

ADJUSTING THE WHEEL BRAKE UNITS

The brakes should be checked and if necessary adjusted every 5,000 km (3,000 miles).

If it is suspected that the linings are worn out, remove the brake drum for checking this. The adjusting device permits adjustment to be carried out even when the linings are worn down to the rivets. Such wear can cause the rivets to damage the drums. Regular examination of the linings should be carried out every 20,000 km (12,500 miles), and more frequently in the case of hard driving.

Adjusting is carried out as follows:

1. Lift up the vehicle and block up under the control arms or rear axle. Release the hand brake.
2. Remove the rubber seal, insert a screwdriver into the recess and apply the brake shoes by moving the screwdriver upwards as shown in Fig. 38. Turn the notched wheel of the adjusting screw until the brake drum is locked.

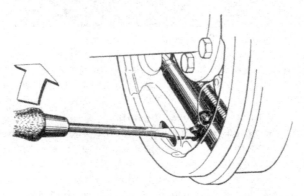

Fig. 38.   Adjusting the wheel brake unit.

3. Turn back the adjusting screw 8 notches. Then check that the drum can rotate freely. If not, depress the brake pedal in order to center the shoes. If this does not help, turn the adjusting screw back a further 2 notches. Repeat the procedure until the drum can rotate freely. Fit the rubber seal.

DISC BRAKES
Replacing the Pad Assemblies

The pad assemblies should be replaced when there is about 3 mm (⅛") left of the lining thickness. In no circumstances may the linings be worn down to under 15. mm (¹⁄₁₆").

1. Remove the hub cap and slacken the wheel nuts slightly.

2. Lift up the front end and block up under the lower control arms. Screw off the wheel nuts and lift down the wheel.
3. Remove the hairpin-shaped locking clips and guide pins for the pads. Pull out the pads as shown in Fig. 39.

Fig. 39. Removing the pads.

4. Press in the plungers of the wheel unit cylinders carefully and fit the new pads. When doing this, note that the brake fluid level in the master cylinder rises and may run over. Re-fit the guide pins and locking clips.
5. **Operate the brake pedal repeatedly and check that the movement feels normal.** It is not generally necessary to carry out bleeding after replacing the pads.
6. Lift on the wheel after having cleaned the contact surfaces between the wheel and hub free from grit and dirt, and then screw up the nuts so that the wheel cannot be disturbed on the hub. Lower the vehicle and tighten the wheel nuts. Tighten every other nut until all of them are tightened to a torque of 10—14 kgm (70—100 lb. ft.). Fit the hub cap.

RECONDITIONING THE WHEEL UNIT CYLINDERS
Removing
1. Remove the wheel, see operations 1—2 under "Replacing the pad assemblies."
2. Clean the front wheel brake unit externally.
3. Unscrew the brake line (3, Fig. 40) and plug the connection. Brake fluid must not be allowed to get onto the brake disc or pads. Bend up the locking washer (6) and screw out the attaching bolts (4 and 5). Lift off the brake unit complete, see Fig. 41.

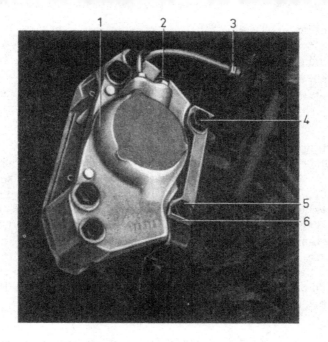

Fig. 40.   Front wheel brake unit.

1. Housing   4. Attaching bolt
2. Air-venting nipple 5. Attaching bolt
3. Brake line   6. Locking washer

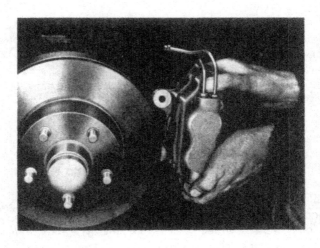

Fig. 41.   Removing the front wheel brake unit.

Dismantling

1. Remove the hairpin-shaped locking clips, (11, Fig. 14) and guide pins (1). Pull out the pads (9).
2. Remove the plungers and pull off the rubber dust covers (8).
3. Take out the packings (3) from the cylinders with the help of a blunt tool. Be careful to avoid damaging the edges of the grooves.

Inspecting

Before inspecting, all parts should be washed in alcohol or hydraulic fluid. The plungers and cylinders should be inspected carefully. There must be no scoring, scratches or rust spots on the polished surface. Damaged plungers must be replaced. Minor damage in the cylinders can generally be put right by honing. When doing this, the two halves of the brake are taken apart. The procedure varies with different types of machines, so that no general description can be given. Follow the manufacturer's instructions carefully. Clean the cylinders thoroughly after honing and check that the channels are clear.

Assembling

1. Coat the working surfaces of the plungers and cylinders with brake fluid.
2. Fit new packings (3, Fig. 14) into the cylinders. Place the rubber dust covers (8) in position and make sure that they enter the cylinder grooves.
3. Fit the plunger with the closed end first. Press the plunger right in and make sure that the rubber dust covers enter the plunger grooves.
4. Place the pads (9) in position. If the two halves of the brake unit have been taken apart, fit these together. Tighten the inner, larger attaching bolts (12) to a torque of 6.2—7 kgm (45—50 lb. ft.) and the outer, smaller bolts (13) to a torque of 3.5—5.2 kgm (25—30 lb. ft.) Fit the guide pins and locking clips.

Fitting

Check that the contact surfaces on the front wheel brake unit and retainer are clean and undamaged since it is vital that the brake unit is located correctly in relation to the brake disc. Fit the brake unit, see Fig. 40.

Check that the brake disc runs freely between the pads. Place on the locking washer (6) and tighten the attaching bolts (4 and 5) and lock them. Connect the brake line (3) and air-vent the wheel unit cylinders. Fit the wheel, see operation 6 under "Replacing the pad assemblies."

BRAKE DISC

The brake disc should be examined as regards the friction surface, run-out and thickness. There must be no rust spots or scoring on the friction surface. The run-out must not exceed 0.1 mm (0.004") and should be measured as shown in Fig. 42. First check that the wheel bearings are correctly adjusted and that the disc fits securely on the hub. The thickness should not vary more than 0.03 mm (0.0012") when the disc is rotated one turn, since this can cause a vibrating brake pedal.

Fig. 42. Checking run-out.

The brake disc can be reconditioned by fine turning or fine grinding. Machining should be done together with the hub. After machining, the thickness of the disc must not be less than 12.2 mm (0.4803"). After reconditioning, the disc must not have a runout exceeding 0.10 mm (0.004") and its thickness must not vary more than 0.03 mm (0.0012").

If the brake disc cannot be put in order in accordance with the above, or if there are cracks or similar damage, the disc together with the hub should be replaced. "Replacing or adjusting the front wheel bearings."

When replacing the wheel studs, the old stud is pressed out after which an oversize stud is fitted. Before the stud can be pressed through the hole in the brake disc, this must be drilled out to 16.6—16.8 mm (0.653—0.661").

REAR WHEEL BRAKE UNIT, ON VEHICLES FITTED WITH DISC BRAKES AT FRONT

Dismantling

1. Remove the hub cap and the split pin in the drive shaft. Slacken the castle nut and wheel nuts slightly. Lift up the vehicle and block up underneath the rear axle. Remove the wheel.
2. Release the handbrake. Pull off the hub with tool SVO 1791, see Fig. 18.
3. Place clamp SVO 4074 over the wheel unit cylinder so that the plungers cannot be pressed outwards. Remove the upper return spring with the help of brake pliers. Pull down the front shoe into the groove on the brake backing plate, hold against the guide pin on the back of the plate and turn and remove the locking washer. Lift off the shoe, see Fig. 43.

Fig. 43. Removing the brake shoe.

4. Remove the rear shoe in a similar manner and disconnect the handbrake cable. Unhook the return springs and if necessary the handbrake link.
5. Screw in the adjusting screw slightly. Remove the adjusting plungers, see Fig. 44.

REPLACING BRAKE LININGS

The brake linings should be replaced at the latest when they are worn down level with the rivet heads. If shoes with linings applied are unavailable:

Fig. 44. Removing the adjusting plunger.

1. Press out the rivets with a special drift in a rivet press. Then wash the shoes clean and dry them.
2. Rivet on the ready-manufactured original linings. The front lining is placed at the bottom of the shoe and the rear one on top, see Fig. 45. Use rivets in accordance with the specications and a rivet press with suitable drifts. Begin to rivet at the center and continue outwards towards the ends. Check after riveting that the brake lining beds down properly along its whole length.
3. In order to obtain best results, the linings should be ground in a special grinding machine. When doing this, make sure that the linings have a radius 0.2—0.4 mm (0.008—0.016") smaller than that of the brake drum.

BRAKE DRUM

The friction surface and radial throw of the brake drums should be checked. The radial throw must not exceed 0.15 mm (0.006"). If the friction surface is concave, scored or cracked, the brake drum must be replaced. Rust spots and minor scratches, can, however, be cleaned up in a machine.

ASSEMBLING

1. Screw back the adjusting screw and fit the cleaned adjusting plungers after having coated them lightly with heat-resistant grease. Check that the plungers move easily.
2. Fit the lever onto the rear brake shoe. Hook on the handbrake cable and return springs. Place the shoe in position and fit the guide pin and locking clip. Make sure that the head of the guide pin enters the recess in the clip.

3. Place the handbrake link in position and make sure that it is turned the right way round. Hook on the lower return spring and fit the front brake shoe with guide pin and locking clip. Hook on the upper return spring with brake pliers. Remove SVO 4074. Fit the spring clip (5, Fig. 45).

4. Check that the key is fitted in the drive shaft and fit the hub with brake drum. Place on the washer and tighten the castle nut. If the wheel unit cylinder has been removed , this should be air-vented. See under "Bleeding the hydraulic system." Lift on the wheel after having cleaned the contact surfaces between the wheel and hub free from dirt and grit, and tighten the nuts sufficiently so that the wheel cannot be disturbed on the hub. Adjust the brakes, see under "Adjusting the wheel brake units." Lower the vehicle and tighten the wheel nuts. Tighten every other nut a little at a time till all are tightened to a torque of 10—14 kgm (70—100 lb. ft.). Tighten the castle nut finally and lock with a split pin. Fit the hub cap.

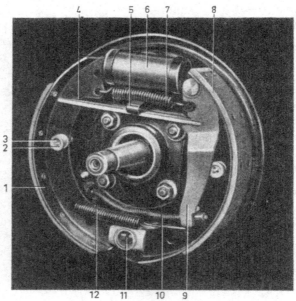

Fig. 45. Rear wheel brake unit.

1.	Front brake shoe	7.	Upper return spring
2.	Locking washer	8.	Rear brake shoe
3.	Guide pin	9.	Lever
4.	Link	10.	Return spring for lever
5.	Spring clip	11.	Adjusting spring for lever
6.	Wheel unit cylinder	12.	Lower return spring

ADJUSTING THE WHEEL BRAKE UNITS

The front wheel disc brakes are so designed that the linings always stand at a certain minimum distance from the brake disc regardless of wear. The front wheel brake units are therefore self-adjusting and it is not necessary to carry out any manual adjustment of the pad assemblies.

If the brake pedal goes far down towards the floorboard when braking, this generally means that the brake linings on the rear wheel are worn and that the brake shoes require adjusting. If it is suspected that the linings are worn out, the brake drum should be removed for checking this. The adjusting device permits further adjustment even if the linings are worn down to the rivets, and this situation can lead to the rivets damaging the drum. The linings should be inspected regularly at least every 20,000 km (12,500 miles), and more frequently in the case of hard driving. Adjusting is carried out as follows:

1. Lift up the rear end and block up under the rear axle. Release the handbrake.

2. Turn the adjusting screw (1, Fig. 46) clockwise until the brake drum locks.
   Then slacken the screw until the drum can rotate freely.

3. Adjust the other rear wheel in the same way. Lower the vehicle.

*Fig. 46.   Adjusting device for rear wheel
brake unit.*

1. Adjusting screw

Fig. 47.   Brake parts.

1. Brake line, rear wheels
2. Connection
3. Brake line, left front wheel
4. Brake contact
5. Brake line, right front wheel
6. Brake line, master cylinder
7. Filling cap
8. Master cylinder
9. Attaching bolt

Fig. 48.   Checking the clearance.

1. Master cylinder
2. Plunger
3. Feeler gauge

MASTER CYLINDER, EARLY PRODUCTION
Removing
1. Remove the split pin and stud for the brake pedal. Disconnect the return spring. Remove the rubber cover.
2. Slacken the connection for the brake line. Collect up the brake fluid which runs out. Remove the two attaching bolts for the master cylinder. Take out the master cylinder carefully. Avoid spilling brake fluid onto the paintwork since this can cause damage.

Dismantling
1. Remove the cap and empty out the brake fluid.
2. Bend back the rubber cover (4, Fig. 2) and remove the locking ring (6), washer and push rod (5). Shake out the parts from the cylinder. Bend up the locking ring on the spring retainer (10) which is placed on the plunger (3) and separate the parts. Remember that the spring (11) is under tension.

Inspecting
Before inspecting, all the parts of the master cylinder should be washed in alcohol or hydraulic fluid.

The cylinder should be inspected thoroughly internally. There must be no scoring, scratches or rust spots on the polished surface.

The clearance between the plunger and cylinder must not exceed 0.15 mm (0.06") and this can be measured as shown in Fig. 48. If the clearance exceeds 0.15 mm (0.006"), test with a new plunger. If this does not help, the master cylinder must be replaced.

Asembling
1. Fit the packings onto the plunger (3, Fig. 2) and valve (13).
2. Assemble the valve. Turn the convex part of the spring washer to face the packing.
3. Fit the spring and spring retainer (3, Fig. 49) onto the push rod (4) and assemble these parts to the plunger, see Fig. 49. Then press down the locking piece (2) on the spring retainer so that the parts are held in position.
4. Dip the packing and plunger in brake fluid and fit them into the cylinder. Fit the push rod, (5, Fig. 2), washer and locking ring (6).

Fitting
Fitting is done in the reverse order to removing. Do not forget the split pin in the pedal stud. Fill up with brake fluid and air-vent the system in accordance with the instructions under "Bleeding the brake system."

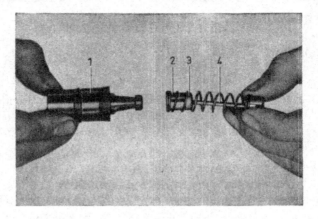

Fig. 49. Assembling the plunger.

1. Plunger   3. Spring retainer
2. Locking piece   4. Push rod

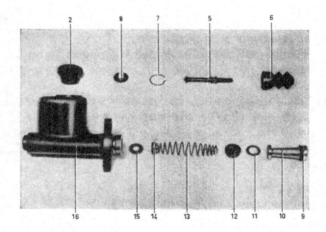

Fig. 50. Master cylinder, late production.

2. Cap   11. Washer
5. Push rod   12. Packing
6. Rubber cover   13. Spring
7. Locking ring   14. Valve
8. Stop washer   15. Washer
9. Packing   16. Cylinder housing
10. Plunger

MASTER CYLINDER, LATE PRODUCTION
Removing

See "Master cylinder, early production."

Dismantling

1. Unscrew the cap (2, Figs. 4 and 50) and empty out the brake fluid.
2. Bend back the rubber cover (6) and remove the locking ring (7), washer (8) and push rod (5). Shake all the parts out of the cylinder, see Fig. 50.

Before inspecting, all the master cylinder parts should be washed in alcohol or hydraulic fluid. The cylinder must be examined thoroughly internally. There must be no scoring, scratches or rust spots on the polished surface. Such damage can as a rule be eliminated by honing the cylinder. The procedure for this varies with different machines so that no general description can be given. Therefore follow the manufacturer's instructions. Clean the cylinder thoroughly after honing and check that the holes are clear.

The clearance between the plunger and cylinder must not exceed 0.20 mm (0.008") which can be measured with a feeler gauge as shown in Fig. 48. If the clearance exceeds 0.20 mm (0.008"), test with a new plunger. If this does not help, the master cylinder must be replaced.

Examine the packings, valves and other parts for wear and damage. Damaged or worn parts must be replaced.

Assembling

1. Fit the washer (15, Fig. 50), in the bottom of the cylinder.
2. Place the packing (12) on the spring guide. Dip the packing in brake fluid and fit it together with the spring and valve. Place the washer (11) into the cylinder.
3. Pull the packing (9) onto the plunger and turn it as shown in the figure. Dip the plunger in brake fluid and fit it. Take care to see that the packing (9) is not damaged. It is best to use a piece of brass foil formed into a ring to act as a guide for the packing, see Fig. 51. Compress the spring and fit the push rod (5), washer (8) and locking ring (7).
   Check that the equalizing hole is clear by inserting a piece of 0.5 mm (25 gauge) wire through the hole, see Fig. 52. It should then be posible to press the plunger in approx. 0.5 mm (0.02") before the wire is gripped. Take care not to damage the packing. Also check that there is clearance for the push rod (5).
5. Fit the rubber cover (6).

Fitting

Fitting is done in the reverse order to removing. Do not forget the split pin in the pedal stud. Fill up with brake fluid and bleed in accordance with the instructions under "Bleeding the brake system."

Fig. 51. Fitting the plunger.

1. Plunger   2. Brass foil   3. Master cylinder

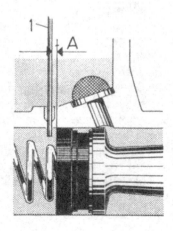

Fig. 52. Checking the equalizing hole.

1. 0.5 mm (25 gauge) wire   A = approx. 0.5 mm (0.02")

WHEEL UNIT CYLINDER

Concerning the wheel unit cylinders of the disc brakes, see under "Front wheel brake unit, disc brakes."

REMOVING DRUM BRAKES, LATE PRODUCTION

1. Remove the hub, see under "Dismantling the wheel brake unit."
2. Place clamp SVO 4047 over the wheel unit cylinder. Move the brake shoes to one side with the help of a screwdriver in order to release the push rods from the shoes, see Fig. 53.

Fig. 53. Removing the wheel unit cylinder.

3. Disconnect the brake lines and unscrew the wheel unit clyinder attaching bolts. Lift off the wheel unit cylinder but make sure that no brake fluid gets onto the linings.

REMOVING, REMAINDER

1. Remove the hub and brake shoes, see under "Dismantling the wheel brake unit."
2. Disconnect the brake line and unscrew the wheel unit cylinder attaching bolts. Lift off the wheel unit cylinder.

RECONDITIONING

Remove the clip, pull off the rubber seals and take out plungers, packings and springs.

349

The cylinder must be examined thoroughly internally. There must be no scoring, scratches, or rust spots on the polished surface. Such damage can as a rule be eliminated by honing the cylinder. Since the procedure for this varies with different machines, follow the instructions of the manufacturer concerned. Clean the cylinder thoroughly after honing, when the bleed nipple should be removed.

The clearance between the plunger and cylinder must not exceed 0.25 mm (0.010") which is measured as shown in Fig. 54. If the clearance exceeds 0.25 mm (0.010"), test with a new plunger. If this does not help, the wheel unit cylinder must be replaced.

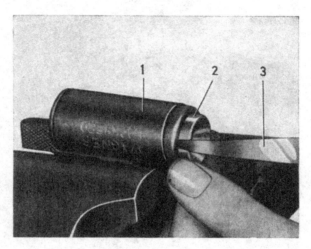

Fig. 54.   Checking the clearance.

1. Wheel unit cylinder   2. Plunger   3. Feeler gauge

Examine the packings and other parts for wear and damage. Damaged or worn parts must be replaced.

Assemble the parts in the reverse order to dismantling. When doing this, dip the plungers and packings in brake fluid.

FITTING

Fitting is done in the reverse order to removing. When working on both front and rear wheel unit cylinders of late production, remember that the front cylinder has a diameter of 1" and the rear of 13⁄16". Bleed the wheel unit cylinder as the final operation.

BLEEDING THE HYDRAULIC SYSTEM

An indication that there is air in the system is that the brake pedal can be depressed with very little resistance or that it feels

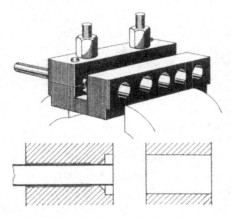

Fig. 55. *Flanging a brake pipe.*

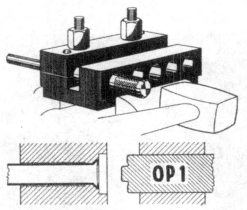

Fig. 56. *Flanging a brake pipe.*

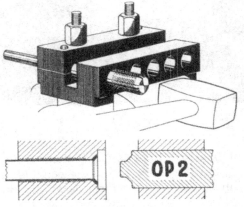

Fig. 57. *Flanging a brake pipe.*

351

"spongy." After any part of the system has been removed for repairs, air-venting must be carried out. Air can also enter the system if there is insufficient brake fluid in the container. If, for example, only one wheel unit cylinder has been removed, it is usually sufficient just to bleed this. If, on the other hand, the master cylinder or lines from this have been removed, then the whole system must be bled.

Bleeding the whole brake system is carried out as follows:

1. Clean around the filling cap on the master cylinder. Screw off the cap and top up with brake fluid if necessary.
2. Clean the bleed nipple. Place the key with hose on the nipple and let the other end of the hose hang down in the fluid in a collecting vessel, see Fig. 58. For front wheel brake units of early production, key SVO 2280 is used, for disc brakes SVO 2381, and for other brakes SVO 1431. An adjustable wrench can be used in an emergency.

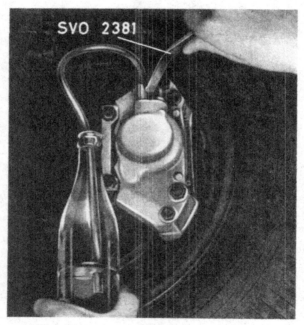

Fig. 58.   Air-venting the disc brakes.

3. Open the nipple and have someone depress the brake pedal gradually. Close the nipple before the pedal is released, otherwise air can be sucked in if there is no non-return valve between the master cylinder and lines. Repeat this procedure as long as there are air bubbles in the fluid running out.

4. Air-vent the other wheels in the same way. Check between every wheel that there is sufficient brake fluid in the container.

BRAKE PEDAL
Adjusting the Pedal Position
When the brake pedal is released, it should take up the same position as the clutch pedal. The position is adjusted by slackening the locknut and turning the push rod for the master cylinder. Do not forget to tighten the locknut.
Replacing the Pedal and Bushings
See under "Reconditioning pedal shaft," in clutch chapter.

HANDBRAKE
Replacing the Handbrake Cable
Removing
1. Apply the handbrake, remove the hub cap, slacken the wheel nuts and castle nut.
2. Lift up the rear end, block up under the rear axle and remove the wheel. Release the handbrake.
3. Pull off the brake drum and hub with puller SVO 1791, see Fig. 18. Disconnect the cable from the brake shoe lever.
4. Remove the bolts of the cable casing attachment on the brake backing plate or the locking spring if the brakes are of early production. Remove the cable casing front attachment with rubber sleeve. Disconnect the cable from the clevis and pull out the cable forwards. In the case of older type cables (up to chassis number 534), this is pulled first backwards so that the locking washer can be removed. If the guide sleeve and locking washer do not come out with the cable, knock the guide sleeve to the rear with a narrow drift.

Fitting
1. Fit the rubber sleeve over the cable casing and connect the cable to the clevis.
2. Thread the sealing ring over the cable spring (does not apply to cables with locking springs). Insert the cable through the brake backing plate. On older type cables the guide sleeve and locking washer are then fitted. Connect the cable to the brake shoe lever.
3. Place on the locking spring or tighten the bolts, whichever the case may be. Fit the cable casing front attachment and make sure that the clamp enters the groove on the sleeve. If necessary, slacken the adjusting nuts. Fit the rubber sleeve in its bracket.

4. Fit on the hub with brake drum and wheel. Tighten the castle nut and wheel nuts sufficiently for the drum and wheel to come into the correct position.
5. Adjust the handbrake. Lower the vehicle and tighten the wheel nuts to a torque of 10—14 kgm (70—100 lb. ft.) Tighten and lock the castle nut. Fit on the hub cap.

REPLACING THE RUBBER COVER

If the handbrake cable rubber cover has been damaged for any reason, it must be replaced, otherwise water and dirt can penetrate, causing rusting.

For this purpose there is a special rubber cover with sealing plug (part numbers 86850 and 86851 respectively). When re-placing, the pull rod is disconnected from lever and the cable disconnected from the clevis. Cut off the old cover and thread on the new one. Connect the cable to the clevis and re-fit the pull rod. Place the slotted sealing plug (1, Fig. 59) onto the cable (2) and press it into the rubber casing (3).

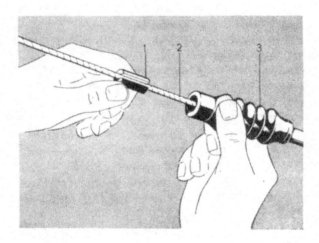

Fig. 59. Fitting the rubber cover.

1. Sealing plug   2. Cable   3. Rubber cover

REPLACING THE HANDBRAKE LEVER OR CATCH PARTS

1. Lift up the rear end and block up the rear axle.
2. Remove the split pin and pull the cables so that the pull rod (2, Fig. 16) can be removed from the lever. Remove the bearing support (1).
3. Turn back the floor mat and remove the rubber cover over the ratchet segment. Remove the ratchet segment.

4. Move the brake lever (15) towards the center of the vehicle until it releases at the outer bearing. Remove the rubber seal and pull out the handbrake lever forwards with shaft and lever, see Fig. 60.

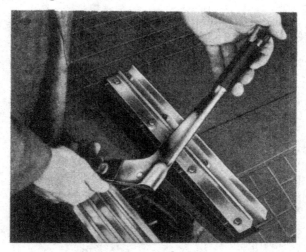

Fig. 60. Removing the handbrake lever.

5. Screw out the locking screw (18) and remove the loop (20) and button (19). Take the spring out of the lever. Remove the pin (13) and take out the push rod (16) and pawl (12).
6. Fit the new parts in the reverse order. Make sure that the pin is properly secured without the movement of the pawl being affected. Lubricate the bushings with a thin layer of ball bearing grease. Do not forget to lock the pull rod and ensure that the rubber on the shaft seals properly.

ADJUSTING THE HANDBRAKE

The handbrake should give full effect at the 4th—5th ratchet notch. If not, the handbrake should be adjusted. Before adjusting, make sure that the fault is not in the wheel brake units. On vehicles with late production wheel brake units (without self-adjusting), the rear wheel brakes should therefore be adjusted first.

The handbrake is adjusted by moving the clevis on the pull rod, see Fig. 61. Tighten the nuts properly after adjusting.

FAULT TRACING

No or Poor Braking Effect

Insufficient brake fluid in the system. Top up with brake fluid. Check for leakage. Air-vent.

Air in the hydraulic system. Air-vent the system.

Leakage in the hydraulic system. Check and repair the leakage. Air-vent.

Defective master cylinder. Recondition the master cylinder. Incorrectly adjusted brakes. Adjust the brakes.

Unsuitable brake linings. Change over to original brake linings.

Grease or oil on the brake linings. Replace the brake linings. Check the sealing ring.

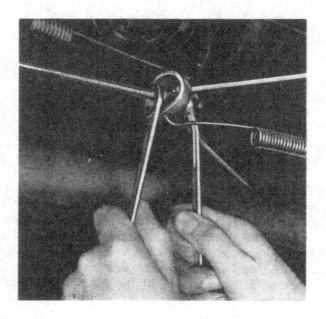

Fig. 61.   Adjusting handbrake.

REPLACING THE HANDBRAKE CABLES—1800
Removing
1. Apply the handbrake, remove the hub cap, slacken the wheel nuts and castle nut.
2. Jack up the rear end, place blocks under the rear axles and remove the whels. Release the handbrake.
3. Pull off the brake drum and hub with puller SVO 1791, see Fig. 7-14. Unhook the cable from the brake shoe lever.
4. Loosen the screws at the cable sleeve attachment in the brake backing plate. Remove the front attachment of the cable sleeve with support rubber. Unhook the cable from the clevis and pull the cable forwards.

Fig. 7-14. Removing the hub

Fitting

1. Place the rubber support on the cable sleeves. Insert the cable into the brake backing plate and hook it onto the lever.
2. Hook the cable onto the clevis.
3. Tighten the bolt in the brake backing plate. Fit the cable sleeve front attachment and ensure that the clamp enters the groove on the sleeve. If necessary, slacken the adjusting nut. Fit the support rubber in its bracket.
4. Fit on the hub with brake drum and wheels. Tighten the castle nut and wheel nuts sufficiently for the drum and wheel to position correctly.
5. Adjust the handbrake. Lower the car and tighten the wheel nuts to a torque of 70—100 lb. ft. (10-14 kgm.). Tighten and lock the castle nuts. Fit on the hub caps.

REPLACING THE BRAKE LEVER
OR RATCHET PART—1800

1. Release the handbrake and remove the protective cover over the segment.
2. Remove the split pin and washer at the shaft lever (6 Fig. 7-31). Turn the pull-rod (7) so that it can be removed from the handbrake lever. Remove the ratchet segment (1).
3. Unscrew the bolts for the support attachment (8) and drive out the stud and attachment. Lift off the lever (3).
4. Unscrew the locking screw and remove the yoke (5) and button (4). Take out the spring from the lever. Remove the rivet (2) and take out the thrust rod (6, Fig. 7-9) and pawl (18).
5. Fit the new parts in the reverse order. Ensure that the rivet is secure but without interfering with the movement of the pawl. Lubricate the bushings with a thin coating of ball-bearing grease. Do not forget to lock the pull-rod.

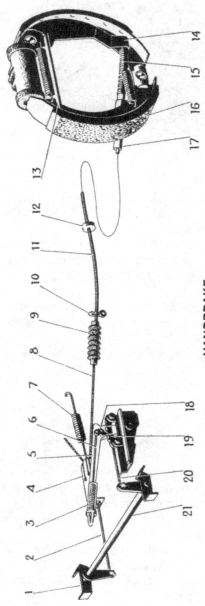

HANDBRAKE

1. Support attachment
2. Pull-rod
3. Spring
4. Clevis (early production)
5. Handbrake lever
6. Thrust rod
7. Return spring
8. Handbrake cable
9. Rubber cover
10. Attachment for outer casing
11. Outer casing
12. Bushing
13. Link
14. Lever
15. Return spring
16. Brake shoe
17. Sleeve
18. Pawl
19. Toothed segment
20. Pull-rod
21. Shaft

REPLACING THE HANDBRAKE SHAFT—1800

1. Lift up the rear end and place blocks under the rear axle.
2. Release the handbrake and disconnect the pull-rod (7, Fig. 7-31) from the shaft lever (6).
3. Remove the split pin and stretch the cables so that the pull-rod (2, Fig. 7-9) can be removed from the shaft lever. Remove the support attachment and lift off the shaft (21).
4. Lubricate the bushings in the new shaft with a thin coating of ball bearing grease. Check that the studs of the support attachments are undamaged. Fit the shaft in the reverse order to removing.

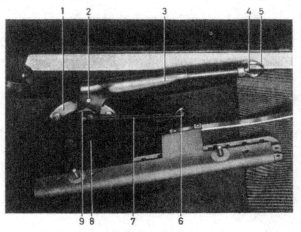

Fig. 7-31. Handbrake lever

1. Ratchet segment	4. Button	7. Pull-rod
2. Rivet	5. Yoke	8. Support attachment
3. Handbrake lever	6. Lever	9. Lever

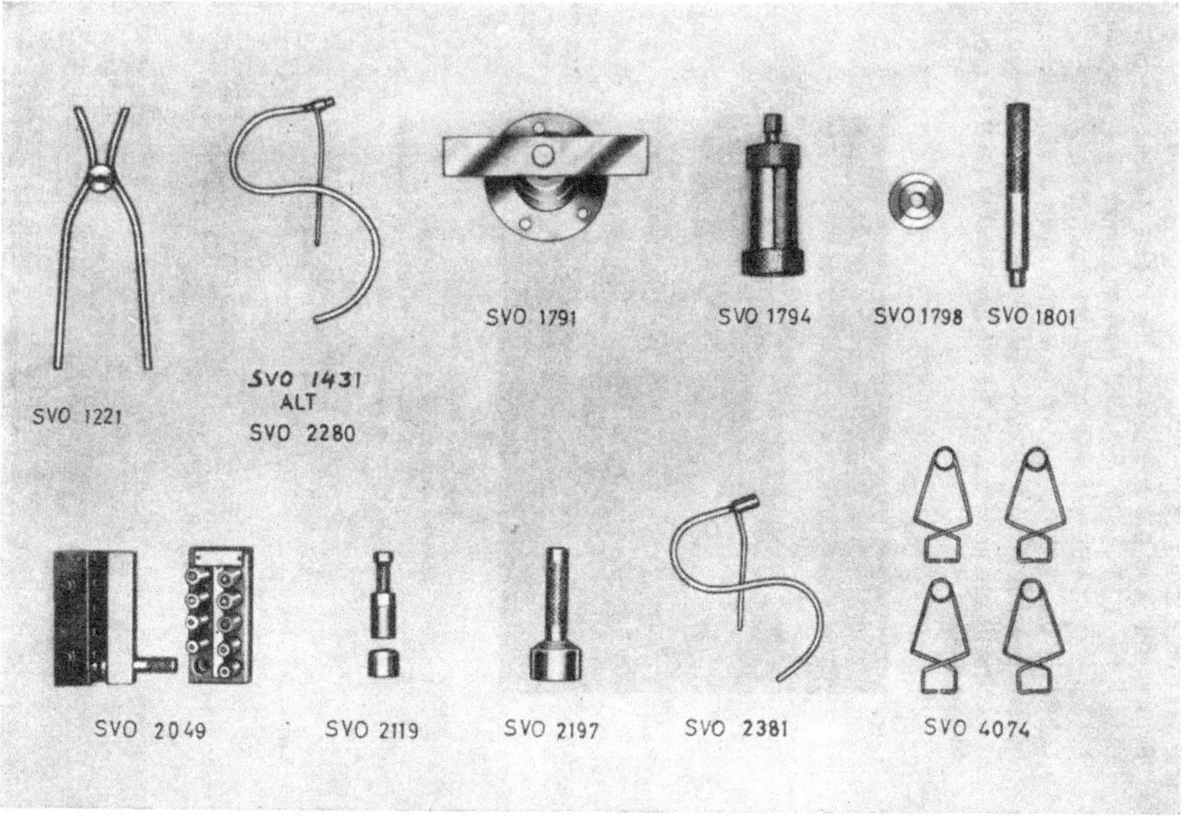

SVO 1798   SVO 1801

SVO 4074

SVO 1794

SVO 2381

SVO 1791

SVO 2197

SVO 1431
ALT
SVO 2280

SVO 2119

SVO 1221

SVO 2049

Fig. 62.   Special tools.

TOOLS

The following special tools are required for repairs to the brake system.

SVO 1221	Pliers for lower spring, rear wheel brake unit, early production.
SVO 1431	Key for air-venting nipple.
SVO 1791	Puller for hub and brake drum.
SVP 1794	Puller for inner bearing on steering knuckle.
SVO 1798	Drift for fitting sealing ring in front wheel hub.
SVO 1801	Standard handle.
SVO 2049	Tool for flanging brake pipe.
SVO 2119	Staving tool for eccentric stud, early production.
SVO 2197	Drift for removing and fitting grease cap for front wheel hub.
SVO 2280	Key for air-venting nipple, front wheel brake unit, early production.
SVO 2381	Key for air-venting nipple, vehicles with disc brakes.
SVO 4074	Spring clip for wheel unit cylinder.

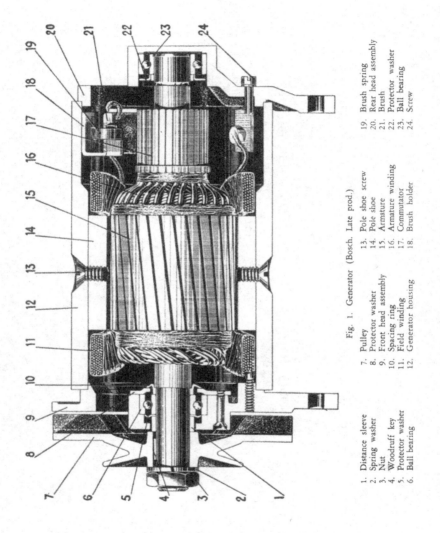

Fig. 1. Generator (Bosch. Late prod.)

1. Distance sleeve
2. Spring washer
3. Nut
4. Woodruff key
5. Protector washer
6. Ball bearing

7. Pulley
8. Protector washer
9. Front head assembly
10. Spacing ring
11. Field winding
12. Generator housing

13. Pole shoe screw
14. Pole shoe
15. Armature
16. Armature winding
17. Commutator
18. Brush holder

19. Brush spring
20. Rear head assembly
21. Brush
22. Protector washer
23. Ball bearing
24. Screw

ELECTRICAL SYSTEM – 6 VOLT

The Volvos equipped with B 14 and B 16 engines have a six-volt electrical system. The system may be suitably divided into battery, generator, charging relay, starter motor, ignition system, lighting and indicator devices as well as the necessary instrumentation.

BATTERY

The battery is mounted on a shelf on the front of the bulkhead. It is a lead battery consisting of three cells and has a capacity of 85 ampere hous.

GENERATOR

The generator is located on the right-hand side of the engine and is driven from the crankshaft by means of a V-belt. It is a shunt-type generator; i.e. the field windings are connected in parallel with the armature. Charging is regulated by means of the charging relay.

CHARGING RELAY

The charging relay is fitted close to the generator on the right-hand wheel housing. The charging control functions on the constant voltage principle. It consists of a cut-out relay, current control and voltage control.

STARTER MOTOR

The starter motor is fitted on the flywheel housing on the right hand side of the engine. It consists of a four-pole series motor. The drive pinion on the rotor shaft of the starter motor is movable axially and thus can engage with the flywheel ring gear. The pinion is controlled by a solenoid.

IGNITION SYSTEM

The ignition system is of the battery type. It consists of the following main parts: Ignition coil, distributor, ignition leads and spark plugs.

IGNITION COIL

The ignition coil is fitted on the left-hand side of the front of the firewall. The purpose of this coil is to transform battery voltage for the spark plugs. It consists of a core of laminated sheet metal around which is wound both a winding of heavy copper wire (the primary winding) and a winding of fine copper wire (the secondary winding).

The primary winding operates on battery voltage. The secondary winding, the high tension winding is connected to the

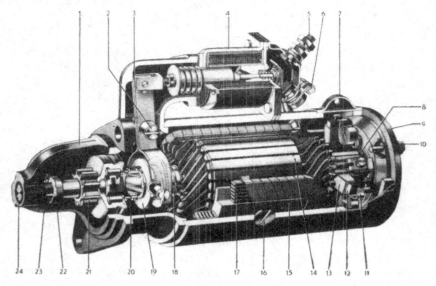

Fig. 3. Starter motor (Bosch with solenoid).

1. Rear head assembly	9. Front head assembly	17. Field winding
2. Screw for coupling arm	10. Screw	18. Spring for guide ring
3. Coupling arm	11. Brush spring	19. Guide ring
4. Solenoid	12. Brush	20. Spring for guide ring
5. Terminal screw for battery lead	13. Brush retainer	21. Pinion
6. Connecting lead for field and	14. Armature	22. Castle nut
armature	15. Pole shoe	23. Split pin
7. Protecting cover	16. Pole screw	24. Bushing
8. Armature brake		

central tapping point on the distributor cover. From here the high-tension current is supplied to the engine spark plugs.

DISTRIBUTOR

The distributor is fitted on the left hand side of the engine and is driven from the camshaft.

The distributor has two separate electrical circuits, low and high-tension.

Low-tension (battery voltage) is supplied to the coil by the breaker contacts, the breaking action of which is imparted by the cam fitted on the distributor shaft.

High tension voltage which is produced in the coil is supplied to the spark plugs by the rotor arm fitted on the distributor shaft.

The adjustment of the distributor in relation to engine speed in controlled by a centrifugal governor under the breaker arm plate. Adjustment in relation to loading is governed by a vacuum regulator.

LIGHTING

Lighting consists of headlamps which can be dimmed, flashing directional signals and parking lights, rear lights and number plate lights.

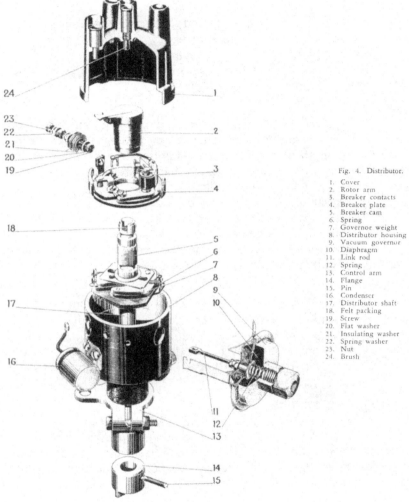

Fig. 4. Distributor.

1. Cover
2. Rotor arm
3. Breaker contacts
4. Breaker plate
5. Breaker cam
6. Spring
7. Governor weight
8. Distributor housing
9. Vacuum governor
10. Diaphragm
11. Link rod
12. Spring
13. Control arm
14. Flange
15. Pin
16. Condenser
17. Distributor shaft
18. Felt packing
19. Screw
20. Flat washer
21. Insulating washer
22. Spring washer
23. Nut
24. Brush

The headlamps are mounted in the fenders. They are switched on and off by the main lighting switch on the instrument panel. The headlanmps are dimmed by means of the foot switch on the floor. The headlamps receive current direct from the battery via the control relay fitted beside the radiator. This is to reduce the voltage drop in the circuit to a minimum. The lighting switch is used only for operating the relay.

The parking lamps are located underneath the headlamps and contain bulbs for the parking lights, direction signal lights and long-time parking lights.

The rear lamps have two separate bulbs for the rear lights, stop lights and directional signal lights.

SWITCHES

The lighting switch consists of a combined pull and turn switch. The car lighting is switched on by pulling out this switch and the strength of the instrument lighting can be adjusted by turning it. The directional signal switch is fitted on the steering column. The switch is self-cancelling.

The switch for the heater is placed beside the heater controls. The switch has positions for both half-speed and full-speed for the fan motor in the heater body.

The windshield wiper switch is also provided with positions for full and half speeds.

HORNS

The horns are fitted in front of the radiator. One of these horns gives a high-frequency note and the other gives a low-frequency note. Operation is by means of the horn ring fitted on the steering wheel. When the ring is depressed a relay is engaged which supplies current to the horns. The relay is integrally built with the lighting relays.

WINDSHIELD WIPERS

The windshield wipers are driven by an electric motor connected to the wiper blades via a gear and linkage mechanism. The motor has two speeds which can be selected by a means of the switch on the instrument panel. The windshield wipers are self-parking.

FUSES

There are two types of fuses. These consist partly of melt-type fuses fitted on porcelain or bakelite bodies and partly of a thermal fuse built in the lighting switch,

The latter protects the position lights, brake lights, glove compartment light, windshield wipers, roof light and clock. The former individual fuses are grouped in a fuse box fitted to the right on the mounting board underneath the hood. A plate under the fuses in the fuse box indicates which components these protect.

INSTRUMENTS

The speedometer is of the eddy current type and is driven by a cable from the transmission. The fuel gauge indicates the quantity of fuel in the tank. The gauge is operated by a level indicator fitted in the tank.

CONTROL LAMPS

The charging control lamp should extinguish when the engine is running.

This shows that the generator is charging the battery. If the lamp lights this means that some fault has arisen in the generator. At low enginespeeds (idling speed) it is normal for the lamp to light.

The oil pressure control lamp receives current from the starter switch via the fuse box and is grounded by means of an oil pressure control unit fitted in the engine. When the engine is running and the oil pressure is normal, contact between the lamp and ground via the pressure control unit is broken. When the oil pressure falls below a predetermined figure, the control unit closes the circuit and the lamp lights.

The control lamp for the directional signals flashes when one of the lamps is switched on. When the headlamps are on "full" the control lamp for same lights with a weak blue glow.

BATTERY REMOVAL

1. Remove cable lamps from battery terminals. Use a puller if the clamps are very tight.
2. Loosen the wing nuts on the retainer band and lift out the battery.
3. Brush off the battery with a brush and rinse clean with warm water.
4. Clean the battery shelf and the cable clamps. Use a wire brush. Use special battery pliers on the cable clamps.

INSTALLATION

1. Place the battery in position. Ensure that it is turned the right way. Tighten in position by means of the retainer band and the wing nuts.
2. Tighten the cable clamps on the battery terminals. **The negative terminal is grounded.**
3. Smear terminals and cable clamps with vaseline.

GENERATOR

Procedure to be carried out before removal and disassembly:

Should the generator not charge or there be any reason to suspect that it does not generate current in sufficient quantities, or should it produce excessive current or voltage, make sure that the fault lies in the generator itself and not in the ammeter, charging relay or cables.

First, check that the connection from the battery to the relay connection marked B (51 B + on Bosch control) is complete. This is carried out with a voltmeter. The voltmeter is connected between the relay connection B (51 B +) and the chassis. The voltage should be noticeably less than the battery voltage. Should there be no reading whatsoever on the voltmeter there is a breakdown in the system.

Should no faults be discovered carry out the following test on the generator:

Unscrew the cables on the generator. Connect the sealed take-off (a small screw) and the generator frame. Start the engine and increase idling up to about 2000 r.p.m. watching the voltmeter reading at the same time. The voltage should increase as the engine speed increases. Return to idling and disconnect the field frame connection. The voltmeter should then return to zero. Should it not do this the field is grounded to the frame inside the generator whereupon the charging cutout device is put out of action which can result in the generator burning out. The test can also be carried out in the following way: Release the generator cables on the charging relay. Connect the field cable to the frame, increase the engine speed slowly at the same time bringing the other generator cable into contact with the charging relay frame several times. Powerful sparks will appear when contact between the cables and the charging relay frame is broken.

Break the contact between the charging relay frame and the field cable, bring the main cable into contact with the charging relay frame again, no sparks will appear. Should there be no sparks the field is grounded inside the generator.

If no sparks are seen or if the voltmeter gives no reading the generator is faulty and must be removed.

REPLACING A CARBON BRUSH

If the carbon brushes have worn more than half way or are damaged, they must be replaced. This is normally recognized by the fact that the generator stops charging. Loosen the protector strip and inspect the carbon brushes and commutators. If the above-mentioned fault is the cause of the trouble, remove the generator.

Clean the outside of the generator carefully or wipe it with a rag which has been moistened with gasoline.

Remove the carbon brushes by loosening the contact on the brush holders, lift up the brush spring and pull up the carbon brush with pliers, see fig. 8.

If the commutator is scratched or unevenly worn the generator must be disassembled and the commutator turned. See under heading "Disassembly, inspection and assembly."

Fit the carbon brushes into place, check that the right type has been used, and refit the protector strip. If there should be a generator testing device in the vicinity it is wise to test the generator before it is refitted into the vehicle.

GENERATOR REMOVAL
1. Remove cable clamp from battery negative terminal.
2. Disconnect cables from generator.
3. Loosen the V-belt tension device and lift off V-belt.
4. Remove the two bolts attaching generator to engine and remove.
5. Clean generator externally with a cloth soaked in gasoline.

Installation
Installation is carried out in the reverse order to removal. The attachment bolts should be secured by means of lock washers or lock nuts and cotter pins. The fan belt is adjusted as follows:
1. Turn the engine by means of the fan in its direction of rotation until compression resistance is felt.
2. Attach a spring balance as shown in Fig. 8 and pull on this. When the belt is correctly tensioned the belt pulley should begin to slip around at pull of 12.1 - 14.3 lb. (5.5 - 6.5 kg.).
3. Adjust belt tension if necessary. Recheck the slipping moment.

CHARGING RELAY REMOVAL
1. Disconnect the three cables from the charging relay.
2. Remove relay from car.
3. Clean thoroughly externally.

INSTALLATION
1. If the relay is to be replaced, make sure that the correct type is fitted.
2. Screw into position.
3. Connect the cables. The cable from the generator armature terminal is connected to the terminal marked A, from the generator field terminal to the terminal marked F, and from the battery to Bat.

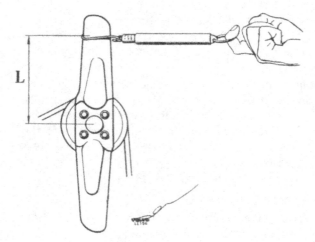

Fig. 8. Checking belt tension.
L=5.9″ (150 mm)

Fig. 9. Charging relay terminals.

1. Ground cable
2. Generator positive and and control lamp, A.
3. Generator field, F.
4. Battery, lighting relay and starter switch, Bat.

STARTER MOTOR REMOVAL

1. Remove cable clamp from battery negative terminal.
2. Disconnect the cables from the starter motor relay or solenoid switch.
3. Remove the screws which hold the starter motor in position on the flywheel housing and remove it.
4. Clean externally with a cloth soaked in gasoline.

Installation is carried out in the reverse order to removal. Tighten nuts evenly but not too hard. Connect cables carefully.

REPLACEMENT OF HEADLAMPS

If a headlamp is to be completely disassembled, follow the instructions below. For partial disassembling, follow the relevant instructions.

1. Remove the headlamp rim screw. Remove rim by pulling out lower part slightly and then lifting upwards.
2. Slacken the headlamp body retaining ring screws a few turns. Turn the retainer until the catches are free from the screws and lift out the retainer and body with bulb holder.
3. Remove the contact plug from the bulb holder by pulling it straight out backwards.
4. Slacken the headlamp adjusting screws 8-10 turns. Unhook the springs from the insert. Remove the insert from the outer casing.
6. Remove the outer casing from fender and pull out the cable and rubber bushing.
7. Fitting is done in the reverse order. Ensure that the leads are connected correctly and the screws are properly tightened.

ALIGNING OF HEADLAMPS

From a traffic safety point of view it is of the utmost importance that the headlamps are adjusted in accordance with the regulations in force.

FLASHERS AND PARKING LAMPS

1. The glass is removed by unscrewing the two screws in the rim.
2. Then unscrew the screw which holds the body and pull this out.
3. The bulb is now accessible for replacement. Use the bulb carton as protection for the bulb when fitting it.

HORN
Removal and Installation

The horns are fitted to the body by means of studs and rubber bushings. When fitting ensure that the rubber bushings are

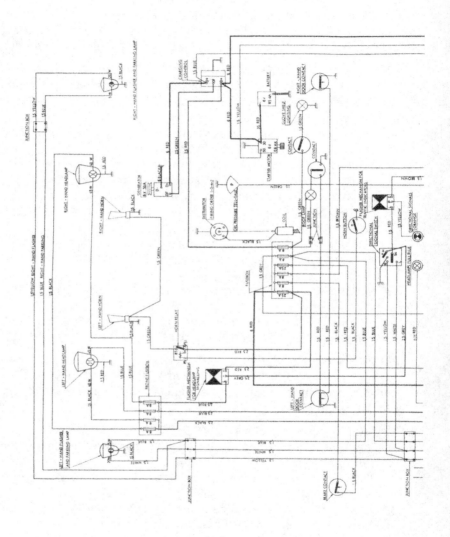

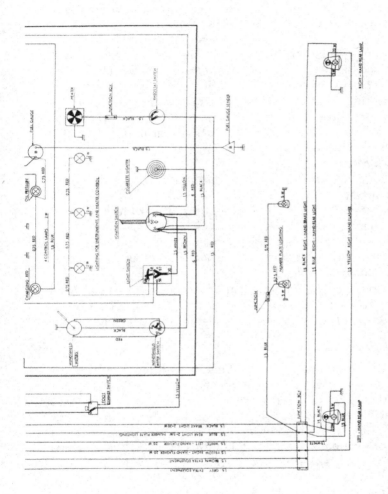

Illustration I. Wiring diagram for Volvo 122S.

not deformed or otherwise damaged. The horns are grounded by means of a short lead bolted to the body. When tracing faults and installing ensure that this lead makes a good contact as otherwise the function of the horns can be impaired.

The horns obtain current from the horn relay. This relay is integrally built with the lighting relay. In case of damage the whole relay must be replaced. The horn relay is operated by a signal ring built in the steering wheel. The ring is removed by loosening the two screws on the underside of the steering wheel, after which the ring can be ifted up. The lead in the steering shaft can be pulled up for replacement after the connection on the steering box has been removed.

The steering shaft is divided and fitted in the middle with a rubber coupling disk. A junction is fitted over the coupling disk and when carrying out adjustments to the horn ensure that this fits securely and makes good contact.

ELECTRIC CABLES

The wiring diagram shows how the various components are connected together and also shows the marking and cross-sectional area of different leads. The leads are of different colors in order to facilitate fitting and fault tracing. When carrying out fault tracing it is important that this should be done in accordance with the wiring diagram. If breakage or grounding occurs in a lead it should be replaced.

When doing so it is important that the new wire has at least the same cross section area (gage) as the old one. Too small a gage can lead to overloading and dangerous overheating of the wire.

FUSES

The fuses consist of eight melt-type fuses fitted in a fuse box and one thermal fuse fitted in the light switch. The fuses in the fuse box should be replaced when they are damaged. The fuses must never be repaired or replaced by nails, iron wire and so on.

The thermal fuse in the lighting switch breaks when short circuiting or overloading occurs. When this happens the powerful current thus passes the bi-metal spring and heats it up so that it bends and thus breaks connection between the contacts. During the time when the contacts are broken (when no current passes, the spring cools and the contacts are reconnected. If the short circuit or overloading persists, breakage occurs again. The contacts will be broken repeatedly as long as short circuiting remains. When repairing, the short circuit must not be allowed to remain on during the whole of this fault tracing time as the fuse can be damaged by this. If the fuse is damaged, then the whole lighting switch must be replaced.

ELECTRICAL SYSTEM–12 VOLT

The ignition system, lighting and accessories are identical in function to those described under the 6 volt heading, the exception being, of course, that they are of different capacity and bear different part numbers. Maintenance and repair are essentially the same, therefore we will present here only those components whose configuration or repair is essentially quite different.

12 VOLT SYSTEM
of Volvos fitted with B 18 engines
Description

The electrical system is made for a voltage of 12V. The equipment can be divided up into the following main parts: battery, dynamo, charging control, starter motor, ignition system, lighting and signalling devices and instruments.

BATTERY

The battery is placed on a shelf on the right of the bulkhead. It is a 12-volt lead type consisting of 6 cells and has a capacity of 60 ampere-hours.

STARTER MOTOR

The starter is fitted on the flywheel housing on the left-hand side of the engine. It consists of a 4-pole series-wound motor. The pinion on the starter motor rotor shaft is movable axialy to obtain engagement with the flywheel ring gear. The pinion is controlled by a solenoid.

CHARGING CONTROL

The charging control is fitted on the bulkhead. It is of the variode type, that is to say, current limitation is done by means of a variode. In addition to the variode, the charging control consists of a reverse current relay and voltage control.

FUSES

The fuses consist of melt wires fitted on porcelain plugs. The wire melts when the current exceeds the value for which the fuse is intended. The fuses used are rated at 8 and 25 amps. The fuses are placed in a fusebox fitted on the bulkhead under the bonnet.

CONTROL LAMPS

The charging control lamp should go out when the engine is running. This indicates that the generator is charging the battery. If the lamp lights, this means that there is a fault in the generator. At low engine speed (idling), it is normal for the lamp to light.

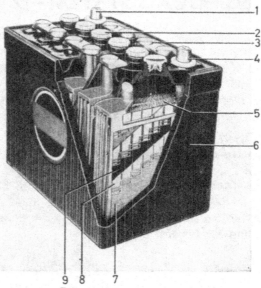

Fig. 1. Battery.

1. Negative terminal
2. Filling plug
3. Cell connection
4. Positive terminal
5. Protecting grid
6. Battery casing
7. Negative plate
8. Spacer
9. Positive plate

Text for Fig. 2. Starter motor.

1. Adjusting washer
2. Locking ring
3. End head
4. Shaft
5. Engaging lever
6. Solenoid switch
7. Terminal stud
8. Main lead
9. Protecting band
10. Brush spring
11. Brush
12. Brush retainer
13. End head
14. Rotor brake
15. Bolt
16. Commutator
17. Field winding
18. Pole shoe
19. Rotor
20. Pole screw
21. Stator
22. Spring
23. Spring
24. Pinion
25. Stop washer
26. Stop washer
27. Bushing

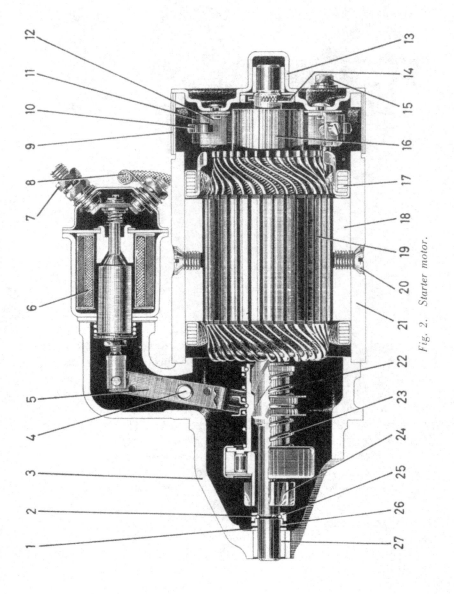

Fig. 2. Starter motor.

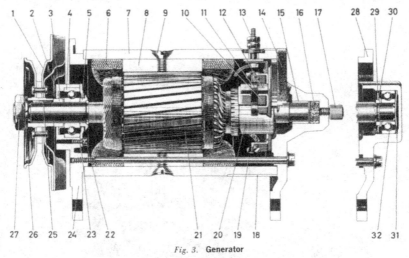

Fig. 3. **Generator**

1. Belt pulley	13. Terminal screw	25. Key
2. Spacing ring	14. End head	26. Spring washer
3. Oil seal washer	15. Bushing	27. Nut
4. Ball bearing	16. Lubricating felt } Dynamo type AR 6	28. End head
5. Spacing ring	17. Lubricating cup	29. Oil seal washer
6. Field winding	18. Protecting band	30. Spacing ring } Dynamo type AR 7
7. Stator	19. Screw	31. Spring ring
8. Pole shoe	20. Commutator	32. Ball bearing
9. Pole screw	21. Rotor	
10. Brush holder	22. Screw	
11. Brush spring	23. Sealing washer	
12. Brush	24. End head	

The oil pressure control lamp receives current from the starting switch via the fusebox and is earthed through a pressure indicator fitted on the engine. When the engine is running and the oil pressure normal, the connection between the lamp and engine frame through the pressure indicator is broken. When the oil pressure has fallen to a predetermined value, the pressure indicator closes the circuit and the lamp lights.

The control lamp for the direction indicators winks when one of the indicators is in use. The control lamp for full headlights lights up with a weak blue glow when full headlights are switched on.

STARTER MOTOR
Removing
1. Remove the cable terminal from the battery negative terminal studs.
2. Disconnect the leads from the starter motor.
3. Unscrew the bolts which hold the starter motor to the flywheel housing and lift it off.

4. Wipe off the starter motor externally with a piece of cloth soaked in solvent.

Fitting

Fitting is carried out in the reverse order to removing. Tighten the bolts evenly, but not too tightly. Connect the leads carefully.

Measures to be taken before dismantling

If the starter motor shows signs of not functioning satisfactorily, or perhaps not at all, first make sure that it is not the battery, leads, starter contact or solenoid that are out of order.

If the trouble is localized to the starter motor, remove it.

Before dismantling is started, it is important to carry out correct testing. Reliable instruments must be available if the results of the test are to be of any value.

Testing is carried out as follows:

Place the starter motor on a test bench and remove the protecting band.

Connect the starter motor to the correct voltage. The starter motor housing is connected with the negative connection. If the starter motor functions without any signs of shorting or stiffness when the current is connected, testing is continued. Connect up a voltmeter and ammeter to a 500 A shunt. Hold a revolution counter against the shaft end of the rotor. Connect the current and read off voltage, amperage and revolutions. Also watch the brushes and commutator. Make a note of the values and observations. Compare the values with those given in the specifications for an unloaded starter motor. The following reasons can now be established:

1. Low revolutions and low amperage.
   Excessive resistance caused by dirty commutator, worn brushes or poor spring pressure.
2. Low revolutions and high amperage.
   Shorting in field windings. The rotor drags against the pole shoes due to worn bearings or bent rotor shaft.
3. Heavy sparking, low rotation.
   Low spring pressure due to worn brushes or fatigued brush springs. Shorting or partial breakage in rotor winding.
4. Excessive movement of brushes.
   Poor spring pressure or out-of-round commutator.

Control solenoid

If the control solenoid does not function, first check that the battery is in good condition. If there is not fault with the battery, connect a lead between the battery positive terminal and the control solenoid contact screw for the control lead. If the control solenoid still does not engage the starter pinion and main current, it should be removed from the starter motor. If, on the other hand, it engages satisfactorily, examine the starter switch and leads.

When the control solenoid has been removed, it should be wiped clean. Then press the armature in several times and test again by connecting it to a battery. If it still does not function, the coil must be measured and the values obtained should agree with those in the specifications. A faulty control solenoid should be replaced.

Before the control solenoid is re-fitted, the distance "a" between the center line through the pivot stud in the engaging forks and the attaching flange should be checked when the iron core is fully withdrawn, see Fig. 30. After the distance has been adjusted and the locknuts tightened, the distance "a" is checked again. The nut and fork stud are then locked with sealing paint.

Concerning the distance "a", see specifications.

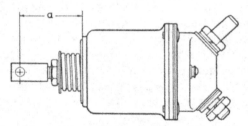

Fig. 30. Adjusting distance for solenoid fork

Replacing the brushes

If the brushes are damaged or worn down more than halfway, they must be replaced.

When replacing the brushes, the starter motor should be removed from the vehicle and cleaned externally.

Brushes are replaced with the starter motor assembled. The lead from the brush is disconnected and the brush spring lifted with a hook, after which the brush is removed from its holder. The new brush is slid down into the holder and secured with the screw.

Lubricating scheme for starter motor

Use Bosch lubricant (or corresponding) in accordance with the following designations:

1. Ft 1v 8. Grease the rotor brake springs lightly.
2. OL 1v 13. Place the bushing in oil 30 minutes before fitting.
3. Ft 1v 8. Grease the adjust washers and shaft end lightly.
4. Ft 1v 8. Apply plenty of grease in the groove.
6. Ft 1v 8 Grease the flange sleeve and coil spring lightly.
7. Ft 1v 8. Grease the shaft end and cams lightly.
8. Ft. 1v 8. Grease the adjusting washers lightly.
9. Ol 1v 13. Place the bushing in oil for 30 minutes before fitting.
10. Ft 1v 8. Grease the pins and their bearing points lightly.

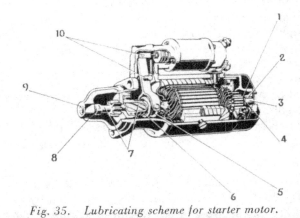

Fig. 35.   Lubricating scheme for starter motor.

GENERATOR
Removing

1. Remove the cable terminal from the battery negative terminal stud.
2. Disconnect the leads.
3. Disconnect the stay for tensioning the V-belt and lift off the V-belt.
4. Remove the two bolts which hold the generator to the engine and lift it off.
5. Wipe off the generator externally with a piece of cloth soaked in solvent.

Examining

After removing, the generator should be cleaned externally. The protecting band for the brushes should be removed and the unit placed on a test bench. The testing to be carried out now is done to establish the type of fault and it is most important that testing is carried out correctly and with reliable instruments.

The generator field terminal is connected to the generator frame and this connected to the battery negative terminal. The positive terminal on the battery is connected in series with an ammeter to the generator output terminal.

The generator should then run as motor at a low, even speed. If not, one of these conditions prevails.

Current low, rotor stationary.
> Brushes worn or bind in their holders and do not reach down to the commutator.

Current low, rotor rotates slowly.
> Poor contact between the brushes and commutator. Breakage in rotor winding.

Current high, rotor stationary.
> Shorting in the rotor. Breakage or shorting in field. A bearing has ceased.

Current high, rotor rotating.
> Scored or burnt commutator. Binding bearings. Excessive brush spring pressure.

Excessive movement of brushes and heavy sparking.
> Out-of-round or burnt commutator. Damaged brushes.

Replacing the brushes

If the brushes are damaged or worn down more than halfway, they must be replaced. This can usually be determined by the fact that the generator ceases to charge. Remove the protecting band and inspect the brushes and commutator. If it is seen that the above-mentioned fault can be the reason for no charging, the generator should be removed.

Take out the brushes by removing the connection at the brush holder, lifting up the brush spring and pulling out the brush with a pair of pliers. If the commutator is scored or unevenly worn, the generator must be dismantled and the commutator turned. Place in the brushes, ensuring that the correct types are used, and fit the protecting band. If there are testing devices available, it is advisable to test the generator before re-fitting it into the vehicle.

Lubricating instructions
Generator with ball bearings at both ends

The ball bearings should be cleaned with solvent and lubricated with ball bearing grease.

Generators with ball bearing and bushing

For the ball bearing, see above.

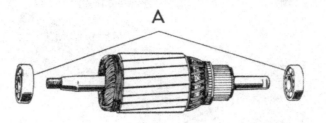

Fig. 50. Dynamo lubricating scheme

A Bearings lubricated with grease, Bosch Ft 1 v 22 or corresponding.

Bushing: The lubricating cup on the commutator end should be filled with engine oil every 10,000 km (6,000 miles). Lubricating is done with an ordinary oil can. A pressure oil can must not be used.

NOTE: A new bushing should lie in an oil bath for at least half an hour before being fitted.

CHARGING CONTROL
Removing
1. Disconnect the leads on the charging control.
2. Remove the charging control from the bulkhead.
3. Wipe off the charging control externally.

Fitting
1. If the charging control has to be replaced, check that the new one is of the correct type.
2. Screw the charging control onto the wheel housing.
3. Connect the leads as shown in Fig. 51.

Adjusting the charging control
Reverse current relay
Cut-in voltage

A voltmeter is connected over D+ on the charging control and generator frame. The engine is started and the speed increased while watching the voltmeter.

The reading should first increase and then fall back to 0.1—0.2 V, when the reverse current relay cuts in, after which it should remain still. The reading given by the voltmeter up to the point when cutting-in takes place is known as the cut-in voltage.

This should be compared with the value given in the specifications and any necessary adjustment carried out.

Adjusting is done by increasing or decreasing the pressure of the spring which influences the relay armature. If the spring pressure is reduced, the cut-in voltage will decrease and vice versa.

Fig. 51.   Charging control terminals.

1. Dynamo field DF
2. Earth lead

3. Dynamo D+
4. Battery B+

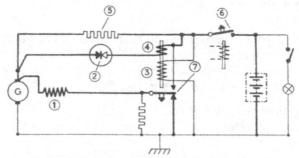

Fig. 52.   Wiring diagram for charging control.

1. Field winding
2. Variode
3. Voltage winding
4. Current winding

5. Variode resistance
6. Cut-in contacts
7. Regulating contacts

Rough adjusting is carried out as shown in Fig. 53, and fine adjusting as shown in Fig. 54.

Reverse current.

An ammeter is connected in series with B+ on the charging control and the lead to the battery. The speed of the generator is increasd until the ammeter shows a reading. The speed is then

Fig. 53. Adjusting the cut-in voltage.

Fig. 54. Fine adjusting the voltage control.

Fig. 55. Rough adjusting the voltage control.

reduced gradually. The ammeter needle will go down to zero and then over to discharge. After this, it will suddenly go up again to zero. The reverse current is read off at the turning point of the needle before it returns to the zero position. The relay has cut out when the needle returns to the zero position. The reverse current should lie between the values given in th specifications.

If the reverse current is too low, the bend of the contact spring should be lessened by bending the contact yoke of the cut-in contact. It may be necessary to file off the pole pin slightly. If the reverse current is too high, the bending of the contact spring must be increased. Check the cut-in contact gap and adjust this if necessary. After adjusting, check the cut-in voltage again.

Voltage control

Disconnect the connection B+ on the charging control. Connect a voltmeter between B+ and the charging control frame and increase the generator speed gradually.

As soon as voltage control has begun, that is to say, when the voltage does not increase further, the control voltage should be read off. The control is adjusted by bending the support lip for the spring tongue as shown in Fig. 54, so that the spring tongue is completely unloaded. After this, a rough adjustment is made by bending the relay angle piece as shown in Fig. 55. If the angle piece is bent downwards, the voltage is increased and vice versa. Rough adjustment should lie about 1—2 V lower than final adjustment. This is done by bending the support lip upwards so that the spring tongue is tensioned, see Fig. 55. Use special tool V 397 (Robert Bosch, Stockholm).

Increase and decrease the speed a few times and ensure that the control is correctly adjusted.

NOTE. This adjustment must be done after the generator has reached full operating temperature, that is to say, at least 12 minutes after the engine has been started from cold.

Checking the variode under loading (cold generator)

Connect an ammeter between B+ and the live lead, and connect an adjustable loading resistance of suitable size between the battery side of the ammeter and the frame. In addition, a voltmeter should be connected between B+ and frame.

Increase the speed and note the meter readings. Adjust the loading resistance so that a loading current = 1 max. is obtained. Check the control voltage under loading.

Run the engine at the above loading. After about 2—3 minutes the current value must not be higher than 2/3 of the max. current stamped on the dynamo (1 max.) If the loading does not fall, this indicates a fault in the variode, so that the charging control must be replaced.

Since the effect of the generator is very high, great demands are placed on the condition and tension of the drive belt. Before carrying out any work on the charging control and generator, therefore, always check that the belt is correctly tensioned.

REMOVING AND REFITTING 544 WIPER MOTOR

1. Pull off wiper arm.
2. Remove the nut (1, Fig. 85) and lift off the washer (2) and seal (3).
3. Mark and remove the leads from the wiper.
4. Unscrew the screw (5, Fig. 85) accessible from under the instrument panel.
5. Fitting is done in the reverse order. Be sure the rubber seals are intact.

LUBRICATING AND ADJUSTING
THE WINDSCREEN WIPER MOTOR

The windscreen wiper motor bushings are of the self-lubricating type. When overhauling the wiper motor, the rotor shaft should be lubricated with a few drops of engine oil and the surplus oil wiped off. The motor gear housing should be filled three-quarters full with gear housing grease (Auto-Lite ST 294 A or corresponding).

During annual overhaul, apply a suitable quantity of grease.

The rotor shaft axial clearance should be between 0.1 and 0.3 mm (0.004 and 0.012"). Adjusting is done with screw 14, Fig. 87.

Changing over self-parking position

When delivered from the factory, the windscreen wiper parks to the right viewed from the driving position. The parking position can be changed over, that is to say, the wiper blades park to the left on the windscreen, by turning the contact plate (Fig. 87) through 180°. (Auto-Lite wipers). The nut (11), steel washer (12) and fibre washer (13) are first removed, after which the contact plate (2), can be lifted up and turned. The SWF wiper can be changed over by removing the shaft (1, Fig. 87) and turning through 180°.

WINDSCREEN WASHER

The windscreen washer pump is driven by an electric motor. The pump is of the gear type.

When overhauling, the bushings and shafts are lubricated with oil. Brushes which are worn down more than half-way must be replaced.

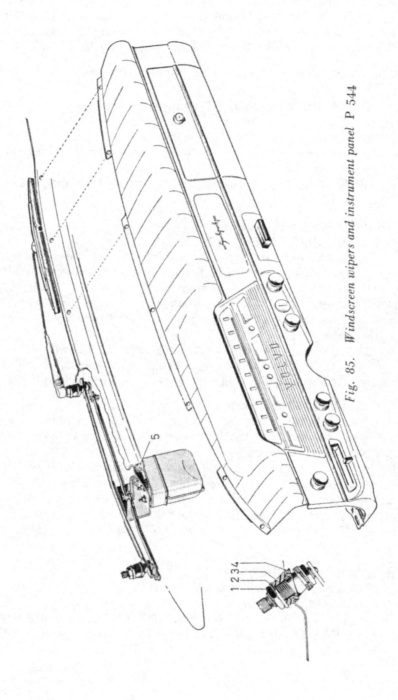

Fig. 85. *Windscreen wipers and instrument panel P 544*

1. Shaft
2. Contact plate
3. Gear wheel
4. Stator
5. Commutator
6. Brush
7. Brush holder
8. Rotor
9. Pole shoe
10. Field coil
11. Nut
12. Steel washer
13. Insulating washer
14. Adjusting screw

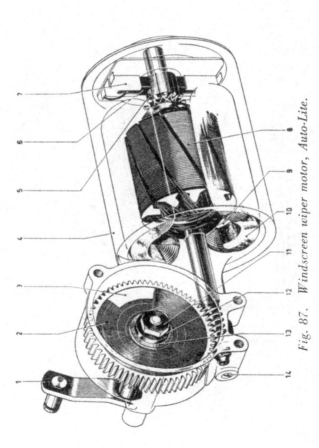

Fig. 87. *Windscreen wiper motor, Auto-Lite.*

1. Contact plate
2. Contact strip
3. Contact strip
4. Switch
5. Shunt winding
6. Series winding
7. Brush
8. Commutator
9. Rotor
10. Rotor winding
11. Field coil
12. Resistance

Lead colours

A Green
B Black
C Red
D Current-carrying lead

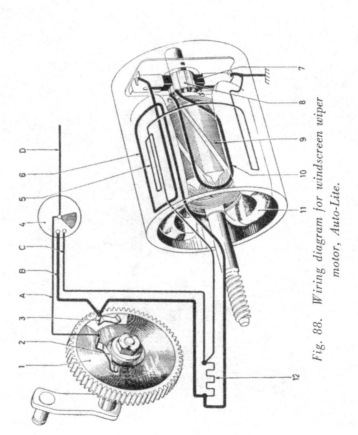

Fig. 88. Wiring diagram for windscreen wiper motor, Auto-Lite.

390

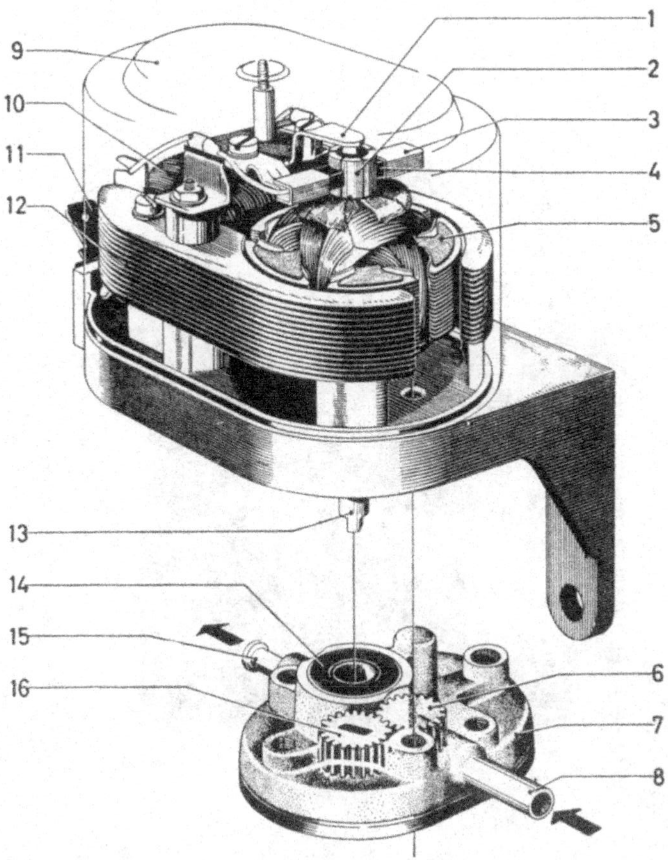

Fig. 95.

Windscreen washer.

1. Stop lip
2. Commutator
3. Brush holders
4. Brush
5. Rotor
6. Pump gear
7. Pump housing
8. Inlet pipe
9. Casing
10. Field winding
11. Terminal
12. Pole shoe
13. Rotor shaft
14. Seal
15. Outlet pipe
16. Pump gear

391

ELECTRICAL LEADS

The wiring diagram shows how the electrical leads connect the various components, and also shows the marking and cross-sectional area of the leads. The leads have different colors to facilitate fitting and fault tracing. When fault tracing, it is important that this is carried out in accordance with the wiring diagram.

If a lead is broken or earthed, it must be replaced.

When doing this, it is most important that the new lead has at least the same cross-sectional area as the old one. If the area is too small, this can lead to overloading and dangerous heating of the lead.

LEADS FOR EXTRA EQUIPMENT

For fitting extra electrical equipment at the rear of the vehicle, for example, rear window fan and reversing lamp, two leads are included in the cable harness. The cable harness is placed along the roof of the vehicle inside the headlining. The extra leads are accessible under the instrument panel and at the rear in the rear in the luggage compartment.

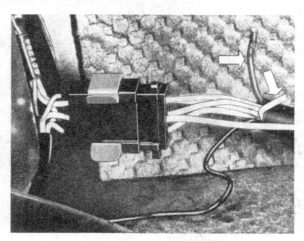

Fig. 89.   Connecting piece for stop light, rear light, direction indicators, and leads for extra equipment (arrows).

FUSES

These consist of four melt-type fuses fitted in a fusebox placed on the left-hand side of the bulkhead.

The fuses in the fusebox must be replaced when burnt out. The fuses must never be repaired or replaced with nails, wire, etc.

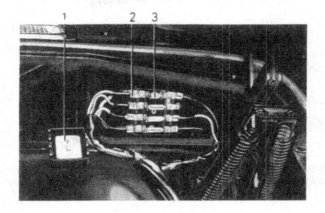

Fig. 91.   Fuses.

1. Cover for fusebox   2. Terminal   3. Fuse

The fuses on cars have a rating of 8 and 25 A.
The table below shows data for the fuses.

Rating	8 A	25 A
Rated current at continuous loading	8 A	25 A
Current which the fuse should withstand for at least one hour	12 A	35 A
Current for which the fuse should melt within one hour	20 A	62.5 A

1. Turbine
2. Terminals for leads
3. Half-speed resistance
4. Fan motor

Fig. 94.   Removing the heater fan motor.

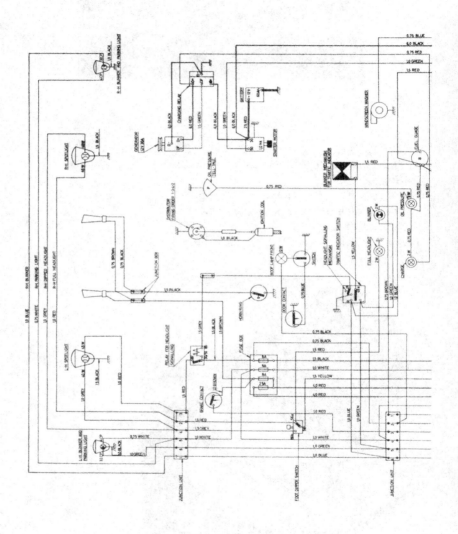

394

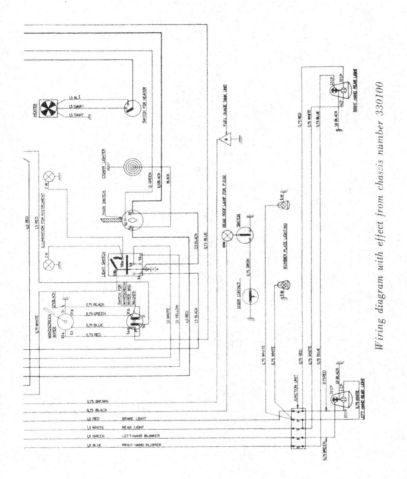

Wiring diagram with effect from chassis number 330100

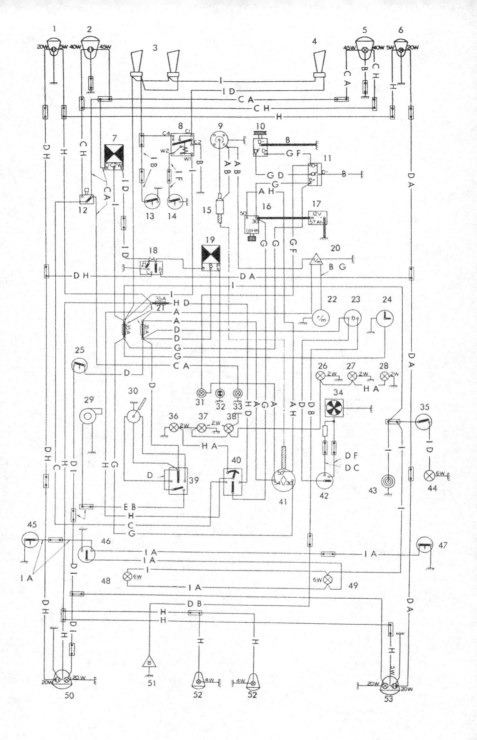

396

Illustration X. Wiring Diagram —1800

1. Flasher and parking light, left
2. Headlight, left
3. Horn
4. Loud tone horn
5. Headlight, right
6. Flasher and parking light, right
7. Relay for headlight flasher
8. Horn relay
9. Distributor
10. Generator
11. Charging control
12. Foot dimmer switch
13. Horn button
14. Lever for loud tone horn
15. Ignition coil
16. Starter motor
17. Battery
18. Directional indicator switch
19. Flasher impulse unit,
    directional indicators
20. Revolution counter sender
21. Fuses
22. Revolution counter
23. Fuel gauge
24. Clock
25. Brake contact
26. Instrument lighting
27. Instrument lighting
28. Instrument lighting
29. Windshield washer
30. Windshield wipers
31. Warning lamp, charging
32. Warning lamp,
    directional indicators
33. Warning lamp
    full headlights
34. Heater
35. Switch, map-reading light
36. Instrument lighting
37. Instrument lighting
38. Instrument lighting
39. Controls for windshield wipers
    and windshield washers
40. Lighting controls
41. Ignition switch
42. Heater controls
43. Cigarette lighter
44. Map-reading light
45. Door contact
46. Switch for roof light
47. Door contact
48. Roof light
49. Roof light
50. Rear light, left
51. Fuel gauge sender
52. Number plate lighting
53. Rear light, right

A = White
B = Black
C = Blue
D = Green
E = Light green
F = Yellow
G = Brown
H = Red
I = Purple

397

REMOVING HEATER FAN MOTOR

1. Disconnect the current-carrying lead on the connecting piece.
2. Unscrew the six screws which hold the fan motor to the radiator casing and lift this out as shown in Fig. 94.

Fitting is done in the reverse order. The fan motor is provided with self-lubricating bushings so that lubricating need not be done after a certain time but only in connection with reconditioning.

DIRECTIONAL SIGNAL SWITCH – 122 S
Removal and Installation
1. Remove the steering wheel.
2. Remove the three screws which hold the casing to the jacket tube and lift this up. Remove the leads on the underside of the switch. These are removed by pulling them out from their retainers.
3. Remove the two screws which hold the switch to the jacket tube. The position of the switch is adjusted by turning the jacket tube. The flange is screwed to the steering wheel. The flange is not adjustable. When worn or damaged it should be replaced.

DIRECTION INDICATOR SWITCH – 444
Removing and fitting
1. Remove the steering wheel.
2. Unscrew the three screws which hold the casing to the jacket tube, and lift this up.
3. Remove the leads on the underside of the switch. This is done by pulling them out of their holders.
4. Unscrew the two screws which hold the switch to the jacket tube.
   Adjusting the position of the switch is done by turning the jacket tube.

TRAFFIC INDICATOR SWITCH -544
Removal and Installation
1. Remove the steering wheel.
2. Remove the leads at the underside of the switch. These are removed by pulling out of their retainers.
3. Slacken the lock nut and screw out the stop screw a few turns.
4. Lift the switch casing with switch straight off from steering column.
5. Fitting is done in reverse sequence.
   The switch is attached to the switch casing by two screws. When these are removed the switch can be taken out of the casing.
   The traffic indicator switch can be adjusted by slackening screw and then turning the casing with switch to desired position. A space of about 2 mm (5/64") should be left between the steering wheel and casing.
   The leads are connected to the traffic indicator switch as shown. The cable terminals are pressed firmly into holders. After fitting, check that the leads fit properly into the holders.

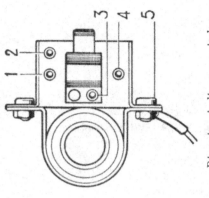

Direction indicator switch terminals (seen from underneath).

1. Right flasher
2. Left flasher
3. Headlight signal
4. Lead from flasher unit
5. Earth lead

Direction indicator switch.

1. Jacket tube
2. Casing
3. Screw
4. Switch
5. Screw
6. Control lever
7. Earth lead

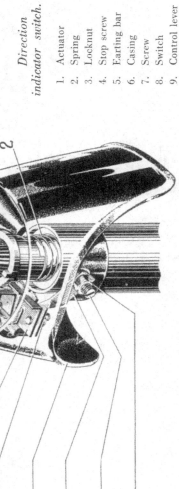

*Direction
indicator switch.*

1. Actuator
2. Spring
3. Locknut
4. Stop screw
5. Earting bar
6. Casing
7. Screw
8. Switch
9. Control lever

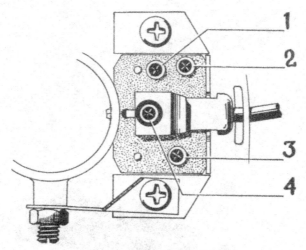

Direction indicator switch connections.
Switch seen from underneath.

1. Terminal for right flashers
2. Terminal for left flashers
3. Terminal for flasher unit
4. Terminal for headlight signal

LUBRICATION

122-1800 LUBRICATION
Engine

The engine oil should be changed after every 5,000 km (3,000 miles) during the summer and in the case of cars which are mainly used for long-distance driving. During the winter the oil should be changed after every 2,500 km (1,500 miles) particularly on cars mainly used for driving short distances. On new cars the oil should also be changed after the first 1,000 km (600 miles).

The oil should be drained off immediately after the car has been driven and while the engine is still warm. When all the oil has run out, check the washer and screw the plug tightly into position again. Oil is added through the rocker arm casing after the filler cap has been removed.

The engine oil to be used must be of a grade corresponding to the specifications laid down in "Service MS". In the case of cars fitted with B 16 A engines which are run under favorable conditions at normal speed and with normal loading, oil of the "Service MM" type can, however, be used. The viscosity of the oil used is chosen from the table below.

Air temperature

below 0° C (32° F) .... SAE 10 W
0—30° C (32°—90° F) .... SAE 20
over 30° C (90° F) .... SAE 30

or SAE 10 W—30 multigrade oil all the year round.

The oil capacity of the B 16 engine when changing oil is 2.75 litres (4⅞ Imp. pints = 5¾ US pints) and for the B 18 engine 3.25 litres (6 Imp. pints = 7¼ US pints). The oil capacity including the lubricating oil filter for the B 16 engine is 3.5 litres (6¼ Imp. pints = 7½ US pints) and for the B 18 engine 3.75 litres (7 Imp. pints = 8 US pints).

Fig. 1. Drain plug on oil sump.

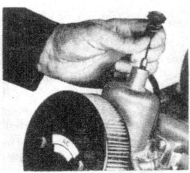

Fig. 2. Checking the oil level.

Carburetors

Each time the oil is changed on cars fitted with twin carburetors, the oil evel in the damping cylinder must be checked. This is done by removing the nut and damping plunger. There should be so much oil there that the center spindle but not the part above it is full when the plunger is fitted. If there is not sufficient oil, top up with SAE 20 engine oil (not multigrade oil).

Gearbox (without overdrive)

The oil should be changed after every 20,000 km (12,000 miles). In the case of a new or reconditioned gearbox, the oil should be changed and the gearbox should be flushed after the first 5,000 km (3,000 miles).

The oil should be drained off immediately after the car has been driven and while the oil is still warm. When draining off the oil, remove the plugs marked 1 and 2 in Fig. 3.

Fig. 3. Gearbox.

1. Filler plug   2. Drain plug

It is advisable to use flushing oil now and again, for example in connection with every other oil change. This flushing oil is added through the filler hole (2, Fig. 3) after the drain plug has been screwed back into position. The engine should then be allowed to run for a minute or so with one of the gears engaged and both the rear wheels jacked up. The engine should then be stopped, the rear wheels lowered and the flushing oil drained out.

Fill up with new oil after the drain plug has been screwed tightly back into position. The oil should be up to the filler hole (1.). Screw the filler plug back tightly into position. Use standard transmission oil SAE 90 for the gearbox. The amount of oil required when changing oil is as follows:

H 6 gearbox approx. 0.5 litres (1 Imp. pint = 1 US pint),
M 4 gearbox approx. 0.9 litres (1¾ Imp. pints = 2 US pints)
M 30 and M 40 gearboxes 0.75 litres (1¼ Imp. pints = 1½ US pints).

In the case of air temperatures continuously below −20° C (−5° F), oil with a viscosity of SAE 80 should be used.

GEARBOX WITH OVERDRIVE

The oil should be changed after every 20,000 km (12,000 miles). In the case of a new or reconditioned gearbox, the oil should also be changed after the first 5,000 km (3,00 miles).

The old oil should be drained off immediately after the car has been driven and while the oil is still warm. The plugs marked 1 and 2 in Fig 3 are opened as well as the drain plug (Fig. 4), and the oil strainer, see page 6, is also cleaned.

Top up with new oil when the drain plugs have been screwed tightly back into position. Fill up with oil slowly so that the oil has time to run over into the overdrive. The oil level should be up to the filler hole (1, Fig. 3). Screw the filler plug tightly into position.

Engine oil with a viscosity of SAE 30 should be used all the year round in a gearbox fitted with overdrive. The oil capacity when changing oil is approximately 1.8 litres (3¼ Imp. pints = 4 US pints).

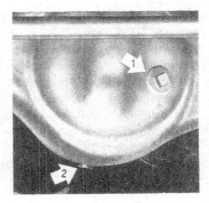

Fig. 4. Drain plug on overdrive.   *Fig. 5. Rear axle (ENV),*
early production.

1. Filler plug   2. Drain plug

Fig. 6. Rear axle (Spicer),
late production.

REAR AXLE

The oil should be changed after every 20,000 km (12,000 miles). It is recommended that the oil is changed immediately after the car has been driven and while the oil is still warm. Drainage is carried out by removing the plug (2, Fig. 5) and also removing the filler plug (1). If there is no drain plug fitted on the rear axle, the oil must be sucked out or the cover must be removed to allow the oil to run out. Great cleanliness must be observed to prevent dirt from getting into the final drive. Check that the cover gasket is in good condition, otherwise replace it.

As in the case of the gearbox, it is recommended now and then, for example in connection with every other oil change, that flushing oil be used. This is added through the filler hole after the drain plug has been screwed into position. The engine is then allowed to run for a minute or so with one of the gears engaged and both the rear wheels jacked up. The car is then lowered again and the flushing oil is drained off.

Normally SAE 90 hypoid oil is used in the rear axle. At air temperatures continuously below −20° C (−5° F), SAE 80 oil should be used. The oil capacity when changing oil is about 1.3 litres (2¼ Imp. pints = 2¾ US pints).

STEERING SYSTEM

It is not usually necessary to change the oil in the steering system except when reconditioning is being carried out. Should the oil be changed for some reason in the steering box when fitted, the old oil can be sucked out by using a suitable device, for example, an oil spray which should be inserted through the filler hole, or the steering box can also be removed and emptied.

The oil used in the steering box is normally SAE 90 hypoid oil all the year round. In the case of air temperatures continuously below −20° C (−5° F), the oil used should have a viscosity of SAE 80.

Fig. 7. *Steering box filler plug.*

Fig. 8. *Distributor.*

1. Lubricating wick for ignition setting mechanism
2. Circumference of cam
3. Lubricator for distributor shaft

INSTRUCTIONS FOR LUBRICATING AND CLEANING DISTRIBUTOR

The distributor must be lubricated regularly otherwise the result will be wear, ignition trouble and increased fuel consumption. The distributor shaft is lubricated by filling the lubricators. The ignition timing mechanism is lubricated by pouring two or three drops of light engine oil (SAE 10) on the wick in the distributor shaft. The circumference of the cam is greased when necessary by using a very thin layer of vaseline. The points mentioned above should be greased after every 10,000 km (6,000 miles). The other moving parts of the distributor should be greased in connection with reconditioning.

LUBRICATING OIL FILTER

The insert in the engine lubricating filter or the complete filter should normally be changed after every 10,000 km (6,000 miles). In the case of a new or reconditioned engine, replacement must however be carried out for the first time after 5,000 km (3,000 miles). The work is carried out as follows.

B 16 Engine

1. Clean the lubricating oil filter housing and the surrounding parts of the engine to prevent dirt from getting into the lubricating system when the fiter is removed.
2. Loosen the center bolt (3, Fig. 9) on the housing. Collect up the oil that runs out.
3. Remove the lubricating oil filter. Remove the old insert and wash the housing with white spirit.
4. Fit a new gasket, filter insert and filter housing. The intermediary plate (1) should be located so that the hole marked "UP" is at the highest point. Make sure that the housing is correctly located on its guide in the bracket. Tighten the bolt (3) to a torque of 2 kgm (15 lb. ft.).
5. If the element is replaced without the oil being changed in the engine at the same time, top up afterwards with about 0.75 litre (1¼ Imp. pints = 1½ US pints) of oil. Check for leakage when the engine has been started.

Fig. 9. Replacing the lubricating oil filter element (B 16).

10. Removing the oil filter (B 18).

1. Intermediate plate   3. Centre bolt
2. Filter cartridge

B 18 Engine

1. Clean the lubricating oil filter and the surrounding parts of the engine to prevent dirt from getting into the lubricating system when the filter is removed.
2. Remove the old filter with the help of the tool as shown in Fig. 10. Scrap the filter.
3. Smear oil onto the new filter rubber gasket and make sure that the contact surface for the oil filter is free from dirt. The coating of oil enables the gasket to slide better against the sealing surface. Screw on the filter by hand until it just touches the block.

4. Tighten the oil filter a further half turn by hand. No tool should be used when fitting. Start the engine and check that there is no leakage. Top up with oil if necessary. It is normally necessary to add about 0.5 litre (1 Imp. pint = 1 US pint) of oil.

AIR CLEANER WITH WIRE FILTER

The air cleaner filter should be cleaned after every 5,000 km (3,000 miles).

The air cleaner as shown in Fig. 11 does not need to be disassembled when cleaning. Instead loosen the nut for the cover and remove the cover. Then remove the filter element (Fig. 11) and clean it with petrol. After the filter has dried, it should be soaked with engine oil which is allowed to run off before the filter is refitted.

The air cleaner shown in Fig. 12 cannot be disassembled and should therefore be removed complete and cleaned in petrol. After cleaning, the air cleaner should be soaked in engine oil which should be allowed to run off before the cleaner is refitted on the engine. Make sure when fitting that the ventilation holes in the cleaner index with the corresponding holes in the gasket and carburetor.

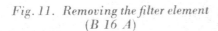

Fig. 11. Removing the filter element (B 16 A)   *Fig. 12. Air cleaner (B 16 B, early production)*

AIR CLEANER WITH PAPER FILTER

The paper filter should be replaced after every 20,000 km (12,000 miles). If the car is mainly driven on dusty roads or in districts with particularly contaminated air, the filter should be changed more often, approx. every 10,000 km (6,000 miles). No cleaning of any sort may be attempted between these replacements. It is absolutely forbidden to moisten or oil in the paper filter.

Fig. 13. Replacing the air cleaner
(B 16 B, B 18 D).

Fig. 14. Replacing the filter insert
(B 18 D, right-hand drive).

On the model shown in Fig. 13, the housing and the filter are in the form of one unit and the complete air cleaner is replaced. This is done by removing the attaching screws. When fitting the new cleaners, check that the gaskets are turned the right way, see Fig. 13. If the gaskets are turned the wrong way, the ventilation holes for the vacuum plungers are blocked and the carburetors cannot function properly.

In the case of cars with right-hand drive fitted with B 18 D engines, the air cleaners have replaceable inserts. When replacing remove the wing nut and lift off the cover as shown in Fig. 14. Make sure that the contact surface for the cleaner element is clean Be careful to ensure that no dirt gets into the air intake or onto the inside of the insert. When replacing the insert in this type of air cleaner loosen the wing nut and the upper hose clamp as shown in Fig. 15. Remove the upper section and replace the insert after the inside of the cleaner has been cleaned with a moist cloth. When fitting make sure that the gaskets are in good condition.

AIR CLEANER OF THE OIL-BATH TYPE

This type of air cleaner should normally be removed and cleaned after every 10,000 km (6,000 miles). If the car is mainly run on dusty roads or in districts with particularly contaminated air, cleaning should be carried out more often.

When cleaning the air cleaner as shown in Fig. 16, the clamps are turned upwards and the lower part is removed. The old oil is drained out and then the insert and housing are cleaned in gasoline or solvent, and then blown dry with compressed air. After the lower part has been fitted, oil of the same type as that

Fig. 15. *Replacing the filter*
insert (B 18 A).

Fig. 16. *Disassembling the air*
cleaner (B 18 B, B 18 D).

being used in the engine is added until the red level ring is just covered. The insert is then fitted and the upper part clamped into position.

On the air cleaner shown in Fig. 17, the upper hose clamp is loosened and then the wing nut is removed so that the upper section can be lifted off. Lift up the inner container and empty out the old oil. Wash the container and insert and clean the other parts. Fit the container in the lower section and add oil up to the level mark. Only add oil to the loose container and not to the lower section. Use the same sort of oil as used in the engine. Finally, fit the upper section.

CLEANING THE OIL FILLER CAP

If the crankcase breather is to function properly, the filter in the oil filler cap should be removed and cleaned after every 10,000 km (6,000 miles). The cap is removed, the three screws loosened (Fig. 18) and the top lifted off. The filter is cleaned in gasoline, dried and then oiled in with light oil. Before the cap is refitted, check and, if necessary, replace the gasket.

CLEANING THE OVERDRIVE OIL STRAINER

The oil strainer should be cleaned in connection with every oil change. After the oil has been drained off through the plug (Fig. 4), cleaning is carried out in the following way:

1. Remove the cover (2, Fig. 19) and remove the oil strainer (1).
2. Clean the oil strainer in gasoline or solvent. Blow dry with compressed air.
3. Check that the gasket (3) is in good condition and lay it in position. Fit the oil strainer, a new gasket (4) and the cover.

Fig. 17. *Disassembling the air cleaner*   Fig. 18. *Oil filler cap.*
(B 18 A, B 16 A).

GREASING PLASTIC-LINED BALL JOINTS

The ball joints for the tie rod and the steering rods are plastic-lined so they require no maintenance greasing and are thus not fitted with nipples. The rubber seals, on the other hand, should be full of grease. On early production cars where there are no lock rings on the rubber seals, these seals should be folded down and filled with chassis grease, see Fig. 20, when being fitted and also once a year. On late production cars where the rubber seals are fitted with a lock ring at the top, the seals only require filling with grease when being replaced. About once a year the rubber seals should be inspected and replaced if damaged.

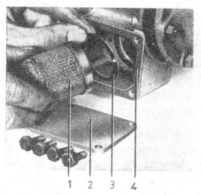

Fig. 19. *The overdrive oil strainer.*   Fig. 20. *Greasing the ball joint,*
1. Oil strainer   *early production.*
2. Cover
3. Gasket for oil strainer
4. Gasket for cover

GREASING THE HANDBRAKE CABLE

The handbrake cable and outer sheath (later production) should be greased a couple of times a year. The forward and rear attachments for the protective sheath are loosened and this is moved backwards and forwards while graphite grease is applied to the cable, see Fig. 21.

Fig. 21. Greasing the handbrake cable.

CHECKING THE BRAKE FLUID LEVEL

After every 5,000 km (3,000 miles) check that the fluid in both the containers (Fig. 22) is up to a point 15—20 mm (⅝ — ¾") below the filler edge.

Top up if necessary with first-class brake fluid which satisfies the conditions laid down in SAE 70 R1 or R3. Avoid spilling brake fluid on the surface finish since it has a damaging effect.

*Fig. 22. Brake fluid container, early production
and clutch fluid container.*

413

Fig. 23. Brake fluid container, late production

LUBRICATING THE WHEEL BEARINGS

The front wheel bearings should be removed after every 20,000 km (12,000 miles) or at least once a year for cleaning and greasing and the rear wheel bearings after every 40,000 km (25,000 miles) or at least every other year.

After the bearings and seal rings have been removed, the hub and grease cap should be thoroughly cleaned.

Make sure that all the old grease inside the hub is removed. Compressed air can be used for rough cleaning of the bearings. The bearing components are then washed in white spirit or a similar solvent and then allowed to dry. Drying should not be done with compressed air since the air often contains moisture and particles of dust. Accessible bearing components should be dried off with linen or cotton cloth (not cotton waste). A new bearing in an unbroken packing should not be cleaned.

Inspect all parts carefully after cleaning. If there are any signs of damage, rust or blueing on the bearing races or rollers, replace the bearing. If the outer or inner races are loose in their recesses, test with a new race. If the looseness does not disappear, the hub or axle in question must be replaced. Replace seal rings if they are worn or damaged.

Use first-class wheel bearing grease for the lubrication of wheel bearings. Do not mix up different makes of grease. A greasing machine should be used for the effective grease-packing of the wheel bearings. Follow the instructions supplied by the manufacturers. If no greasing machine is available, pack the bearings by hand with as much grease as there is room for between

414

the roller cage and the inner race. Also apply grease to the outside of the rollers and cages. The space between the outer and inner bearing in the front wheel hub should be filled with grease as shown in Fig. 24.

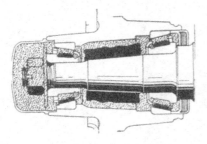
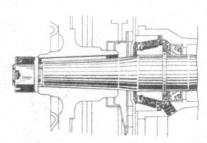

Fig. 24. Front wheel bearing.　　*Fig. 25. Rear wheel bearing.*

1. Hinge (light oil)
2. Door check (paraffin wax)
3. Hinge (light oil)

1. Lubricating hole (silicon oil)
2. Latch (paraffin wax)

Grease with paraffin wax

Lubricating the body

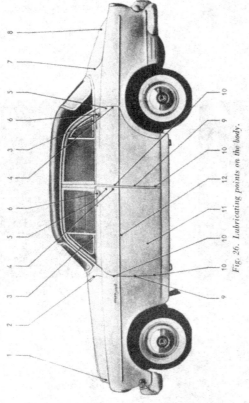

Fig. 26. Lubricating points on the body.

To avoid squeaking in the doors and locks, the body should be greased after every 10,000 km (6,000 miles). During the winter the locks should also be lubricated with some form of anti-freeze preparation which prevents the locks from freezing.

No.	Lubricating point	Lubricant
1	Bonnet catch	Paraffin wax
2	Bonnet hinges	Oil
3	Ventilator catch and hinges.	Oil
4	Door catch	Paraffin wax
5	Door lock	Silicon oil
6	Door handle lock buttons ..	Paraffin wax
	Key holes	Silicon oil
7	Luggage compartment hinges	Oil
8	Luggage compartment lock .	Oil
9	Door checks	Paraffin wax
10	Door hinges	Oil
11	Driving seat slide rails and catches	Paraffin wax and oil
12	Window lifts	Oil and grease
	Locks .... (accessible after door upholstery panels have been removed)	Silicon grease

PV 444, 544 LUBRICATION

ENGINE

During the summer and on cars that are mainly used for long-distance driving, the engine oil should be changed after 5000 km (3000 miles). An exception to this rule consists of cars without oil filters (PV 444 chassis Nos 1—12005) in which case the oil should be changed after every 2500 km (1500 miles), especially on cars mainly used for short-distance running. On new cars the oil should also be changed after the first 1000 km (600 miles).

The oil should be drained off immediately after the engine has been run and while it is still warm. The oil drain plug is shown in Fig. 1. When all the oil has run out check the washer and then screw the plug tightly back into position. Remove the filler cap on the rocker arm cover and add the new oil through the hole.

The engine lubricating oil used should be of a grade corresponding to the conditions laid down in "For Service MM" or "MS". Oil of the "For Service MS" type is used under difficult conditions of operation, for example, driving of a mainly short-distance character with excessively low working temperatures, driving for long periods at high speed or other conditions where a high degree of loading on the engine results in a high working temperature. Otherwise oil of the "For Service MM" type should be used. Only oil of the "For Service MS" type should be used on cars fitted with sports engines. The viscosity of the oil used is as follows:

below 0° C (32° F) SAE 10 W
between 0° C (32° F) and 30° C (90° F) SAE 20
over 30° C (90° F) SAE 30

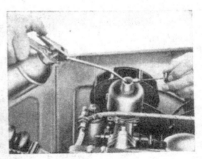

Fig. 2.

Topping up the carburetter

Fig. 1. Draining the engine oil.   *damping cylinders.*

The oil capacity of PV 444 cars up to chassis No. 131917 is 3.25 litres (6 Imp. pints = 7 US pints). For PV 444 cars from chassis No. 131918 onwards and PV 544 cars, the capacity is 2.75 litres (4¾ Imp. pints = 5¾ US pints). The corresponding capacities including the oil filter are 3.75 litres (6¾ Imp. pints = 8 US pints) and 3.5 litres (6¼ Imp. pints = 7½ US pints).

Each time the oil is changed the twin carburetors on B 14 A and B 16 B engines should have their damping cylinders topped up with light engine oil (SAE 10 W). The cap nut and the damping plunger (Fig. 2) should be removed on each carburetor and the damping cylinders should be filled with oil. Do not fill the part above the cylinder.

GEARBOX

The oil should be changed after every 20,000 km (12,000 miles). With a new or reconditioned gearbox, the oil should be changed and the gearbox should be flushed after the first 5000 km (3000 miles).

The oil should be drained off immediately after the car has been run while the oil is still warm. To drain off the oil remove plugs 1 and 2 as shown in Fig. 3. It is recommended that now and then, for example, in connection with every other oil change, flushing oil should be used. This flushing oil is added through the filler hole (2, Fig. 3) after which the drain plugs should be screwed back into position.

The engine should then be allowed to run for a minute or so with one of the gears engaged and one of the rear wheels jacked up. The engine should then be stopped, the rear wheel lowered and the flushing oil drained off.

The new oil should be added after the drain plug has been screwed tightly back into position. The level of oil should be up to the filler hole (2). Then screw the filler plug tightly back into position.

Fig. 3. Gearbox.
Drain plug 2. Filler plug

Use SAE 30 gearbox oil all the year round. When changing the oil, the capacity of the three-speed gearbox is 0.5 litres (⅞ Imp. pint = 1 US pint) and for the four-speed box 0.9 litres (1¾ Imp. pints = 1 US quart).

REAR AXLE

The oil should be changed after every 20,000 km (12,000 miles). In the case of a new or reconditioned rear axle, the oil should be changed and the rear axle should be flushed after the first 5000 km (3000 miles).

The oil should be drained off immediately after the car has been driven and while the oil is still warm. To drain off the oil, remove plugs 1 and 2 as shown in Fig. 4.

As in the case of the gearbox, it is recommended that now and then, for example in connection with every other oil change, flushing oil is used. This oil is added through the filler hole (1) after the drain plug has been screwed back into position. The engine should be allowed to run for a minute or so with one of the gears engaged and one of the rear wheels jacked up after which the engine is stopped. the rear wheel lowered and the flushing oil drained off.

Add the new oil after the drain plug has been screwed tightly back into position. The level of oil should be up to the filler hole (1). Screw the filler plug tightly back into position.

Use SAE 80 hypoid oil all the year round. On PV 444 cars from chassis No. 131918 onward and for PV 544 cars the oil capacity when changing oil is 1.3 litres (2¼ Imp. pints = 2¾ US pints). For PV 444 cars up to chassis No. 131917 the oil capacity when changing oil is 0.9 litres (1¾ Imp. pints = 2¼ US pints) for model I and 1.3 litres (2¼ Imp. pints = 2¾ US pints) for model II. Model I and model II can be recognized by their design, see Fig. 5.

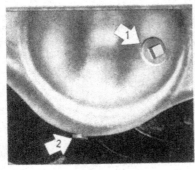

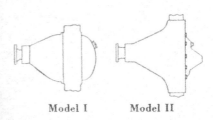

Model I   Model II

Fig. 5.   Rear axle.

Fig. 4.   Rear axle.

1. Filler plug   2. Drain plug

STEERING GEAR

The oil in the steering gear does not usually require changing except in the case of reconditioning. If, however, the oil must be changed for some reason when the steering system is fitted in the car, the old oil must be sucked out with some suitable device, for example, a grease gun which is inserted through the filling hole.

Oil is then add through the filling hole after the plug has been removed, Fig. 6. The level of oil should be up to the filler hole. Screw the plug tightly back into position.

For the steering gear on PV 544 cars SAE 80 gear oil should be used all the year round and on PV 444 cars one of the following special oils: Caltex Special Oil 250, Castrol B Special Gear Oil, Esso Gear Oil 250 Special, Kendall 400, Kopra Gear Oil Special, Mobilube Special Steering Gear Oil or Shell Dentax Oil 250. The capacity of the steering gear for an early production PV 444 when all the oil oil has been removed is 0.3 litres (⅜ Imp. pint = ½ US pint), for late production PV 444 0.13 litres (¼ Imp. pint = ⅜ US pint) and for PV 544 0.25 litres (½ Imp. pint = ⅝ US pint).

Fig. 6. Removing the steering gear filler plug.

Points to be lubricated:
After every 1250 km (750 miles)

Fig. 7. Upper control arm.

Fig. 8. King pin.

Fig. 9. Lower control arm.

Fig. 10. Steering linkage.

Fig. 11. Tie rod.

Fig. 12. Steering idler arm.

After every 5000 km (3000 miles)

Fig. 13.

1. Clutch shaft 2. Pedal shaft

Fig. 14. Forward universal joint.

Fig. 15.

1. Centre universal joint 2. Slip joint

Fig. 16. Rear universal joint.

Fig. 17.   Distributor.

Fig. 18.   Cooling water pump.
Lubricate sparingly.

Fig. 19.   Dynamo.
(PV 444 cars up to chassis No.
131917 and PV 544 cars, late
production).

REPLACING THE OIL FILTER ELEMENT

The oil filter element fitted may be of the by-pass type (PV 444 cars up to chassis No. 131917) or of the full-flow type (PV 444 cars from chassis No. 131918 onwards and PV 544 cars). The oil filter element should normally be changed after every 10,000 km (6000 miles). When a full-flow type filter is fitted the element should also be replaced after 5000 km (3000 miles) in the case of a new or reconditioned engine. Use only Volvo original elements.

The oil filter element is replaced as follows.

BY-PASS TYPE OIL FILTER

1. Clean the cover and loosen the centre bolt. See Fig. 20. Lift up the cover and the element.
2. Fit the new element. Check the cover gasket and replace if damaged. Fit the cover and tighten the bolt.
3. Check the oil filter for leakage after the engine has been started.

Fig. 20. Removing the cover. Fig. 21. Removing the oil filter.

FULL-FLOW TYPE OIL FILTER

1. Clean the oil filter housing and the adjacent parts of the engine to prevent dirt from getting into the lubricating system while the replacement work is going on.
2. Loosen the center bolt, see Fig. 21. Allow the oil running out to collect in a suitable vessel.
3. Remove the oil filter and take out the old element. Clean the housing in white spirit.
4. On late production units check that the intermediate plate is fitted with the mark "UP" at the top.
   Fit a new gasket in the cylinder block and a new filter element. Fit the oil filter and make sure that it comes cor-

rectly into the groove. Tighten the center bolt to a torque of 2 kgm (15 lb.ft.).

5. If the element is replaced and the engine oil is not changed at the same time, top up with 0.75 litres (1¼ Imp. pints = 1½ US pints) of oil. Check the oil filter for leakage after the engine has been started.

LUBRICATING WHEEL BEARINGS

The front wheel bearings should be disassembled for cleaning and greasing after every 20,000 km (12,000 miles) or at least once a year and the rear wheel bearings should be disassembled for cleaning and greasing after every 40,000 km (25,000 miles) or at least once every other year.

The hub and grease cap should be carefully cleaned after the bearing and seal ring have been removed. Make sure that all old grease is removed from inside the hub. First clean the bearings by using compressed air and then wash the bearing components in white spirit and allow them to dry. Drying should not be carried out with compressed air since the compressed air often contains water and particles of dust. The parts of the bearing that are accessible should be dried off with linen or cotton cloth (not cotton waste). A new bearing that is delivered in a sealed package should not be cleaned.

Inspect all the components after cleaning. If any signs of damage, rust or blueing are noticed on the bearing races or rollers, the bearings should be replaced. If the outer or inner races are loose, test with a new ring. If this looseness still persists, the hub or the axle shaft in question should be replaced. Replace the seal rings if they are worn or damaged.

Use only high quality wheel bearing grease to lubricate the wheel bearings. Do not mix different makes of grease. A special greasing apparatus should be used to pack the wheel bearings effectively. Follow the instructions supplied by the manufacturer. If an apparatus of this type is not available, the bearings can be packed by hand with as much grease as there is place for between the roller bearing cage and the inner race. The insides of the rollers and the cage should also be greased. The space in the front wheel hub between the outer and inner bearings should be filled with grease as shown in Fig. 22.

LUBRICATING PLASTIC-LINED BALL JOINTS

If there are no lubricating nipples on the tie rod and steering linkage this means that they are fitted with plastic-lined ball joints. The rubber seals on these should be turned back once a year and filled with chassis grease, see Fig. 23.

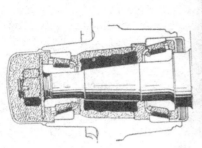 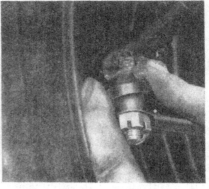

Fig. 22. Greasing a hub.   *Fig. 23. Lubricating a ball joint.*

LUBRICATING HANDBRAKE CABLE

The handbrake cable with its sleeve (late production) should be lubricated about twice a year. The front and rear attachments for the sleeve should be loosened and moved backwards and forwards while graphite grease is smeared on the cables, see Fig. 24.

CLEANING THE OIL FILLER CAP

In order to ensure that crankcase ventilation is satisfactory, the filter in the oil filler cap should be removed and cleaned after every 10,000 km (6000 miles). The filler cap should be removed, the three screws (Fig. 25) taken out and the top lifted off. The filters should be cleaned in petrol, dried and then oiled in with light oil. Before refitting the cap, check the gasket and replace if necessary.

Fig. 25. Oil filler cap.

Fig. 24. Lubricating the handbrake cable.

CLEANING THE AIR CLEANER

The air cleaner filter should be cleaned after every 5000 km (3000 miles). An exception to this is the air cleaner of the oil-bath type (extra equipment) which only needs cleaning after every 10,000 km (6000 miles).

Cleaning is carried out in the following way.

AIR CLEANERS ON B 14 A AND B 16 B ENGINES (EARLIER PRODUCTION)

Two air cleaners are fitted on B 14 A and B 16 A engines and the appearance of these is shown in Fig. 26. Since it is not possible to disassemble them, they should be removed as a unit and washed in petrol. After this cleaning the filter should be oiled in with engine oil and this should be allowed to run off before the air cleaners are refitted on the engine. Make sure that the air cleaner and gasket come in the correct position when fitting. The ventilation holes (see illustration) must index with the corresponding holes on the carburetors if they are to function properly.

Fig. 26. Air cleaners for B 14 A and B 16 B engines.

AIR CLEARNER WITH PAPER ELEMENT, B 16 B ENGINE (LATE PRODUCTION)

The elements in the air cleaners are made of specially-treated paper.

The air cleaners must not be washed in liquid or be oiled in.

If they should become moist in any way they must be replaced since the flow through them will then be greatly reduced.

If the car in question is run under relatively dust-free conditions then the only servicing operation necessary is to replace the air cleaners with new units after each 20,000 km (12,000 miles) and the old cleaners should be thrown away since the air cleaner and element are manufactured in one unit.

When the car is being run on dusty roads or the air cleaners become clogged more rapidly than usual, it is recommended that, in addition to the replacement mentioned above, they should be blown clean with compressed air after every 5000 km (3000 miles). The air cleaners should be removed and blown **from the inside outwards** with dry, clean compressed air. Hold the compressed air nozzle in the hole and not close to the cleaner element since this can damage it.

Remember to turn the gasket between the air cleaner and the carburetor the right way round when re-fitting the air cleaner.

OIL BATH-TYPE AIR CLEANER

This air cleaner can be encountered on PV 444 cars from chassis No. 131918 onwards and on PV 544 cars.

Fig. 27.   Disassembling the air cleaner.

Remove the complete air cleaner unit and then disassemble it, Fig. 27. Empty out the old oil and then clean the housing and the filter element in petrol before blowing it dry with compressed air. Fill the air cleaner up to the level mark with engine oil of the same type as used in the engine. Then reassemble the cleaner and refit it on the engine.

OTHER AIR CLEANERS

These do not need to be disassembled for cleaning. The nut on the cover is removed and the cover is taken off. The air cleaner element is then removed (see Fig. 28 which shows an early production unit) and cleaned in petrol. After the element has dried it should be oiled in with engine oil and this should be allowed to run off before the element is replaced in the container.

CHECKING THE BRAKE FLUID LEVEL

After every 5000 km (3000 miles) the level of brake fluid should be checked. Remove the plug from the master cylinder

Fig. 28. Removing the filter element.

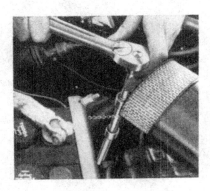

Fig. 29. Removing the master cylinder
filler plug.

which is located under the steering column after it has been cleaned to prevent dirt from getting into the fluid container. To remove the plug on PV 444 cars up to chassis No. 20004 a special wrench SVO 1457 is used and for other models a box spanner (1⅛") and an extension as shown in Fig. 29.

The master cylinder should be almost full and should, if necessary, be topped up with high quality brake fluid, i.e. fluid satisfying the conditions laids down in SAE 70 R 1 (HD grade).

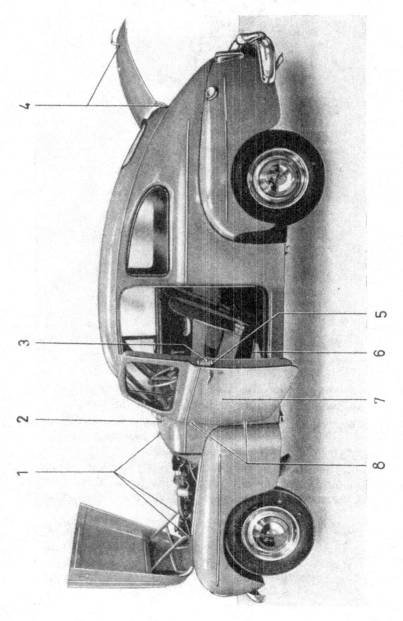

Fig. 30. Lubricating points on body.

BODY LUBRICATION

In order to avoid squeaks and unnecessary wear the body should be lubricated at the points shown in Fig. 30. Unless otherwise stated, a few drops of light engine oil should be added after every 10,000 km (6000 miles).

1. Hood lock and hinges.
2. Windscreen wiper anchorages and spindles.
3. Door lock cylinders.
4. Rear compartment lock and hinges. The lock is lubricated by blowing a little powdered graphite into the keyhole. The key is then dipped in graphite, inserted in the lock and turned a few times.
5. Lock cylinders, dovetails and striker plates. Lubricate with paraffin wax.
6. Front seat slide rails and catches.
7. Lock mechanism with linkage, remote control system, window regulators with rollers and adjusters. These are accessible by removing the door inner panel. Lubrication is only necessary after every 20,000 km. (12,000 miles) or once a year. The cable and chain should be lubricated with grease. See point 4 concerning the lubrication of the lock.
8. Door hinges.

SPECIFICATIONS

B 4 B Engine (PV 444 up to chassis No. 131917)

```
Lubricating oil, type .............................   Engine oil
              quality  ........................   Service MM or MS
              viscosity: Below 0° C (32° F)  .......   SAE 10 W
                         0° C—30° C (32° F—90° F)   SAE 20
                         Above 30° C (90° F) ......   SAE 30
Oil change quantity, without oil cleaner ............   3.25 litres
                                                        (6 Imp. pints = 7 US pints)
              with oil cleaner  ..............   3.75 litres
                                                        (6¹/₂ Imp. pints = 7³/₄ US pints)
```

B 16 A Engine (PV 444 from chassis No. 131918 onwards, PV 544)

```
Lubricating oil, type .............................   Engine oil
              quality  ........................   Service MM or MS
              viscosity: Below 0° C (32° F)  .......   SAE 10 W
                         0° C—30° C (32° F—90° F)   SAE 20
                         Above 30° C (90° F) ......   SAE 30
Oil change quantity, without oil cleaner ............   2.75 litres
                                                        (4³/₄ Imp. pints = 5³/₄ US pints)
              with oil cleaner  ..............   3.5 litres
                                                        (6¹/₄ Imp. pints = 7¹/₂ US pints)
```

B 16 B Engine

```
Lubricating oil, type .............................   Engine oil
              quality  ........................   Service MS
              viscosity: Below 0° C (32° F)  .......   SAE 10 W
                         0° C—30° C (32° F—90° F)   SAE 20
                         Above 30° C (90° F) ......   SAE 30
Oil change quantity, without oil cleaner ............   2.75 litres
                                                        (4³/₄ Imp. pints = 5³/₄ US pints)
              with oil cleaner  ..............   3.5 litres
                                                        (6¹/₄ Imp. pints = 7¹/₂ US pints)
```

Gearbox

```
Lubricating oil, type .............................   Gear oil
              viscosity, all year round ............   SAE 80
Oil change quantity, 3-speed ......................   0.5 litre
                                                        (1 Imp. pint = 1¹/₄ US pints)
              4-speed  ......................   0.9 litre
                                                        (1¹/₂ Imp. pints = 2 US pints)
```

Rear axle

```
Lubricating oil, type .............................   Hypoid oil
              viscosity, all year round ............   SAE 80
Oil change quantity, PV 444 up to chassis No. 131917,
    rear axle type  I (see page 2) ...................   0.9 litre
                                                        (1¹/₂ Imp. pints = 2 US pints)
    rear axle type II (see page 2) ..................   1.3 litres
                                                        (2¹/₄ Imp. pints = 2³/₄ US pints)
    PV 444 from chassis No. 131918 onwards and PV 544 .   1.3 litres
                                                        (2¹/₄ Imp. pints = 2³/₄ US pints)
```

SPECIFICATIONS

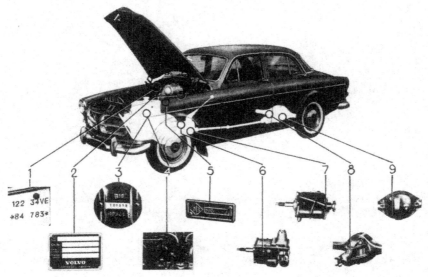

1. The chassis number on late production models is stamped in the bulkhead.
2. Type designation of vehicle, chassis number and code number for surface finish and upholstery.
3. Engine type designation (B 16), serial and part number (on right-hand side of early production engines).
4. Engine type designation (B 18) serial number and part number.
5. Body number.
6. Gearbox type designation, serial number and part number.
7. Gearbox type designation, serial number and part number.
8. ENV rear axle. Number of teeth and serial number stamped on forward part of housing.
9. Spicer rear axle. Number of teeth and ratio on plate attached to lower part of inspection cover.

B 16 ENGINE

General

	B 16 A	B 16 B
Type designation		
Output, b.h.p./r.p.m.	60/4500 (DIN)	76/5500 (DIN)
	66/4500 (SAE)	85/5500 (SAE)
Max. torque, kgm (lb. ft.)/r.p.m.	11.3 (81.7)/2500 (DIN)	11.5 (83.1)/3300 (DIN)
	11.8 (85.4)/2500 (SAE)	12 (86.8)/3500 (SAE)
Compression pressure (warm engine) when turning over by using starter engine, 200 r.p.m., kg/cm^2	9.5—10.5	10—11
lb./sq. in.	135—150	142—156
Compression ratio	7.4 : 1	8.2 : 1
Number of cylinders	4	4
Bore	79.37 mm (3.125″)	79.37 mm (3.125″)
Stroke	80 mm (3.15″)	80 mm (3.15″)
Displacement	1.58 litres (96.4 cu. in.)	1.58 litres (96.4 cu. in.)
Weight, including clutch, carburetter, starter motor, dynamo and air cleaner	approx. 150 kg (330 lb.)	approx. 150 kg (330 lb.)

Cylinder block

The cylinder bores are drilled directly in the block.

Material	Special-alloy cast-iron
Bore, standard	79.37 mm (3.125″)
0.020″ oversize	79.88 mm (3.145″)
0.030″ ,, ...	80.13 mm (3.155″)
0.040″ ,, ...	80.39 mm (3.165″)
0.050″ ,, ...	80.64 mm (3.175″)

Pistons

	B 16 A	B 16 B
Material	Light-alloy	
Weight	410±5 grams (14.46±0.18 oz.)	
Permissible weight difference between pistons on the same engine	10 g (0.35 oz.)	
Total height	86 mm (3.390″)	
Height from piston pin centre to piston top	46 mm (1.81″)	
Piston clearance	0.03—0.05 mm (0.0012—0.0020″)	
Diameter, standard, at right angle to piston pin at lower edge of piston	79.33 mm (3.1230″)	
0.020″ oversize	79.84 mm (3.1431″)	
0.030″ ,,	80.09 mm (3.1535″)	
0.040″ ,,	80.35 mm (3.1638″)	
0.050″ ,,	80.60 mm (3.1736″)	

Piston rings

Piston ring gap measured in ring opening .... 0.25—0.50 mm (0.0027—0.0031″)
Piston ring oversizes .... 0.020″   0.040″
                                                  0.030″   0.050″

Compression rings

Both rings are beveled on the inner edge and this bevel should be turned upwards.
The rings are also marked "TOP" on the upper surface.
The upper ring on each piston is chromed.
Number of rings on each piston 2
Height .... 1.97 mm (0.078″)
Piston ring clearance in groove .... 0.068—0.079 mm (0.0027—0.0031″)

Oil rings

Number on each piston 1
Height .... 4.73 mm (0.1865″)
Piston ring clearance in groove .... 0.045—0.073 mm (0.0017—0.0029″)

Piston pins

Fully floating. Circlips at both ends in piston.
Fit:
In connecting rod .... Close running fit
In piston .... Slide fit
Diameter, standard .... 19 mm (0.748″)
0.05 mm oversize .... 19.05 mm (0.750″)
0.10 mm   ,, ... 19.10 mm (0.752″)
0.20 mm   ,, ... 19.20 mm (0.754″)

Cylinder head

Height, measured from cylinder head contact surface to cylinder head nut flats .... 99 mm (3.90″)   97.5 mm (3.84″)

Crankshaft

Replaceable bearing shells for main bearings and connecting rod bearings.

	B 16 A	B 16 B
Crankshaft end play	0.01—0.10 mm (0.0004—0.0040″)	0.01—0.10 mm (0.0004—0.0040″)
Main bearings, radial play, flange bearing	0.014—0.064 mm (0.0005—0.0025″)	0.014—0.064 mm (0.0005—0.0025″)
others	0.014—0.064 mm (0.005—0.0025″)	0.051—0.100 mm (0.0020—0.0034″)
Connecting rod bearings, radial play	0.051—0.091 mm (0.0020—0.0036″)	0.051—0.087 mm (0.0020—0.0034″)

Main bearings

Main bearing journals

Diameter, standard	53.950—53.960 mm (2.1240—2.1244″)
0.010″ undersize	53.696—53.706 mm (2.1140—2.1144″)
0.020″ „	53.442—53.452 mm (2.1040—2.1044″)
0.030″ „	53.188—53.198 mm (2.0940—2.0944″)
0.040″ „	52.934—52.944 mm (2.0840—2.0844″)

Width on crankshaft for flange bearing shell:

Standard	38.935—38.975 mm (1.5329—1.5344″)
Oversize 0.1 mm (undersize shell 0.010″)	39.035—39.075 mm (1.5369—1.5384″)
0.2 mm („ „ 0.020″)	39.135—39.175 mm (1.5407—1.5423″)
0.3 mm („ „ 0.030″)	39.235—39.275 mm (1.5447—1.5463″)
0.4 mm („ „ 0.040″)	39.335—39.375 mm (1.5486—1.5502″)

Main bearing shells

Flange bearing shells:

Thickness, standard	1.911—1.918 mm (0.0752—0.0755″)
0.010″ undersize	2.038—2.045 mm (0.0802—0.0805″)
0.020″ „	2.165—2.172 mm (0.0852—0.0855″)
0.030″ „	2.292—2.299 mm (0.0902—0.0905″)
0.040″ „	2.419—2.426 mm (0.0952—0.0955″)

Other bearing shells:

Thickness, standard	1.911—1.918 mm (0.0752—0.0755″)	1.894—1.900 mm (0.0746—0.0748″)
0.010″ undersize	2.038—2.045 mm (0.0802—0.0805″)	2.021—2.027 mm (0.0796—0.0798″)
0.020″ „	2.165—2.172 mm (0.0852—0.0855″)	2.148—2.154 mm (0.0854—0.0848″)
0.030″ „	2.292—2.299 mm (0.0902—0.0905″)	2.275—2.281 mm (0.0895—0.0898″)
0.040″ „	2.419—2.426 mm (0.0952—0.0955″)	2.402—2.408 mm (0.0946—0.0948″)

Connecting rod bearings

Connecting rod bearing journals

Bearing seat width	32.900—33.000 mm (1.2953—1.2992″)
Diameter, standard	47.589—47.600 mm (1.8736—1.8740″)
0.010″ undersize	47.335—47.347 mm (1.8635—1.8640″)
0.020″ „	47.081—47.092 mm (1.8536—1.8540″)
0.030″ „	46.827—46.838 mm (1.8436—1.8440″)
0.040″ „	46.573—46.584 mm (1.8336—1.8520″)

Connecting rod bearing shells

	B 16 A	B 16 B
Thickness, standard	1.560—1.568 mm (0.0614—0.0617″)	1.562—1.568 mm (0.0615—0.0617″)
0.010″ undersize	1.687—1.695 mm (0.0664—0.0667″)	1.689—1.695 mm (0.0665—0.0667″)
0.020″ ,,	1.814—1.822 mm (0.0715—0.0717″)	1.816—1.822 mm (0.0715—0.0717″)
0.030″ ,,	1.941—1.949 mm (0.0764—0.0767″)	1.943—1.949 mm (0.0765—0.0767″)
0.040″ ,,	2.068—2.076 mm (0.0814—0.0817″)	2.070—2.076 mm (0.0815—0.0817″)

Connecting rods

Marked 1—4 on side away from camshaft. Classified A—D showing weight range. Only connecting rods with the same weight classification may be used in the same engine.

Weight class A	578—608 grams (20.39—21.44 oz.)
B	608—638 grams (21.44—22.50 oz.)
C	638—668 grams (22.50—22.56 oz.)
D	668—698 grams (23.56—24.62 oz.)
Side clearance at crankshaft	0.15—0.35 mm (0.0060—0.0140″)
Length, centre—centre	150±0.1 mm (5.905±0.004″)

Flywheel

Permissible axial play	0.20 mm (0.008″)
Ring gear (chamfer facing inwards)	116 teeth

Flywheel housing

Maximum axial play for rear surface	0.08 mm (0.0016″)
Maximum radial play for rear guide	0.15 mm (0.0060″)

Camshaft

Drive	Gear drive with fibre gear on camshaft
Number of bearings	3
Forward bearing journal, diameter	46.975—47.000 mm (1.8494—1.8504″)
Centre bearing journal, diameter	42.975—43.000 mm (1.6919—1.6929″)
Rear bearing journal, diameter	36.975—37.000 mm (1.4557—1.4567″)
Radial clearance	0.025—0.075 mm (0.0010—0.0029″)
Valve clearance for check of camshaft setting (cold engine)	1.1 mm (0.043″) 1.15 mm (0.045″)
Inlet valve should then open at	10° before T.D.C. 0° (T.D.C.)

Camshaft bearings

Forward bearing, diameter	47.025—47.050 mm (1.8514—1.8524″)
Centre bearing, diameter	43.025—43.050 mm (1.6939—1.6949″)
Rear bearing, diameter	37.025—37.050 mm (1.4577—1.4587″)

Timing gears

Crankshaft gear	20 teeth
Camshaft gear	40 teeth
Backlash	0.01—0.04 mm (0.0004—0.0016″)

Valve system

Valves

Inlet

	B 16 A	B 16 B
Disc diameter	37 mm (1.46")	
Stem diameter	7.859—7.874 mm (0.3094—0.3100")	
Valve seat angle	44.5°	
Cylinder head seat angle	45°	
Seat width in cylinder head	1.5 mm (0.060")	

Exhaust

Disc diameter	34 mm (1.34")	
Stem diameter	7.830—7.845 mm (0.3082—0.3089")	
Valve seat angle	44.5°	
Cylinder head seat angle	45°	
Seat width in cylinder head	1.5 mm (0.060")	

Valve clearances

Clearance, inlet valves, warm engine	0.40 mm (0.016")	0.50 mm (0.020")
Clearance, exhaust valves, warm engine	0.45 mm (0.018")	0.50 mm (0.020")

Valve guides

Length	62 mm (2.44")
Inner diameter	7.905—7.920 mm (0.311—0.312")
Height above cylinder head upper surface	21 mm (0.83")
Clearance, valve stem—valve guide, inlet valves	0.031—0.061 mm (0.0024—0.0035")
Clearance, valve stem—valve guide, exhaust valves	0.060—0.090 mm (0.0024—0.0035")

Valve springs

Length, unloaded	45 mm (1.77")
Length with loading of 25.5±2 kg (56±4 1/2 lb.)	39 mm (1.20")
Length with loading of 66±3.5 kg (145±8 lb.)	30.5 mm (1.2")

Lubricating system

Oil capacity, including oil cleaner	3.5 litres (3 Imp. quarts = 3 1/4 US quarts)
Oil capacity excluding oil cleaner	2.75 litres (2 1/2 Imp. quarts = 3 US quarts)
Oil pressure at 2000 r.p.m. (approx. 50 km.p.h. = 30 m.p.h. in top gear, warm engine)	2.5—3.5 kg/cm² (36—50 lb./sq. in.)

Lubricant	Engine oil, Service MM or MS	Engine oil, Service MS
viscosity, below 32° F (0° C)	SAE 10 W	SAE 10 W
from 32° F (0° C) to 90° F (30° C)	SAE 20	SAE 20
above 90° F (30° C)	SAE 30	SAE 30
Oil cleaner, make	AC, Mann or Fram	

Relief valve spring

Length, unloaded	40±0.5 mm (1.575"±0.002")
Length, loaded with 2.5±0.2 kg (5 1/2±1/2 lb.)	34 mm (1.34")
3.5—0.2 kg (8±1/2 lb.)	31.5 mm (1.24")

Lubricating oil pump

Oil pump, type	Gear pump
number of teeth	10
axial clearance	0.02—0.10 mm (0.0008—0.004″)
radial clearance	0.01—0.10 mm (0.0004—0.004″)
backlash	0.15—0.35 mm (0.006—0.014″)

Fuel system

Fuel pump, make and type	AC diaphragm pump
Fuel pressure	min. 0.14 kg/cm² (2 lb./sq. in.)
	max. 0.25 kg/cm² (3.5 lb./sq. in.)
Capacity at idling speed	0.5 litres/min. (7/8 Imp. pint = 1 US pint/min.)
Fuel gauge, type	Electric
Fuel tank, capacity	35 litres (7 ³/₄ Imp. galls. = 9 ¹/₄ US galls.)

Carburetters
B 16 A

	Designation	Dimensions
Type	Down-draught	
Make and designation	Zenith 34 VN	
Venturi	27	—
Main jet, standard	97	0.97 mm
bentyl fuel	102	1.02 mm
Compensation jet	97	0.97 mm
Idling jet	50	0.50 mm
Idling air jet	50	0.50 mm
Acceleration jet	40	0.40 mm
Float valve	1.75	
Float valve washer, thickness		1.0 m
Fuel level when running		18 mm under float bowl top
Idling speed	400—600 r.p.m.	

B 16 B

Type	Horizontal (2)
Make and designation	SU H4
Number of carburetters	2
Size (air intake diameter)	38 mm (1¹/₂″)
Fuel control jet, designation	AUC 2112
Fuel needle, designation	GT
when using intake silencer air cleaner	GW
Rapid idling, setting of rod in cam-shaped lever	Position 2
Idling speed	500—700 r.p.m.

Cooling system

Type	Pressure
Filler cap valve opens at	0.23—0.30 kg/cm² (3.2—4.2 lb./sq. in.)
Capacity	approx. 8.5 litres (1 ⁷/₈ Imp. galls = 2 US galls.)

Thermostat balanced. Does not open under effect of water pump pressure.

Marked	170
Starts to open at	75—78° C (167—172° F)
Fully open at	90° C (194° F)
Fan belt, designation	HC .380″×33″

Wear tolerances

Cylinders:
Rebore when worn (if oil consumption abnormal) . . . . 0.25 mm (0.010")

Crankshaft:
Permissible out-of-round on main bearing journals, max. . . . . . . 0.05 mm (0.0020")
Permissible out-of-round on connecting rod bearing journals, max. 0.07 mm (0.0028")
Max. crankshaft end play . . . . 0.15 mm (0.0060")

Valves:
Permissible clearance between valve stems and valve guides, max. 0.15 mm (0.0060")
Valve stems, permissible wear, max. . . . . 0.02 mm (0.0008")

Camshaft:
Permissible out-of-round (with new bearings) max. . . . . 0.07 mm (0.0028")
Bearings, permissible wear . . . . 0.02 mm (0.0008")

Timing gears:
Permissible backlash, max. . . . . 0.12 mm (0.0047")

Tightening torques, B 16 A and B 16 B engines

	Kgm	Lb. ft.
Cylinder head	7—8	50—60
Main bearings	8—10	60—70
Connecting rod bearings	4—5	30—35
Flywheel	2.3—2.7	17—20
Dynamo bolts (3/8"—16)	4	30
Oil cleaner centre bolts	5	36
Spark plugs, steel washers	4	30
copper washers	3.5	25
Crankshaft pulley nut and camshaft nut	15	108

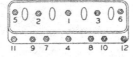

Tightening sequence for cylinder head nuts on B 16 engines.

B 18 ENGINE

General

	B 18 A	B 18 D
Type designation	B 18 A	B 18 D
Output, b.h.p. at r.p.m. (SAE)	75/4500	90/5000
(DIN)	68/4500	80/5000
Max. torque, kgm (lb. ft.) at r.p.m. (SAE)	14.0 (103)/2800	14.5 (105)/3500
(DIN)	13.5 (98)/2600	14.0 (103)/3000
Compression pressure (warm engine) when turned over		
with starter motor, 200 r.p.m., kg/cm²	12—14	12—14
lb./sq. in.	170—200	170—200
Compression ratio	8.5:1	8.5:1
Number of cylinders	4	4
Bore	84.14 mm (3.312")	84.14 mm (3.312")
Stroke	80 mm (3.15")	80 mm (3.15")
Displacement	1.78 litres	1.78 litres

Cylinder block

Material	Special-alloy cast-iron
Bore, standard	84.14 mm (3.313″)
0.020″ oversize	84.65 mm (3.363″)
0.030″ „	84.90 mm (3.342″)
0.040″ „	85.16 mm (3.353″)
0.050″ „	85.41 mm (3.362″)

Pistons

Material	Light-alloy
Weight	425 ± 5 g (15 ± 0.18 oz.)
Permissible weight difference between pistons in same engine	10 g (0.35 oz.)
Height, total	83.5 mm (3.29″)
Height from piston pin centre to piston top	46 mm (1.81″)
Piston clearance	0.03—0.05 mm (0.0012—0.0020″)
Diameter, measured at right angles to piston pin	12.5 mm (0.10″)

12.5 mm (0.10″) from lower edge of piston:

Standard Class C	84.095 mm (3.3108″)
Class D	84.105 mm (3.3112″)
Class E	84.115 mm (3.3116″)
0.020″ oversize	84.615 ± 0.01 mm (3.3313 ± 0.0004″)
0.030″ „	84.685 ± 0.01 mm (3.3411 ± 0.0004″)
0.040″ „	85.125 ± 0.01 mm (3.3514 ± 0.0004″)
0.050″ „	85.375 ± 0.01 mm (3.3612 ± 0.0004″)

Piston rings

Piston ring gap measured in ring opening	0.25—0.50 mm (0.010—0.020″)
Piston ring oversizes	0.020″ 0.040″
	0.030″ 0.050″

Compression rings

Marked ”TOP”. Upper ring on each piston chromed.

Number of rings on each piston	2
Height	1.98 mm (0.078″)
Piston ring clearance in groove	0.054—0.092 mm (0.0021—0.0036″)

Oil control rings

Number on each piston	1
Height	4.76 mm (0.187 = ³/₁₆″)
Piston ring clearance in groove	0.044—0.072 mm (0.0017—0.0028″)

Piston pins

Floating fit. Circlips at both ends in piston.
Fit:

In connecting rod	Close running fit
In piston	Slide fit
Diameter, standard	22 mm (0.866″)
0.05 mm (0.002″) oversize	22.05 mm (0.868″)
0.10 mm (0.004″) „	22.10 mm (0.870″)
0.20 mm (0.008″) „	22.20 mm (0.874″)

Cylinder head

Height, measured from cylinder head contact surface to
bolt head level .... 88 mm (3.46″)
Distance from upper surface of cylinder head to upper
end of relief pipe (pipe located under thermostat) .... 35 mm (1.38″)

Crankshaft

Crankshaft axial clearance .... 0.017—0.108 mm (0.007—0.0042″)
Main bearings, radial clearance .... 0.026—0.077 mm (0.0010—0.0030″)
Connecting rod bearings, radial clearance .... 0.039—0.081 mm (0.0015—0.0032″)

Main bearings
Main bearing journals

Diameter, standard .... 63.441—63.454 mm (2.4977—2.4982″)
        undersize 0.010″ .... 63.187—63.200 mm (2.4877—2.4882″)
             0.020″ .... 62.933—62.946 mm (2.4777—2.4782″)
             0.030″ .... 62.679—62.692 mm (2.4677—2.4682″)
             0.040″ .... 62.425—62.438 mm (2.4577—2.4582″)
             0.050″ .... 62.171—62.184 mm (2.4477—2.4482″)
Width on crankshaft for flange bearing shell
  Standard .... 38.930—38.970 mm (1.5327—1.5342″)
  Oversize 1 (undersize shell 0.010″) .... 39.031—39.072 mm (1.5367—1.5383″)
       2 (,, ,, 0.020″) .... 39.133—39.173 mm (1.5407—1.5422″)
       3 (,, ,, 0.030″) .... 39.235—39.275 mm (1.5447—1.5463″)
       4 (,, ,, 0.040″) .... 39.336—39.376 mm (1.5487—1.5502″)
       5 (,, ,, 0.050″) .... 39.438—39.478 mm (1.5527—1.5543″)

Main bearing shells

Thickness, standard .... 1.985—1.991 mm (0.0781—0.0784″)
        undersize 0.010″ .... 2.112—2.118 mm (0.0831—0.0834″)
             0.020″ .... 2.239—2.245 mm (0.0881—0.0884″)
             0.030″ .... 2.366—2.372 mm (0.0931—0.0934″)
             0.040″ .... 2.493—2.499 mm (0.0981—0.0984″)
             0.050″ .... 2.620—2.626 mm (0.1031—0.1304″)

Connecting rod bearings
Connecting rod bearing journals

Bearing seat width .... 31.950—32.050 mm (1.2579—1.2618″)
Diameter, standard .... 54.089—54.102 mm (2.1295—2.1300″)
             0.010″ .... 53.835—53.848 mm (2.1195—2.1200″)
             0.020″ .... 53.581—53.594 mm (2.1095—2.1100″)
             0.030″ .... 53.327—53.340 mm (2.0995—2.1000″)
             0.040″ .... 53.073—53.086 mm (2.0895—2.0900″)
             0.050″ .... 52.819—52.832 mm (2.0795—2.0800″)

Connecting rod bearing shells

Thickness, standard .... 1.833—1.841 mm (0.0722—0.0725″)
        undersize 0.010″ .... 1.960—1.968 mm (0.0772—0.0775″)
             0.020″ .... 2.087—2.095 mm (0.0822—0.0825″)
             0.030″ .... 2.214—2.222 mm (0.0872—0.0875″)
             0.040″ .... 2.341—2.349 mm (0.0922—0.0925″)
             0.050″ .... 2.469—2.476 mm (0.0972—0.0975″)

Connecting rods

Axial clearance at crankshaft	0.15—0.35 mm (0.006—0.014")
Length, centre—centre	145±0.1 mm (5.710±0.004")
Maximum permissible difference in weight between connecting rods in same engine	6 g (0.21 oz.)

Flywheel

Permissible axial throw, max.	0.20 mm (0.008")
Ring gear (bevel facing forwards)	142 teeth

Flywheel housing

Permissible axial throw, max.	0.05 mm/100 mm diam. (0.002"/4" diam.)
Max. radial throw for rear guide	0.15 mm (0.006")

Camshaft

Number of bearings	3
Front bearing journal, diameter	46.975—47.000 mm (1.8494—1.8504")
Centre bearing journal, diam.	42.975—43.000 mm (1.6919—1.6929")
Rear bearing journal, diam.	36.975—37.000 mm (1.4557—1.4567")
Radial clearance	0.020—0.075 mm (0.0008—0.0030")
Axial clearance	0.020—0.060 mm (0.0008—0.0024")
Valve clearance for check of camshaft setting (cold engine)	1.1 mm (0.043")
Inlet valve should then open at	10° after T.D.C.

Camshaft bearings

Front bearing, diameter	47.020—47.050 mm (1.8512—1.8524")
Centre bearing, diameter	43.025—43.050 mm (1.6939—1.6949")
Rear bearing, diameter	37.020—37.045 mm (1.4575—1.4585")

Timing gears

Crankshaft gear, number of teeth	21
Camshaft gear, (fibre), number of teeth	42
Backlash	0.04—0.08 mm (0.0016—0.0032")
Axial clearance, camshaft	0.02—0.06 mm (0.0008—0.0023")

Valves

Inlet

Disc diameter	40 mm (1.58")
Stem diameter	8.685—8.700 mm (0.3419—0.3425")
Valve seat angle	44.5°
Cylinder head seat angle	45°
Seat width in cylinder head	1.5 mm (0.060")
Clearance, warm and cold engine	0.40—0.45 mm (0.016—0.018")

Exhaust

Disc diameter	35 mm (1.38")
Stem diameter	8.645—8.660 mm (0.3403—0.3409")
Valve seat angle	44.5°
Cylinder head seat angle	45°
Seat width in cylinder head	1.5 mm (0.060")
Clearance, warm and cold engine	0.40—0.45 mm (0.016—0.018")

Valve guides

Length	63 mm (2.48")
Inner diameter	8.725—8.740 mm (0.3435—0.3441")
Height above upper surface of head	21 mm (0.83")
Clearance, valve stem—guide, inlet valves	0.025—0.055 mm (0.0010—0.0022")
exhaust valve	0.065—0.095 mm (0.0026—0.0037")

Valve springs

Length, unloaded, approx.	45 mm (1.77")
loaded with 25.5±2 kg (56±4 1/2 lb.)	39 mm (1.54")
66±3.5 kg (145±8 lb.)	30.5 mm (1.20")

Lubricating system

Oil capacity, including oil cleaner	3.75 litres (3 1/2 Imp. qts.=4 US qts.)
excluding oil cleaner	3.25 litres (3 1/4 Imp. qts.=3 1/2 US qts.)
Oil pressure at 2,000 r.p.m. (with warm engine and new oil cleaner)	4.0—6.0 kg/cm² (56—85 lb./sq. in.)
Lubricant	Engine oil, Service MS
viscosity, below 0° C (30° F)	SAE 10 W
between 0° C (30° F) and +30° C (90° F)	SAE 20
above +30° C (90° F)	SAE 30

or multigrade oil SAE 10 W—30

Lubricating oil cleaner

Type	Fullflow
Make	Wix or Mann

Lubricating oil pump

Oil pump, type	Gear pump
number of teeth on each gear	10
axial clearance	0.02—0.10 mm (0.0008—0.0040")
radial clearance	0.08—0.14 mm (0.0032—0.0055")
backlash	0.15—0.35 mm (0.0060—0.0140")

Relief valve spring (in oil pump)

Length, unloaded	31 mm (1.22")
loaded with 4.0±0.2 kg (9±1/2 lb.)	27.5 mm (1.08")
9.5±0.3 kg (21±3/4 lb.)	22.5 mm (0.88")

Fuel system

Fuel pump

Fuel pump, type	AC diaphragm pump UG
Fuel pressure, measured at same height as pump	min. 0.1 kg/cm² (1.5 lb./sq. in.)
	max. 0.18 kg/cm² (2.5 lb./sq. in.)

Carburetter, B 18 A

Type	Down-draught
Type and designation	Zenith 36 VN
Venturi	30
Main jet	117
Compensation jet	115
Idling jet	70
Idling air jet	70
Air jet for acceleration	140
Acceleration jet	40
Acceleration pump stroke	Short
Float valve	1.75
Washer for float valve, thickness	1 mm
Idling speed (warm engine)	500—700 r.p.m.

Carburetter, B 18 D

Type .... Horizontal, twin
Make and type .... SU—HS 6
No. of carburetters 2
Size (air intake) .... 44.5 mm (1³/₄")
Fuel needle, designation .... K . A
Idling speed .... 500—700 r.p.m.
Oil for damping cylinders .... SAE 20 engine oil (*not* multigrade)

Ignition system

Voltage .... 12 V
Order of firing .... 1—3—4—2
Ignition timing setting with stroboscope at 1500 r.p.m.
97 octane (Research Method) (vacuum regulator
disconnected). Accurate adjustment cannot be carried
out on stationary engine .... 21—23° before T.D.C. (B 18 A)
                                             22—24° before T.D.C. (B 18 D)
Spark plugs .... Bosch W 175 T1 or corresponding
Spark plug gap .... 0.7—0.8 mm (0.028—0.032")
            tightening torque .... 3.8—4.5 kgm (28—32 lb. ft.)

Distributor

Type .... Bosch
Designation .... VJU 4 BL 33
Contact breaker gap .... 0.4—0.5 mm (0.016—0.018")
               pressure .... 0.4—0.5 mm (0.016—0.018")
Dwell angle .... 60°
Direction of rotation .... Counter-clockwise

Cooling system

Type .... Pressure
Radiator cap valve opens at .... 0.23—0.30 kg/cm² (3—4 lb./sq. in.)
Capacity .... Approx. 8.5 litres (2 Imp. galls =
                                             2¹/₄ US galls)
Fan belt, designation .... HC 38×35"
    tension: the pulley should start slipping when
          the force applied is .... 6.5—8.5 kg (14—19 lb.)/lever of
                                             150 mm (6")

Anti-freeze

Amount of glycol required for frost protection down to
   —10° C (15° F) .... 2 litres (3¹/₂ Imp. pints = 4 US pints)
   —20° C (—5° F) .... 3 litres (5¹/₄ Imp. pints = 6 US pints)
   —30° C (—22° F) .... 4 litres (7 Imp. pints = 9 US pints)
   —40° C (—40° F) .... 4.5 litres (1 Imp. gall. = 1¹/₄ US galls)

Thermostat

Type .... Fulton Sylphon 1-1700-D 3
Marking 170
Starts to open at .... 75—78° C (167—172° F)
Fully open at .... 89° C (192° F)

Tightening torques, B 18 A and B 18 D

	Kgm	Lb. ft.
Cylinder head	8.5—9.5	61—68
Main bearings	12—13	87—94
Connecting rod bearings	5.2—5.8	38—42
Flywheel	4.5—5.5	33—40
Spark plug	3.8—4.5	28—30
Camshaft nut	13—15	94—108
Crankshaft pulley bolt	7—8	50—58
Dynamo bolt ($^3/_8$"×16)	3.5—4	25—29
Oil cleaner nipple	4.5—5.5	32—39
Oil sump bolts	0.8—1.1	6—8

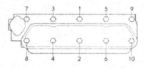

Tightening sequence, cylinder head, B 18 engine.

Wear tolerances

Cylinders:
To be rebored when wear reaches (if engine shows
abnormal oil consumption) ... 0.25 mm (0.010")

Crankshaft:
Permissible out-of-round on main bearing journals,
max. ... 0.05 mm (0.002")
Permissible out-of-round on connecting rod bearing
journals, max. ... 0.07 mm (0.003")

Valves:
Permissible clearance between valve stems and valve
guides, max. ... 0.15 mm (0.006")
Valve stems, permissible wear, max. ... 0.02 mm (0.0008")

Camshaft:
Permissible out-of-round (with new bearings) max. ... 0.07 mm (0.003")
Bearings, permissible wear ... 0.02 mm (0.0008")

Timing gears:
Permissible backlash, max. ... 0.12 mm (0.005")

CLUTCH

For B 16

Type ... Single dry disc
Size ... 8"
Friction area, total ... 340 cm^2 (52.7 sq. in.)
Thickness of clutch plate when fitted ... 7.0—7.5 mm (0.276—0.295")
Rivets for clutch facings:
Number ... 16
Size ... $^9/_{64}$"×$^1/_4$" (3.5×6.5 mm)
Distance between the flywheel and clutch release lever
contact surface with the relief bearing ... 46 mm (1.81")

445

Clutch springs:
  B 16 A, early production and B 16 B:
  Colour: Neutral
  Length, loaded with 85.5—90.5 kg (188—199 lb.) ....   38 mm (1.496")
  B 16 A, late production:
  Colour: Light yellow and light green
  Length, loaded with 82—86 kg (180—189 lb.) ......   40 mm (1.575")
  Number   6
Adjusting the clutch release levers:
  Alternative I 7.5 mm (0.295") lower than the hub in
  adjusting jig SVO 2065 within a limit of ± 1.5 mm
  (0.06") and within 0.25 mm (0.010") of each other.
  Alternative II, adjustment 40.5 in clutch fixture SVO
  2322, packing blocks number 0.
Clutch fork free travel ....   10—15 mm (0.39—0.59")
Clutch pedal stroke ....   140 mm (5¹/₂")
Tightening torque for master cylinder push rod adjuster
nuts ....   1.1—1.2 kgm (8—9 lb. ft.)

For B 18

Type ....   Single dry disc
Size ....   8¹/₂" (215.9 mm)
Friction area, total ....   440 cm² (68.2 sq. in.)
Clutch plate thickness when fitted ....   7.0—7.5 mm (0.276—0.295")
Rivets for clutch facings, number   16
Distance between the clutch release lever contact surface
for the release bearing and flywheel ....   46 mm (1.81")
Clutch springs:
  Number   6
  Marking ....   Neutral
  Length, loaded with 85.5—90.5 kg (188—199 lb.) ....   38 mm (1.496")
Adjustment of clutch release levers:
  Adjustment 41.5 in clutch fixture SVO 2322, packing
  blocks number 0.
Clutch pedal free travel ....   10—15 mm (0.39—0.59")

GEARBOX

H 6

Type designation, serial number and part number stamped on name plate fixed to left-hand side of gearbox.
2nd and 3rd speeds synchronized.

Type designation ....   H 6
Ratios:
  1st speed ....   3.13 : 1
  2nd speed ....   1.62 : 1
  3rd speed ....   1 : 1
  Reverse ....   2.66 : 1
Number of teeth on the different gears:
  Input shaft   17
  Countershaft, drive gear   24
  Gear for 1st speed   14
  Gear for 2nd speed   20
Main shaft, gear for 1st speed   31
  Gear for 2nd speed   23
Reverse gears ....   17 and 20
Lubricant ....   Gear oil
  Viscosity ....   SAE 80
Oil capacity ....   0.5 litre (⁷/₈ Imp. pint = 1 US pint)

M 4

Type designation, serial number and part number stamped on nameplate fixed to lower side of gearbox.
4-speed, fully synchronized.

Type designation	M 4
Ratios:	
1st speed	3.45: 1
2nd speed	2.18: 1
3rd speed	1.31: 1
4th speed	1: 1
Reverse	3.55: 1
Number of teeth on the different gears:	
Input shaft	18
Countershaft, drive gear	28
Gear for 1st speed	14
Gear for 2nd speed	20
Gear for 3rd speed	25
Gear for reverse	14
Main shaft, gear for 1st speed	31
Gear for 2nd speed	28
Gear for 3rd speed	21
Gear for reverse	32
Reverse gear	19
Lubricant	Gear oil
viscosity	SAE 80
Oil capacity	Approx. 0.9 litre ($1^{1}/_{2}$ Imp. pints = $1^{7}/_{8}$ US pints)

M 30, M 40

	M 30	M 40
Type designation	M 30	M 40
Reduction ratios:		
1st speed	3.13: 1	3.13: 1
2nd speed	1.55: 1	1.99: 1
3rd speed	1: 1	1.36: 1
4th speed	—	1: 1
Reverse	3.25: 1	3.25: 1
Number of teeth on the different gears:		
Input shaft	19	19
Countershaft, drive gear	27	27
Gear for 1st speed	15	15
Gear for 2nd speed	22	20
Gear for 3rd speed	—	23
Gear for reverse	14	14
Main shaft, gear for 1st speed	33	33
Gear for 2nd speed	24	28
Gear for 3rd speed	—	22
Gear for reverse	32	32
Reverse gear	19	19
Lubricant	Gear oil	
viscosity	SAE 80	
Oil capacity	0.75 litre ($1^{1}/_{4}$ Imp. pints = $1^{1}/_{2}$ US pints)	

Speedometer gears

Rear axle ratio	Tyre size	Speedometer gears		Ratio	Theoretical percentage error of mileometer
		Number of teeth			
		Large	Small		
4.56: 1 (9/41)	5.90—15	5	18	3.6	+1.5
4.10: 1 (10/41)	5.90—15	5	16	3.2	+2.6

Number of revolutions of speedometer cable per km (mile) registered 630 (1008)

M 41 (Gearbox with overdrive)

Type designation, gearbox with overdrive	M 41
Ratio, overdrive	0.756: 1
Oil pump stroke	3.2 mm (0.13")
Clearance, plunger—cylinder in oil pump	0.005—0.040 mm (0.0002—0.0016")
Oil pressure	37—40 kg/cm² (525—570 lb./sq. in.)
Lubricant	Engine oil
viscosity (all the year round)	SAE 30
grade	Service ML, MM, MS, DG, DM or DS
Oil capacity, gearbox and overdrive	1.8 litres (2 US quarts = 1³/₄ Imp. quarts)

PROPELLER SHAFT

Type	Tubular, divided, three universal joints, intermediate bearing
Universal joints, make and type	Hardy-Spicer with needle bearings
Lubricant, universal joints	Special chassis lubricant

REAR AXLE

ENV: Number of teeth and serial number stamped on the front part of casing.

Spicer: Number of teeth and reduction ratio stamped on nameplate on lower part of inspection cover.

Type	Semi-floating
Track width	1315 mm (51³/₄")
Axial clearance for drive shafts, ENV	0.02—0.12 mm (0.0008—0.0047")
Spicer	0.07—0.20 mm (0.0027—0.0079")

Rear axle

Type	Hypoid
Reduction ratio	4.56: 1 (9/41)
Axial throw, crown wheel	max. 0.08 mm (0.0031")
Tooth flank clearance (pinion—crown wheel)	
ENV Spicer model 23	0.10—0.20 mm (0.0039—0.0079")
Spicer model 27	0.08—0.15 mm (0.0032—0.0059")
Tension for pinion bearing, ENV	2—4 kgcm (1.74—3.48 lb. in.)
Spicer	9—14 kgcm (7.82—12.2 lb. in.)
Lubricant	Hypoid oil
viscosity	SAE 80
Oil capacity	1.3 litres (2¹/₄ Imp. pints = 2³/₄ US pints)

Tightening torques

ENV	Kgm	Lb. ft.
Flange	max. 20	max. 150
Cap	„ 5.5—6	„ 40—45
Crown wheel	„ 5.0—5.5	„ 36—40
Spicer		
Flange	„ 28—30	„ 200—220
Cap, model 23	„ 8.5—10	„ 60—70
model 27	„ 5.5—7	„ 40—50
Crown wheel	„ 5.5—7	„ 40—50

FRONT AXLE AND STEERING GEAR

Front axle

Shims at front axle cross—member	Thickness = 2 mm
	„ = 3 mm
Shims at upper control arm	„ = 0.15 mm
	„ = 0.5 mm
	„ = 1 mm
	„ = 3 mm
	„ = 6 mm

Steering gear

Steering wheel diameter	430 mm (17″)
Number of turns (from lock to lock)	3¹/₄
Steering box, type	Gemmer, cam and roller
ratio	15.5: 1
Shims for steering worm bearing	Thickness = 0.10 mm
	„ = 0.12 mm
	„ = 0.15 mm
	„ = 0.30 mm
Washer between adjusting screw and Pitman arm shaft (0.05 mm = 0.002″ steps)	Thickness = 2.20—2.45 mm
Lubricant for steering box	SAE 80 Hypoid oil
Oil capacity	0.2 litres (¹/₂ US pint = ³/₈ Imp. pint)
Idler arm:	
Tightening torque	1.5—8.5 kgcm (1.3—7.4 lb. in.)
Shims	Thickness = 0.1 mm
	„ = 0.35 mm
Tightening torque for nyloc nut on idler arm shaft	8.5 kgm (60 lb. ft.)
steering wheel nut	3.5—5 kgm (25—35 lb. ft.)
pitman arm nuts	13.5—16.5 kgm (100—120 lb. ft.)
castle nut for steering rod and tie rod	3.2—3.7 kgm (23—27 lb. ft.)
tie rod clamp	1.1—1.4 kgm (8—10 lb. ft.)
clamps for upper and lower control arms	2.1—2.4 kgm (15—17 lb. ft.)

Wheel alignment (unloaded vehicle)

Caster up to chassis number 2610	—¹/₂° to +¹/₂°
Caster with effect from chassis number 2611 onwards	0 to +1°
Camber	0 to +¹/₂°
"King pin" inclination with 0° camber	8°
Toe-in	0 to 4 mm (0.16″)
Steering geometry:	
When the outer wheel is turned 20°, the inner wheel should be turned	21.5 to 23.5°
Max. turning angle outwards	40°

BRAKES

Wheel brake units

Cars with drum brakes

Brake drum:	
Diameter, front, early production	228.6 mm (9″)
late production	254 mm (10″)
rear	228.6 mm (9″)
Radial throw, max.	0.15 mm (0.006″)

Brake linings, production I
Width .... 2"
Thickness .... 3/16"
Length, front wheels .... 260 mm (10 1/4")
rear wheels, front shoe .... 260 mm (10 1/4")
rear shoe .... 200 mm (7 7/8")
Effective brake lining area, front............... 520 cm² (81 sq. in.)
rear .... 465 cm² (72 sq. in.)
total .... 985 cm² (153 sq. in.)

Effective brake lining area, production II
Width .... 2"
Thickness, rear lining, front wheel .... 1/4—3/16" (ground)
others .... 3/16"
Length, front wheel .... 275 mm (10 3/4")
rear wheel .... 250 mm (9 27/32")
Effective brake lining area, front............... 560 cm² (87 sq. in.)
rear .... 508 cm² (79 sq. in.)
total .... 1068 cm² (166 sq. in.)

Effective brake lining area, production III
Width .... 2"
Thickness, rear lining, front wheel .... 1/4—3/16" (ground)
others .... 3/16"
Length, front wheel, front shoe .... 192 mm (7 1/2")
rear shoe .... 250 mm (9 27/32")
rear wheel, front shoe .... 212 mm (8 11/32")
rear shoe .... 250 mm (9 27/32")
Effective brake lining area, front............... 497 cm² (77 sq. in.)
rear .... 451 cm² (70 sq. in.)
total .... 948 cm² (147 sq. in.)
Return spring for brake shoes, early production:
Pulling force with a total length of
154 mm (6 1/16") front .... 13.5—20.5 kg (30—45 lb.)
rear .... 15.5—20.5 kg (34—45 lb.)
Clearance between brake shoe and drum, early production 0.1 mm (0.004")
Rivets for brake linings, size .... 9/64" × 5/16" (3.5 × 8 mm)

Hydraulic system

Master cylinder:
Internal diameter .... 22.2 mm (7/8")
Clearance between plunger and cylinder .... 0.025—0.127 mm (0.001—0.005")
Wheel unit cylinders:
Internal diameter, front wheel, early production .... 22.23 mm (7/8")
late production .... 25.4 mm (1")
rear wheel, early production .... 22.23 mm (7/8")
late production .... 20.64 mm (13/16")
Clearance between plunger and cylinder .... 0.025—0.127 mm (0.001—0.005")
Brake lines:
External diameter 3/16
Tightening torque for master cylinder push rod adjuster
nuts .... 1.1—1.2 kgm (8—9 lb. ft.)

Cars with disc brakes
Front wheel brakes
Type .... Disc brakes
Brake disc:
External diameter .... 276.5 mm (10.88")
Thickness, new .... 12.7—12.8 mm (0.500—0.501")
reconditioned .... min. 12.2 mm (0.480")
Lateral throw .... max. 0.1 mm (0.004")

Brake linings:
Number on each wheel 2
Thickness .... 10.7 mm (0.421")
Effective brake friction area per wheel .... 92.5 cm² (14.3 sq. in.)
Wheel unit cylinder:
Number on each wheel 3
Diameter, inner cylinder .... 53.98 mm (2¹/₈")
              outer cylinders .... 38.1 mm (1¹/₂")
Tightening torque, internal bolts .... 6.2—7.0 kgm (45—50 lb. ft.)
                   outer bolts .... 3.5—4.2 kgm (25—30 lb. ft.)

Rear wheel brakes

Type .... Drum brakes
Brake drum:
Diameter...................................... 228.6 mm (9")
Radial throw .... max. 0.15 mm (0.006")
Brake linings:
Width .... 50.8 mm (2")
Thickness .... 4.76 mm (³/₁₆")
Length .... 210 mm (8.27")
Effective brake lining area per wheel .... 210 cm² (32 sq. in.)
Rivets for brake linings, size .... 6.7—4.4 mm (¹¹/₆₄ × ¹⁷/₆₄")
                  number per shoe 10
Wheel unit cylinders:
Internal diameter .... 25.4 mm (1")
Clearance between plunger and cylinder .... 0.038—0.090 mm (0.0015—0.0035")
Return spring for brake shoe:
Pulling force for a total external length of:
for upper spring 95 mm (3.74") .... 10.0—12.5 kg (22¹/₂—27¹/₂ lb.)
for lower spring 132 mm (5.20") .... 8—10 kg (17¹/₂—22 lb.)

Master cylinder

Internal diameter .... 22.2 mm (⁷/₈")
Clearance between plunger and cylinder .... 0.025—0.127 mm (0.001—0.005")

WHEELS AND TYRES

Wheels

Type and designation .... Disc wheel, 4J×15
Number of wheel nuts 5
Radial throw .... Max. 2.5 mm (0.10")
Run-out .... Max. 2.5 mm (0.10")
Unbalance (complete wheel) .... Max. 900 gcm (0.8 lb.in.)
Tightening torque for wheel nuts .... 10—14 kgm (70—100 lb.ft.)

Tyres

Type .... Tubeless
Size .... 5.90—15
Number of plies 4
Rolling radius .... 315 mm (12 ³/₈")
Number of wheel turns per km (mile) .... Approx. 492 (787)
Tyre pressure (cold tyre), front .... 1.4 kg/cm² (20 lb./sq.in.)
                           rear .... 1.6 kg/cm² (23 lb./sq. in.)
for continuous driving between
140—160 km. p.h.
(90—100 m.p.h.), front ...... 1.8 kg/cm² (26 lb./sq.in.)
              rear ...... 2.0 kg/cm² (28 lb/sq.in.)

SPRINGS AND SHOCK ABSORBERS

Front springs

Type	Coil springs
Material thickness	14.1—14.3 mm (0.555—0.563")
External diameter	121—122.5 mm (4.763—4.823")
Total number of coils	8
Test values:	
Loading for compression of 1 cm (25/64") (measured within a spring length range of 175—215 mm = 6.89" —8.46")	47.8—51.8 kg (105—114 lb.)
Length when fully compressed	max. 120 mm (4.72")
Loading for a spring length of 195 mm (7.68")	
Yellow marked springs	481—491 kg (1060—1083 lb.)
Blue marked springs	491—501 kg (1083—1104 lb.)
Red marked springs	501—511 kg (1104—1127 lb.)

Rear springs

Type	Coil springs
Material thickness	11.7—11.9 mm (0.461—0.468")
External diameter	114.5—116.0 mm (4.507"—4.567")
Number of coils	10.7
Test values:	
Loading for compression of 1 cm (25/64") (measured within a spring length range of 225—265 mm = 8.85 —10.43")	19.4—21.4 kg (43—47 lb.)
Length, fully compressed	max. 123 mm (0.484")
Loading for a spring length of 245 mm (9.64")	
Yellow marked springs	276—282 kg (608—622 lb.)
Blue marked springs	282—288 kg (622—635 lb.)
Red marked springs	288—294 kg (635—648 lb.)

Shock absorbers

Type	Double-acting, hydraulic telescopic shock absorbers
Total length:	
Front shock absorbers, compressed	approx. 300 mm (12")
extended	approx. 415 mm (16.3")
Rear shock absorber, compressed	approx. 355 mm (14")
extended	approx. 530 mm 20.9")

ELECTRICAL SYSTEM

Early type. For vehicles with B 16 engine

Battery

Make and designation	Tudor 3 Df6 or corresponding
Earthed	Negative terminal
Voltage	6 V
Battery capacity, standard	85 Ah (13 plate)
Electrolyte specific gravity, fully charged battery	1.275—1.285
Electrolyte specific gravity when battery need recharging	1.230

Ignition system

	B 16 A	B 16 B
Firing order	1—3—4—2	

Ignition setting:
basic setting

octane rating (Research Method) 87	2—4° B.T.D.C.	—
93	—	4° B.T.D.C.
97	2—4° B.T.D.C.	4—6° B.T.D.C.

stroboscope setting, 1500 engine r.p.m.
(vacuum regulator disengaged)

octane rating (Research Method) 87	19—21° B.T.D.C.	—
93	—	21° B.T.D.C.
97	19—21° B.T.D.C.	21—23° B.T.D.C.
Sparking plugs, normal driving	Bosch W 175 T3	Bosch W 225 T3
	Champion J7	Champion J6
	or corresponding	or corresponding
hard driving	Bosch W 225 T3	Bosch W 240 T3
	Champion J6	Champion J6
	or corresponding	or corresponding
Sparking plug gap	0.7—0.8 mm (0.028—0.032")	
Ignition coil	Bosch ZS/KZ 1/6/4	

Distributor

Make and type .... Bosch VJU 4 BR 20

Test values

Rotation .... Clockwise

Ignition setting curves:
Centrifugal governor

| Crankshaft degrees .... | 0 | 10 | 20 | 27±3 |
| Crankshaft r.p.m. .... | 400—800 | 700—1100 | 1600—2500 | 3100—3800 |

Vacuum regulator

Crankshaft degrees	0°	16±2°
Vacuum, cm (in.) Hg	7—14	50
	(2.76—5.51")	(19.68")

Contact breakers, gap	0.4—0.5 mm (0.016—0.020")
contact pressure	0.4—0.5 kg (0.88—1.10 lb.)
closing angle	50±3°

Dynamo

| Make and designation, early production | Bosch LJ/GG 200/6-2300 R7 | Bosch LJ/GG 200/6-2300 R7 |
| late production | Bosch LJ/GG 200/6-2300 R6 | Bosch LJ/GG 200/6-2300 R7 |

Voltage .... 6 V
Earthed .... Negative terminal
Effect, continuous .... Max. 49 A
Direction of rotation .... Clockwise
Ratio, engine—dynamo .... 1 : 1.8
Brushes, designation, 2 .... WSK 40 L6

Test values

Brush spring tension .... 0.45—0.60 kg (1.0—1.3 lb.)
Field winding .... 4 A at 5 V
Dynamo as motor .... 8 A at 5 V

Charging, cold dynamo:
6.4 V 0 A .... 1850—1900 r.p.m.
8 V 40 A .... 2575—2675 r.p.m.

Charging, warm dynamo:
6.4 V 0 A .... 1875—1950 r.p.m.
8 V 40 A .... 2750—2850 r.p.m.

Charging control

Make and designation	Bosch RS/UA 200/6/23
Equalizing resistance AR	5.5—6.0 Ohm
Control resistance W1	3.2—3.7 Ohm
Control resistance W2	5—6 Ohm

Test values

Reverse current relay:	
Adjusted for cutting-in at	5.5—6.3 V
Adjusted for cutting-out at, reverse current	4—9 A (closed circuit)
Voltage control:	
Control voltage adjusted to	7.0—7.5 V
Control current:	
Control current adjusted to	47—51 A
The test values for an ambient temperature of approx. 20° C (70° F).	

Starter motor

Make and designation	Bosch EGD 0.6/6 AR 19
Control solenoid, type designation	SSM 120/2
Voltage	6 V
Earthed..	Negative terminal
Direction of rotation	Clockwise
Output	0.6 h.p. at —10° C (15° F)
	0.75 h.p. at 20° C (70° F)
Number of teeth on the pinion	9
Brushes, designation	DSK 35/5
number	4

Test values

Mechanical:	
Axial clearance of rotor	0.15—0.30 mm (0.006—0.012″)
Brush spring tension	0.8—0.9 kg (1.76—2.0 lb.)
Distance from pinion to ring gear	3 mm (0.12″)
Friction torque of rotor brake	3—5 kg. cm (2.6—4.3 lb. in.)
Pinion idling torque	0.4—0.8 kg. cm (0.35—0.7 lb. in.)
Electrical:	
Starter motor unloaded:	
Test time	Max. 15 seconds
5.5 V and 65—75 A	3,500—4,000 r.p.m.
Starter motor loaded:	
4.5 V and 260—280 A	750—850 r.p.m.
Starter motor locked (r.p.m. = 0):	
3.5 V and 450—480 A	Min. 1.33 kgm (9.4 lb. ft.)

Control solenoid

Test values

Current consumption of winding:	
Between terminal 50 and earth	9—12 A at 5.0 V
Between terminal 50 and 30	31—35 A at 5.0 V
Control voltage, cutting-in	2.5—3.3 V
Control voltage, cutting-out	0.8—1.6 V
Distance "a" (see Fig.)	32.2±0.1 mm (1.27±0.004″)

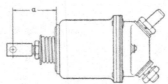

Adjusting the control solenoid (iron core withdrawn).

Fuses

Fuse box under bonnet on left-hand side of cowl 4 8A, 2 25A
Fuse box under bonnet on left-hand wheel housing
(with effect from chassis number 21000) 4 8A

Bulbs

	Watts	Socket	Number
Headlights	45/40	BA 20 d	2
Long-time parking (up to chassis number 20999)	2	BA 9 s	4
Number plate lighting	5	BA 15 s	2
Stop lights (up to chassis number 20999)	20	BA 15 s	2
Rear lights (up to chassis number 20999)	5	BA 15 s	2
Combination stop and rear lights (up to chassis number 21000)	20/5	BA 15 d spec.	2
Instrument lighting	2	BA 9 s	2
Direction indicator and parking lights, front	20/5	BA 15 d spec.	2
Direction indicator lights, rear	20	BA 15 s	2
Glove compartment light	2	BA 9 s	1
Clock light	2	BA 9 s	1
Roof light	10	S 8	1
Control lamp for direction indicators	2	BA 9 s	1
headlights	2	BA 9 s	1
oil pressure	2	BA 9 s	1
charging	2	BA 9 s	1

Late production. For vehicles with B 18 engine

Battery

Type .... Boliden 107GM60 or corresponding
Earthed .... Negative terminal
Voltage .... 12 V
Battery capacity, standard .... 60 Ah

Electrolyte specific gravity:
    Fully charged battery 1.230
    When recharging is necessary .... 1.275—1.285
Recommended charging current .... 4.5 A

Ignition system

Firing order .... 1—3—4—2
Ignition setting, with stroboscope at an engine speed of
1500 r.p.m. (vacuum regulator disconnected) octane rating
97 (Research Method). (Accurate adjusting with
stationary engine must not be done) .... 21—23° B.T.D.C. B 18 A
                                                      22—24° B.T.D.C. B 18 D

Ignition coil .... Bosch ZS/KZ/1/12A (14/3)
Sparking plugs, type .... Bosch W 175 T 1 or corresponding
           thread .... 14 mm
           gap .... 0.7 mm (0.028″)

Distributor

Type .... Bosch VJU 4 BL 33

Test values

Direction of rotation .... Clockwise
Ignition setting curves:
Centrifugal regulator:

	0	10	22	22±3
Crankshaft degrees	0	10	22	22±3
Crankshaft r.p.m.	750—1050	1300—1850	2300—2900	2800—3300

Vacuum regulator:

Crankshaft degrees	6	15±4
Vacuum, cm (in.) Hg	6—10 (2.36—3.94″)	18 (7.09″)

Contact breaker, gap, ... 0.4—0.5 mm (0.016—0.020″)
contact pressure .... 0.4—0.5 kg (0.88—1.10 lb)
closing angle .... 60°

Dynamo

B 18 A, type .... Bosch LJ/GG 240/12/2400 AR6
B 18 D, type .... Bosch LJ/GG 240/12/2400 AR7
Voltage .... 12 V
Rated effect .... 240 W
Max. continuous effect .... 30 A (cold dynamo)
Earthed .... Negative terminal
Direction of rotation .... Clockwise
Ratio, engine—dynamo .... 1 : 1.8
Brushes, designation .... WSK 43 L1
number 2
contact pressure .... 450—600 g (16—21 oz.)

Test values

Field winding resistance .... 4.8 + 0.5 Ohm
Charging, cold dynamo, 240 W .... 2300 r.p.m.
warm dynamo, 240 W .... 2500 r.p.m.
Speed for rated voltage, unloaded .... 1700 r.p.m.

Charging control

Type .... Bosch RS/VA 240/12/2
Equalizing resistance aR .... 15.5—16.5 ohm
Control resistance wR .... 8—9 ohm

Test values

Reverse current relay:
Adjusted for, cutting-in at .... 12.4—13.1 V
reverse current at .... 2.0—7.5 A
Voltage control:
Control voltage, dynamo unloaded (idling) .... 14.1—14.8 V
loaded .... 13.0—14.0 V
Loading current:
Cold dynamo and control .... 45 A
Warm dynamo and control .... 30 A

Starter motor

Type	Bosch EGD 1/12 AR 37
Voltage	12 V
Earthed	Negative terminal
Direction of rotation	Clockwise
Output	Approx. 0.9 h.p. at —10° C (15° F)
	Approx. 1.2 h.p. at 20° C (70° F)
Number of teeth on pinion	9
Brushes, designation	DSK 35/5
number	4

Mechanical

Rotor axial clearance	0.1—0.3 mm (0.004—0.012″)
Brush spring tension	0.8—0.9 kg (1.76—2.0 lb.)
Distance from pinion to ring gear	2.5—3.0 mm (0.10—0.12″)
Friction torque of rotor brake	3—5 kg.cm (2.6—4.3 lb.in.)
Pinion idling torque	1.3—1.8 kg.cm (1.13—1.56 lb.in.)
Tooth flank clearance	0.35—0.6 mm (0.014—0.023″)
Pinion modulus	2.11

Electrical

Starter motor unloaded: 11.5 V and 40—60 A	5500—7500 r.p.m.
Starter motor loaded: 10 V and 200 A	1100—1300 r.p.m.
Starter motor locked: r.p.m. = 0	8 V 400—450 A
Control solenoid: Cut-in voltage	Max. 7 V
Adjusting measurement "a" (see Fig.)	32.2±0.1 mm (1.27±0.004″)

Bulbs

	Watts	Socket	Number
Headlights	45/40	Ba 20 d	2
Direction indicators/parking lights, front	20/5	Ba 15 d spec.	2
Direction indicators, rear	20	BA 15 s	2
Brake lights, parking lights, rear	20/5	Ba 15 d spec.	2
Number plate lighting	5	S 8	2
Internal lighting	10	S 8	1
Instrument lighting	2	Ba 9 s	2
Control lamp, direction indicators	2	Ba 9 s	1
Full headlights	2	Ba 9 s	1
Charging	2	Ba 9 s	1
Oil pressure	2	Ba 9 s	1

LUBRICATION

B 16 Engine

	B 16 A	B 16 B
Lubricant	Engine oil for Service MM or MS	Engine oil for Service MS
viscosity, summer	SAE 20	SAE 20
winter	SAE 10 W	SAE 10 W
Oil capacity, with oil cleaner	3.5 litres (3 Imp. quarts =3 ¼ US quarts)	3.5 litres (3 Imp. quarts =3 ¼ US quarts)
without oil cleaner	2.75 litres (2 ½ Imp. quarts =3 US quarts)	2.75 litres (2 ½ Imp. quarts =3 US quarts)
Oil for damping cylinders of carburetters	—	SAE 10 W

B 18 Engine

Lubricant	Engine oil Service MS or multi-grade oil 10 W—30
viscosity below 0° C (32° F)	SAE 10 W
above 0° C (32° F)	SAE 20
Oil capacity with oil cleaner	3.75 litres (3 1/2 Imp. quarts = 4 US quarts)
without oil cleaner	3.25 litres (3 1/4 Imp. quarts =3 1/2 US quarts)

Gearbox
Early type (H 6)

Lubricant, type	Gear oil
viscosity	SAE 80
oil capacity	0.5 litre (7/8 Imp. pint =1 1/2 US pints)

Late type (M 4)

Lubricant, type	Gear oil
viscosity	SAE 80
oil capacity	approx. 0.9 litre (1 5/8 Imp. pints =1 7/8 US pints)

M 30, M 40

Lubricant, type	Gear oil
viscosity	SAE 80
oil capacity	0.75 litre (1 1/4 Imp. pints =1 1/2 US pints)

M 41 (with overdrive)

Lubricant, type................................	Engine oil
viscosity	SAE 30
capacity	1.8 litres (2 US quarts =1 3/4 Imp. quarts)

Rear axle

Lubricant, type	Hypoid oil
viscosity	SAE 80
oil capacity	1.3 litres (2 3/8 Imp. pints =2 3/4 US pints)

Steering box

Lubricant, type	Hypoid oil
viscosity	SAE 80
oil capacity	0.3 litre (3/8 Imp. pint =3/4 US pint)

OTHER BOOKS CURRENTLY AVAILABLE FROM

www.VelocePress.com

AUTOBOOKS SERIES OF WORKSHOP MANUALS

ALFA ROMEO GIULIA 1750, 2000 1962-1978 WORKSHOP MANUAL
AUSTIN HEALEY SPRITE, MG MIDGET 1958-1980 WORKSHOP MANUAL
BMW 1600 1966-1973 WORKSHOP MANUAL
FIAT 124 1966-1974 WORKSHOP MANUAL
FIAT 124 SPORT 1966-1975 WORKSHOP MANUAL
FIAT 500 1957-1973 WORKSHOP MANUAL
FIAT 850 1964-1972 WORKSHOP MANUAL
JAGUAR E-TYPE 1961-1972 WORKSHOP MANUAL
JAGUAR MK 1, 2 1955-1969 WORKSHOP MANUAL
JAGUAR S TYPE, 420 1963-1968 WORKSHOP MANUAL
JAGUAR XK 120, 140, 150 MK 7, 8, 9 1948-1961 WORKSHOP MANUAL
LAND ROVER 1, 2 1948-1961 WORKSHOP MANUAL
MERCEDES-BENZ 190 1959-1968 WORKSHOP MANUAL
MERCEDES-BENZ 230 1963-1968 WORKSHOP MANUAL
MERCEDES-BENZ 250 1968-1972 WORKSHOP MANUAL
MG MIDGET TA-TF 1936-1955 WORKSHOP MANUAL
MINI 1959-1980 WORKSHOP MANUAL
MORRIS MINOR 1952-1971 WORKSHOP MANUAL
PEUGEOT 404 1960-1975 WORKSHOP MANUAL
PORSCHE 911 1964-1969 WORKSHOP MANUAL
RENAULT 8, 10, 1100 1962-1971 WORKSHOP MANUAL
RENAULT 16 1965-1979 WORKSHOP MANUAL
ROVER 3500, 3500S 1968-1976 WORKSHOP MANUAL
SUNBEAM RAPIER, ALPINE 1955-1965 WORKSHOP MANUAL
TRIUMPH SPITFIRE, GT6, VITESSE 1962-1968 WORKSHOP MANUAL
TRIUMPH TR2, TR3, TR3A 1952-1962 WORKSHOP MANUAL
TRIUMPH TR4, TR4A 1961-1967 WORKSHOP MANUAL
VOLKSWAGEN BEETLE 1968-1977 WORKSHOP MANUAL

OTHER WORKSHOP MANUALS, MAINTENANCE & TECHNICAL TITLES

AUSTIN HEALEY SIX CYLINDER CARS 1956-1968
BMW ISETTA FACTORY REPAIR MANUAL
FERRARI 250/GT SERVICE AND MAINTENANCE
FERRARI GUIDE TO PERFORMANCE
FERRARI OPERATING, MAINTENANCE & SERVICE HANDBOOKS 1948-1963
FERRARI OWNER'S HANDBOOK
FERRARI TUNING TIPS & MAINTENANCE TECHNIQUES
MASERATI OWNER'S HANDBOOK
OBERT'S FIAT GUIDE
PERFORMANCE TUNING THE SUNBEAM TIGER
PORSCHE 356 SERVICE AND MAINTENANCE MANUAL 1948-1965
PORSCHE 912 WORKSHOP MANUAL
VOLVO ALL MODELS 1944-1968 WORKSHOP MANUAL

MOTORCYCLE WORKSHOP MANUALS, MAINTENANCE & TECHNICAL TITLES

ARIEL MOTORCYCLES WORKSHOP MANUAL 1933-1951
BMW MOTORCYCLES FACTORY WORKSHOP MANUAL R26 R27 (1956-1967)
BMW MOTORCYCLES FACTORY WORKSHOP MANUAL R50 R50S R60 R69S R50US R60US R69US (1955-1969)
HONDA MOTORCYCLES FACTORY WORKSHOP MANUAL 250cc TO 305cc C/CS/CB 72 & 77 SERIES 1960-1969
NORTON MOTORCYCLES FACTORY WORKSHOP MANUAL 1957-1970
NORTON MOTORCYCLES WORKSHOP MANUAL 1932-1939
TRIUMPH MOTORCYCLES FACTORY WORKSHOP MANUAL NO. 11 (1945-1955)
TRIUMPH MOTORCYCLES WORKSHOP MANUAL 1935-1939
TRIUMPH MOTORCYCLES WORKSHOP MANUAL 1937-1951
VINCENT MOTORCYCLES MAINTENANCE AND REPAIR 1935-1955

CLASSIC AUTO TITLES & REFERENCE BOOKS

ABARTH BUYERS GUIDE
DIALED IN ~ THE JAN OPPERMAN STORY
FERRARI 308 SERIES BUYER'S AND OWNER'S GUIDE
FERRARI BERLINETTA LUSSO
FERRARI BROCHURES & SALES LITERATURE 1946-1967
FERRARI SERIAL NUMBERS PART I ~ STREET CARS TO SERIAL # 21399 (1948-1977)
FERRARI SERIAL NUMBERS PART II ~ RACE CARS TO SERIAL # 1050 (1948-1973)
FERRARI SPYDER CALIFORNIA
IF HEMINGWAY HAD WRITTEN A RACING NOVEL ~ THE BEST OF MOTOR RACING FICTION 1950-2000
LE MANS 24 ~ WHAT THE MOVIE COULD HAVE BEEN
MASERATI BROCHURES AND SALES LITERATURE ~ POSTWAR THROUGH INLINE 6 CYLINDER CARS

CHECK OUR WEBSITE AT

www.VelocePress.com

OR CONTACT YOUR DEALER FOR PRICING

CPSIA information can be obtained
at www.ICGtesting.com
Printed in the USA
FSOW04n1355100917
38339FS